Forty years ago I dreamed of teaching *gurukula* students with Śrīla Prabhupāda's *Śrīmad-Bhāgavatam* serving as the central text. Toward realizing that goal, I had compiled the *Bhāgavatam* into its essential stories, for I trusted Śrīla Prabhupāda's words that such study would truly educate and prepare my students on every level for a satisfying and worthwhile life.

But Kṛṣṇa had a more wonderful plan. The opportunity to fulfill Śrīla Prabhupāda's desire – like a fragrant lotus in the form of this *Śrīmad-Bhāgavatam: A Comprehensive Guide for Young Readers* – has been carefully placed in the open hands of Mātājī Aruddhā Devī Dāsī and her team of parents and educators. May the fortunate children who take advantage of their love-laden offering gain a taste for this sweet, potent literature. May those children continue throughout their lives to taste and distribute to others what they have relished in their childhood and youth. May the *Śrīmad-Bhāgavatam* safeguard their rapid journey to the lotus feet of Śrī Kṛṣṇa. And may Śrīla Prabhupāda bless those who have sought to fulfill his desire by compiling this offering and placing it into his lotus hands.

BHŪRIJANA DĀSA

Śrīmad-Bhāgavatam: A Comprehensive Guide for Young Readers, to our reading, and from all reports, is an unsurpassed resource for teachers of *Śrīmad-Bhāgavatam,* both in families and in schools. The variety of materials and amount of work that went into producing the book as a gift to Śrīla Prabhupāda are astonishing.

HANUMATPREŚAKA SWAMI (PROF. H. H. ROBINSON)

As I travel around the United States, I get to personally witness how much devotee families have benefitted from Aruddhā Devī Dāsī and her homeschooling methods, which are completely based on Śrīla Prabhupāda's books and teachings. I am an ardent supporter of her and the models of education which she develops and promotes through her books and various homeschooling seminars.

It is very pleasing to note that she and her team have come up with a second project, *Śrīmad-Bhāgavatam: A Comprehensive Guide for Young Readers*. The series' main objective is to provide children with a *Bhāgavatam*-centered education, with lots of activities created by parents and teachers that are geared toward different learning styles, while meeting devotional, cognitive and language objectives of a growing child in Kṛṣṇa consciousness. This innovative and systematic compilation of various activities in book form is a great resource for any homeschooling parents who want their children to go deeper into the messages of *Śrīmad-Bhāgavatam*.

ROMAPĀDA SWAMI

From my reading of Aruddhā Devī Dāsī's book on studying *Śrīmad-Bhāgavatam*, it is evident that she is fulfilling Śrīla Prabhupāda's desire that our children get the best Kṛṣṇa conscious education. As Śrīla Prabhupāda said in a lecture on *Śrīmad-Bhāgavatam* 1.5.13 given in New Vrindaban in 1969: "When one can understand *Śrīmad-Bhāgavatam* in true perspective, then it is to be understood that he has finished all his educational advancement. *Avadhi*. *Avadhi* means 'this is the limit of education.' *Vidyā-bhāgavatāvadhi*."

This book gives the highest knowledge in an interesting way, so that children may access the *Bhāgavatam* on many levels, including higher-level thinking and application to their lives, as well as artistic, dramatic and journalistic approaches. I recommend this book for all parents who want to give their children a higher taste for reading Śrīla Prabhupāda's *Śrīmad-Bhāgavatam*.

NĀRĀYAṆĪ DEVĪ DĀSĪ

ŚRĪMAD BHĀGAVATAM

A Comprehensive Guide for Young Readers

CANTO 7

ŚRĪMAD BHĀGAVATAM

A Comprehensive Guide for Young Readers

CANTO 7

COMPILED BY

Aruddhā Devī Dāsī

Krishna Homeschool

Library of Congress Cataloging-in-Publication Data

Srimad-Bhagavatam: a comprehensive guide for young readers, Canto 7 /
compiled by Aruddha devi dasi.
342 pages
ISBN 978-1-7369610-7-0
1. Puranas. Bhagavatapurana–Textbooks. 2. Hinduism–Textbooks.
I. Aruddha, devi dasi.
BL1140.4.B436S745 2014
294.5'925--dc23
2014005526

Cover and book design:
Eight Eyes
www.eighteyes.com

Cover illustration: by Prithvi Kumar

For more information, contact:

Krishna Homeschool

aruddha108@yahoo.com

CONTENTS

Acknowledgments ix
Introduction xi

1 / The Supreme Lord is Equal to Everyone 1
2 / Hiraṇyakaśipu, King of the Demons 24
3 / Hiraṇyakaśipu's Plan to Become Immortal 47
4 / Hiraṇyakaśipu Terrorizes the Universe 67
5 / Prahlāda Mahārāja, the Saintly Son of Hiraṇyakaśipu 91
6 / Prahlāda Instructs His Demoniac Schoolmates 116
7 / What Prahlāda Learned in the Womb 136
8 / The Lord Slays the King of the Demons 156
9 / Prahlāda Pacifies the Lord with Prayers 177
10 / Prahlāda, the Best Among Exalted Devotees 199
11 / The Perfect Society: Four Social Classes 224
12 / Four Spiritual Classes 244
13 / The Behavior of a Perfect Person 262
14 / Ideal Family Life 284
15 / Instructions for Civilized Human Beings 302

This book is a tribute to the spiritual master of the entire world, His Divine Grace A. C. Bhaktivedanta Swami Prabhupāda, who gave us the invaluable gift of *Śrīmad-Bhāgavatam*. Śrīla Prabhupāda spent many hours translating this vast literature from Sanskrit to English and promised that anyone who studies his books will be liberated from the miseries of material life and directly connected to Kṛṣṇa.

ACKNOWLEDGMENTS

This book is a tribute to the spiritual master of the entire world, His Divine Grace A. C. Bhaktivedanta Swami Prabhupāda, who gave us the invaluable gift of *Śrīmad-Bhāgavatam*. Śrīla Prabhupāda spent many hours at night translating this vast literature from Sanskrit to English and promised that anyone who studies his books will be liberated from the miseries of material life and directly connected to Kṛṣṇa.

My humble obeisances and gratitude to my spiritual master, His Holiness Gopal Krishna Goswami, a dear and dedicated disciple of Śrīla Prabhupāda, who was untiring in his efforts to preach Kṛṣṇa consciousness throughout the world. He always encouraged me to share my experiences of Kṛṣṇa conscious parenting with devotees.

My gratitude to my husband, Anantarūpa Prabhu, my sons, Rādhikā Ramaṇa and Gopāla Hari, and my daughters-in-law, Amṛta Keli and Devī Mūrti, who greatly supported my efforts in completing these series of books.

My profound thanks to all the contributors of this book who spent many hours studying the topics in Canto 7 and creating suitable resources for children. They hail from countries around the world. I offer my heartfelt gratitude to the following contributors for their committed and excellent efforts in specific areas:

India

- Prithvi Kumar for the front cover artwork, beautiful book illustrations, and an artistic activity.
- Pūrṇeśvarī Rādhā Devī Dāsī for critical-thinking, analogy, language, and science activities.
- Śyāmalī Devī Dāsī for action, introspective, writing, and language activities.
- Girija Ramanan for introspective, theatrical, and language activities.
- Rāsapriyā Gopikā Devī Dāsī for action and language activities.
- Vṛndā Priyā Līlā Devī Dāsī for artistic activities.

Portugal

- Nikuñja Vilāsinī Devī Dāsī for chapter summaries, themes, higher-thinking questions, general activities, and art suggestions.

South Africa

- Indulekhā Sakhī Devī Dāsī for theatrical, writing, and language activities.

Canada

- Tanvi Sharma for artistic activities.

United States

- Amṛta Sundarī Devī Dāsī for action, language, artistic, and theatrical activities.
- Amala Nāma Dāsa for adding diacritics and reviewing the text.

My profuse thanks to Nikuñja Vilāsinī Devī Dāsī (Nirvana Kasopersad) for her excellent editorial work. Her expertise in checking content, correcting grammar, and proofreading, with constant attention to quality and detail, proved to be a great blessing as we put together this voluminous work.

Many thanks to Raghu and Govinda of Eight Eyes for their excellent design and layout and cover design, which make the book polished, attractive, and friendly to children.

I am also grateful to Amala Nāma Dāsa (Amol Bakshi) for reviewing the content with care and attention, for his valuable feedback, and for spotting minute errors with an eye for detail.

This book is the product of many hands, and it would not have existed without the dedication of all these devotees. I am deeply indebted to them for taking time from their busy schedules to create a valuable resource for children everywhere.

INTRODUCTION

While conducting seminars on homeschooling and Kṛṣṇa conscious parenting throughout the world during the last seven years, I met many parents who wanted to teach their children *Śrīmad-Bhāgavatam* but who needed more guidance on how to do it. It was then that I started doing workshops, during which we would sit together with their children and I would demonstrate how to guide a discussion in a way that evoked the child's curiosity about the nature of the world, God, the self, and the purpose of life. Together, we would read the translations of a chapter of *Śrīmad-Bhāgavatam* and discuss the stories, main themes, and great personalities. We would talk about the relevance of *Śrīmad-Bhāgavatam* in our own lives – how it provides spiritual solutions to material problems. Both the children and parents were thoroughly enlivened and absorbed in the discussions.

When I explained at seminars how I taught my boys *Śrīmad-Bhāgavatam* through interactive reading and discussion, hundreds of parents were inspired to follow. However, many parents who wanted to study the *Bhāgavatam* with their children were uncertain about how to do it. They needed a formal curriculum, *and* I pondered how I could help. I decided to start a collaborative project, involving devotee parents from around the world. I formed an online group in which approximately 15 parents – from Australia, New Zealand, India, South Africa, the United Kingdom, and the United States – worked together to create study resources for each chapter of Canto 1. Every parent would send their creations to others in the group, who would use the material with their own children and offer feedback.

All the parents brought special skills – our team included English teachers, musicians, artists, and computer professionals. With children of their own, they were highly motivated to give them a *Bhāgavatam*-centered education. The result? An innovative collection of material on every chapter of Canto 1. The creators used the curriculum with their own children as they designed it, seeing the results firsthand.

However, having all this material in email

attachments was beneficial only to a certain extent – it had to be edited, organized, and compiled. So we began the painstaking task of systematically compiling a book for use by parents and teachers anywhere, which was published as *Śrīmad Bhāgavatam: A Comprehensive Guide for Young Readers, Canto 1.* We then went through a similar process for Cantos 2, 3, 4, 5, and 6, and now we are pleased to present to you Canto 7. This book is primarily geared for children between the ages of 13 and 18, but much of the material can be adapted for children younger than 13, or even older than 18. You will find fewer yet longer chapters for this canto. So we suggest that you take more time to go over each chapter with your students, since the chapters cover themes and concepts that require extra learning and discussion. However, we've provided additional resources and activities for each chapter, addressing the themes more in detail, so that you would be able to assist your students with ease.

WHY STUDY ŚRĪMAD-BHĀGAVATAM?

Śrīla Prabhupāda said that from the very beginning, children "should be taught Sanskrit and English, so in the future they can read our books. That will make them MA, Ph.D. Because the knowledge in these books is so advanced, children would be well-educated, happy, satisfied, and even go back home, back to Godhead." (Jagadīśa, April 6, 1977)

As is evident in many of his lectures, Śrīla Prabhupāda desired that children in his *gurukula* schools read *Śrīmad-Bhāgavatam.* In 1974, speaking on *Śrīmad-Bhāgavatam* (1.16.22), Śrīla Prabhupāda emphasized that the *Bhāgavatam* would equip one to know any subject: "So in *Śrīmad-Bhāgavatam* you will find everything, whatever is necessity, for the advancement of human civilization, everything is there described. And knowledge also, all departments of knowledge, even astronomy, astrology, politics, sociology, atomic theory, everything is there. *Vidyā-bhāgavatāvadhi.* Therefore, if you study *Śrīmad-Bhāgavatam* very carefully, then you get all knowledge completely. Because *Bhāgavatam* begins from the point of creation: *janmādy asya yataḥ.*" (July 12, 1974, Los Angeles)

If we give children this foundation, they become confident of their spiritual identity and also do well academically. Śrīla Prabhupāda's books inspire critical reasoning and creative thinking, which are the main elements of academic education. In addition, *Śrīmad-Bhāgavatam* is pure and perfect and can equip them with the highest knowledge, both material and spiritual.

Parents and teachers who have taught their children *Śrīmad-Bhāgavatam* from their early lives have experienced how easily they pick up English language skills, especially reading, comprehension, and analytical reasoning. *Śrīmad-Bhāgavatam* is full of analogies, allegories, figurative speech, and metaphors. Even a seven-year-old child can grasp difficult concepts because the subject matter of *Śrīmad-Bhāgavatam* encourages higher-thinking skills.

Śrīmad-Bhāgavatam is a wonderful book to teach from because it gives the philosophy of the *Bhagavad-gītā* through stories, and children love stories. These stories are not fictitious; rather, they are the lives of great saintly personalities and the pastimes of Kṛṣṇa and His *avatāras.* By reading these, they directly associate with the great personalities and their teachings and begin to emulate the character of these personalities. As children grow older, they learn to appreciate the instructions given by Queen Kuntī, Prahlāda Mahārāja, Dhruva Mahārāja, Kapiladeva, and so many others. In fact, many of the devotees described in the *Bhāgavatam*, such as Prahlāda and Dhruva, are children themselves, so our children have perfect examples and heroes to follow.

The scriptures tell us that Śrī Caitanya Mahāprabhu heard the stories of Dhruva Mahārāja and Prahlāda Mahārāja hundreds of times while growing up, and still he was never bored. The example and instructions of these saints are so valuable that no other moral book can compare with them. Children develop good character, saintly qualities, and pure *bhakti* by reading *Śrīmad-Bhāgavatam*. Indeed, *Śrīmad-Bhāgavatam* is the very essence of Lord Caitanya's *saṅkīrtana* movement.

HOW TO USE THIS BOOK

(A) *Discussion*

In my book, *Homeschooling Kṛṣṇa's Children*, I emphasize the necessity of giving our children a Kṛṣṇa conscious education based on Śrīla Prabhupāda's books. I discuss the methodology of studying *Śrīmad-Bhāgavatam* through interactive reading and discussion – the most important element of the process. We sit in a circle and take turns reading only translations, pausing frequently for discussion. (For children who cannot read, they can listen as their parents read and paraphrase the translations). This method has been followed for thousands of years by the great sages of Vedic India as we see in the *Bhāgavatam* itself.

Discussion is an important part of reading. For children it breaks up the monotony of reading and can add both interest and challenge. By using *Śrīmad-Bhāgavatam* as their basic text, children can learn all aspects of language skills: composition, comprehension, vocabulary, critical thinking, and analytical reasoning. The children often drive the discussion by asking questions, raising doubts, or making observations about what they read. By expressing themselves, children understand the material better, gain self-confidence, and learn communication skills. Parents can pick up on their children's cues and ask questions of their own to encourage deeper understanding. Parents can also present their own realizations, play devil's advocate, and relate the stories to practical life, thus making the *Bhāgavatam* study a dynamic learning experience.

Reading and discussion also lead to good speaking, debate, and logical thinking. The nature of *Śrīmad-Bhāgavatam* is such that it encourages a person to ask questions, think critically, and work creatively because the *Bhāgavatam* is full of analogies, metaphors, and figurative speech. For example, the analogy of the car and the driver that Prabhupāda uses to describe the difference between the body and the soul is practical and simple, but it allows a child to appreciate a foundational principle of Kṛṣṇa consciousness. Some analogies may be difficult for a four- or five-year-old, but as he or she grows older, these analogies will become the basis for strong reasoning skills.

Before reading a chapter (translations) with their children, parents should read the chapter and purports on their own and go through the discussion (higher-thinking questions) provided in this book. These questions give parents ideas of how to inspire discussion as they read with their children. Please remember, however, that the discussion questions are only for the purpose of stimulating ideas, not to create a highly structured "oral exam" atmosphere while reading. The key is to keep the discussion dynamic and student-driven, using the sample questions when needed and adapting/rephrasing them appropriately for the age and personality of the child. During a vibrant discussion, you and your child will, no doubt, come up with questions and topics that were not mentioned in this book, and we encourage you do so. Here are some suggestions for raising interesting and thought-provoking questions:

- Take turns reading the translations, going in a circle. This keeps the child's attention because children eagerly await their turn. If your child cannot read, you should read and pause frequently to paraphrase the story at the child's level. Ask your child to tell the story in his or her own words.

- Whenever possible, ask "why" and "how" questions rather than "what" (factual) questions, thus encouraging your child to think and reason.
- Don't be afraid to ask open-ended questions that do not have a clear-cut answer. These questions often lead to beneficial discussions.
- Discuss the many analogies and metaphors in Śrīla Prabhupāda's purports, which are good opportunities to connect the *Śrīmad-Bhāgavatam* to your child's experience and imagination.
- Frequently encourage your child to make comments and raise questions. When your child raises a question for which you don't know the answer, don't be afraid to say so. Discuss his or her question thoroughly, read through purports to find guidance, and you will see many fresh realizations arise.
- Try to relate the story to daily life: "Why did Parīkṣit Mahārāja not retaliate against the boy's curse?" or "What can we learn from Parīkṣit Mahārāja's behavior?" However, don't put your child on the spot by pointing fingers: "How should you have behaved with your friend Johnny the other day?" Such finger-pointing destroys the discussion and intimidates the child.
- Draw connections with other stories from the scriptures that your child may already know: "The boy Śṛṅgi showed anger in an inappropriate way, but when is it okay to feel angry? Can you give an example from other stories in the scriptures?"
- Continue reading until you come to a translation that raises a question or comment. Don't worry if a particular section doesn't raise discussion – some sections will be more interesting to a child than others.
- Have a "realizations session" at the end of a chapter where your child can tell you what they learned from the chapter, and you can tell your child what you learned. Or bring the family together and ask your child to give a short class on the chapter.
- If you have not read *Śrīmad-Bhāgavatam* before, that is okay. As a parent (or teacher), you have more life experience, and you know your child, which will allow you to lead a discussion and engage your child.
- When you read with an older child (the specific age will vary based on the maturity of the child), take the stance of a fellow reader and learner. This will help your child open up and feel comfortable. Of course, as the teacher, you will still need to correct a mistaken line of reasoning or raise points that are important but try to do it as a partner rather than as a master.
- Consider these readings/discussions as your time with *Śrīmad-Bhāgavatam*. Stay focused and become absorbed in *Śrīmad-Bhāgavatam*. Just because your study partner is a seven-year-old child does not mean that you will gain any less from studying *Śrīmad-Bhāgavatam*.

(B) *Written and Oral Exercises*

Once you have read a chapter of the *Bhāgavatam* translations together, you can use a variety of exercises provided in the book to teach language skills – including writing, comprehension, and vocabulary – which will help in understanding the chapter. This book provides comprehension questions, key themes and messages, language puzzles, arts and crafts, and many other activities. In this volume we have eliminated some language activities and extra resources to not make it too thick and unwieldy for children. We also encourage you to use your creativity to compile interesting new activities that would stimulate your child. To decide which verses children can memorize, please use the verse references under the key messages. Our goal is to provide you with practical tools to make *Śrīmad-Bhāgavatam* a central part of your children's education. Regardless of whether you are homeschooling or sending your children to school, we hope these tools will inspire you to create other innovative ways to help your children.

Here are the different sections you will find in this book:

- Story Summary
- Themes and Key Messages
- Discussion and Higher-Thinking Questions
- Analogy Activities
- Critical-Thinking Activities
- Introspective Activities
- Science Activities
- Writing and Language Activities
- Crossword Puzzles, Games, and Action Activities
- Arts, Crafts, Drama, and other Hands-On Activities
- Answers (includes answers to specific questions and puzzles)

The instructions for each activity are addressed directly to the child, but if your child is younger, we encourage you to explain and supervise the activities.

LEARNING OUTCOMES

The book's main objective is to provide children from the ages of 13–18 with spiritual knowledge from the *Śrīmad-Bhāgavatam* and the opportunity for personal realization.

The primary process for doing this is by reading chapter translations with the children, discussing the stories and philosophical content of the chapter, and providing the children with the opportunity to make their own inquiries and share their personal experiences.

In addition, the activities in this book develop the key themes and philosophical points presented in each chapter by accommodating different learning styles in a range of learning modes (visual, auditory, and kinesthetic).

The activities also meet the following cognitive and language objectives:

Developing thinking skills (based on Bloom's *Taxonomy of Educational Objectives*)

- Developing comprehension skills
- Acquiring knowledge
- Applying knowledge
- Using knowledge to be creative
- Analyzing information
- Promoting self-evaluation

Language objectives:

- Written language (includes reading and writing)
- Visual language (includes communicating through the visual arts, such as drama and static imagery)
- Oral language (includes communication through speaking)

This book also supplements any existing curriculum that parents or teachers may use to teach language skills. This is not a course designed to teach reading and writing in itself, but it can work together with a formal curriculum to further develop language skills, while providing children with a resource for studying *Śrīmad-Bhāgavatam*.

Śrīmad-Bhāgavatam lies at the heart of Śrī Caitanya Mahāprabhu's philosophy and movement. I pray that this book will help children and their parents develop a lifelong love for this great literature, following in the footsteps of Śrīla Prabhupāda and our previous *ācāryas*. *Śrīmad-Bhāgavatam* is very profound, and this book only skims the surface. I humbly request you to forgive any faults and shortcomings in our humble endeavors.

Aruddhā Devī Dāsī
March 2024

1

THE SUPREME LORD IS EQUAL TO EVERYONE

Story Summary

Mahārāja Parīkṣit's time was running out, but, being immersed in this sublime discussion with Śukadeva Gosvāmī, the King felt as if time had stood still. There was so much more he wanted to know, not just to benefit him but to benefit all of us.

He had heard [in the Sixth Canto] how Diti had burned with anger when her sons, Hiraṇyākṣa and Hiraṇyakaśipu, were killed by Lord Viṣṇu on the plea of King Indra. Was the Lord then partial to the demigods and inimical to the demons?

To remove his doubt, Parīkṣit Mahārāja asked, "O dear Śukadeva Gosvāmī, since the Lord is everyone's well-wisher and is equal and dear to everyone, how is it that He acted like a common man?"

Śukadeva Gosvāmī frowned and cleared his throat.

"Errr . . . I mean, it seemed that he was partial to Indra and so killed Indra's enemies," Parīkṣit Mahārāja continued. "How can the Lord, who is equal to everyone, be partial to some and inimical to others?

"Lord Viṣṇu, the Supreme Personality of Godhead, is already full of bliss. So what happiness will He gain if He sides with the demigods? And since He is transcendental and has nothing to do with material qualities, how could He fear the demons or be envious of them?

"O learned *brāhmaṇa*, kindly remove my doubt with evidence that Nārāyaṇa is always neutral and equal to everyone."

Śukadeva Gosvāmī smiled and exclaimed, "That's an excellent question!

"How wonderful are these discussions about the Lord's activities, which please the devotees and counteract the miseries of material life. Therefore great sages like Nārada Muni always speak from *Śrīmad-Bhāgavatam* about the Lord's glories. Let me offer my respectful obeisances first to Śrīla Vyāsadeva and then begin discussing these topics."

Śrīla Śukadeva Gosvāmī folded his palms together and closed his eyes. He muttered a prayer and then looked affectionately upon the King.

"O my dear King, you are right. Lord Viṣṇu

is *nirguṇa*, always transcendental to material qualities. He doesn't have a material body – so how can he have hatred or attachment? How can He be envious of someone and then be friendly to another? However, through His spiritual potency He appeared and acted like an ordinary human being, accepting duties apparently like a conditioned soul. But know for certain that the Lord is pure and untouched by the material modes of nature.

"My dear King Parīkṣit, the material modes of *sattva*, *rajas*, and *tamas* – goodness, passion, and ignorance – belong to the material world. Everyone is controlled by these modes except the Lord. In fact, He controls these qualities. So there is no question of His being partial.

"On the universal level as well, Kṛṣṇa controls the modes of nature. When goodness is prominent in the world, Kṛṣṇa allows the sages and demigods to flourish; when the mode of passion and ignorance are prominent, the demons, Yakṣas, and Rākṣasas flourish. As the Supersoul in everyone's heart, He invokes different proportions of goodness, passion, and ignorance, depending on our *karma*, or fruitive actions.

"So the Lord is not partial. Everyone works under the influence of the various modes of nature, and when the various modes are prominent, the demigods or demons appear victorious under their influence."

"Mmm . . ." said Parīkṣit Mahārāja. "So, in other words, everyone reaps the fruits of their activities."

"Exactly! The Supreme Lord in everyone's heart simply awards the results of one's activities, which are influenced by the various modes of material nature. He supervises victory and loss, but He does not take part in them."

"So He's not responsible for the demigods' victory?" asked Parīkṣit Mahārāja.

"No; when the demigods are surcharged with *sattva-guṇa*, they are naturally victorious. It is not because of the Lord's partiality. Just as fire [goodness] is in wood, water [passion] is in a waterpot, and ether [ignorance] in a pot, one can understand whether one is a devotee or a demon by the activities one performs. Someone can understand how the Lord is favoring a person by seeing the person's actions.

"It's like a teacher instructing a student. If a student is receptive and accepts the teacher's instructions, he will progress in his understanding. It has nothing to do with partiality. In the same way, Kṛṣṇa wants to give *bhakti-yoga* to everyone, but one must be capable of receiving it."

"Aha!" exclaimed Parīkṣit Mahārāja, his eyes glinting in amazement. "So if we don't want to receive, how can we say that Kṛṣṇa is partial?"

"Yes," said Śukadeva Gosvāmī, nodding. "Like a neutral judge, Kṛṣṇa simply awards the results of one's *karma*. As far as His devotees are concerned, Kṛṣṇa is not partial to them; He simply responds to their receptiveness, to their devotion.

"Furthermore, these three *guṇas* cannot increase and decrease on their own – they do so because of time. Time forces these modes to change. And who is the controller of time?"

"Kṛṣṇa!" exclaimed Mahārāja Parīkṣit.

"Indeed! He controls time, as we see in the creation, maintenance, and annihilation of the universe, which are all under Kṛṣṇa's supreme will. He controls the material modes through time and thus allows the living beings to act within the limits of time.

"For example, He favors the demigods because they are situated in the mode of goodness under the influence of time, and He kills the demons who are under the influence of ignorance also due to the time factor. But He is still never partial. Just as an electrician who can manipulate electrical energy according to his desire (to power a heater or a cooler) but has nothing to do with causing heat or cold, the Lord similarly does not have anything to do with the results of the living beings' actions. He simply induces time to act according to their activities within the modes of nature."

"So, time controls the material energy, and Kṛṣṇa controls time," said Parīkṣit Mahārāja, trying to follow the philosophical discussion.

"Yes. Besides this, even though Kṛṣṇa favors His devotees because of their receptivity and devotion, He is still the friend of everyone. When He kills the demons, like Pūtanā, for example, He liberates them. He gave Pūtanā, the demon who tried to kill Him by feeding Him her poisoned breast milk, the exalted position of His nurse in the spiritual world. This is how impartial Kṛṣṇa is. Therefore He is called Uruśravā, one whose glories are widespread."

Mahārāja Parīkṣit beamed from ear to ear, hearing about Kṛṣṇa's mercy. Indeed, Kṛṣṇa's glories are widespread because He is not only glorified everywhere but His mercy is spread everywhere and to everyone.

"I will tell you another story," continued Śukadeva Gosvāmī, "to show you how the Lord is impartial, even to the demons."

"Oh yes, please tell me," said Mahārāja Parīkṣit, eager to hear of Kṛṣṇa's mercy.

"Once," Śukadeva Gosvāmī began, "Mahārāja Yudhiṣṭhira, the eldest of the Pāṇḍava brothers, invited kings and exalted personalities from far and wide for a Rājasūya sacrifice. Kṛṣṇa, the well-wisher, friend, and loving cousin of the Pāṇḍavas, was there. And so was Kṛṣṇa's enemy, Śiśupāla. You see, Śiśupāla had always despised Kṛṣṇa even from his childhood. Fueled by the fire of envy that raged in his heart, he constantly blasphemed the Lord. His brother, Dantavakra, did the same.

"So on this special day, in the prestigious assembly, Kṛṣṇa was glorified as the most exalted personality and chosen to be worshiped first. Yudhiṣṭhira Mahārāja joyfully washed Kṛṣṇa's feet while Śiśupāla watched in fury. He could not tolerate Kṛṣṇa's worship, and with a sudden outburst, he blasphemed Kṛṣṇa and rebuked the elders for choosing Kṛṣṇa above anyone else. Many of the guests blocked their ears and left the assembly while the Pāṇḍavas raised their weapons to kill the envious Śiśupāla. Kṛṣṇa stopped them, and with His *Sudarśana cakra* decapitated Śiśupāla. At that moment, a tiny spark left Śiśupāla's body and entered Kṛṣṇa's body. Śiśupāla was liberated by merging into Kṛṣṇa's divine body.

"Mahārāja Yudhiṣṭhira was struck with wonder. He asked Nārada Muni, who had also witnessed the spectacular incident, how could such an envious person attain this exalted destination, which even great transcendentalists could not achieve."

Śukadeva Gosvāmī narrated how Yudhiṣṭhira and the sages present were eager to hear from Nārada Muni.

Yudhiṣṭhira Mahārāja asked, "How is it that these two envious persons – Śiśupāla and Dantavakra – who constantly blasphemed the Lord were not attacked by leprosy nor enter the darkest regions of hell? Even King Vena, who blasphemed the Lord, was sure to go to hell. So, Śiśupāla should've also. Yet how did he merge into the Lord's existence, which is almost impossible to attain?"

Nārada Muni answered: "The conditioned souls in this world are affected by praise and blasphemy. They suffer under the influence of the Lord's external energy. They consider their bodies to be their real self and everything related to the body to be theirs. Because of this wrong conception of life, they create friends and enemies and feel the effects of chastisement or praise.

"But not the Lord – He has no material body and no false conception of 'I' and 'mine.' So don't think that He feels pleasure or pain when blasphemed or offered prayers. He has no enemy or friend."

"But then why did He kill Śiśupāla?" thought Yudhiṣṭhira Mahārāja.

Nārada Muni, who knew everything, continued, "Kṛṣṇa is very kind. When Kṛṣṇa chastises the demons it is for their good, and when He accepts the prayers of His devotees it is for their good. He is affected neither by prayers nor blasphemy, but He is so kind that He may punish such demons in one life, like he did with Citraketu (who became Vṛtrāsura), and then take them back to Godhead.

"So, my dear King, if you simply concentrate

your mind on the Lord, either by enmity or devotional service, by fear, affection, or lusty desire, the result is the same, because the Lord is never affected by enmity or friendship."

Nārada Muni didn't mean that we should think of Kṛṣṇa unfavorably like Śiśupāla or any other demon. We should serve Kṛṣṇa favorably. Nārada Muni wanted to emphasize that if we are intensely absorbed in thoughts of Kṛṣṇa, we will receive Kṛṣṇa's mercy and become purified. Kṛṣṇa's enemies can never be more elevated than Kṛṣṇa's devotees.

Nārada Muni continued, "Believe it or not, one can be more absorbed in Kṛṣṇa through enmity than by devotional service. Just as a grassworm who's confined by a bee in the hole of a wall and later becomes bee-like because of remembrance and fear of the bee, conditioned souls who somehow or the other think of Kṛṣṇa can become free of their sins and regain their spiritual bodies.

"Many persons were liberated just by thinking of Kṛṣṇa with great attention and gave up their sinful activities. I shall now explain how someone receives Kṛṣṇa's mercy by concentrating one's mind upon Him."

Mahārāja Yudhiṣṭhira could understand that Nārada Muni, out of humility, felt that the absorption of the demons surpassed his, and therefore he spoke like this. But his essential message remained – by focusing on the Lord with rapt attention we can receive Kṛṣṇa's favor and go back to Godhead. If an envious mind can be so absorbed in the Lord and receive such results, imagine the results a devotee can achieve by constant absorption in Kṛṣṇa.

"My dear King Yudhiṣṭhira," Nārada said, "the *gopīs* obtained Kṛṣṇa's mercy by their lusty desires, Kaṁsa by his fear, Śiśupāla and other kings by envy, the Yadus by their familial relationship, you Pāṇḍavas by your affection for Kṛṣṇa, and we, the general devotees, by our devotional service.

"One must concentrate on the form of Kṛṣṇa in any of these five ways to achieve Kṛṣṇa. King Vena was unable to think of Kṛṣṇa's form in any of these ways and was therefore not eligible for salvation. So, my dear King, simply remember Kṛṣṇa, one way or the other.

"O best of the Pāṇḍavas, your two cousins Śiśupāla and Dantavakra were associates of Lord Viṣṇu in Vaikuṇṭha. They were the Lord's gatekeepers, Jaya and Vijaya, but because they were cursed by *brāhmaṇas*, they fell to this material world."

"What kind of curse could affect such liberated souls who are completely spiritual, and who would even dare curse the Lord's associates?" asked Yudhiṣṭhira Mahārāja, surprised.

Nārada Muni smiled and said, "Once, the four sons of Brahmā, Sanaka, Sanandana, Sanātana, and Sanat-kumāra, while wandering through the three worlds, came to Viṣṇuloka. They appeared like small, naked children although they were even older than Brahmā's other sons. Thinking they were ordinary children, the gatekeepers Jaya and Vijaya forbade them to enter. The four Kumāras were enraged. They cursed Jaya and Vijaya to take birth as demons in the material world.

"As the guards of Vaikuṇṭha fell to the material realm, the Kumāras took pity on them and said that after three births they would return to their positions in Vaikuṇṭha.

"In this way, Jaya and Vijaya had three births. The first was as the two sons of Diti, Hiraṇyakaśipu and Hiraṇyākṣa. Lord Varāha killed Hiraṇyākṣa when he hindered the Lord in his attempts to save the earth from the Garbhodaka Ocean. And Hiraṇyakaśipu, well, he was the worst of all. He wanted to kill his own son, Prahlāda, who was a great devotee of Viṣṇu. Just imagine! But the Lord protected Prahlāda, and so his father couldn't kill him.

"Then Jaya and Vijaya took birth as Rāvaṇa and Kumbhakarṇa, who troubled the world in many ways. Lord Rāma appeared to kill them, not only to rid the world of miscreants but so they could be relieved of their curse."

"How merciful is the Lord!" exclaimed Yudhiṣṭhira Mahārāja.

Nārada Muni continued, "O King Yudhiṣṭhira, in their third birth, the same Jaya and Vijaya took birth in a family of *kṣatriyas*, as your cousins Śiśupāla and Dantavakra. With His disc, Lord Kṛṣṇa severed their heads, and as a result all their sinful reactions were destroyed. Now they are free from their curse and have regained the shelter of the Lord in Vaikuṇṭha."

"So although they merged into the body of Kṛṣṇa, they didn't remain there?" asked the King.

"No, no one can fall from Vaikuṇṭha. It was the arrangement of the Lord's internal energy that Jaya and Vijaya descend to the material world – to fulfill the Lord's desire to fight."

"How remarkable are the Lord's pastimes," said Yudhiṣṭhira Mahārāja, who now appreciated what had just happened in his Rājasūya sacrifice.

"But there's just one more thing I'd like to know," said the King, now that he felt invigorated from hearing the Lord's pastimes. "Why were Hiraṇyakaśipu and his son, Prahlāda, enemies? And how did Prahlāda become such a great devotee of Kṛṣṇa?"

Themes and Key Messages

Please go through this table of themes and key messages, with corresponding verses, and discuss each topic further.

THEMES	REFERENCES	KEY MESSAGES
The Lord is impartial although He appears to be partial.	7.1.1–6	Mahārāja Parīkṣit questioned that if the Lord is impartial how is it that He seemed to have favored the demigods and killed the demons? Śrīla Prabhupāda explains that the Lord is transcendental and has nothing to do with material qualities; He is absolute whether He kills or gives His favor. Therefore, He liberated even the demons when He killed them. He doesn't have attachment or hatred towards anyone. He only appears to act under material influence because He appeared in this material world and acted like an ordinary human being. Only a devotee can understand the truth of how the Lord acts.
The Lord is not influenced by the modes of nature. He simply awards the results of the activities of the living entities, who are influenced by the modes. Therefore He cannot be partial.	7.1.7–8	The three modes of material nature – goodness, passion, and ignorance – cannot touch the Supreme Lord. He controls material nature, which works under His order. Conditioned living beings, however, become influenced by and work under the various modes, and they act accordingly. The Supreme Lord simply gives the results of the living entity's actions. He supervises victory and loss, but He does not take part in them. Because the demigods are in *sattva-guṇa,* they are victorious when they fight with the demons. This is not due to the partiality of the Lord.
Kṛṣṇa is favorable to someone not because He is impartial but because of the person's devotional activities and receptiveness to Him.	7.1.9–10	Kṛṣṇa favors His devotee because of the devotee's advanced position in devotional service. One can judge a demigod or a demon according to the quantities of *sattva-guṇa, rajo-guṇa,* and *tamo-guṇa* they possess and how they conduct their activities. The Lord, who is in everyone's heart, directs the soul, but it depends on the soul to take direction and follow the instructions of the Lord. Kṛṣṇa is open to everyone, but one has to be capable of understanding Him. Therefore, Kṛṣṇa is not impartial; He is equal to everyone and simply responds to our receptiveness.

THEMES	REFERENCES	KEY MESSAGES
The Lord favors the demigods and kills the demons not because of His partiality but because of the influence of the time factor.	7.1.11–12	Kṛṣṇa is the creator of time and is therefore not limited or subject to the actions and reactions of time. He controls time, seen in creation (passion), maintenance (goodness), and annihilation (ignorance), which are all under His supreme will. Therefore, when He favors the demigods and kills the demons, it's not because He is partial but because they are influenced by the material energy through the time factor. Just as an electrician who can manipulate electrical energy according to his desire (to use a heater or a cooler) but has nothing to do with causing heat or cold, the Lord similarly does not have anything to do with the results of the living beings' actions. He simply induces time to act according to their activities within the modes of nature, but He is never partial.
One should be intensely absorbed in thought of the Lord favorably and be engaged in favorable devotional service to attain the highest perfection of life.	7.1.25–27	The Lord is not affected by blasphemy or prayers, or enmity or friendship. (When He chastises the demons, it is for their good, and when He accepts the prayers of His devotees, it is for their good.) But that doesn't mean that we should blaspheme Him. Devotional service should be done favorably as Kṛṣṇa desires (*ānukūlyena kṛṣṇānuśīlanam*). One should never blaspheme the Lord otherwise the blasphemer will suffer in hellish life. Even though Nārada Muni says that one is more intensely absorbed in thoughts of the Lord as an enemy than a friend, this doesn't mean that we should think of the Lord as an enemy or that the demons are more elevated than Kṛṣṇa's pure devotees.
Any remembrance of the Lord can purify one from all sins.	7.1.28–32	Even Kṛṣṇa's enemy can become purified and liberated by thinking of Kṛṣṇa, in His personal form, just as Śiśupāla did. The *gopīs* obtained Kṛṣṇa's mercy through "lust," Kaṁsa by his fear, Śiśupāla and other kings by their envy, the Yadus by their familial relationship, the Pāṇḍavas by their great affection, and the general devotees by their devotional service. However, the destination of the devotee and the enemy is not the same; the Lord's enemies, such as Kaṁsa, Hiraṇyakaśipu, and Śiśupāla merged into Brahman, whereas the Lord's pure devotees attain the association of the Lord in the spiritual world.

Higher-Thinking Questions

Now try to deepen your understanding of this chapter by delving into Śrīla Prabhupāda's purports and reflecting on the following questions:

1. What is the difference between material and spiritual explained by Śrīla Prabhupāda in his purport to verse 2? How is Kṛṣṇa spiritual in relation to His impartiality?
2. If someone thinks that Kṛṣṇa is under the influence of material qualities, like attachment and hatred, envy and friendship, why are their thoughts considered foolish? (See verse 6 purport.)
3. Verse 9 explains that we can judge whether the Lord favors someone by seeing their actions. This implies that the Lord favors His devotees. Is this because of the Lord's partiality or because of the devotee's actions? Explain.
4. Briefly explain which elements relate to which modes of material nature and how one can judge a person by the mode in which he acts. (Refer to verse 9 purport.)
5. Explain how the living being receives different kinds of bodies as outlined in verse 10 purport.
6. According to verse 11 purport, describe briefly how the Lord is not under the limitations of time.
7. Based on verse 12 purport, explain how the Lord's killing of Pūtanā shows His impartiality.
8. Verse 25 states that the Lord is neither affected by blasphemy nor prayers. Does this mean that one should blaspheme the Lord? Regarding this, what is Śrīla Prabhupāda's advice in verse 26 purport?
9. Nārada Muni's opinion is that one can become absorbed more intensely on the Lord through enmity than through devotional service, just as Śiśupāla did. Does this mean that the enemies of the Lord are greater than His devotees? Explain. (See verse 27 and purport.)
10. If no one can fall from the spiritual world, how is it that Jaya and Vijaya fell from Vaikuṇṭha and became demons? Recall what you've learned in Canto 3 and refer to verse 35 purport.

ACTIVITIES

In this section you will find many exciting things to do. These activities will get you thinking, moving, drawing, and having loads of fun.

Analogy Activity

... to bring out the scholar in you

POTS OF PERCEPTION

"The all-pervading Personality of Godhead exists within the heart of every living being, and an expert thinker can perceive how He is present there to a large or small extent. Just as one can understand the supply of fire in wood, the water in a waterpot, or the sky within a pot, one can understand whether a living entity is a demon or a demigod by understanding that living entity's devotional performances. A thoughtful man can understand how much a person is favored by the Supreme Lord by seeing his actions." *SB* 7.1.9

This verse shows that an expert thinker can judge who a devotee or a demon is based on their activities – how nicely they receive and utilize the mercy of the Lord. To the extent they accept the Lord's favor, they are not influenced by the modes.

Further in the analogy, fire, water, and sky represent the modes of goodness, passion, and ignorance respectively. Śrīla Prabhupāda says that just like we can "measure" fire in terms of the capacity of a container of coal or petrol, water in terms of the capacity of the waterpot, and sky based on the size of the container it fills, we can understand the extent to which a person is affected by the modes by understanding how much he has accepted the mercy of the Lord.

Furthermore, Śrīla Prabhupāda says that the mercy of the Lord, the chance to be situated in His service (*śuddha sattva*), is available to everyone.

Let us try to understand this analogy better.

Look at each of the circles below:

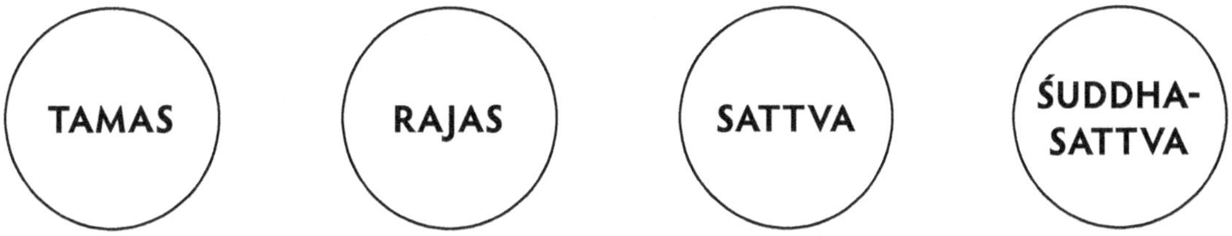

Color the mode of ignorance blue, the mode of passion red, and the mode of goodness yellow. Finally, leave transcendental goodness, *śuddha-sattva*, white.

Now look at each of the waterpots below. They represent different types of people. Each of them has a mixture of goodness, passion, ignorance, and *śuddha-sattva* in them.

Color the waterpots in proportion to the amount of goodness, passion, ignorance, and pure goodness (using the colors in the previous diagrams) you think these people have:

Śrīla Prabhupāda

A devotee who has no desire other than to serve Śrīla Prabhupāda's mission

A devotee who wants to serve, but also has a bucket list of ways he wants to enjoy the world

A person who wants to work hard and enjoy his money

A thief

Demons who came to kill Kṛṣṇa

An atheist

After you have colored in the pots, decide:

1. To whom is Kṛṣṇa ready to give mercy?
2. Who is ready to take mercy from Kṛṣṇa easily?
3. Why are some people eager to receive the mercy, while others aren't?

Śrīla Prabhupāda uses another analogy in the purport of students who are receptive to the teacher. Reflect on the following:

1. To whom is the teacher ready to give instructions?

2. Who is ready to act according to the teacher's instructions?
3. Why do some students listen to the teacher, while others don't?
4. Do you think that regardless of the modes we are in, we can still make a choice to accept the teacher's instructions?

What can you conclude from these two analogies in relation to Kṛṣṇa?

Challenge: What do you think will happen if we focus on performing devotional service, activities in *śuddha-sattva*? Will the lower modes have less hold on us?

Artistic Activity

... to reveal your creativity

KṚṢṆA ABSORPTION BOX

Absorption in Kṛṣṇa means to remember Kṛṣṇa. The essence of *bhakti* is to always remember Kṛṣṇa and never forget Him.

In this chapter we learn of how the grassworm becomes bee-like by meditating on the bee. Similarly, by remembering Kṛṣṇa, we become purified and regain our eternal spiritual bodies.

In this fun activity, you will make a photo box of four of your favorite devotional activities, which increase your remembrance of Kṛṣṇa. In this example, we use chanting of the holy names, reading *Śrīmad-Bhāgavatam*, serving with devotees in *saṅkīrtana*, and visiting the holy *dhāma* (Māyāpur).

Materials needed: Light-colored card stock paper enough to make one 6x16-inch (15x40 cm) rectangle and another 2x2-inch (5x5 cm) rectangle; scissors; ruler; pencil; pen; 1 to 2 crayons; glue; 12-inch (30 cm) colored ribbon; 4 photos of your favorite devotional activities, each a bit smaller than 2x2 inches (5x5 cm).

Steps:

1. From your stock paper, measure and then cut out a 2x2-inch (5x5 cm) rectangle. Draw and color in the worm and bee as shown in the resource. Keep this aside.
2. Now, from your stock paper, cut a rectangle of 6x16 inches (15x40 cm). Make a grid of 24 squares 2x2 inches (5x5 cm) each. (See Image 1)
3. Beginning from the top, draw two hearts on the outer squares of each alternating row. You will have four rows with two hearts each. (See Image 2)

Resource

Image 1

Image 2

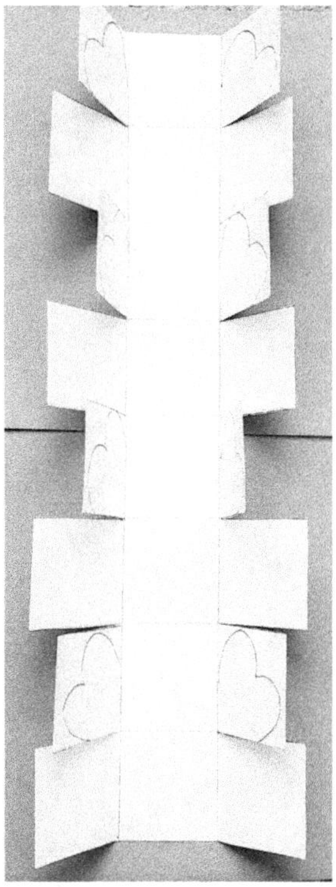

Image 3

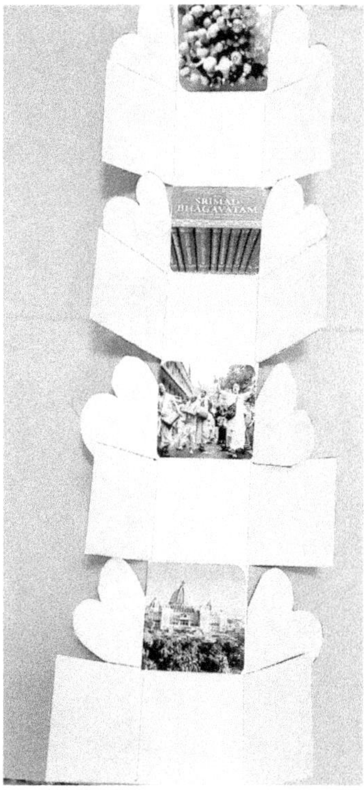

Image 4

4. Fold the paper to divide it into three columns. Cut below and above the heart drawing to make "tabs" as shown in Image 3.

Image 5

5. Glue the four photos in between the hearts in all four rows. (See Image 4)

6. Now, add your personal experiences and reflections on each activity around the photo. (See Image 5)

7. Now fold the sheet to make a box. Begin at the bottom by folding the last row over the middle square of the row above. (See Image 6)

8. Grab the two hearts on each side and fold the whole thing onto the next square together. Continue folding until you reach the end. (See Images 7 to 9)

9. Secure the cube with a ribbon, and glue the art onto the photo cube. (See Image 10)

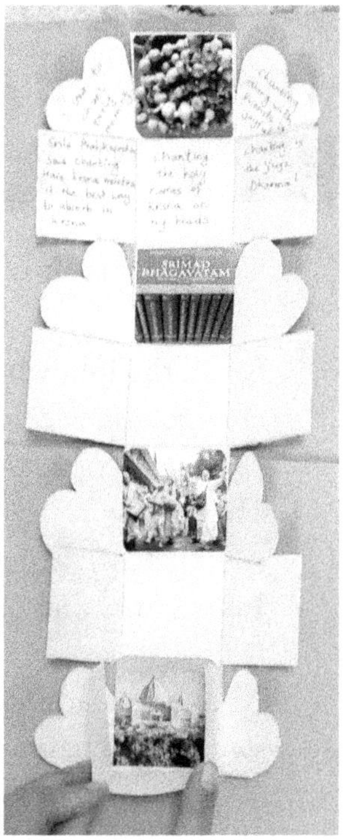

Image 6

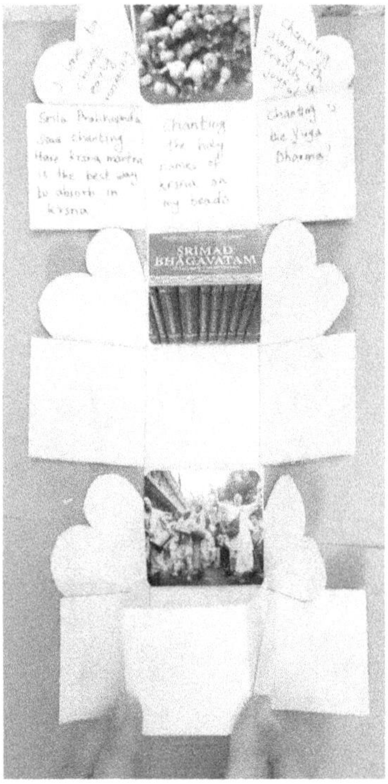

Image 7

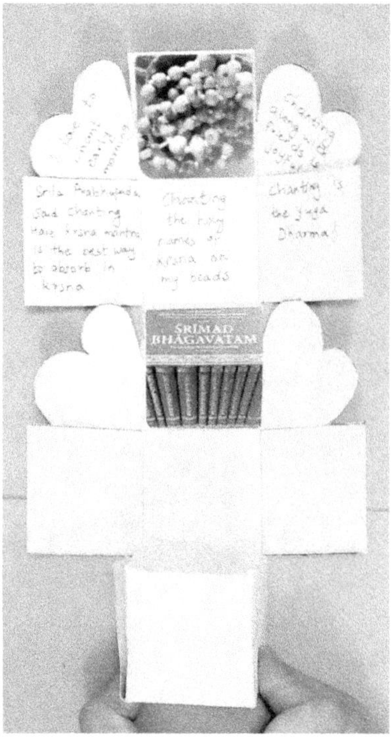

Image 8

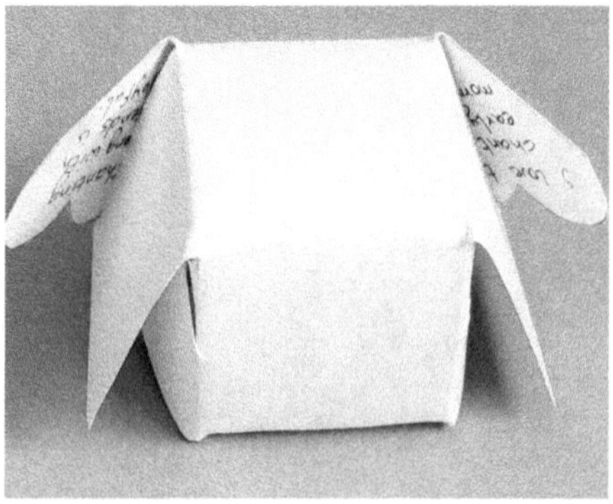

Image 9

Image 10

Now you have a wonderful piece of art reminding you of the most essential principle of devotional service: absorption in Kṛṣṇa!

Theatrical Activity

... to bring out the actor in you

SKIT: ONE STEP CLOSER

Enact the following skit with your friend. It is written for two male protagonists, but you can change this depending on who are available for the roles.

Two people are sitting at individual desks on roller office chairs, their backs to each other. They are working on their laptops.

Jake: No . . . no . . . oh . . . no no no. (Swings around in his chair) Nitai! Nitai!

Nitai has headphones on so he cannot hear Jake. Jake pulls out Nitai's headphones, and Nitai swings his chair around.

Nitai: What's up? I was working and listening to a beautiful *kīrtana*.

Jake: I'll tell you what's up. What's this? (points to his screen)

Nitai: A person.

Jake: (moves his mouse) What's this?

Nitai: A person.

Jake: And what's this?

Nitai: I'm going out on a limb here, but I'll say it's another person. Jake, did you take your blood pressure meds today? It looks like you are having a heart attack.

Jake: I'm perfectly fine, thank you very much. But what's not fine is this algorithm you wrote for our social media app.

Nitai: What's wrong with it?

Jake: The people. The people in the app. I just tested it, and it came up with these people (points to the screen and moves his hand in a circular motion).

Nitai: And what's wrong with these people?

Jake: This one is average looking, this one is below average, and this one is just plain ugly.

Nitai: Jake, that's hurtful to those people. So what if these people aren't movie stars? (points to the people on the screen) This one is talented, this one is hilarious, and this one is an innovative genius.

Jake: Boring. People using this app want to see beautiful people. I want to see beautiful people. Pretty privilege exists for a reason.

Nitai: That's old news. Can't we be different? Can't our app be different?

Jake: (Thinking for a moment and walks up and down) You're always talking about Kṛṣṇa, aren't you? But Kṛṣṇa isn't different, is He? Kṛṣṇa favors certain people; otherwise why would some people be more beautiful, more rich, or more intelligent?

Nitai: You have it all wrong. Kṛṣṇa is not partial to anyone. It is clearly stated in the *Śrīmad-Bhāgavatam* that He is equal to both the devotees and nondevotees.

Jake: (with sarcasm) Oh well, in that case please enlighten me. Why is there so much difference in the world if Kṛṣṇa is equal to us all?

Nitai: Because WE are different. We've been given different bodies related to our past lives' *karma*.

Jake: So now we're stuck here?

Nitai: No, we are never stuck. We can get out of this entanglement through devotional service. Kṛṣṇa gives everyone and anyone that opportunity. It's up to us to take it.

Jake: Devotional service, you say. Sounds like hard work. And you know how I feel about hard work.

Nitai: Jake, Jake, Jake. The whole world is hard work. But devotional service is blissful.

Jake: Blissful . . .hmm . . . that almost sounds tempting.

Nitai: You know, today is Lord Nṛsiṁhadeva's appearance day. Let's forget about work and go help the devotees clean vegetables for the feast tonight.

Jake: Feast! I don't mind a feast. (They walk off together) Will they pay us to clean vegetables?

Nitai: I wouldn't count on that! Your reward will be that you will be one step closer to Kṛṣṇa.

Critical-Thinking Activity

... to bring out the spiritual investigator in you

PROVING THE IMPARTIALITY OF THE LORD

Mahārāja Parīkṣit asks Śukadeva Gosvāmī how the Lord could be impartial if He seemed to side with Indra. In this chapter Śukadeva Gosvāmī proves to Mahārāja Parīkṣit the impartial nature of the Lord.

Let's try to apply what you learned from their discussion to another scenario.

Imagine you are asked to visit Vṛtrāsura's demon associates, who do not understand the position of the Lord or His devotee, Vṛtrāsura. They simply think that Indra killed Vṛtrāsura and that Lord Nārāyaṇa sided with Indra. They are upset about Lord Nārāyaṇa's partiality toward Indra. Your job is to convince these demons about the impartial nature of the Lord.

You decide to create the following bulletin board to help you. Some messages are only partially written out, with the purport number in brackets.

Complete the first and second columns of the bulletin board from the purports. Then use this information to complete the speech bubbles on the right. (You need not match the speech bubbles point by point, but you need to address all points overall.)

Vṛtrāsura's associates think the Lord is partial because . . .	**But I know that . . .**	**So I'll try to convince them by saying . . .**
1. The Lord seemed to favor Indra over Vṛtrāsura in the battle.	The Lord clearly states that He is impartial in the *Bhagavad-gītā* 9.29 (purport 1)	
2. The Lord chooses only to listen to the demigods, not to them.	The Lord is present as the same Supersoul within everyone, devotee or demon, and listens to everyone's desires.	

Vṛtrāsura's associates think the Lord is partial because . . .	But I know that . . .	So I'll try to convince them by saying . . .
3. The Lord caused the victory of Indra and the defeat of Vṛtrāsura.	It is the material qualities that cause victory or defeat, not the Lord – He is transcendental and allows the modes to act, without interfering in any way. So everyone receives the result they deserve.	
4. The Lord got Vṛtrāsura killed (by Indra) because He considered Vṛtrāsura His enemy.	The Lord has no friends or enemies. (Refer to *BG* 9.29.) He is therefore not vengeful to anyone. He awards the same result to both devotees and demons who always think of Him, either due to affection or envy. They both get liberated.	

Introspective Activity

. . . to bring out the reflective devotee in you

IS THE LORD FAIR TO ME?

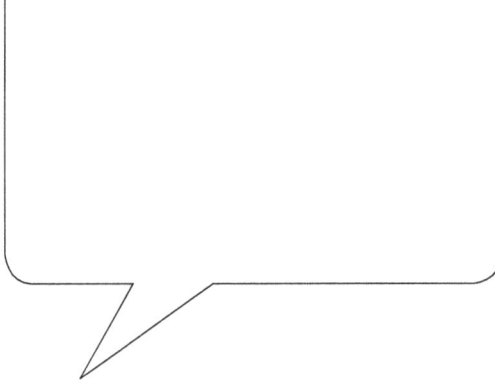

Have you ever felt that the Lord was unfair to you? Have you desired something that you didn't get and felt hurt that the Lord didn't fulfill your desire despite your faith in Him?

Think of such a time, and fill out the reflection sheet below, while trying to understand the nature of the Lord's hand in the situation:

Was the Lord Fair to Me?

1. Which incident or situation shows this to me?

   ----

2. In what way do I think things turned out unfair to me?

   ----

3. In this incident, do you think:
   a) The Lord knew your desire/action as the Paramātmā?

      ----

   b) The Lord was involved in the situation in some way? In other words, do you believe that the result you obtained, even though unfavorable, was by the Lord's sanction?

      ----

4. The result obtained was seemingly unfavorable, but the Lord is always impartial as we've learned from this chapter. Let us evaluate why the Lord may have sanctioned something unfavorable despite your strong opinion that you may have deserved better.

5. Although the result was not favorable, consider:
   a) Did you learn or grow from the experience?
   b) Did you often think of Kṛṣṇa when you were going through the difficult situation?
   c) Did you perhaps benefit in other ways (if not the way you wanted to) in the situation?
   d) Did you experience or feel, at least a little bit at some point, that the "unfair" result may have been because of something else (your *karma*) rather than Kṛṣṇa wanting something bad for you?

Analyze the situation by thinking about these questions and trying to see Kṛṣṇa's hand and "favor" in the situation. Discuss your thoughts with your group.

Writing Activity

... to bring out the writer in you

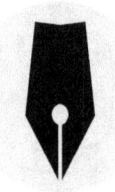

HAIKU: COVERED BY THE CLOUDS

We advance in Kṛṣṇa consciousness according to our ability to receive Kṛṣṇa's mercy. Kṛṣṇa's mercy is always there, but because we are covered by the three modes of nature, due to our *karma*, we are unable to accept Kṛṣṇa's mercy.

In the purport to verse 9, Śrīla Prabhupāda discusses an analogy given by Śrīla Viśvanātha Cakravartī Ṭhākura to understand this better: The sun and the moon are brilliant, but when they are covered by the clouds, they are not clearly visible. Similarly, when we are in the lower modes of nature, we are covered, and the more we come to the mode of goodness, the more brilliant our devotion shines.

Using the analogy of the sun or moon, write a haiku showing how Kṛṣṇa is not partial and that we are responsible for our covered condition because of the influence of the modes.

What is a haiku?

A haiku is an ancient Japanese form of poetry with a specific structure, style, and philosophy. Traditionally, haiku poetry discusses abstract subjects or those from the natural world. The structure can be looser and traditional rules ignored.

The traditional haiku includes the following features:

- There are only three lines, totaling 17 syllables.
- The first line contains five syllables, the second line seven syllables, and the third line five syllables.
- Punctuation and capitalization are left to the poet.
- A haiku usually does not rhyme.
- It can include the repetition of words or sounds.

Here's an example. Check if it follows the above rules:

Glossy golden sun
dark hissing clouds devour you
Shine, shine, shine stronger

Guidelines to help you:

1. Read examples of haiku to learn more about its structure.
2. Make a list of words that relate to the subject you have chosen. Be as descriptive as possible. Think about feelings and emotions too.

3. The last line usually observes or reflects on your subject. It may be interesting to add a surprise here. Looking through the list you wrote, can you create an unexpected relationship between the first two lines and the third?

Language Activities

... to help you understand better

TYPES OF ABSORPTION IN KṚṢṆA AND WHERE THEY TAKE US

Verse 31 discusses five different devotees or demons who have attained Kṛṣṇa through intensely thinking of him in different ways. Match the personalities in the left column with their kind of absorption in Kṛṣṇa in the right column.

DEVOTEE / DEMON	TYPE OF ABSORPTION
1. Śiśupāla and Dantavakra	A. Familial mood
2. Gopīs	B. Devotional service
3. Pāṇḍavas	C. Lust
4. Yadus	D. Affection
5. General devotees	E. Envy

1. Do each of these devotees have the same destination? Explain.
2. How is the destination of Śiśupāla and Dantavakra, Hiraṇyākṣa and Hiraṇyakaśipu, and Rāvaṇa and Kumbhakarṇa different from the destination of other demons in Kṛṣṇa's pastimes?
3. What can you conclude from this?

SHOULD WE BECOME KṚṢṆA'S ENEMIES?

In this chapter we learn that even the demons are absorbed in Kṛṣṇa. In verses 26 and 27 Nārada Muni explains that the demons' absorption in Kṛṣṇa is even more intense than the devotees' absorption. Does this mean that we should become Kṛṣṇa's enemies?

Let's compare the demons' absorption to the devotees'.

We can use two examples: Hiraṇyakaśipu and his son Prahlāda, and Śiśupāla and Yudhiṣṭhira Mahārāja.

In the Venn diagrams on the next page, write the similarities of their absorption in the center where the two circles cross, and in the respective circles write the differences in the quality of their absorption. Analyze their absorption through their mind, body, and words. Use descriptive words. What do you notice about the quality of each of their minds, words, and actions? In other words, is it favorable or unfavorable to Kṛṣṇa?

In the previous activity, we concluded that the destination for the demons and devotees are different. The demons in *Kṛṣṇa-līlā* were special because they were intensely absorbed in Kṛṣṇa and became liberated by being killed by Kṛṣṇa.

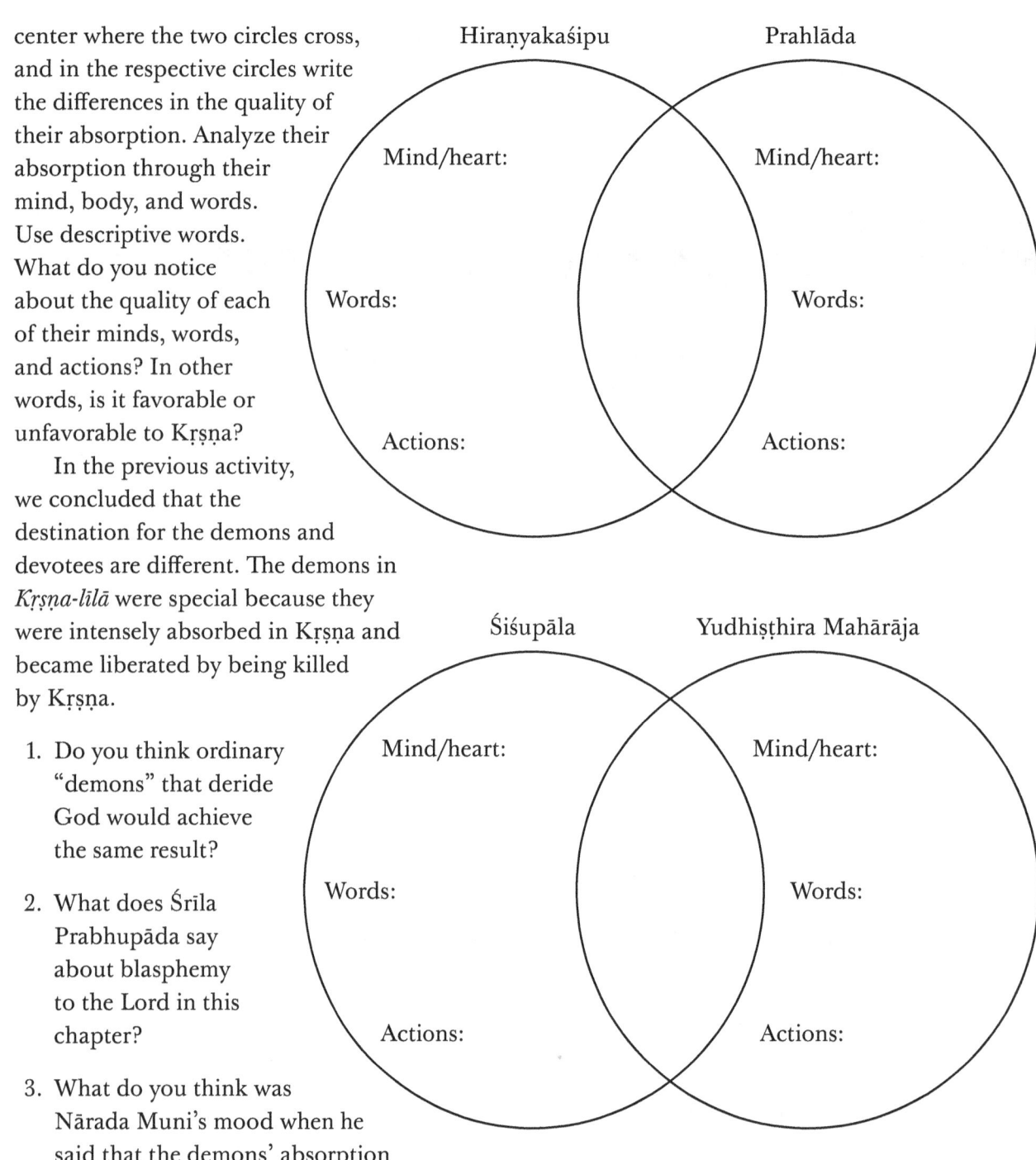

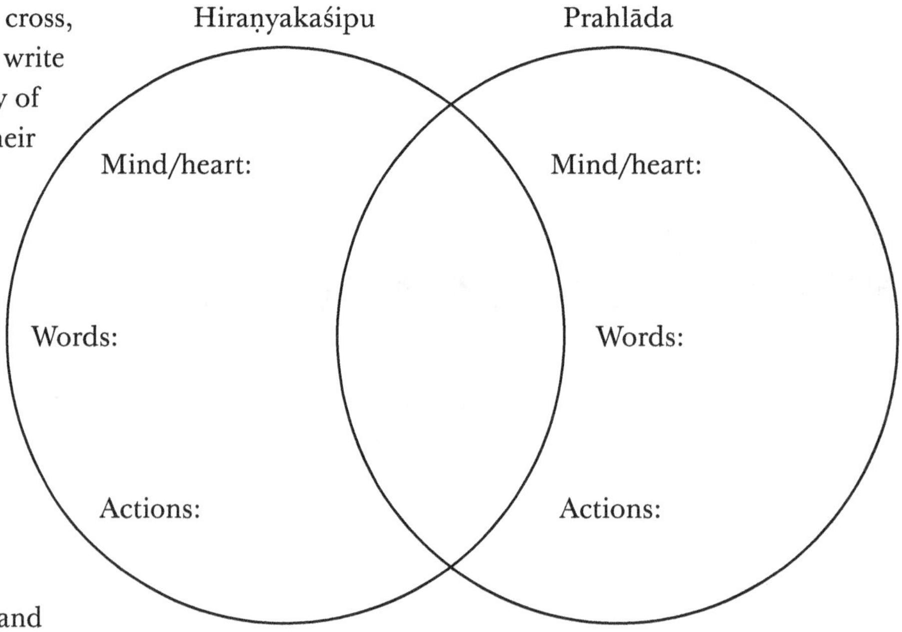

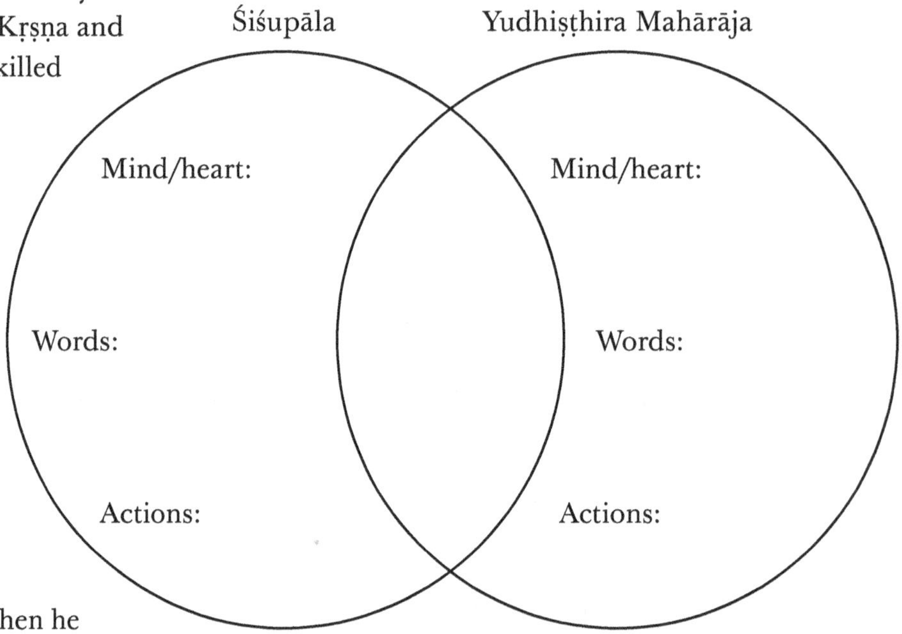

1. Do you think ordinary "demons" that deride God would achieve the same result?
2. What does Śrīla Prabhupāda say about blasphemy to the Lord in this chapter?
3. What do you think was Nārada Muni's mood when he said that the demons' absorption in Kṛṣṇa is the greatest?

CHAPTER 1 ANSWERS

Pots of Perception

Śrīla Prabhupāda – pot: white; devotee serving Prabhupāda's mission – pot: white; devotee serving and also enjoying – pot: mix of all four colors; hard-working man – pot: no white, minimal yellow, mostly red and little blue; thief – pot: no white, minimal yellow, mix of red and blue; demons – pot: mostly mix of blue and red; atheist – mostly blue, little red.

Kṛṣṇa is ready to give mercy to all these people, but based on the modes they act in, they may or may not take the mercy. Similarly, the teacher is ready to give instruction to everyone, but only the diligent student will accept and carry out the instructions. Conclusion: We should try to develop at least the mode of goodness, which can help elevate our consciousness so we can make good choices and accept Kṛṣṇa's instructions. This, however, doesn't mean that those tainted with the modes of passion and ignorance cannot become purified and accept Kṛṣṇa's mercy. We are all tainted by the modes, but by performing devotional service, we become purified and we can thus make the right choices.

Proving the Impartiality of the Lord

1. It may seem like Indra won the battle and got his way, but Vṛtrāsura also got his way – he was a devotee and wanted to associate with the Lord directly in the spiritual world, and the Lord granted his wish. The Lord was, therefore, equal to both parties; 2. The Lord heard Vṛtrāsura's desire to go back to the spiritual world and serve Him, as much as He heard Indra's desire to want to kill Vṛtrāsura. He simply fulfilled both people's desires, proving His impartial nature; 3. If Vṛtrāsura was actually defeated, then how did he attain eternal life as an associate of the Lord, with opulence and position that Indra cannot even imagine? Indra's victory is material and temporary, while Vṛtrāsura attained spiritual victory, which is permanent; 4. Vṛtrāsura was a devotee although he appeared in the body of a demon. He was dear to the Lord and desired His personal service – the Lord simply awarded him personal service, while externally acting through the agency of Indra. He awarded Vṛtrāsura a benediction far superior to Indra's.

Types of Absorption in Kṛṣṇa

Matching: 1. E; 2. C; 3. D; 4. A; 5. B

1. They don't have the same destination. They achieve different types of liberation (*mukti*) depending on their mood and intense desire. The *gopīs*' lust, which is based on their intense love for Kṛṣṇa, allows them to associate with Kṛṣṇa personally in the spiritual world. This also applies to Kṛṣṇa's other pure devotees. However, the demons killed by Kṛṣṇa attained impersonal liberation and therefore can fall back into the material world. Kṛṣṇa's pure devotees in Vṛndāvana or Vaikuṇṭha do not.

2. They were Jaya and Vijaya in Vaikuṇṭha and only fell to the material world to fulfill the Lord's desire to fight and have pastimes. After merging into the Lord's existence, they once again attained their original positions in Vaikuṇṭha in a personal relationship with the Lord.

3. Conclusion: The destination of the spiritual world is better than the impersonal Brahman. It is therefore better to be absorbed in Kṛṣṇa favorably, through affection and love, than through envy or hatred.

Should We Become Kṛṣṇa's Enemies? *(Potential Answers)*

Hiraṇyakaśipu and Śiśupāla:

Differences: mind/heart – evil, cunning, envious, angry, fearful; words – blasphemous, insulting, negative, hurtful, harsh; actions – violent, ruthless, vengeful, evil, cruel/wicked, hurtful, hostile.

Prahlāda and Yudhiṣṭhira Mahārāja:

Differences: mind/heart – loving, affectionate, devotional, friendly; words – prayerful, respectful, glorifying the Lord, humble, gracious, tolerant, patient; actions – worshipful, kind, generous, serving mood, loving, affectionate, warm, caring.

Similarities among all: absorbed in thinking of Kṛṣṇa intensely

1. Demons have unfavorable thoughts, words, and actions toward the Lord, while the devotees have favorable thoughts, words, and actions toward the Lord.
2. No. Those who are blasphemous to the Lord go to hellish conditions of life.
3. He was being humble, not thinking himself a great devotee (that even the demons had greater intensity in thoughts of Kṛṣṇa than he). And he wanted to impress upon Yudhiṣṭhira Mahārāja that the conditioned souls should somehow become absorbed in thoughts of Kṛṣṇa.

2

HIRAṆYAKAŚIPU, KING OF THE DEMONS

Story Summary

Nārada Muni started to explain from the beginning. It was a long story but one that would give great spiritual nourishment to all who hear it.

Nārada Muni described how furious Hiraṇyakaśipu was when Lord Viṣṇu, in the form of Lord Varāha, had killed his brother Hiraṇyākṣa.

Biting his lips and his eyes ablaze in anger, Hiraṇyakaśipu picked up his trident and spoke to the assembled demons: "O Dānavas and Daityas! Listen to me! My enemies, the demigods, have united to kill my brother. You may think that the Supreme Lord Viṣṇu is always equal to the demons and the demigods. But don't be fooled! Lord Viṣṇu has taken the demigods' side and helped them kill Hiraṇyākṣa."

Frowning and showing his terrible teeth, the king of the demons continued, "Influenced by *māyā*, Lord Viṣṇu has taken the form of a boar to please His devotees. I shall therefore sever His head with my trident. With the blood from His body I shall please my brother, who was fond of sucking blood. Then I will be peaceful!

"When the root of a tree is cut, the entire tree

is destroyed and dries up. Similarly, when I kill Lord Viṣṇu, the demigods will die, for He is the source of their life."

Pacing the floor, Hiraṇyakaśipu hissed like a serpent at the thought of Lord Viṣṇu. Then he stopped and smiled a cunning smile. He looked at his followers and said: "While I am busy trying to kill Viṣṇu, go to the planet earth and kill all the *brāhmaṇas* and *kṣatriyas*! The earth is flourishing because of them, because of their austerity, sacrifice, Vedic study, vows, and charity. We cannot allow them to flourish! If you kill the *brāhmaṇas*, there'll be no one to encourage the *kṣatriyas* to perform *yajñas*. And when the demigods don't get their share of the *yajñas*, they will automatically die without the shelter of Lord Viṣṇu."

Hiraṇyakaśipu laughed loudly, invoking terror in the hearts of the demons. "Go immediately to wherever the cows and the *brāhmaṇas* are protected. Set fire to those places and cut the trees, which are the source of life, from their roots."

The demons offered their obeisances at the feet of their king and hurried to do as they were told. They set fire to the cities, villages, pasturing grounds, forests, and agricultural fields. They burned the hermitages, mines, the mountain villages, the villages of the cowherd community, and the government capitals. They even broke down the bridges, walls, and gates of the cities. With their axes they chopped down mango, jackfruit, and other trees that were sources of food. They destroyed almost everything!

People had no choice but to neglect their activities of Vedic culture. They couldn't perform any *yajña*, and as a result the demigods suffered without the results of sacrifices. They left the heavenly planets and began wandering the earth, not noticed by the demons, to see the disasters.

In the meantime, Hiraṇyakaśipu was observing the rituals for the death of his brother.

His heart broke when he saw his nephews crying bitterly at their father's side. How could he comfort them? Anger again rose within him, but he restrained it, wanting to pacify his nephews, his sister-in-law, and his mother.

Looking at Diti's tear-stained face, he said, "Dear mother, thirsty travelers come together in a restaurant or a place for drinking water, and after drinking water, they continue their journeys. Similarly, living beings come together in a family, and later, because of their own actions, they depart to different destinations.

"The spirit soul, the living being, is eternal. It doesn't die. And the pure soul, free from contamination, can go anywhere in the material or spiritual worlds. Such a soul is in full knowledge and is completely different from the material body. But because the soul misuses its slight independence, it accepts subtle and gross bodies created by the material energy. With these bodies the living being enjoys or suffers. So you should not lament for the passing of the soul from the body."

Diti looked up, surprised. Her son was speaking like a *sādhu*.

"Trees on the bank of a river seem to move when reflected on the water. Similarly, when

someone's mind is unstable or disturbed, he sees the ground moving in front of him. In the same way, O mother, when the mind is agitated by material nature, the living being thinks that his condition has changed from one form to another. Actually, Hiraṇyākṣa has attained his next destination, so there's no reason to lament. Don't lament for the death of a great hero, for a hero's death in front of his enemy is glorious and desirable.

"Don't be bewildered, my dear relatives. The bewildered living being thinks the body and mind to be the self. As a result, he thinks that some people are his friends and others his enemies. Because of this misconception, he suffers. He has to take birth again and again in different species and with various types of consciousness in this cycle of *saṁsāra*."

Hiraṇyakaśipu's sister-in-law burst out crying. Diti stroked her shoulder to comfort her. The nephews also still looked upset. Weren't they listening to anything he had said thus far? Hiraṇyakaśipu grew impatient and then angry again, thinking of his sworn enemy, Lord Viṣṇu, who had caused such trauma and heartache.

He let out a deep breath and then decided to take a different approach. He began to relate a story from ancient history: "Please listen to this old history. It involves a discussion between Yamarāja and the friends of a dead person."

Hiraṇyakaśipu's audience gathered their composure and tried to listen attentively.

Hiraṇyakaśipu forced a smile and said, "Once, the great king Suyajña of Uśīnara was killed in battle. His friends sat around the dead body, grieving for their loss. When the queens saw their husband lying slain on the battlefield with his hair scattered, his eyes lifeless, his entire body covered in blood, and his heart pierced by arrows, they cried: 'O lord, because you've been killed, we've also been killed.' Repeating these words, they pounded their breasts and fell at the feet of the dead king.

"Their tears glided onto their chests, becoming reddened with the *kuṅkuma* powder on their breasts. While loudly crying, their hair and clothes became disheveled and their ornaments were scattered on the ground. Everyone around felt pity for them.

"The queens cried, 'O lord, cruel fate has now removed you from our sight. You've sustained the people of Uśīnara and made them happy, but now you've made them unhappy. O hero, you were our best friend. How can we live without you? Take us with you!'

"The queens didn't allow the body to be burned. They held the dead body in their laps and wailed piteously. As the sun set, Yamarāja, from his abode far away, heard the loud cries of the queens. He took the form of a young boy and approached the heartbroken relatives.

"'How amazing it is!' Yamarāja told them. 'These people have lived longer than me. They have seen that hundreds and thousands of living beings have taken birth and died. So shouldn't they understand that they are sure to die? But no, they are still bewildered. The conditioned soul comes from an unknown place and then after death returns to that same unknown place. There is no exception to this rule. So if they know this, then why do they lament?' "

Hiraṇyakaśipu described that the grieving friends and relatives looked at this young boy, mystified by his presence. They wondered who he was.

Glancing at the mourning queens, the boy continued, "Just look at these elderly women. Isn't it amazing that they don't have a higher understanding of life? Yet, we weak children, who are not protected by a mother or father, are still alive and not eaten by ferocious animals that lurk in these forests. So, we firmly believe that the Supreme Personality of Godhead, who protected us in the womb, will protect us anywhere."

"Then how is it that He hasn't protected our husband?" asked a queen amidst her sobs.

The boy then approached the crying ladies and said, "O weak women, the Vedic knowledge declares that the Supreme Personality of Godhead creates, maintains, and destroys this world. This material creation is like His plaything. He is completely free to do as He pleases – to destroy or protect. He can do anything; otherwise how can He be supreme?"

The queens stopped sobbing and began listening to this fascinating young boy.

"Have you ever wondered why someone may lose his money in a public street and then get it back because no one had noticed it there? And yet someone who keeps his money securely at home is robbed of it all. Everything happens by the Lord's will. If the Lord protects someone, even if they are in the jungle, they remain alive, and someone who is well protected at home may die.

"Everyone gets a body according to their *karma*. The Lord is not directly responsible for this. The soul is completely different from the body. Just as someone may think his house is identical with him, the conditioned soul incorrectly thinks that the body is himself. This body is made of material elements and in time is vanquished. The soul has nothing to do with the creation and destruction of the body. Just as fire is different from the wood, air is different from the mouth and nostrils that it fills, and as the sky pervades everything yet is also separate, so the living being is separate from the material body even though he is encaged within it."

The queens wiped the tears from their eyes as they listened to the wise words of Yamarāja.

"O lamenters, you are all fools!" the boy chastised. "There's your husband lying before you!" He pointed to the King's carcass. "He hasn't gone anywhere, so why do you lament?"

The queens looked down, embarrassed yet brought to their senses by the boy's jarring words. They knew that even a common man could understand the difference between a living body and a dead body. The soul cannot be seen when it occupies the body, but it is the actual living force. If the queens hadn't even seen the real person, the soul, then why were they lamenting for that which they never saw?

"The soul cannot do anything without the direction of the Supersoul," the boy continued. "When the soul is covered by the subtle body (the mind, intelligence, and false ego), the living being is forced to accept the results of his actions. In this way the soul is connected with the material energy

and has to suffer or enjoy, continually, life after life. This happiness and distress caused by the material senses are like dreams – they are mental concoctions. But those who are self-realized, who understand that the soul lives forever and that the body perishes, do not lament. They are never illusioned.

"Let me tell you a story so you understand better," said the boy, now feeling compassion for these illusioned souls.

"There was a hunter who captured birds in his net, luring them with food. Once, two *kuliṅga* birds flew nearby, and the female bird got caught in the net.

"O queens, the male *kuliṅga* bird became distressed when he saw that his wife was in danger. He was unable to release her and began to lament: 'How merciless in Providence! What will Providence gain by taking away this poor bird? My wife is half of my body. What is the use of my living with half of my body if she dies? The unfortunate baby birds, who haven't even grown their wings, are waiting in their nest for her to feed them. I won't be able to maintain them.'

"Meanwhile, the hunter, who was watching in the distance, released an arrow and killed the male *kuliṅga* bird.

"O queens! You are all so foolish that you lament but don't see your own death coming. You don't know that even if you lament for your dead husband for hundreds of years, he's not going to come back. And in the meantime your lives will be finished!"

Hiraṇyakaśipu continued the narration: "The relatives and wives of the King were wonderstruck by the philosophical words of Yamarāja, in the form of a small boy. When Yamarāja disappeared, they performed the funeral ceremonies of King Sujyajña, understanding that all material things are temporary and cannot continue to exist."

Hiraṇyakaśipu had tried to console and enlighten his relatives with transcendental knowledge. He concluded, "So none of you should grieve for the loss of the body. Only an ignorant person makes bodily distinctions, thinking 'Who am I? Who are the others? What is mine? What is for others?"

Nārada Muni, who had been relating this entire episode to Mahārāja Yudhiṣṭhira, in answer to his question, said, "Diti, the mother of Hiraṇyakaśipu and Hiraṇyākṣa, heard these instructions of Hiraṇyakaśipu along with her daughter-in-law. She forgot her grief and focused on understanding the real philosophy of life."

Themes and Key Messages

Please go through this table of themes and key messages, with corresponding verses, and discuss each topic further.

THEMES	REFERENCES	KEY MESSAGES
Varṇāśrama-dharma is essential for the peace and wellbeing of human civilization.	7.2.9–12	Hiraṇyakaśipu wanted to kill the *brāhmaṇas*, because their purpose was to please Lord Viṣṇu through the performance of *yajña*. If they were killed no one would encourage the *kṣatriyas* to perform *yajña*, and thus the demigods would die. He also wanted to destroy the places where the *brāhmaṇas* and cows were protected. Without the *brāhmaṇas* to guide, *kṣatriyas* to rule perfectly, and *vaiśyas* to produce food and protect the cows, people would not live peacefully. In Kali-yuga there is a lack of real *brāhmaṇas*, *kṣatriyas*, and *vaiśyas*, and therefore there is a rise in the demonic population. Through the *saṅkīrtana* movement, the brahmincial culture and *kṣatriya* government can be restored and people can be happy.
Everyone in society should be trained to satisfy the Supreme Personality of Godhead.	7.2.14–16, 21	Hiraṇyakaśipu and his followers destroyed all the paraphernalia, including the trees that produced fruit and flowers, which were meant to please the Lord. Similarly, in this age, people, like the demons of previous ages, do not know that the highest goal of human life is to please Lord Viṣṇu. On the contrary, they simply plan to "kill" Lord Viṣṇu and be happy by sense gratification. Everyone should be trained to satisfy the Supreme Lord by their actions and occupation. Even though demons, like Hiraṇyakaśipu, may be elevated in knowledge, they don't use their good intelligence for the service and satisfaction of the Lord. Thus, they are called demons.
We are entangled in the material world because of bodily identification.	7.2.21–26	Because we think we are the body instead of the soul, which is eternal (has no death), full of knowledge, and bliss, we try to enjoy the material world independently. As a result, we have to accept bodies one after another in different lifetimes created by the material energy. The mind also becomes agitated by the modes of material nature. In such a bewildered state, the conditioned soul discriminates between friends and enemies and thus suffers and enjoys in different material bodies, in the *saṁsāra* of birth and death. Hiraṇyakaśipu advised his relatives that they need not lament for the passing of Hiraṇyākṣa because there is no death for the soul, and family relations are all temporary, just as travelers come together to drink water at a place and then move on to their respective destinations.

THEMES	REFERENCES	KEY MESSAGES
One should not lament for the dead body, for the body is different from the soul.	7.2.37, 42, 49	Death is certain for everyone, Yamarāja explained to the grieving queens, and the soul is eternal, so they should not lament for the loss of the body. Everyone receives a body according to their *karma*, yet the soul is different from the body. Due to ignorance the conditioned soul accepts the body to be himself. Yamarāja rebuked the queens saying that the body that they were attached to was in front of them, yet they were lamenting. Even a common man can understand that the soul, which is invisible, is different from the body and has now gone away. So why lament for something that was never seen? Those who have knowledge of self-realization, knowing the soul to be eternal and the body perishable, do not lament.
The Lord is the supreme protector; nothing happens without His will, so we should surrender to Him and seek His protection.	7.2.38–40	The Lord present in everyone's hearts gives protection to everyone and gives the different kinds of bodies that the living entity wants to enjoy. Everything is done by His order according to what the living being wants. He creates, maintains, and annihilates the entire world. Sometimes if the Lord does not give protection, even money that is kept securely is lost, whereas if He gives His protection, one who loses one's money on a public street where everyone can see it, gets it back. Since everything is dependent on the Lord's will, we should surrender to Him and seek His protection.
Everyone thinks that they are deathless even if they know that thousands of living beings are dying at every moment. Not preparing for death, they waste their valuable human life.	7.2.57–58	Yamarāja, in the guise of a small boy, related the story of the *kuliṅga* bird to convince the queens that they were foolish lamenting for their dead husband – even if they lamented for hundreds of years, they would never get him back, and in the meantime their lives would be finished. Similarly, even though people see others dying at every moment, they think that they will never die. They do not prepare for death and waste their valuable human life. Conversely, people usually think of philosophy when their relatives die and for that moment become interested in God, but as time passes, they forget this reality.

Higher-Thinking Questions

Now try to deepen your understanding of this chapter by delving into Śrīla Prabhupāda's purports and reflecting on the following questions:

1. In verse 6 Hiraṇyakaśipu brings up the Lord's impartiality. What argument, similar to what you've learned in Chapter 1, does Śrīla Prabhupāda use in the purport to refute the demon's statement?
2. What are some of the differences between the demigods and demons as described in verses 9 and 10 purports.
3. In what way is Hiraṇyakaśipu indirectly glorifying the demigods' relationship with the Lord in verse 9?
4. How can the brahminical culture and *kṣatriya* government come back according to verse 11 purport? Why is this so?
5. Why shouldn't trees generally not be cut down, especially fruit bearing trees? (Refer to verse 12 and 15 purports.) However, how is the publication of ISKCON literature, produced from trees, the performance of *yajña*, as Śrīla Prabhupāda describes in verse 12 purport.
6. What does Śrīla Prabhupāda compare in modern society to Hiraṇyakaśipu's and the demons' acts in verse 13 purport?
7. From verses 21 to 26 Hiraṇyakaśipu speaks transcendental knowledge to his mother and grieving nephews. How can we understand that although he knew the position of the Supreme Lord and the living beings, he was still a demon? (Refer to the note to verse 6 to see the distinguishing factor of a demon. How else is a demon different from a demigod or devotee of the Lord as explained in verse 21 purport?)
8. Why should the material body be cremated soon after death? (See verse 36 purport.) How does this relate to bodily misidentification?
9. Śrīla Prabhupāda explains in verse 37 purport that whether one believes in the existence of the soul or not, one should not lament for the loss of the body. Why is that?
10. For what greater reason does the Lord give the conditioned soul the opportunity to enjoy in the material world? (Refer to verse 38 purport.)
11. If everything happens by the Lord's will, is the Lord responsible for our accepting different types of bodies or are we responsible? Explain. (See verse 41 purport.)

ACTIVITIES

In this section you will find many exciting things to do. These activities will get you thinking, moving, drawing, and having loads of fun.

Critical-Thinking Activity

... to bring out the spiritual investigator in you

MUNDANE PLANS TO KILL VIṢṆU

In this chapter Hiraṇyakaśipu makes an elaborate plan of defeating the demigods by killing Lord Viṣṇu and destroying brahminical culture. He reasons that Lord Viṣṇu, the killer of Hiraṇyākṣa, flourishes when the *kṣatriyas* perform *yajña* under the guidance of the *brāhmaṇas*. The demigods depend on both Lord Viṣṇu and the *yajñas* for their strength. By cutting these two sources of their strength, Hiraṇyakaśipu thought he could defeat the demigods and avenge his brother's death.

Below is a World Nourishment Yajña Tree. Read verses 9 to 12 and label the different parts of the tree and what each represents.

Generally, the root provides nourishment to the tree, and the trunk carries nutrients to the leaves and branches. If the tree is cut off from the root, it ceases to receive nourishment and dries out.

If we take the universe to be a tree and Lord Viṣṇu to be the root, Lord Viṣṇu provides nourishment to the whole creation. Brahminical culture, when properly executed, also nourishes the demigods by giving them their share of *yajña*, and thus the whole tree of creation flourishes.

Now, look at a few entries in Hiraṇyakaśipu's logbook on the right with plans to destroy this tree from its roots.

Do you think Hiraṇyakaśipu will succeed in destroying this healthy tree by his plans? Think about why or why not, and use the following guidelines to write a short paragraph:

Plan 1: I am the strongest in creation. Fight Viṣṇu and kill Him. To weaken Viṣṇu beforehand, stop *yajña*, on which Viṣṇu depends for His strength.

Plan 2: Destroy brahminical culture. Ask my friends to destroy brahminical culture and *yajñas* on Earth. Without their *yajña* share, both demigods and Viṣṇu will become weak.

Plan 3: Destroy demigods. With no *yajña* and no Viṣṇu, demigods have no strength to fight and will surrender.

- Study each part of the plan carefully and determine which parts can be executed and which parts cannot.
- Try to reason why in each case. Draw upon your study of the previous cantos as you analyze.
- Use the imagery of the tree to explain your reasoning to the class.
- To conclude, comment on whether your reasoning would hold for anyone else trying to destroy Lord Viṣṇu and His associates.

Analogy Activity

... to bring out the scholar in you

WANDERINGS OF THE SOUL

"In a restaurant or place for drinking cold water, many travelers are brought together, and after drinking water they continue to their respective destinations. Similarly, living entities join together in a family, and later, as a result of their own actions, they are led apart to their destinations." *SB* 7.2.10

This verse summarizes the way souls wander in the material world. We have come across a similar analogy in Canto 6, and in this purport Śrīla Prabhupāda presents more analogies on the same topic to help us understand. Read the translation and purport, and looking at the images in the table below, label the different analogies.

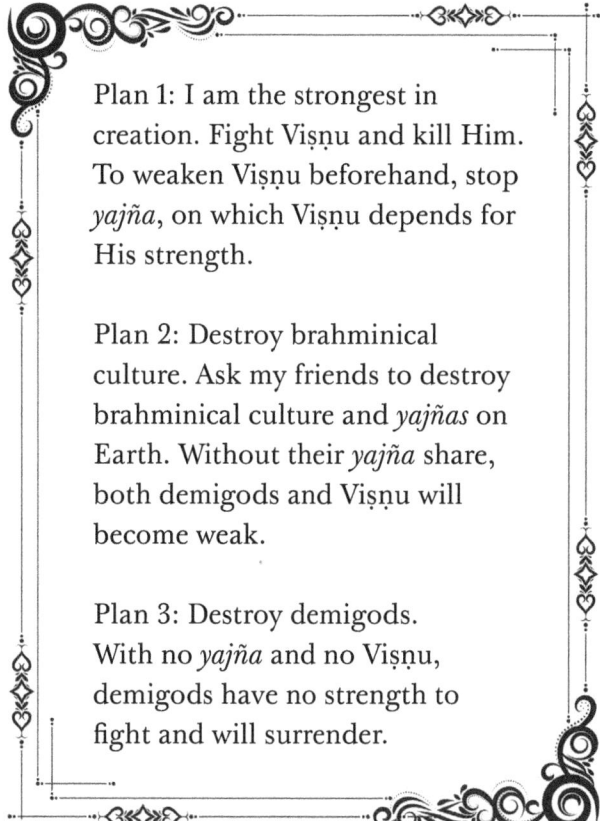

1 A.

1 B.

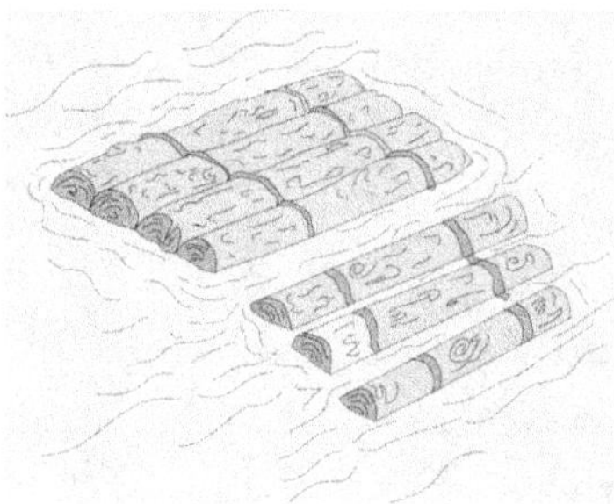

1 C.

Now, look at the soul being part of different "families" in the material world, coming together in different groups and dispersing (at death). Can you label the "families" below?

2 A.

2 B.

2 C.

For our purposes, let us suppose that the same soul travels through all these six situations.

1. Which situations can the soul find it easy to walk away from? Which situations are harder to leave?
2. Why do you think so? Is there any factor that differentiates the two situations?
3. What should a person do to be properly situated in all situations?

Action Activity

... to get you moving and learning

BOARD GAME: THE SUPREME PROTECTOR

We've seen many examples in the *Bhāgavatam* of devotees who, in times of difficulty, surrendered to Kṛṣṇa's will and sought His protection. They offered beautiful prayers to the supreme protector, grateful for the protection they received.

Let's play a board game to help us think of the Lord as our supreme protector.

Directions:

1. Use Resource 1 at the end of this chapter as your board.
2. Photocopy and cut out Resource 2 to make a dice. Only mark the numbers 1 to 3 on the sides. (So there will be two number 1s, two number 2s, and two number 3s on the dice.)
3. The game can be played by two to four players. Start the game with each player placing their tokens where indicated.
4. Each player throws the dice and moves the number of spaces indicated on the dice. Wherever the player lands, he or she must answer the question or guess who the speaker of the prayer is. (You may recite the prayer out loud.) Move from left to right.
5. If you get the answer right, you remain in the same place, but if you get it wrong you move one step back. Then for your next turn, you throw the dice again and move ahead.
6. Whoever reaches the end first is the winner.

Introspective Activity

... to bring out the reflective devotee in you

TAKING TIME TO PLEASE KṚṢṆA

Mama: "Hey, sweetheart! Look at this photo of you as a toddler! You looked so cute trying to offer incense to our Deities, and look at you playing the *mṛdaṅga*! Such wonderful days! You spent so much time at the temple . . ."

Child: "Yeah, Mama! I was just a kid. You know I don't have time now to do anything else besides homework!"

Do you recognize this scenario in your life?

It's true that as you get older, you need time for other things. However, knowing that your relationship with Kṛṣṇa is most important and that your life is meant to please Him, let's see how you can still satisfy Kṛṣṇa.

Śrīla Rūpa Gosvāmī mentions the 64 limbs of devotional service in *Bhakti-rasāmṛta-sindhu*, or the *Nectar of Devotion*. Many of them don't require any time but only require a change of consciousness and attitude. Let's look at some of them:

a) Avoid enjoyments that will not please Kṛṣṇa.
b) Keep your needs simple.
c) Give up company of those who are opposed to Kṛṣṇa.
d) Do not let lamentation and other extreme emotions control you.
e) Do not disrespect the demigods.
f) Do not inflict pain on other living entities.
g) Do not tolerate criticism of the Lord and His devotees.

Think about which is your favorite attitude-rectifying activity from the above list and why?

Discuss in a class group and write down:

1. Which other Kṛṣṇa conscious activities do you do that don't take extra time?

2. What do you think you can improve on?

3. What would you like to do that takes more time and which pleases Kṛṣṇa?

4. How could you manage your time better to do these activities?

Writing Activities

... to bring out the writer in you

LETTER OF CONDOLENCES

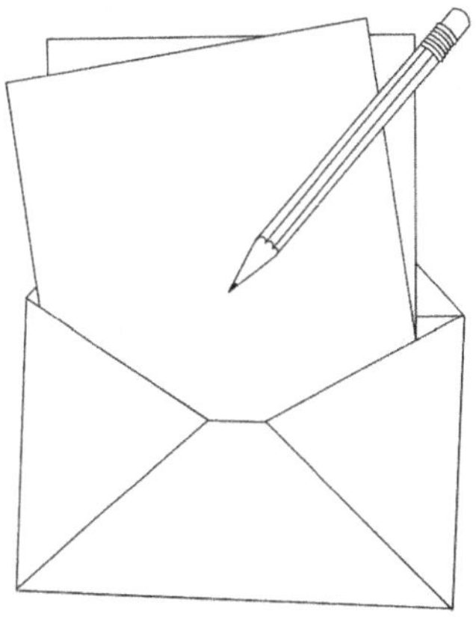

Your close friend, who is favorable to Kṛṣṇa consciousness, is devastated by the loss of a beloved pet (a cat, dog, goldfish, rabbit . . . you decide). Write a letter of condolence to your friend. In the letter use the pastime of the *kuliṅga* bird, narrated by Yamarāja, to explain why it is foolish to lament for an extended period. Explain that while the body remains perishable, the soul is eternal. You may choose to use the prompt below or begin in another way.

Dear John,

I'm so sorry to hear about your pet iguana. Grogu was the best pet anyone could hope for. I remember how he loved having his head patted and how much he enjoyed avocados. When I look at pics of Grogu, it saddens me that he is no longer with us.

As much as we all loved him, we also have to realize that time does not stop. Last night I was paging through the *Śrīmad-Bhāgavatam*, and I stumbled upon the pastime of the *kuliṅga* bird. . . .

SHORT STORY: THE MOST AMAZING THING

The most amazing thing, according to Yamarāja, is that people don't think they will die although they see death every day. In the *Mahābhārata,* Yamarāja also tested Mahārāja Yudhiṣṭhira, asking him what the most amazing thing was, and the King gave the right answer.

Write a short story on one of the following prompts to show that people are illusioned, thinking they will live forever. As a result, they refuse to mend relationships or forgive others, they continue to enjoy despite knowing that everything is taken away at death, they continue to harbor grudges and resentment, and they do not surrender to the Supreme Lord, knowing that death is close.

a). An 80-year-old man or woman does not forgive his or her child for something that happened in the past. They know they will die soon, but they still hold on to resentment. Does something or someone help change their understanding?

b). A boy buries his pet dog who dies in an accident. He grieves for a while, but soon he goes about his life normally, thinking that nothing like that will happen again . . . until one day.

c). A selfish shop owner refuses to give charity to the *sādhu* who visits his shop. He thinks that he will live forever, enjoying the comforts of life, when he has a startling reminder that all this could end. Does he change and become more generous?

AN OFFERING THAT PLEASES

Śrīla Prabhupāda mentions in his purport to verse 14: "Whatever we do and whatever our occupation, our main purpose should be to please the Supreme Lord." As spirit souls, part of Kṛṣṇa, we become happy when we please Him.

A common activity in all societies and cultures is cooking. As devotees, we offer food to the Lord that we've cooked with devotion, and only then do we honor or consume it. We know that the Supreme Lord is always pleased to accept our cooked dishes offered with love.

Think of your favorite dish and write down the recipe. If you don't know the recipe, use your imagination. Then get the right recipe, and compare it to yours. You may end up having a good laugh!

Now present the correct recipe in a format you like best.

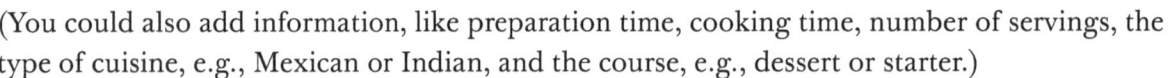

Guidelines for your recipe:

a) Title
b) Introduction to the dish, where you tasted it first, why you love it, and/or why you think the Lord would love it.
c) Picture of the dish
d) Ingredients
e) Method of cooking

(You could also add information, like preparation time, cooking time, number of servings, the type of cuisine, e.g., Mexican or Indian, and the course, e.g., dessert or starter.)

Reflect on the two versions of the recipe and discuss the following: While trying to do anything to please the Lord, we should learn to do it well. That effort in itself shows our desire to please.

Language Activities

... to help you understand better

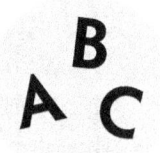

MAKE YOUR OWN JIGSAW PUZZLE

A jigsaw puzzle teaches the basic mental skill of matching. This activity will teach you to match concepts related to *varṇāśrama-dharma*, which ensures a happy and peaceful society. If any of the *varṇas* or *āśramas* are removed, as Hiraṇyakaśipu wanted to do, the whole of society suffers.

Choose two of the following key concepts:

- Perfect human civilization
- Demonic civilization
- Brāhmaṇa
- Kṣatriya
- Vaiśya

Then write down six concepts to match each key concept (see examples below).

Perfect human civilization (examples):
- *Brāhmaṇas* encourage *kṣatriyas* to perform *yajñas*
- *Kṣatriyas* rule according to the *śāstra.*
- *Vaiśyas* produce food and protect the cows.
- The demigods flourish.
- Religious principles are maintained.
- Brahminical culture is upheld.

Demonic civilization (examples):
- The *brāhmaṇas* and cows are destroyed.
- Brahminical culture is lost.
- The demons flourish.
- People only work for sense gratification.
- Trees are indiscriminately cut.
- The government becomes corrupt.

Similarly, you can choose any one of the four *varnas* and expand on them, using concepts related to them. See template below.

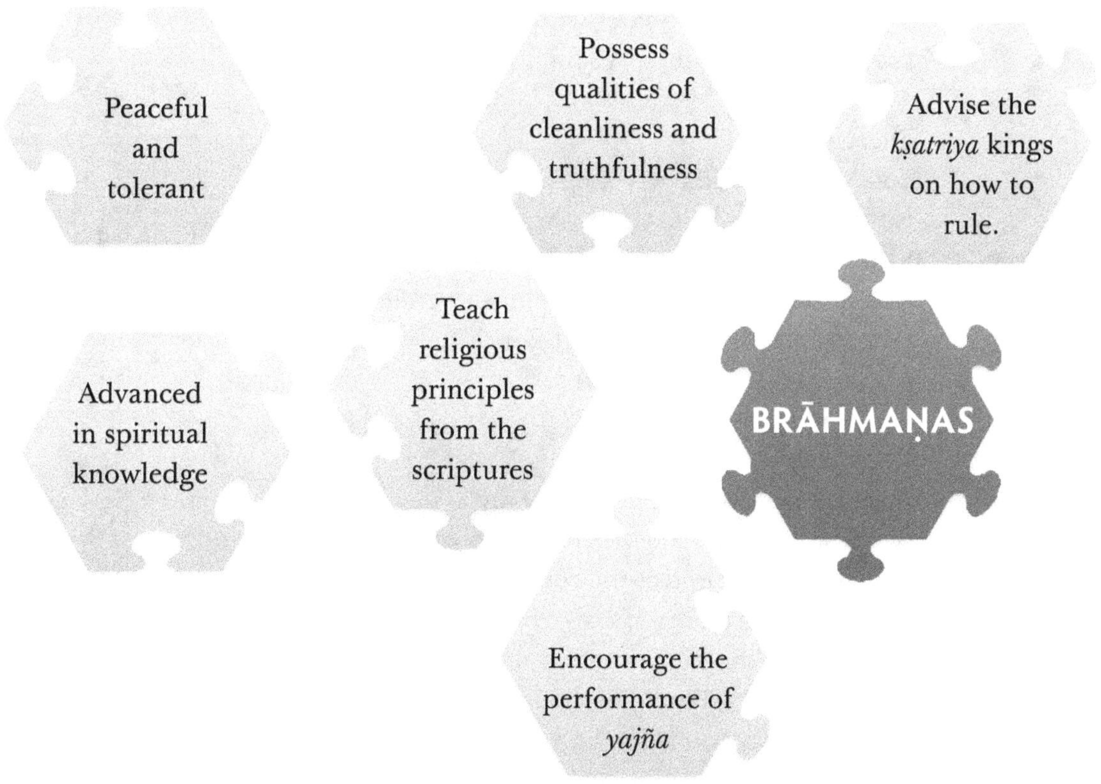

Once you've decided on your main concept and six matching concepts, cut out the puzzle pieces in Resources at the end of the chapter. You may glue them to cardboard and then cut them out.

On your central puzzle piece, write out your main concept.

Then write out the matching concepts on the other pieces. Color them all with different colors if you like.

Now mix the pieces up and put them all together to create your mini jigsaw puzzle.

Do the same with your next puzzle.

DIARY OF A DELUDED DEMON

Read the following excerpts from the recently unearthed diary of Hiraṇyakaśipu and then answer the questions that follow.

Excerpt 1:
I blame Viṣṇu. He killed my brother Hiraṇyākṣa today. I mean what did he even do to deserve such an inglorious death? You hide one measly planet and suddenly you're public enemy number one. Those pitiful demigods complain to Viṣṇu even if they get a paper cut. And of course, Viṣṇu always sides with them. I will avenge my brother's death and kill Viṣṇu if it's the last thing I do.

Excerpt 2:
Today I reminded everyone that Viṣṇu was influenced by *māyā* to kill my beloved brother. One would think that Viṣṇu would be above the clutches of *māyā*. Pathetic really. Anyway, I asked my fellow demons to go down to that most miserable of planets: earth. It flourishes under brahminical culture and I want it stopped.

Excerpt 3:
Revenge tastes delicious. Today my associates wreaked the sweetest havoc on those that dare to worship the demigods, give charity, or protect the cows and the *brāhmaṇas*. They chopped the fruit trees, broke bridges, and burned houses. I laughed as the earth went up in flames. Those sad, sad demigods will not get the results of any *yajñas*, and hopefully they will shrivel up and die. Victory is mine.

Questions:

1. Explain why Hiraṇyākṣa's death was not inglorious?
2. Why does it seem to Hiraṇyakaśipu that Lord Viṣṇu always sides with the demigods? Explain how Lord Viṣṇu is impartial?

3. Quote and explain an example of dramatic irony in excerpt 1. (Hint: Dramatic irony occurs when the audience/reader has a piece of knowledge that a character does not have.)

4. Hiraṇyakaśipu says Lord Viṣṇu is influenced by *māyā*. Recalling what you learned in Chapter 1, refute his statement.

5. Hiraṇyakaśipu wanted to destroy the *brāhmaṇas* and the cow protectors. Explain why the downfall of *varṇāśrama-dharma* is the downfall of society and why the world suffers today.

6. In this extract Hiraṇyakaśipu is not willing to accept responsibility for his actions. Try to recall a time when you didn't take responsibility, and recount what you could have done differently.

RAKHE KṚṢṆA MĀRE KE MĀRE KṚṢṆA RAKHE KE

In *Teachings of Queen Kunti* Śrīla Prabhupāda describes the struggles the Pāṇḍavas faced, which appear in the *Mahābhārata*. The Pāṇḍavas were devotees of Kṛṣṇa, and although they were materially weaker than their enemies, they were victorious because Kṛṣṇa protected them and empowered them.

Śrīla Prabhupāda mentions the aphorism:* *Rakhe kṛṣṇa māre ke māre kṛṣṇa rakhe ke* – if Kṛṣṇa wants to kill someone no one can protect him, and if Kṛṣṇa wants to protect someone, no one can kill him.

Let us review different scenarios from the *Mahābhārata* to understand this better.

A. The table below gives a few difficult and life-threatening situations that the Pāṇḍavas went through. Research them with the help of your teacher. Can you tell how Kṛṣṇa saved the Pāṇḍavas in each case?

	PĀṆḌAVAS' TRIALS	HOW KṚṢṆA SAVES THEM
1.	Bhīma is poisoned by Duryodhana and his friends.	
2.	Duryodhana conspires to send the Pāṇḍavas to Vāraṇāvata to kill them in the lac house by setting it on fire.	

* a short statement regarding a general truth or principle

PĀṆḌAVAS' TRIALS		HOW KṚṢṆA SAVES THEM
3.	Duryodhana attacks the kingdom of Virāṭa knowing that the Pāṇḍavas were hiding there.	
4.	Duryodhana and his friends disrespected Draupadi in full view of everybody in the royal court.	

Some thought-provoking questions:

1. Only in the case of Draupadi, Kṛṣṇa directly comes and helps the Pāṇḍavas. In other cases, He is not seen. How can we say that Kṛṣṇa actually saved them?
2. Why did Kṛṣṇa only save the Pāṇḍavas? Why did He not help the Kauravas?
3. Which part of the aphorism applies to these situations?
4. Can you think of any situation in your life or in the life of someone you may know that this applies to?

B. Now, look at the picture below of the Lord's universal form in the Battle of Kurukṣetra. Can you tell what is happening?

Some thought-provoking questions:

1. Many people were killed in the Kurukṣetra war. How did they die? Was their fate already decided by Kṛṣṇa?
2. How do you know that Kṛṣṇa was behind their losing the war?
3. Which part of the aphorism applies to this case?
4. Can you think of any situation in the world that this applies to?

Can you foresee how this aphorism would apply to the story of Hiraṇyakaśipu and his son, Prahlada?

RESOURCE 1: BOARD GAME – THE SUPREME PROTECTOR

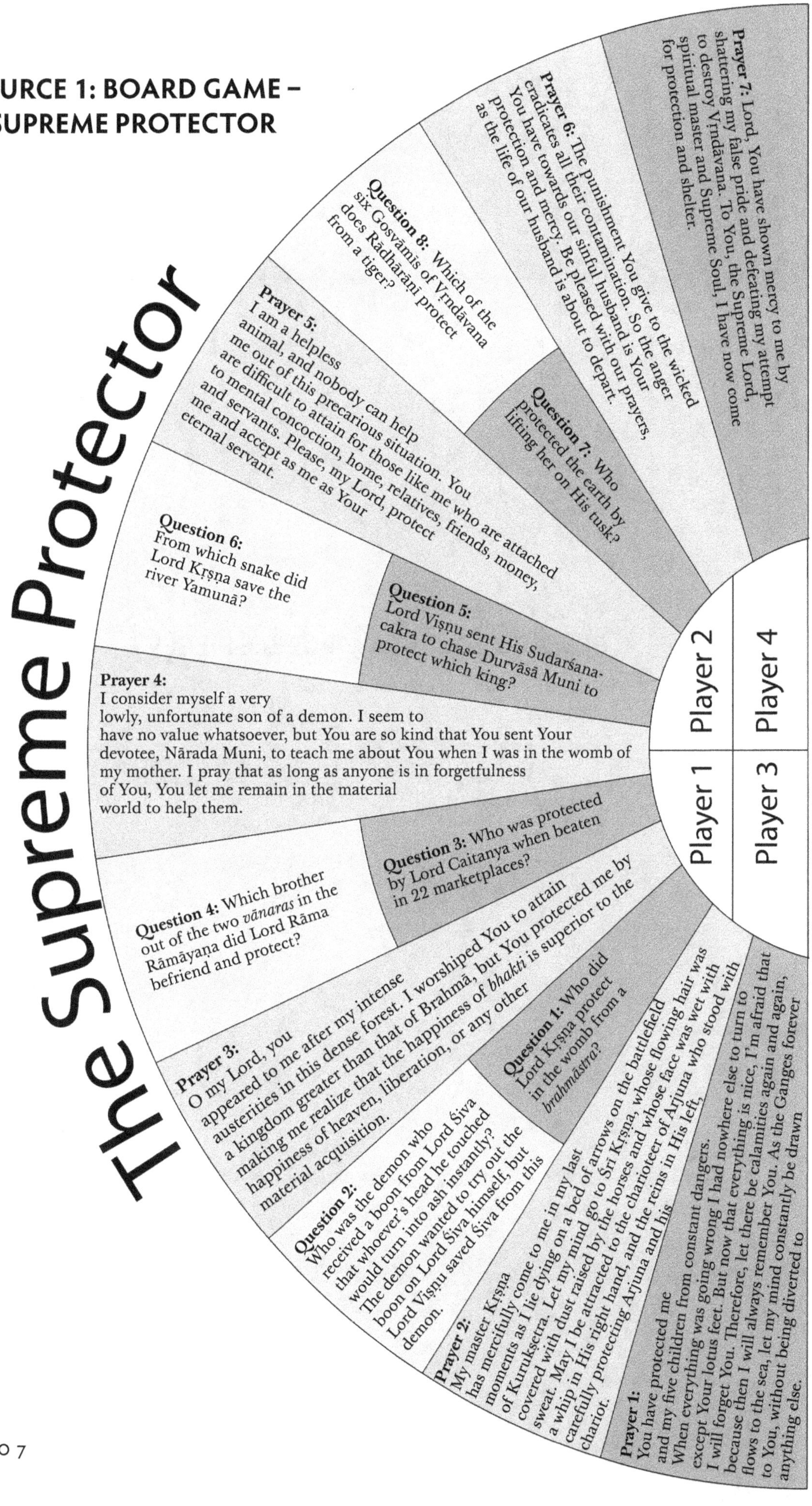

RESOURCE 2: DICE FOR BOARD GAME

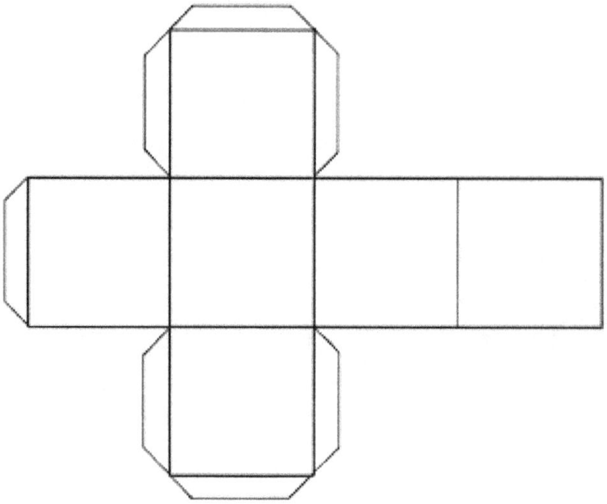

RESOURCE 3: JIGSAW PUZZLE PIECES

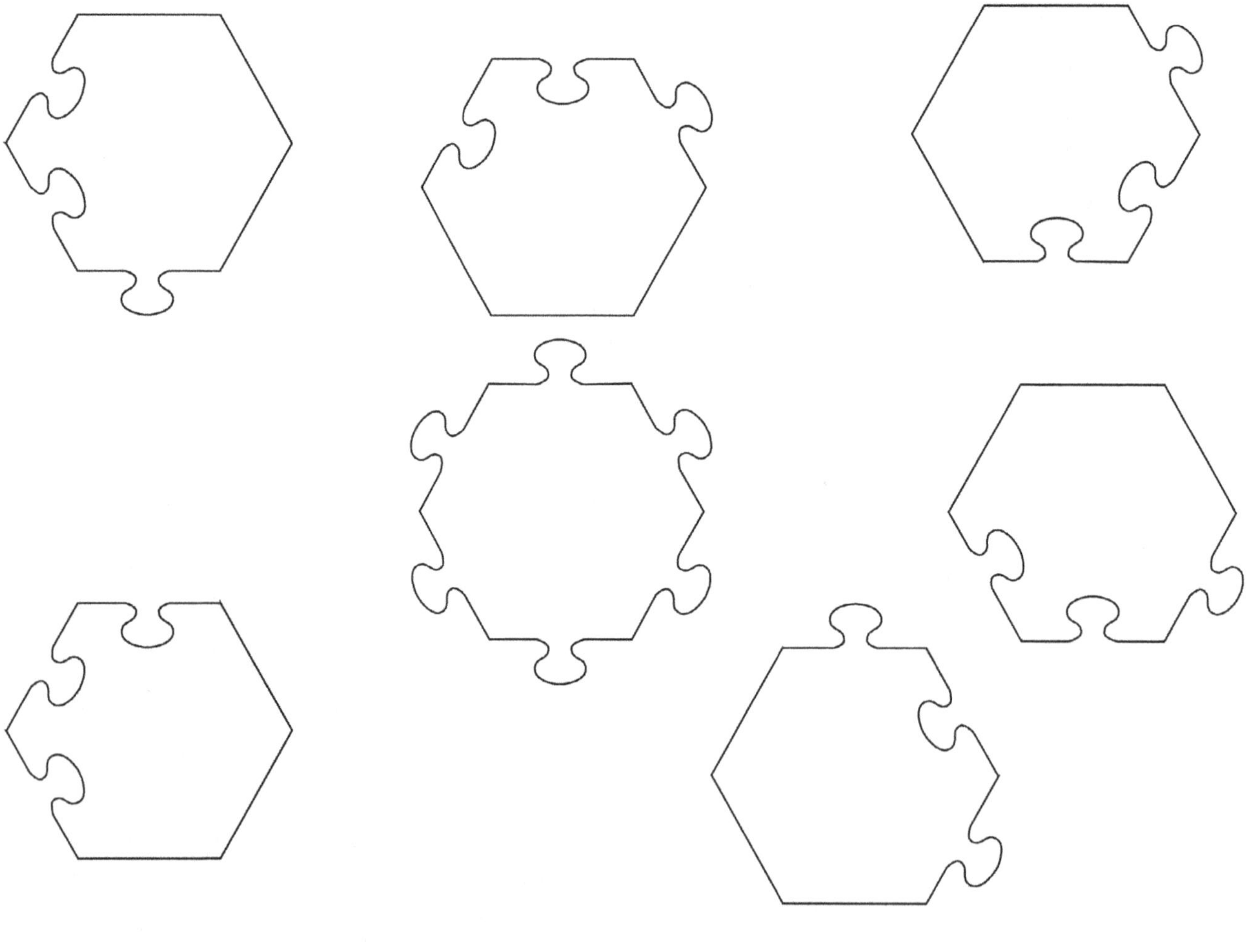

CHAPTER 2 ANSWERS

Mundane Plans to Kill Viṣṇu

Tree image: root – Lord Viṣṇu; leaves and twigs – demigods; trunk – *brāhmaṇas* and *kṣatriyas* who perform *yajña*.

(reasoning): Hiraṇyakaśipu will not be able to destroy the tree. Brahminical culture can be weakened, demigods can be conquered (which happens as the canto progresses), but Lord Viṣṇu and the strength He provides to the rest of the tree cannot be destroyed. Therefore, the tree will continue to flourish despite Hiraṇyakaśipu's attempts.

Hiraṇyakaśipu fails to realize that the root of the tree is not ordinary – the Lord is transcendental and completely independent of everyone (*svarāṭ* – *SB* 1.1.1). Hiraṇyakaśipu thinks that he can destroy the strength of the Lord by destroying the system the Lord has created to nourish this world – but the Lord can continue providing nourishment to those who surrender to Him independent of any system. He also thinks that the Lord depends on the system of *yajña* for His own nourishment, and by destroying the system of *yajña*, Viṣṇu can be weakened – this is also false, because the independent Lord does not depend on anything and can continue to remain complete under all circumstances. Finally, he also fails to realize that the success of his plan also depends on the mercy of Lord Viṣṇu, because he, like all other living beings, is also situated on the same tree (of creation) he is trying to cut down. Hiraṇyakaśipu's calculation is therefore erroneous and will fail. This holds true for anyone.

Wanderings of the Soul

1a. travelers dispersing to their respective destinations; 1b. straws coming together and dispersing; 1c. criminals being released and moving in opposite directions; 2a. family of a dog; 2b. a common family; 2c. a Vaiṣṇava family; 1. The soul would find it easier to get out of the first three situations, where he is a traveler, straw, or criminal; and it would be harder to get out of the second set of three situations, where he is a family member in each case. 2. In the first set of cases, the person is aware that he is present at a certain place for a purpose and that his stay is only for the period to fulfill that purpose. But in the second case, the person does not know the purpose for which he is put into the family (except in the case of a Vaiṣṇava family) or in other conditions in the material world, nor does he realize that he will have to leave for a different situation after some time; therefore, he gets attached to it as though it were a permanent situation. Knowledge and detachment (as mentioned in *SB* 1.2) are therefore the differentiating factors. 3. To adjust properly in the material world to any situation, one should understand that it is temporary and not be attached to it. One should also understand that only one's relationship with the Supreme Lord is permanent and should work towards becoming a member of the Lord's family. If one is part of a Vaiṣṇava family, one can use the rare opportunity to together advance in spiritual life and continue with that relationship even after death (in the spiritual world).

The Supreme Protector

Prayer 1: Queen Kunti
Prayer 2: Bhīṣma
Answer 1: Parīkṣit Mahārāja
Answer 2: Vṛkāsura
Prayer 3: Dhruva
Answer 3: Haridāsa Ṭhākura
Answer 4: Sugrīva
Prayer 4: Prahlāda
Answer 5: King Ambarīṣa
Answer 6: Kālīya
Prayer 5: Gajendra
Answer 7: Lord Varāhadeva
Answer 8: Raghunātha dāsa Gosvāmī
Prayer 6: Nāgapatnīs, wives of Kālīya
Prayer 7: Indra

Taking Time to Please Kṛṣṇa (*Potential Answers*)

Students should discuss activities that don't require extra time, such as taking *prasāda*, serving *prasāda*, talking about Kṛṣṇa, seeing things in nature related to Kṛṣṇa, glorifying devotees, etc. They should see that something like cooking a dish and eating it can be converted into an act of devotion. Similarly, their studies could engage them in their propensities, allowing them to help devotees or propagate the mission by earning money in the future and using it directly in the Lord's service.

Then direct the discussion to the direct devotional activities Śrīla Rupa Gosvāmī recommends that do require extra time and which pleases Kṛṣṇa the most, such as chanting the holy names, worshiping *tulasī*, studying the *Bhāgavatam*, visiting the temple, worshiping the Deities, etc., which are meant to purify our consciousness and hearts and come closer to Him.

Also discuss that as we continue to serve and please the Lord in this way, we will be amazed to see how the Lord will facilitate the time needed to perform these direct services while enhancing our taste for them.

Diary of a Deluded Demon

1. Hiraṇyākṣa is Vijaya, a gatekeeper in the spiritual world. His role as a demon was fulfilling the Lord's desire and pastime. When he was killed by the Lord, he was liberated and entered the body of Kṛṣṇa, and then he returned to Vaikuṇṭha, so his death was glorious.
2. Because it seems that the Lord allows the demigods to be victorious. However, the Lord is impartial to both the demons and demigods as explained in Chapter 1. When the demigods are favored and the demons killed, it is not the Lord's partiality but the influence of the time factor in the modes of material nature. The demigods, who are mainly situated in the mode of goodness, are naturally victorious, and the demons, who are influenced by the mode of ignorance, are defeated. The Supreme Lord influences the time factor to act in different ways according to the influence of the modes, but He is never partial.
3. "I will avenge my brother's death and kill Viṣṇu if it's the last thing I do."
4. The reader knows that Hiraṇyakaśipu does not kill Lord Viṣṇu, but it is the last thing he tries to do before he is killed by Lord Nṛsiṁhadeva.
5. Time cannot control the activities of the Lord because time is created by the Lord, and it acts under His control. The Lord is always transcendental to the influence of the modes of nature, *māyā,* the Lord's external energy, which acts in creation and annihilation. Thus all the demons killed by the Supreme Lord attain salvation immediately.
6. The *varṇāśrama-dharma* system is a program offered by the Lord to engage the conditioned souls in a complete social and religious system that eventually takes them back to Godhead. The *brāhmaṇas* can guide society. The *brāhmaṇa* is compared to the brain of a human being, and without a good brain one will act like a madman. So if the society does not follow *varṇāśrama-dharma* and is led by the wrong person, society will be in chaos.
7. Students' own answers.

Rakhe Kṛṣṇa Māre Ke Māre Kṛṣṇa Rakhe Ke

A. Table:

1. Bhīma goes to the kingdom of snakes where he gains the strength of 10,000 elephants; 2. The Pāṇḍavas escape through a secret tunnel; 3. The Pāṇḍavas defeat Duryodhana in a battle; 4. Kṛṣṇa provides Draupadi with unlimited cloth when she took full shelter of Him.

Questions:

1. If Kṛṣṇa was not present personally, He sent someone; He gave them the strength and expertise to fight; He guided them as their well-wisher.

2. The Pāṇḍavas were devotees of Kṛṣṇa and were completely surrendered to Him. Therefore they were assured of Kṛṣṇa's protection. Kṛṣṇa says in *BG* (9.31): "Declare it boldly that my devotee never perishes."

3. *Rakhe Kṛṣṇa māre ke:* If Kṛṣṇa protects someone no one can kill him.

B. 1. Yes; nothing happens without the will of the Lord.

2. Kṛṣṇa promises that He protects His devotees and shows through many incidents and examples how He did that. He also declares in *BG* (4.7) that whenever there is a decline in religious principles, He comes to establish religious principles. This happens when He kills the demons and protect His devotees.

3. *Māre Kṛṣṇa rakhe ke*: when Kṛṣṇa wants to kill someone, no one can protect him.

3

HIRAṆYAKAŚIPU'S PLAN TO BECOME IMMORTAL

Story Summary

You would think that after speaking philosophical truths, Hiraṇyakaśipu would act differently. But he didn't. His selfish desires were too strong – he wanted to be unconquerable, to never get old or die. So he had a plan.

Hiraṇyakaśipu stood on his toes, his arms stretched above his head as he looked to the heavens. A week passed, then a month, then a year, and then a hundred years – but not human years, heavenly years, of which one day of the demigods is equal to six months of our time. That's a long, long time. And all this time, Hiraṇyakaśipu stood unmoved in his pose on Mandara Mountain, resolute in his mind and purpose to become the most powerful being in the universe – even greater than Lord Brahmā.

Then one day, the demigods, who were wandering the universe, became blinded by a brilliant light that was as intolerable as the sunrays during cosmic dissolution. Little did they know that it was coming from the hair on Hiraṇyakaśipu's head! Anxious, they rushed back to their heavenly homes. As if the blinding light weren't enough, fire and smoke permeated the sky, engulfing the upper and lower planets with scorching heat. The demigods soon learned that the fire was coming from Hiraṇyakaśipu's head.

Hiraṇyakaśipu's severe austerities agitated the rivers

and oceans and made the mountains and islands tremble. Even the stars and planets began to fall. All directions were ablaze.

The demigods fled from the raging heat to Brahmaloka. Only Lord Brahmā could help them now.

Lord Brahmā furrowed his four brows when he saw the state of the demigods. He got up from his regal throne as they ran and fell at his feet. "O chief of the universe, please help us!" they exclaimed, as they held their chests and gasped. "Hiraṇyakaśipu . . . he's . . . he's destroying everything! He's doing the most severe austerity that is destroying the universe. O lord, please stop him!"

Lord Brahmā's four mouths broke into a gentle smile. He raised one of his arms, signalling them to calm down.

The demigods tried to compose themselves and bowed their heads in respect. "O lord of the demigods," one of them said, "Hiraṇyakaśipu knows that you're the most worshipable demigod, and you yourself have become powerful because of your severe austerities and mystic powers. He thinks that he can become like you if he performs such austerity. In fact, he wants to take your position!"

Lord Brahmā frowned and listened attentively.

One of the demigods, not able to maintain his composure, went in front of Lord Brahmā. He stood on the tips of his toes and, looking upward, lifted his arms to the sky. With intense focus and in the voice of Hiraṇyakaśipu, he imitated the demon and said, "I shall reverse the results of pious and impious activities so that even the demigods will suffer in the heavens. I shall overturn all the customary practices of this world. I don't want Dhruvaloka, because it is also vanquished at the end of the millennium. I prefer to be Brahmā!"

Lord Brahmā shook his heads with a grim expression on his faces.

Another demigod came forward and declared: "O lord, your position in this universe is most auspicious for everyone. You assure that brahminical culture – including the cows and *brāhmaṇas* – is taken care of. As a result, there is material happiness and prosperity. But if Hiraṇyakaśipu takes your seat, everything will be lost!

"No one has ever tried to take your position. So, please, my lord, do something immediately!"

Soon, Lord Brahmā, along with Bhṛgu, Dakṣa, and other great sages were at Mandara Mountain where Hiraṇyakaśipu was performing his penances and austerities. With his swan airplane, Lord Brahmā approached the site. The demigods had come too, but they couldn't see Hiraṇyakaśipu. All they could see was a giant anthill covered with grass and bamboo sticks.

Looking closer and following the source of the heat, Lord Brahmā spotted Hiraṇyakaśipu underneath the anthill, his body just a skeleton. After so many long years, the ants had devoured the demon's flesh and blood, but he was still alive.

Lord Brahmā was astonished at Hiraṇyakaśipu's extraordinary power to perform *tapasyā*. He smiled and addressed the demon: "O son of Kaśyapa Muni, please get up, get up! I'm amazed by your endurance. Despite being

eaten by all kinds of worms and ants, you are keeping your life air circulating within your bones. Even saintly persons haven't been able to perform such austerities, nor will anyone in future. Who within these three worlds can sustain his life without even drinking water for one hundred celestial years?

"My dear son of Diti, you've now perfected your austerities and done the impossible because of your great determination. You've conquered me. So ask of me any benediction and I shall try to fulfill your wish."

The spark within the skeleton glowed brighter, while the demigods looked at one another, stupefied.

"O best of the *asuras*," Brahmā continued, "We demigods of the celestial world do not die like human beings. But even though you are subject to death, know that your audience with me won't go in vain."

With these words, Lord Brahmā took out his waterpot and sprinkled potent, sanctified water on Hiraṇyakaśipu's skeleton.

From the anthill a dazzling golden form emerged, with limbs so strong that they could bear the blow of thunderbolts. It was Hiraṇyakaśipu, transformed into a radiant young man. The demigods almost fainted in shock.

Nārada Muni told Mahārāja Yudhiṣṭhira how Hiraṇyakaśipu was elated to see his lord seated on his swan carrier in the sky. Hiraṇyakaśipu fell flat on the ground in obeisance. He got up, and seeing Lord Brahmā again, his body trembled and his eyes filled with tears. He folded his palms together and said in a faltering voice, "I offer my respectful obeisances to you, the supreme lord within this universe. You manifest, maintain, and destroy the entire universe through the material energy, which is infused with the three modes of material nature. You are the shelter of these modes of goodness, passion, and ignorance.

"O lord, you are the cause of all manifestations, the original personality within this universe. You are the origin of life and the master and controller of all living beings. You inspire the yajnic *brāhmaṇas* to perform rituals mentioned in the *Vedas*. Being the Supreme Soul and Supersoul, you are beginningless, endless, and omniscient. You are eternal time, reducing the duration of life for all living beings. But you are unchanged. There is nothing separate from you, yet you are transcendental to the material world. You have unlimited potencies: the external, internal, and marginal."

The demigods looked on, still dazed but knowing that Hiraṇyakaśipu's words were only applicable to the Supreme Lord Viṣṇu, their Lord and master.

Hiraṇyakaśipu thought carefully, considering how he could get the benediction he wanted. He wanted to become immortal, yet he, as a human being, couldn't be. But there had to be a way . . .

"O my lord," Hiraṇyakaśipu continued, "you are the best giver of benedictions. Kindly grant me that I will not die from any of the living entities created by you, living or nonliving. Please benedict me that I won't die within any residence or outside any residence, during the daytime or at night, nor in the ground or sky. Grant me that I will not be killed by any being beyond even you, nor by any weapon, human being, or animal."

The demigods stared in disbelief. Would Lord Brahmā fulfill his wish? they thought.

"Grant me, further, that I won't be killed by any demigod, demon, or great snake from the lower planets. Grant me that I may have no rival in battle, just like you who has no competitor. Give me control over all living beings and deities and all the glory that comes with that position.

"Furthermore, my lord, give me all the mystic powers attained by my long austerities and *yoga* practice, for these cannot be lost at any time."

Themes and Key Messages

Please go through this table of themes and key messages, with corresponding verses, and discuss each topic further.

THEMES	REFERENCES	KEY MESSAGES
Demons want to take the position of God whereas devotees want to forever serve the Lord.	7.3.1, 12–13	Hiraṇyakaśipu wanted to receive a benediction from Lord Brahmā to become immortal and then conquer Lord Brahmā's abode and take his place. He wanted to become the most powerful being in the universe and was determined to perform severe austerities to achieve his goal. Demons want to become greater than their benedictors and take over their position whereas devotees want to be eternal servants of God.
Society managed by demons kill brahminical culture, and when that is lost, the entire society suffers.	7.3.13	Lord Brahmā, who is a servant of Lord Kṛṣṇa and who imparts Vedic knowledge to his disciples and sons, is the secondary creator in each universe. On every planet the king must be a representative of Lord Brahmā to maintain brahminical culture and God consciousness. Therefore, the demigods were afraid that if Hiraṇyakaśipu takes the place of Lord Brahmā, brahminical culture and the protection of cows will come to an end. Even today, society is being managed by demons who do not protect brahminical culture and the cows, which are essential for all kinds of good fortune. As a result, society suffers.

THEMES	REFERENCES	KEY MESSAGES
One who performs severe austerities for sense gratification becomes feared by the entire world whereas a devotee who performs even a little devotional service is a friend to everyone.	7.3.16	Hiraṇyakaśipu performed more severe austerities than great saintly persons, but still he was a Rākṣasa and Daitya feared by the entire world. This is because his austerities were ultimately meant for his own sense gratification. On the other hand, five-year-old Prahlāda performed devotional service, according to the instructions of Nārada Muni, and acted for everyone's good fortune. Thus he became dear to the Lord, so much so that the Lord appeared to save him.
Less intelligent persons worship the demigods for material benedictions while devotees worship the Supreme Lord to fulfill their desires.	7.3.24	Human life, through *varṇāśrama-dharma*, is meant to satisfy Viṣṇu, yet less intelligent persons worship demigods for temporary benefit. They therefore fall down in material life and don't achieve spiritual perfection. Although Hiraṇyakaśipu worshiped Lord Brahmā, who is dependent on Lord Viṣṇu, Hiraṇyakaśipu was inimical to Lord Viṣṇu. *Asuras* worship the demigods as separate from the Lord, but if the Lord was to withdraw the powers of the demigods, the demigods would no longer be able to offer benedictions to their worshipers. The devotee knows that Lord Viṣṇu is the Supreme Lord and everyone gets their power from Him, so if he worships Lord Viṣṇu even with material desire, his desires will be fulfilled.
Although there is a Brahmā who is the engineer of each universe, Kṛṣṇa is the origin of all of them.	7.3.27–29	Hiraṇyakaśipu glorifies Lord Brahmā as the original personality within this universe. But the Supreme Absolute Person is Kṛṣṇa, from whom Brahmā receives his mind, intelligence, and everything else. He is the engineer (the secondary creator) of the universe while Kṛṣṇa is the original creator. Lord Brahmā is not independent, for he receives help from the Supreme Lord within his heart. There are many Lord Brahmās created by Lord Viṣṇu, each of whom manages the affairs of his particular universe. Kṛṣṇa is the original source of Brahmā, who is the original engineer and secondary creator of this universe.

Higher-Thinking Questions

Now try to deepen your understanding of this chapter by delving into Śrīla Prabhupāda's purports and reflecting on the following questions:

1. What kind of "demoniac austerity" is being described in verse 1 purport? What is the performer's action and motive?
2. Why was it impossible for Hiraṇyakaśipu to occupy the post of Brahmā according to verse 10 purport?
3. Demons are also determined. But how is their determination different from a Vaiṣṇava's. (Refer to verse 11 purport.)
4. In verse 15–16 purport Śrīla Prabhupāda explains that although Hiraṇyakaśipu performed severe austerities for a long time, which even great saintly persons couldn't do, he was still considered a Daitya and Rākṣasa. Why was this?
5. How are demigods not subject to death as Śrīla Prabhupāda explains in verse 21 purport?
6. Why doesn't Kṛṣṇa approve the worship of demigods according to verse 24 purport? What does He recommend?
7. Do you think that Lord Brahmā is the original cause of the material creation as Hiraṇyakaśipu declares in verse 28? How does Śrīla Prabhupāda describe Lord Brahmā's position as creator in relation to Lord Kṛṣṇa?

ACTIVITIES

In this section you will find many exciting things to do. These activities will get you thinking, moving, drawing, and having loads of fun.

Analogy Activity

... to bring out the scholar in you

ROLE PLAY: BRIBING THE DEMIGODS IS ILLEGAL

"The demigods are, so to speak, different officers and directors in the government of the Supreme Lord. One has to follow the laws made by the government, not by the officers or directors. Similarly, everyone is to offer his worship to the Supreme Lord only. That will

automatically satisfy the different officers and directors of the Lord. The officers and directors are engaged as representatives of the government, and to offer some bribe to the officers and directors is illegal. This is stated in *Bhagavad-gītā* as *avidhi-pūrvakam*. In other words, Kṛṣṇa does not approve the unnecessary worship of the demigods." *SB* 7.3.24 purport

In the previous cantos, we saw how the demigods are officers appointed by the Lord and how Kṛṣṇa is the supreme controller of everyone, including the demigods. Kṛṣṇa calls any worship offered directly to the demigods as "unnecessary," and Śrīla Prabhupāda compares such worship to a bribe given to the officers of a government and is therefore "illegal." Let us understand why direct worship of the demigods is not recommended.

To start this activity, first read Lord Kṛṣṇa's perspective on demigod worship from the following verses in the *Bhagavad-gītā*: 4.12, 7.20, 7.21, 9.23. Discuss these verses among the members of your study group and summarize your understanding. Remember that even though the worshipers themselves do not have this understanding, the demigods understand what Kṛṣṇa is saying here.

Now, imagine three demigods – Brahmā, Indra, and Śiva – meeting to discuss why people worship them and how the faith of their worshipers is so strong that they are unable to see the demigods as dependent on the Supreme Lord. Choose three people from your study group to take on the roles of each of these demigods.

Lord Brahmā could discuss why Hiraṇyakaśipu worshiped him rather than Lord Kṛṣṇa; Lord Śiva could discuss why Rāvaṇa worshiped him; and Lord Indra could discuss why Prācīnabarhi worshiped him. (Lord Indra could also cite the Govardhana-*līlā* as an example of how Kṛṣṇa Himself stopped the *vrajavāsīs* from worshiping him.) Consider the following points for the discussion:

1. What prompts the worshipers to have more faith in the demigods than in the Lord?
2. What methods do they use to worship the demigods? Are they always approved, and if not, why do people choose to use them?
3. What could be the different reasons these worshipers do not approach the Supreme Lord, who is perfectly capable of granting their desires?

Based on the above discussions, the "demigods" should conclude why the Supreme Lord thinks demigod worship is unnecessary. Present these conclusions to your study group through role play.

Artistic Activity

... to reveal your creativity

ANALOGOUS ART: LORD BRAHMĀ

Hiraṇyakaśipu understood that Lord Brahmā had obtained his exalted position due to severe austerities and *yoga* but failed to see that he was a great devotee of the Supreme Lord.

In this activity you will make a painting of Lord Brahmā using analogous colors, which evoke calmness and harmony. This color scheme has at least three hues/colors that are next to each other on the color wheel. For example: violet, red-violet, and red; yellow, orange-yellow, and orange.

Materials needed:

1. Template of Lord Brahmā provided in the resources.
2. At least three analogous colors in any media: watercolors, color pencils, crayons, etc.
3. Brushes and water if using watercolors.
4. Paper to practice coloring.
5. Pencil to draw an object like a leaf or a fruit.

Directions:

1. Research online and pick your favorite analogous color scheme. On the spare paper, draw with pencil an autumn leaf or a fruit (Image 1).
2. Add yellow first (Image 2). Add orange color next (Image 3), and in the end, add red and some finishing touches (Image 4). Practice applying the colors to your drawing to create a pleasing effect.
3. Once you are confident, you can paint Lord Brahmā. A template of Lord Brahmā is given in Resource 1 at the end of this chapter, and you can color it in any analogous color scheme of your choice.

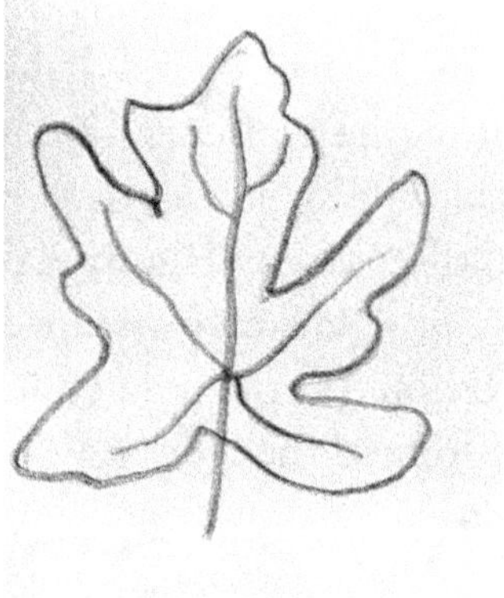

Image 1

Image 2

Image 3

Image 4

Image 5

4. In the example pictures, we used yellow-green, blue, and blue-violet. The lightest color, yellow-green, was added to the face, body, and jewels (Image 5). Next, blue color was added to Lord Brahmā's dress and crown, and to the feathers of the swan (Image 6). Finally, the darkest color blue-violet was used in the shadow areas to add volume and tone (Image 7).
5. You can add finishing touches, like clouds, birds, and a crown for the swan carrier.

Image 6

Image 7

Introspective Activity

... to bring out the reflective devotee in you

AUSTERITY IN THE MODES AND BEYOND

The *Bhagavad-gītā* describes austerity in the three modes:

Austerity in goodness: When austerities are performed with transcendental faith by men not expecting material benefits but engaged only for the sake of the Supreme. *BG* 17.17

Austerity in passion: Penance performed out of pride and for the sake of gaining respect, honor, and worship. It is neither stable nor permanent. *BG* 17.18

Austerity in ignorance: Penance performed out of foolishness, with self-torture or to destroy or injure others. *BG* 17.19

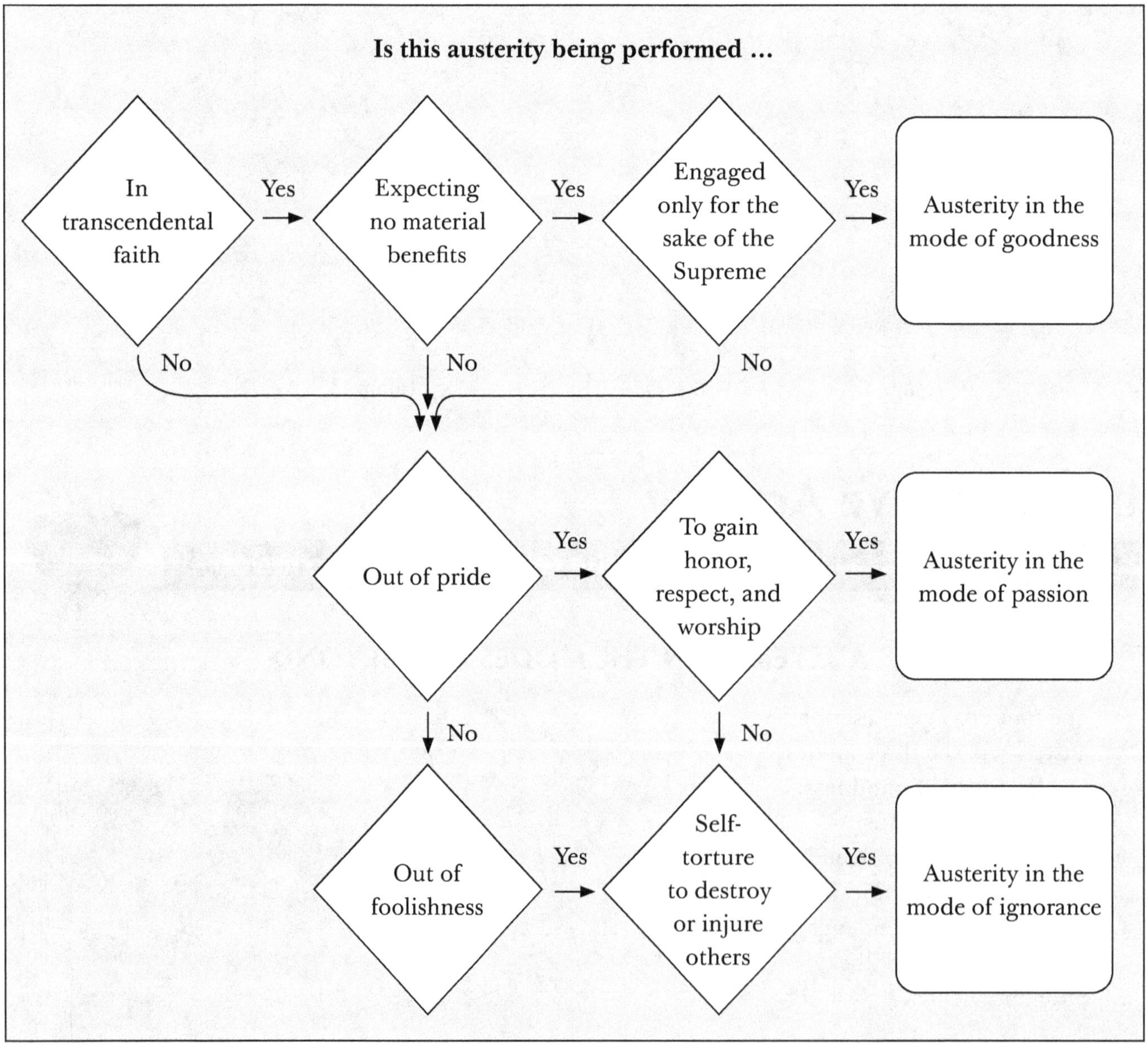

Using the flow chart above, see which mode the following austerities belong to and why:

A. List of Austerities:

1. Brahmā meditated for one thousand celestial years before engineering the secondary creation as instructed by the Lord.
2. Dhruva did *aṣṭāṅga-yoga* for six months to see the Supreme Personality of Godhead and ask for a kingdom bigger than his father's, grandfather's, or great-grandfather's.
3. Hiraṇyakaśipu did mystic *yoga* for many thousands of years to become the most powerful man in the universe and to live forever.

B. The following list of austerities all belong to the mode of passion or ignorance. Give an example of how you can transform each of these activities to goodness or transcendental goodness and practice this in your own life.

1. Politicians doing *satyāgraha* for a political or social cause.
2. A person goes on a strict diet and does vigorous exercises to lose weight.
3. You observe Nirjala-ekādaśī fasting and go around telling everybody about it, because you want to get the admiration of your friends.
4. People observe fasting for Navarātri festival.
5. You want to get selected in the school volleyball team. You go on a strict regimen of diet and exercise only with the aim of making the team.
6. You have an important exam coming up tomorrow, so you skip dinner and burn the midnight oil.
7. People pierce sharp needles in their tongue or cheek as an austerity for their beloved demigod, Kārtikeya.

Critical-Thinking Activity

… to bring out the spiritual investigator in you

DEVOTIONAL SERVICE IS THE GREATEST

In verse 17 purport Śrīla Prabhupāda compares the results of Hiraṇyakaśipu's and Prahlāda's austerities: "One who performs severe austerities for sense gratification is fearful to the entire world, whereas a devotee who performs even a slight amount of devotional service is a friend to everyone (*suhṛdaṁ sarva-bhūtānām*)."

Śrīla Prabhupāda also beautifully brings out the irony that Hiraṇyakaśipu got the opposite of what he expected – while he wanted to be famous, powerful, and immortal, he became an unpopular, hated demon-king and was later killed; and Prahlāda gained the eternal shelter of the Lord, who also blessed him with the power and fame his father so badly sought.

Let us analyze why Prahlāda's devotional service was superior to Hiraṇyakaśipu's austerities and understand why he rightly received superior benefits.

David is new to Vedic philosophy and has just met the devotees. He recently heard the pastime of Prahlāda and Hiraṇyakaśipu at a Sunday program. The speaker focused on how the different motivations of Hiraṇyakaśipu and Prahlāda brought each of them results they neither sought nor expected, and how Prahlāda emerged the hero in the end.

To encourage David, his devotee friend lent him a pack of cards, printed in resource 2. Each card has one statement, either pertaining to Hiraṇyakaśipu's austerity or Prahlāda's devotional service. David has to sort the cards out into two piles and needs to understand why devotional service is superior. Help him by following these steps:

1. Cut up the cards in Resource 2 and stack them in a pile.
2. Sort the cards into two piles. Read each card and tell David whether he should put them in the "Hiraṇyakaśipu pile" or the "Prahlāda pile."
3. Once sorted, read the cards in each pile separately and carefully. See what you can learn from them.
4. Then help David complete his journal entry below to get a proper understanding of the superiority of devotional service:

From Hiraṇyakaśipu's example, I understand that one with the wrong 1. .... cannot achieve lasting success. Hiraṇyakaśipu was motivated by 2. .... and 3. ...., which makes you selfish. When you become selfish, you could also become 4. .... and 5. .... Then, you could lose all your 6. .... In conclusion, by performing severe 7. .... you may gain power and opulence, but you cannot sustain it unless you are a well-wisher of all. And to become a well-wisher and friend to all, you should be a 8. .... of 9. .... Prahlāda showed this by example.

The best thing I learned by Prahlāda's example is that the Lord is the 10. .... of all power, and by 11. .... this, I can become peaceful. We need not pray to different 12. .... or perform severe, life-threatening 13. .... to gain power or fame or opulence – these things are easily bestowed on a 14. .... But then, a devotee is not as interested in these great material facilities as he is in the 15. .... of the Lord. That is because the 16. .... a devotee derives from 17. .... the Lord is far more than even the joy derived from enjoying kingship of the universe. Prahlāda again clearly shows this by example. I don't think I have read a better pastime that shows the power of devotional service.

Writing Activities

... to bring out the writer in you

PETITION TO STOP A DEMON

Write a petition from Lord Indra and the demigods to Lord Brahmā, asking him to stop the demon Hiraṇyakaśipu. Referring to this chapter, please include information on how society will suffer if it is ruled by a demon.

A petition is a tool to raise awareness and make demands. A well-worded one can convince those who support your message to sign and those that receive the request to consider the changes you hope for.

An effective petition contains three parts:

1. The first part describes the problem.

2. The second part discusses what changes you expect to see as a result of the petition.

3. The last part is a call to action.

Ensure you include all three parts when crafting Lord Indra's petition.

PRAYERS MEANT FOR LORD KṚṢṆA

The prayers of Hiraṇyakaśipu in this chapter, although referring to Lord Brahmā, reflect the qualities and glories of the Supreme Lord and should be meant for Him.

Refer to verses 26–34 and choose three qualities that refer to the Supreme Lord, Kṛṣṇa, rather than Lord Brahmā, and write a short paragraph explaining why they refer to Kṛṣṇa, using references from the *Bhagavad-gītā* and/or *Śrīmad-Bhāgavatam*.

MONOLOGUE: BECOMING GREATER THAN YOUR MASTER!

Have you sometimes met people who want to become greater than their masters and even want to take over their positions? Śrīla Prabhupāda condemns this as demonic mentality. The demon Hiraṇyakaśipu wanted to do the same with Lord Brahmā. He wanted benedictions from Lord Brahmā to make himself immortal. Then he planned to conquer Lord Brahmā's abode and take over his position.

In the pastimes of Lord Caitanya, there is the story of a Muslim servant of Subuddhi Rāya. Subuddhi Rāya provided for his servant, but the servant wanted to take the master's position and make Subuddhi Rāya the servant. The servant ended up becoming Nawab Hussein Shah of Bengal.

This story is told by Śrīla Prabhupāda in his purport to verse 12.

Directions:

1. First read the story and make notes.
2. Then write a monologue of Nawab Hussein Shah. A monologue is a speech by a single character in a drama or film that either addresses other characters in the scene or themselves or the audience.
3. The scene can be of Nawab Hussein Shah sprinkling water from his waterpot on Subuddhi Rāya, and thus converting him to a Muslim.
4. Write down the monologue of the Nawab talking to himself in a villainous manner, (before sprinkling water), reminding him of the times that Rāya was the master and he was the servant, and how now he is more powerful than his master. (Also mention the role of his wife in the whole story.)
5. You may enact the monologue in front of the class or your teacher.

POEM: GRANT ME

Hiraṇyakaśipu knew he could not become immortal, so he asked Lord Brahmā for boons that could make him defy death.

Read through verses 35 to 38 and write down all the boons Hiraṇyakaśipu asked from Lord Brahmā. Then compose them in a poetic form.

Here is a sample:

Grant me that I do not die
On the ground nor in the sky
Nor inside places nor outside
Nor at daytime or night

Grant me that my death is not brought
By any of the creations of yours
By no animal or human
Nor mystical or magical weapon

Grant me that my death is not met
By demigods, demons, or those of lower planets
No entity can be the cause of my dying
No entity, living or non-living

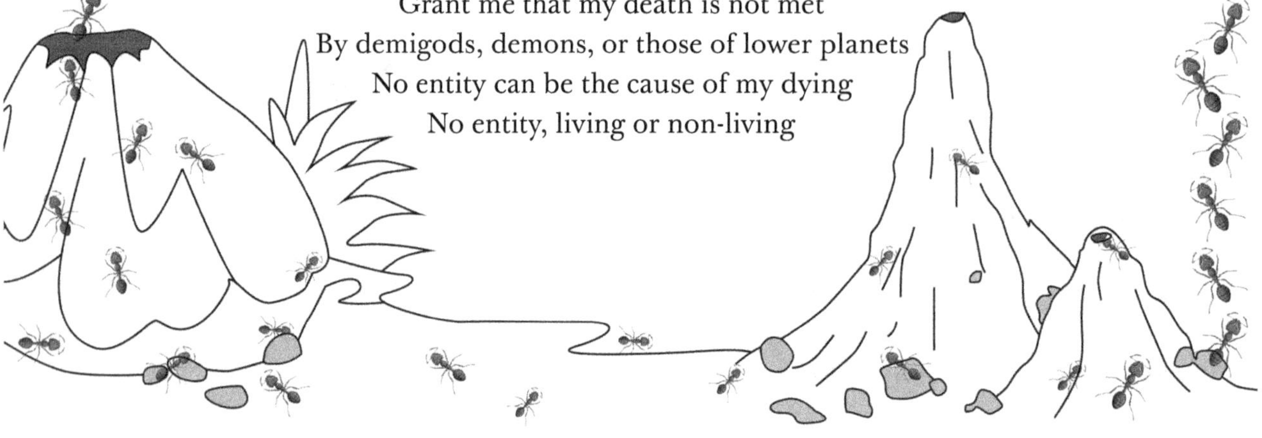

Language Activity

... to help you understand better

A SURPRISE FOR LORD BRAHMĀ

Read the comic strip below and answer the questions that follow:

Questions:

1. What is the setting of the cartoon? Support your answer by a visual clue.

2. What is Lord Brahmā's tone in Panel 1? Explain how the word choice helps decipher the tone. (Hint: Tone is the attitude of the character to the subject.)

3. Kṛṣṇa is all-knowing, yet in Panel 3 He asks the doorman to clarify which Lord Brahmā has come to visit Him. Explain this seeming incongruity.

4. In Panel 4 how has Lord Brahmā's tone changed?

5. Why is Lord Brahmā a "rabbit among elephants"? How does his body language match his words?

6. Try to recall a time when you felt insignificant. Briefly describe your experience.

CROSSWORD

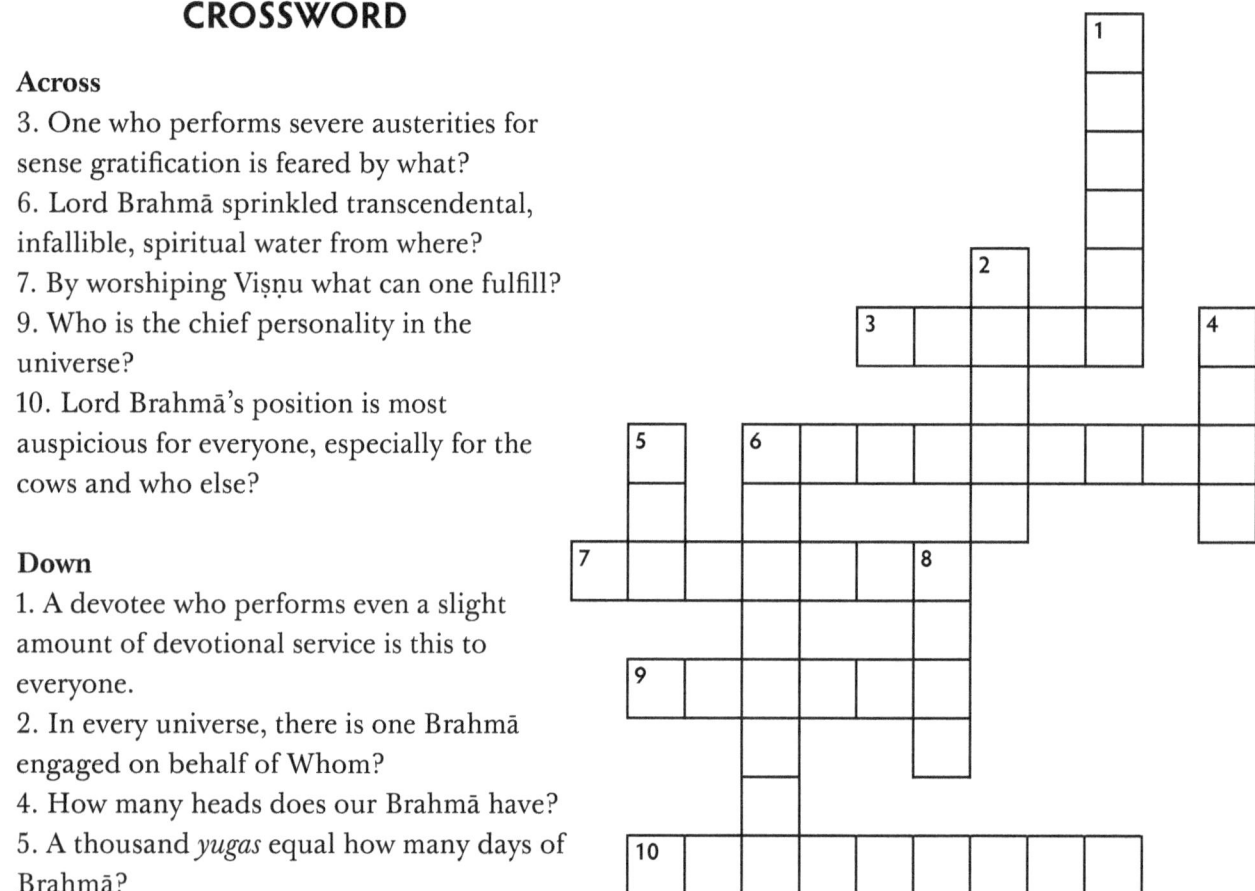

Across

3. One who performs severe austerities for sense gratification is feared by what?
6. Lord Brahmā sprinkled transcendental, infallible, spiritual water from where?
7. By worshiping Viṣṇu what can one fulfill?
9. Who is the chief personality in the universe?
10. Lord Brahmā's position is most auspicious for everyone, especially for the cows and who else?

Down

1. A devotee who performs even a slight amount of devotional service is this to everyone.
2. In every universe, there is one Brahmā engaged on behalf of Whom?
4. How many heads does our Brahmā have?
5. A thousand *yugas* equal how many days of Brahmā?
6. In the beginning of creation, Lord Brahmā was attacked by two demons, Madhu and who else?
8. Lord Brahmā's carrier.

AUSTERITY MAZE

Every day we are performing different austerities knowingly or unknowingly. But if we direct austerity for becoming Kṛṣṇa conscious rather than getting material gains, we will be happier.

In the maze, the main objective is to move from the entry point to the exit point.

There are two entry and exit points. To complete the maze, use the following guidelines:

- Where does austerity for one's own sense gratification lead to?
- Where does the austerity for the Lord's pleasure lead to?

So when you are performing austerities, remember your motivation and destination and make a wise choice.

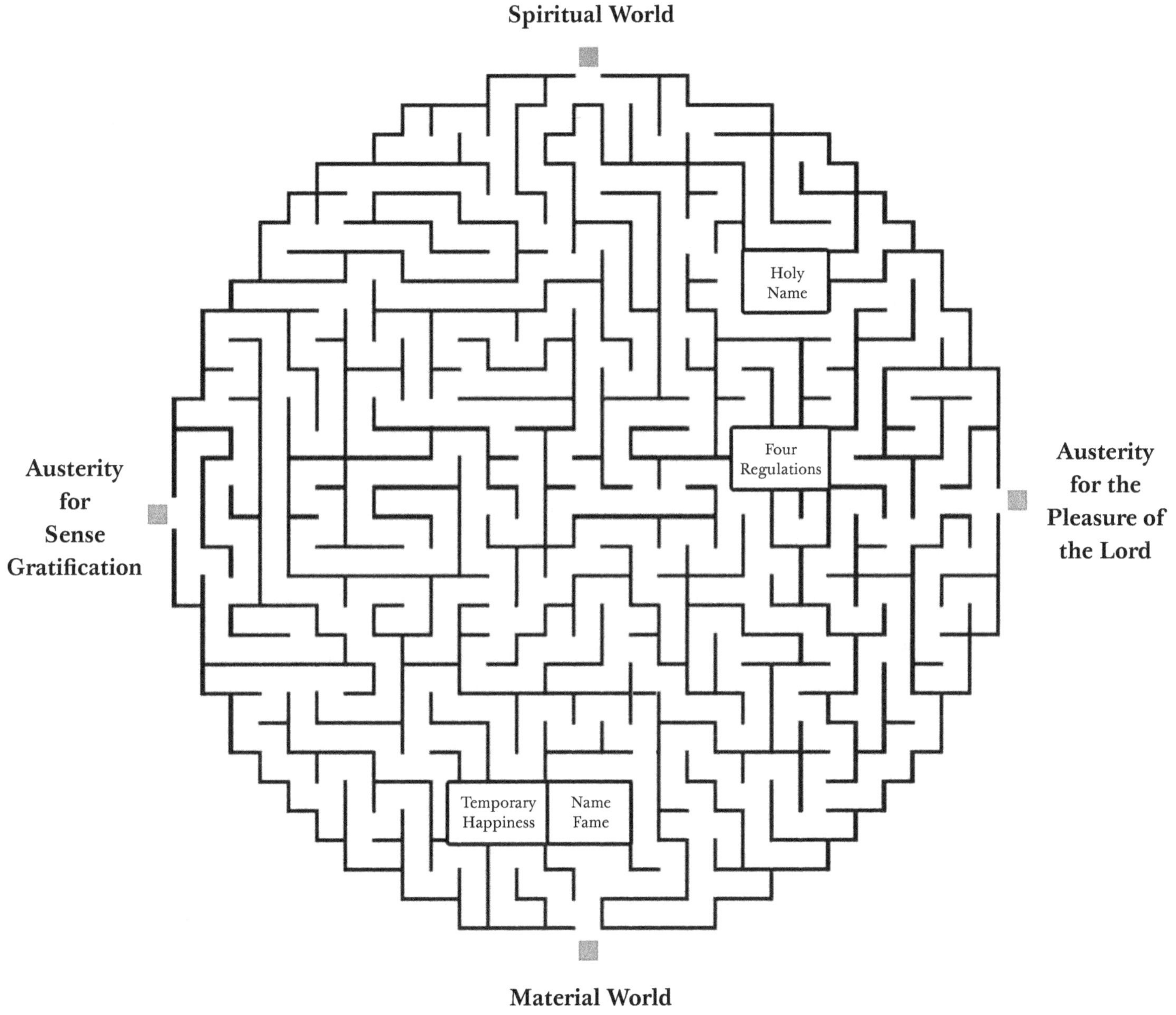

CHAPTER 3 ANSWERS

Bribing the Demigods is Illegal

Possible answers to prompts (to be brought out as roleplay):

1. The Lord says in *BG* 7.21 that as the Paramātmā He strengthens the faith of those who want to achieve

only material benefits from the demigods. The *karma-kāṇḍa* section of the *Vedas* also encourages those who are enamored by material gains to worship the demigods; 2. Some may adopt authorized methods like performing *yajñas* or prescribed austerities. Others may resort to unauthorized austerities, made-up worship, and glorification to please the demigod. People who resort to either of these methods may not always have firm faith in or desire to please the demigod but may be simply motivated by getting their desire fulfilled; 3. They may not be mature enough to understand the position or role of the Lord. They may be skeptical towards the Lord or may not have the faith that He will grant their wishes.

Conclusion: The mentality of demigod worshipers is to enjoy the material world, one way or another. Kṛṣṇa calls demigod worship unnecessary because even if it fulfills their material desires, it will not give them spiritual benefits. Kṛṣṇa says that demigod worship is *avidhi-pūrvakam*, unapproved and akin to a bribe; worshipers can sometimes adopt dishonest or disapproved ways to get the favor of the demigods. They do not recognize that demigods cannot grant their desires without Kṛṣṇa's sanction.

Austerities in the Modes and Beyond

A.

1. goodness: Lord Brahmā did this austerity to please the Lord and was able to be the secondary creator as directed by the Lord.
2. passion: In the beginning Dhruva started his austerities for gaining a kingdom. Later, when the Lord gave His benediction and His *darśana*, Dhruva was completely transformed and became a pure devotee.
3. ignorance: He didn't have faith in the Supreme and did austerity to gain power and harm others.

B. (*Potential Answers*)

1. ignorance – devotees working many hours in the book distribution marathon.
2. passion and ignorance for personal gain – a devotee goes on a healthy diet and exercises regularly so he can have a fit and healthy body to serve Kṛṣṇa. He sees his body as the Lord's property and takes proper care of it.
3. passion – You fast and chant extra rounds without boasting about it, and you do it to absorb yourself in the Lord and to please Him.
4. worship of demigods for material gain is in the mode of passion – They can observe festivals in glorification of the Supreme Lord.
5. passion and ignorance – You play a sport so that you can remain fit and strong and interact with your friends in a healthy way, without thinking of winning or losing.
6. passion and ignorance – You can study methodically and consistently throughout the year, remembering that you will offer the results of your studies to Kṛṣṇa.
7. ignorance – You can chant 64 rounds on Ekādaśī or special holy days or do any other austerity in devotional service.

Devotional Service Is the Greatest

Hiraṇyakaśipu cards: 1, 3, 4, 6, 10, 12;
Prahlāda cards: 2, 5, 7, 8, 9, 11.

Journal answers: 1. Motivation; 2. Sense gratification; 3. Sense gratification; 4. Cruel; 5. Insensitive; 6. Opulences; 7. Austerity; 8. Devotee; 9. Lord Viṣṇu; 10. Source; 11. Understanding; 12. Demigods; 13. Austerities; 14. Devotee; 15. Service; 16. Pleasure; 17. Satisfying

A Surprise for Lord Brahmā

1. Lord Kṛṣṇa's palace in Dvārakā. The palace is visible in Panel 1.
2. Brahmā is feeling proud. He tells the doorman to announce him "at once," which shows he thinks he is important.
3. Kṛṣṇa is all knowing, but He is doing this as part of His pastime so that Brahmā can understand His position.
4. Brahmā is surprised.
5. Brahmā realizes he is not as important as he thought. He feels insignificant compared to the other Lord Brahmās and to Lord Kṛṣṇa. His hands folded in prayer match his words.

Crossword

Across: 3. world; 6. kamandalu; 7. desires; 9. Brahma; 10. brahmanas

Down: 1. friend; 2. Krsna; 4. four; 5.one; 6. kaitabha; 8. swan

RESOURCE 1: ART ACTIVITY – LORD BRAHMĀ

RESOURCE 2: CRITICAL-THINKING ACTIVITY

1 He succeeded in gaining control of the universe and all the planets in it through severe austerity to please Brahmā.	2 By association of Nārada Muni (his spiritual master), and service to *brāhmaṇas*, cows, and the spiritual master, he became a pure devotee of the Lord.	3 His determination and endurance to perform severe austerity, not possible even for great sages, amazed Lord Brahmā. Brahmā offered him any benediction he was capable of giving.	4 He had great powers, and could do wonderful things, but he wanted to use his skills just to fulfill his own ambitions.
5 He was the well-wisher of everyone, since he knew the Lord cares about all living entities.	6 His great power and qualifications were not adequate to save him from the Lord's wrath, and despite his great qualifications, he was killed by the Lord.	7 When the Lord easily bestowed him the powers and privileges that his father endeavored so hard to achieve, he remained detached and considered worshiping the Lord and his *guru* more important.	8 He never thought of devotional service to Viṣṇu as just another way to obtain fame, power, or good fortune – he genuinely was attached to the lotus feet of the Lord.
9 By devotional service, he became free from all designations and material desires despite being from a demoniac family, and thus he pleased the Lord.	10 Ambitious and full of himself, he forgot that the source of his power is the Supreme Lord and that he should use his abilities to please the Lord. Instead, he tormented *brāhmaṇas*, cows, demigods, and Vaiṣṇavas and displeased the Lord.	11 By personal example, he showed how anyone, from any background, and under any circumstance can gain the favor of the Lord.	12 Ambition, talent, and success didn't help him become soft-hearted, because he simply followed his own sense desires. He neither thought about the heavy price others paid for his success, nor thought of their welfare in return.

4

HIRAṆYAKAŚIPU TERRORIZES THE UNIVERSE

Story Summary

Hiraṇyakaśipu's body glistened like gold. He felt invincible after receiving Lord Brahmā's boons and was convinced that he had defeated death. Lord Brahmā had told him that these benedictions were rare to obtain for most humans, yet he had granted them.

However, Hiraṇyakaśipu was still haunted by his brother's death. The thought of his brother's killer, Lord Viṣṇu, made him seethe with anger and envy. "I will show everyone who is most powerful in the universe!" he promised himself.

And sure enough, he conquered the entire universe. He took over all the planets in the three worlds, including the planets of the humans, Gandharvas, Vidyādharas, Siddhas, Cāraṇas, the great saints, Yamarāja, the Manus, the Yakṣas, and the Rākṣasas. Except for Lord Viṣṇu, Brahmā, and Śiva, all the demigods were under his control. He even defeated King Indra and resided in Indra's opulent celestial palace in the heavens. Now the famous Nandana Garden of the demigods was his.

With his head held high, he walked up the coral steps of the palace and stepped onto its floor bedecked with emeralds. He could see himself in the crystal walls and pillars of *vaidūrya* stone. The seats were laden with rubies, and the white silk bedding decorated with pearls. He watched the exquisite palace ladies scurry here and there, their ankle bells tinkling while admiring their beautiful reflections in the gem-studded walls.

Seeing some demigods passing him, Hiraṇyakaśipu sneered and then hollered at them for no reason. They trembled and bowed at his feet. He kicked one away and then laughed, his voice resonating throughout the palace and instilling terror in everyone's hearts.

Nārada Muni continued his narration to Yudhiṣṭhira Mahārāja: "My dear King, Hiraṇyakaśipu sat on King Indra's throne, his coppery eyes rolling, always drunk on strong wines and liquors. Even though he was abominable, because of his power, we were terrified of him. Together with the Gandharvas, Vidyādharas, Apsarās, and sages, I had to offer

prayers to this horrible *asura* and glorify him again and again. We even had to worship him and offer him gifts and sacrifices!"

Nārada Muni winced at the thought and shook his head in disgust. "But instead of offering the share of the oblations to the demigods, he accepted them for himself."

Yudhiṣṭhira Mahārāja shook his head in disbelief.

"If that wasn't enough, the planet earth and the seven islands delivered food grains to him, and the cows supplied abundant milk," Nārada continued. "The various oceans in the universe, along with their rivers and tributaries, supplied gems and jewels, and the trees produced fruits in all seasons, just for his pleasure. Hiraṇyakaśipu became so powerful that he himself did the activities of Indra, Vāyu, and Agni by pouring rain, drying it up, and burning everything.

"But, my dear King, although Hiraṇyakaśipu controlled in all directions and gratified his senses to the fullest, he was always dissatisfied. Do you know why? Because instead of controlling his senses, he became their servant."

Nārada described how the greatest of demons continued to create havoc in the world and transgress all the laws of the *śāstras*. Thus he was cursed by the four Kumāras.

The rulers of the various planets were distressed and without any shelter. At last they surrendered to the Supreme Personality of Godhead. Not sleeping and controlling their minds and living only on their breath, they worshiped Hṛṣīkeśa with this meditation: "We offer our respectful obeisances to the direction where the Supreme Lord is situated, where the great saintly souls go, and from which, having gone, never return."

Then they heard a voice as grave as the rumbling of a cloud, which drove away their fear. It was the voice of the Lord!

"O best of learned persons, don't be afraid," said Lord Viṣṇu. "I wish you all good fortune. Become My devotees by hearing and chanting

about Me and offering prayers to Me, for this certainly gives the greatest benedictions to all beings. I know all about Hiraṇyakaśipu's activities and shall surely stop them very soon. Please wait patiently until then.

"Rest assured, my dear demigods, when anyone is envious of you, who represent Me; the *Vedas*, which give all knowledge; the cows; the *brāhmaṇas* and the Vaiṣṇavas; religious principles; and ultimately Me, they will be vanquished.

"When Hiraṇyakaśipu harasses My great devotee, Prahlāda, who is his own son and who is peaceful and has no enemy, I shall kill Hiraṇyakaśipu despite the benedictions of Brahmā."

The demigods smiled in relief. Tears of joy rolled down their faces as they offered obeisances to their Lord and left. They were confident that Hiraṇyakaśipu was now practically dead.

Nārada Muni continued, "O King Yudhiṣṭhira, Hiraṇyakaśipu had four qualified sons, of whom Prahlāda was the best. He was a reservoir of all wonderful, divine qualities. That's because he was an unalloyed devotee of the Supreme Lord."

"Please tell me more about him," implored Yudhiṣṭhira Mahārāja.

"This young boy was determined to know the Absolute Truth. Unlike Hiraṇyakaśipu, he fully controlled his senses and mind. He was kind to every living being and was a friend to everyone. He was a servant to his elders, like a father to the poor, and like a brother to his equals. He was never proud of his education, riches, beauty, and aristocratic birth. Although he was born in an *asura* family, he was a great devotee of Lord Viṣṇu. Unlike the *asuras*, he was never envious of Vaiṣṇavas. He was not agitated when put into danger nor attracted to the fruitive activities described in the *Vedas*. He had not a trace of material desire, having subdued all lusty desires with his steady intelligence and determination.

"O King, saints and Vaiṣṇavas till this day glorify Prahlāda Mahārāja's great qualities. Just as all good qualities exist in the Supreme Lord, they also forever exist in His devotee Prahlāda.

"O Yudhiṣṭhira, even the demigods would cite Prahlāda Mahārāja as an example of an exalted devotee. Who can describe his countless divine qualities? He had unflinching faith in and devotion to Lord Kṛṣṇa.

"You see, his devotion was natural because of his previous devotional service. He was a *mahātmā*, a great soul. From the very beginning of his childhood he was uninterested in childish play. He appeared silent and dull because he was always absorbed in Kṛṣṇa. He couldn't understand how the world could go on absorbed in material enjoyment.

"Being fully immersed in the Lord, he wasn't aware of how his bodily needs, such as sitting, eating, sleeping, drinking, and talking were taking place. Sometimes he cried, sometimes he laughed, and sometimes he sang loudly. Sometimes, seeing the Supreme Lord, he would loudly and anxiously call out His name. He would dance in ecstasy, losing his shyness, and sometimes he imitated the Lord's pastimes.

"Sometimes he even felt the touch of the Lord's lotus hands, and thus tears would glide down his half-closed eyes in love.

"Prahlāda constantly served the Lord, and seeing his ecstatic mood, his friends became blissful. Their hearts were purified just by witnessing the ecstatic love of Prahlāda Mahārāja.

"Alas, Hiraṇyakaśipu tormented this exalted devotee, even though Prahlāda was his own son."

"But why would a father do such a thing?" asked Mahārāja Yudhiṣṭhira, furrowing his eyebrows. "Parents are always affectionate to their children. When children are disobedient, the parents chastise them out of love, only for the child's welfare. But how did Hiraṇyakaśipu chastise such a noble son? How was it possible for a father to be so violent toward such an obedient, respectful, and well-behaved son with the intention of killing him? I've never heard of such a contradiction before. Kindly remove my doubts."

Themes and Key Messages

Please go through this table of themes and key messages, with corresponding verses, and discuss each topic further.

THEMES	REFERENCES	KEY MESSAGES
Materialists who enjoy all kinds of sense gratification are still dissatisfied because they become servants of their senses.	7.4.7–8, 19–20	Hiraṇyakaśipu became the conqueror of the entire universe. He conquered all the planets in the three worlds and resided in the opulent heavenly palace of Indra. He was always drunk on strong wines and liquor, and all the demigods personally worshiped him. He even controlled material nature to supply him with the best produce. With his power he alone took charge of the functions of the demigods. But he was still dissatisfied because he became a slave to his senses. His senses controlled him, and thus his greed and envy grew and consumed him. He transgressed the laws of *śāstra* and therefore entered a path of destruction.
Kṛṣṇa is our well-wishing friend and supreme shelter.	7.4.21–29	In distress we want to seek the shelter of a well-wishing friend. Kṛṣṇa is the best well-wishing friend, and if we seek His shelter from the beginning, He will protect us. Like this, even the demigods take shelter of the Lord and He awards them protection. But if we seek the shelter of the demigods or others it's like trying to cross the ocean by catching hold of a dog's tail. It is a foolish thing to do, and our efforts will be useless.
On the spiritual platform, there is no difference between seeing the Lord, offering prayers, and hearing transcendental sound.	7.4.25–26	People are sometimes very eager to see God. In *bhakti*, all devotional activities are absolute – there's no difference between worshiping the Deity, seeing the Lord, and chanting His names and glories. All of these are ways of seeing Him. Everything done in devotional service is a means of direct contact with Him. Thus, although the demigods couldn't see Lord Viṣṇu, they were still hearing the Lord and offering prayers to Him, and so were actually "seeing" Him.

THEMES	REFERENCES	KEY MESSAGES
If one offends a Vaiṣṇava, all one's auspicious activities are uprooted and one's life is ruined.	7.4.27–28, 43	Lord Viṣṇu assured the demigods that Hiraṇyakaśipu's life would be ruined because of his offenses to his son, Prahlāda, a pure devotee of the Lord. Of all sinful activities, an offense to a pure Vaiṣṇava is the most severe. Śrī Caitanya Mahāprabhu compared it to a mad elephant that enters a garden and uproots many plants and trees. In the same way, one's offenses to a Vaiṣṇava uproot all one's auspicious activities. A devotee does not create enemies, but if someone becomes his enemy, that person will be vanquished by the Supreme Lord. The Lord cannot tolerate violence to His devotee. One should therefore be very careful of offending a devotee.
The Lord's devotee has all good qualities, both material and spiritual, and sees Kṛṣṇa everywhere. Such a devotee purifies everyone he comes in contact with.	7.4.30–42	Prahlāda was the son of a demon, but he was a perfect *brāhmaṇa* because he was the Lord's devotee and possessed all wonderful qualities. He was fully absorbed in Kṛṣṇa consciousness, and therefore he saw Kṛṣṇa everywhere. He thus experienced ecstatic symptoms and felt the Lord's personal presence and touch. He was undisturbed by the torture of his father because of his absorption in Kṛṣṇa. When his friends saw his love for Kṛṣṇa, they became influenced by him and became devotees. They became blissful just by seeing Prahlāda's behavior and getting his association.

Higher-Thinking Questions

Now try to deepen your understanding of this chapter by delving into Śrīla Prabhupāda's purports and reflecting on the following questions:

1. How can material benedictions become a curse as explained in verse 3 purport?
2. Why are the Vedic descriptions of the universe more accurate than the scientists'? See verses 7 and 8 purports.
3. According to verse 20 purport, what is the meaning of "*śāstra*" and what happens when we don't follow *śāstra*?
4. Why does taking shelter of the holy *dhāma* allow us to advance in Kṛṣṇa consciousness quickly? (See verse 23 purport.)
5. How can one see the Lord and speak to Him as described in verses 25–26 purports.

6. Why should one not worship the demigods, who are themselves harassed by the demons, but take shelter of the Supreme Lord? (See verse 29 purport.)
7. How was Prahlāda Mahārāja, a Vaiṣṇava, automatically a *brāhmaṇa*? Refer to verses 31 to 33 and purports.
8. How is the pure devotee like the Lord as described in verse 34 purport?
9. According to verse 42 and purport, explain how *bhakti* is unconditional and doesn't depend on anything external.

ACTIVITIES

In this section you will find many exciting things to do. These activities will get you thinking, moving, drawing, and having loads of fun.

Analogy Activity

... to bring out the scholar in you

ŚRĪLA PRABHUPĀDA ACTED FOR ALL

"As the moon never refuses to distribute its pleasing rays even to the home of a *caṇḍāla*, a Vaiṣṇava never refuses to act for everyone's welfare." *SB* 7.5.31–32, purport

This analogy compares the act of the moon to a devotee's acts – Śrīla Prabhupāda comments that both act for others' welfare and bring them pleasure.

As a class,

1. Think of at least three ways Śrīla Prabhupāda acted for everyone's welfare; e.g., prasadam distribution, temple construction, book translation, etc.
2. Then, research at least one pastime of Śrīla Prabhupāda for each way you've mentioned.
3. Share the pastime(s) with the class.
4. Discuss how Śrīla Prabhupāda's actions brought peace and pleasure to those whose lives he touched.

Artistic Activity

... to reveal your creativity

STENCIL ART: KṚṢṆA IN VṚNDĀVANA

Stencil art or Sanchai art is a traditional art form, common in Vṛndāvana, which depicts Kṛṣṇa and His pastimes. Let us do a stencil collage using three simple stencils. Please make sure you get assistance or the supervision of your teacher or parent.

Materials needed: Three stencil templates printed from Resources; three thick transparent plastic sheets for the stencils; acrylic paints; brushes or sponges; sticky tape; a thick sheet of paper for the collage; precision knife; and cutting board.

Steps:

1. Photocopy the templates in Resources on plain paper and assemble your materials together (Image 1). Take the first template and place it on a sturdy, thick cutting board, securing it with tape (Image 2).
2. Then secure a plastic sheet over the template with a paper clip or tape (see Image 3).
3. With the supervision of an adult, very carefully cut out the darkened parts of the template with the precision knife (see Image 3). Start from the corners, making short and precise strokes along the edge of the dark parts.
4. Make sure to take your time so that all the black parts are cut out properly and that you do not injure yourself.

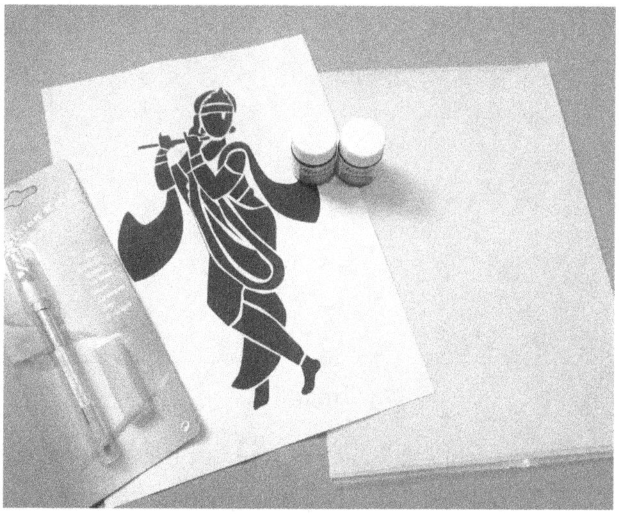

Image 1

Image 2

Image 3

5. Now start with the second template and then the third template.
6. When all your stencils are cut out, carefully remove them from the template underneath. Now you have all your stencils ready (Image 4).
7. Place your tree stencil in the middle of the collage paper and secure with tape (Image 5). Then carefully dab brown paint with a brush or sponge in the trunk area of the stencil. Then apply green paint on the leaves of the stencil (Image 6). Carefully remove the plastic stencil sheet so that you do not smudge the paint. Then leave to dry (Image 7).

Image 4

Image 5

Image 6

Now place the cow stencil in front of the tree and secure it with tape. Dab gray or black paint in the stencil spaces (Image 8).

Image 7

Image 8

Image 9

Remove plastic stencil and leave to dry (Image 9).

8. Then place the Kṛṣṇa stencil to the side of the cow and color Him in (Image 10). For His body use blue paint and for His clothes use yellow and red. You may also use black or blue for the entire stencil.
   Remove the plastic stencil carefully and now your collage is ready (Image 11). You may add any embellishments with a brush and frame your stencil painting.

Image 10

Image 11

Introspective Activity

... to bring out the reflective devotee in you

HOW NOT TO JUDGE

(Concept adapted from *Revealing the Heart* by Sukhāvahā Dāsī)

Kṛṣṇa is displeased when we offend His devotees. Lord Caitanya compares Vaiṣṇava-*aparādha* to a mad elephant. A mad elephant enters a garden, and without discretion uproots numerous plants and trees. Similarly, our offenses to a devotee uproots all our auspicious activities.

To avoid being offensive to devotees, we have to practice avoiding being offensive to everyone we meet. (Why just people! We should treat inanimate objects also with some degree of respect, like picking up something lying on the floor with one's hands rather than kicking it further into a corner.) Being respectful and not being hurtful to people in general will help us avoid offending devotees.

We generally tend to offend others by being judgmental about them. (While it is necessary to make judgments about right and wrong, it is not healthy or beneficial to be judgmental about anyone.)

Let us do an exercise on reframing our judgments into something we actually witness. For example:

Judging: Dev doesn't like to study.
Witnessing: Dev got Ds in four subjects.

Can you see that the former sentence is more hurtful than the latter one?

Here is another example:

Judging: Devotees don't take care of their property.
Witnessing: I haven't seen the devotee families at the apartments around the corner mow their lawn all summer.

Now rewrite the following judgmental statements as witnessing statements:

Judging: She is a messy girl.
Witnessing: I noticed yesterday that ....

Judging: You procrastinate.
Witnessing: I noticed the last three times that you ....

Rewrite the following judgmental statements that imply that our opinions about other's feelings, thoughts, and intentions are the absolute truth.

Judging: She won't call back.
Witnessing: I think that ....

Judging: You are a miser.
Witnessing: You said that ....

We often pass judgments too quickly without pausing to think about the reason behind a person's action.
Write down probable reasons for the following actions you judge:

Judgment: He is too lazy to pay obeisances at the temple.
Reason 1: He has hurt his knee.
Reason 2:
Reason 3:

Judgment: She is a rowdy girl.
Reason 1: She could have some health challenges.
Reason 2:
Reason 3:

Judgment: He seems too nice.
Reason 1: He wants to flatter you.
Reason 2:
Reason 3:

Now try to put this in practice whenever you or anyone else is judging someone.

Critical-Thinking Activity

... to bring out the spiritual investigator in you

THE MISERY OF SENSE "ENJOYMENT"

Verse 19 describes how Hiraṇyakaśipu was dissatisfied in spite of enjoying heavenly pleasures, because he was a servant of his senses. Let us try to understand what the phrase "servant of the senses" means and why one always remains dissatisfied when one is a servant of the senses.

In the *Bhagavad-gītā*, Lord Kṛṣṇa describes that sense gratification is the pleasure we derive when our senses come in touch with sense objects. He also does not approve sense enjoyment, stating its nature as: 1. Capable of carrying a man's intelligence away (2.60); 2. Temporary, having a beginning and an end (5.22); 3. In the end, resulting in misery for the person rather than enjoyment (5.22).

Let us study each of these characteristics of sense gratification and see how it affected Hiraṇyakaśipu but not Prahlāda (who didn't indulge in it).

1. Even one uncontrolled sense can carry a man's intelligence away.

Śrīla Prabhupāda gives the example of different animals to illustrate this. Look at the following pictures, and in each case, identify the animal, the uncontrolled sense, and the consequence of not controlling the senses.

		Animal/ situation	Uncontrolled sense	Consequence
A				
B	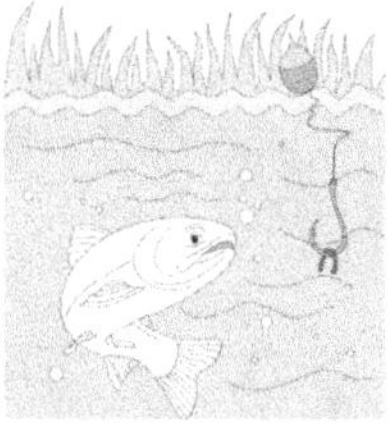			
C				
D				

2. Sense enjoyment is temporary; it has a beginning and an end.
   Śrīla Prabhupāda explains that sense enjoyment is temporary in the following ways.
Solve these picture clues to find out:

A	Sense enjoyment is temporary because the...		is/are temporary.
B	Sense enjoyment is temporary because the...		is/are temporary.

C	Sense enjoyment is temporary because the...		is/are temporary.

3. Unrestricted sense gratification ends in misery rather than enjoyment.
   It's not hard to understand how unrestricted sense enjoyment can end in misery.
Solve these picture clues and fill in the table to understand some examples.

	Image	Uncontrolled activity	Uncontrolled sense	Misery
A				
B				
C				
D				

4. Now consider what you just learned in the context of the pastime:
   a) Why did Hiraṇyakaśipu remain dissatisfied in spite of indulging in virtually unlimited sense gratification?
   b) Why did Prahlāda remain satisfied in spite of choosing not to indulge in uncontrolled sense enjoyment?

Science Activity

... to bring out the spiritual scientist in you

EVALUATING SENSE PERFECTION

Verses 5 to 8 describe how Hiraṇyakaśipu conquered the heavenly planets and lived there in great opulence that is beyond our sense perception or imagination.

In purports 7 and 8, Śrīla Prabhupāda comments that although life exists on different planets in the universe, it is not possible to convince modern scientists about it, since the methods they use to study the universe are different from the Vedic methods. In previous cantos, especially in Canto 5, we learned about these two methods of obtaining knowledge and why their findings don't always match?

Narayani is a first-year science student at the Vedic Sciences Institute, an institute that studies the workings of the world from a Vedic scientific perspective. Narayani is learning that research about the universe can be done in two ways:

1. The ascending process (*āroha-panthā*): We observe the world through our senses, create a theory to explain a certain phenomenon, design an experiment to test the theory, and finally, come up with an explanation for what was observed in nature.

2. The descending process (*avaroha-panthā*): We find an authority on the topic, accept his or her explanation of a phenomenon, and then apply this knowledge to test or take advantage of the phenomenon; for example, a person may accept the instructions in a smart phone manual as correct based on the authority of the manufacturer, and then "tests" or "applies" that knowledge by operating the phone according to the instructions in the manual.

Narayani has further learned that knowledge acquired by the ascending process is subject to four defects. Recall these defects and discuss with your class.

The descending process, however, provides perfect knowledge as long as the authority is chosen properly and the knowledge is passed on without change.

Narayani has been asked to complete an assignment to show how imperfect senses can yield imperfect knowledge. She has been asked to evaluate* the following two statements. The first one is a comment from an expert on the ascending process, and the second is a statement about the descending process of acquiring knowledge.

* to evaluate means to make a judgment about something.

“Even if we photograph the stars, we must eventually ‘take in’ by our senses what the photograph shows. Furthermore, without our senses, we could not handle a photographic camera. Clearly, all knowledge comes to us ultimately through our senses.”

(Eugene Wigner, 1963 Nobel Laureate in Physics)

“Telescopes and the other imperfect instruments of scientists are inadequate for evaluating the upper planetary system. Although such instruments are needed because the vision of the so-called scientists is imperfect, the instruments themselves are also imperfect. Therefore the upper planets cannot be appraised by imperfect men using imperfect man-made instruments. Direct information received from the Vedic literature, however, is perfect. We therefore cannot accept the statement that there are no opulent residences on planets other than this earth.” (*Śrīmad-Bhagavatam* 7.4.8 purport)

Narayani’s teacher gave her some quiz questions to help her with her evaluation:

1. What is meant by “Nobel Laureate”? What is he implying about the images captured through a telescope when viewing the stars?
2. Why is his statement significant?
3. What comment is Śrīla Prabhupāda making about knowledge acquired through telescopes? How is it same or different from the Nobel Laureate’s statement?
4. What conclusion can we draw from this? How does this conclusion help you evaluate the two statements?

Writing Activities

... to bring out the writer in you

NARRATIVE ESSAY: REAL SATISFACTION

Write a narrative essay on one of the following topics, showing that material enjoyment leads to dissatisfaction:

1. Mr. Kumar is a famous, wealthy businessman who owns Kumar Enterprises, and although he has everything and controls many people, he is not satisfied. When he is tired of becoming a slave to his senses, he has an awakening.
2. Sara is a popular girl in school. She has good grades, many friends, a wealthy family, and everything a girl could want. She goes to nightclubs and gets involved in all sorts of nefarious activities, becoming a slave to her senses. An incident occurs which reveals to her how unhappy she has been and prompts her to change.

LETTER TO THE BEST WELL-WISHING FRIEND

Write a letter to Kṛṣṇa expressing to Him your gratitude and happiness for being your best friend and well-wisher. Perhaps describe an incident or a realization that showed you He is always your protector and guide. Express to Him the futility of taking shelter of the demigods or any other so-called protector. You may also express your desire to increase your faith in Him, because having faith that He is your best friend can make you fearless (just as Prahlāda Mahārāja became) and more confident to face life's challenges (as Prahlāda Mahārāja did).

NO ORDINARY SOUND

Read the following interesting story, which relates how the holy name is not ordinary, and then in your own words write a paragraph of 200 to 300 words, explaining what key messages about the holy name come through for you.

(From *Dancing White Elephants, Traveling with Śrīla Prabhupāda in India, August 1970–March 1972* by Giriraj Swami)

In Madras I had kept hearing a cinema song being played—*Dam Maro Dam, Hare Krishna Hare Rama.* When I had asked my host what the words meant, he had replied, "With every breath I take, Hare Krishna Hare Rama"—which had sounded quite nice—but later I found out that they meant, "With every puff I take, Hare Krishna Hare Rama."

When, on Prabhupāda's instruction, I went to Calcutta, en route to Mayapur, the movie featuring the song was playing there too. We didn't know what the movie was, but in those days whenever the musical or the movie *Hair* would show in America, devotees would do *hari-nāma-saṅkīrtana* in front of the theater and distribute books, because *Hair* featured a song with the full Hare Krishna maha-mantra. We thought that this too would be a great opportunity, so we had *hari-nāma* and distributed books outside the theater.

One evening, when most of the patrons had entered the theater, I thought, *Let me steal a peek and see what the movie is.* It began with shots of ocean waves hitting the shore. In a deep, resonant voice, the narrator intoned, "For centuries, India's spiritual culture remained within the shores of India, but one man"—then it showed a picture of Srila Prabhupada—"took India's spiritual culture across the ocean." A shot of the London Ratha-yatra followed, and I thought, *Wow! This is amazing!* Then the film showed a bunch of hippies—boys and girls together—smoking ganja and chanting Hare Krishna Hare Rama. It was really bad. The theme of the movie was that Srila Prabhupada was degrading the sacred Indian culture by giving it to hippies who were just misusing it, chanting Hare Krishna Hare Rama while smoking dope and indulging in free sex.

That was a blow. Later, Prabhupada said that the government was behind the film, because they were afraid that our movement would become too popular and they wanted to turn people away from it. Communists in the government also started rumors that we were CIA. It was the same: they knew we weren't CIA, but they didn't want people to take to Krishna consciousness. They claimed that spiritual life would keep the people down, but actually, it was they who wanted to do that.

Still, Prabhupada had such faith in the holy name that he said, "In the long run the song will actually help us, because eventually people will forget the *dam maro dam* and just remember the Hare Krishna Hare Rama." And it came true. After Calcutta and Mayapur, I went to Bombay, and especially the street urchins there—so many street urchins stood on corners and begged, or sold magazines—whenever they saw us, they would gather around us and put their hands to their mouths, as if they were smoking chillums with charas (hashish), and mockingly sing, "*Dam maro dam, dam maro dam . . .*" Most of the time they wouldn't even get to the "Hare Krishna Hare Rama"—just "*Dam maro dam.*" It went on like that for some time, and only after a year or so—the song was extraordinarily popular—did the emphasis shift, and the two parts—"*Dam maro dam*" and "Hare Krishna Hare Rama"—became equal. And eventually, just as Prabhupāda had predicted, the "*Dam maro dam*" dropped out altogether. It was a mundane sound vibration and had no real attraction or long-lasting appeal. But the "Hare Krishna Hare Rama" was transcendental and ever fresh. Then when people saw us, they would just smile and say, "Hare Krishna Hare Rama."

Language Activities

... to help you understand better

ADVERT: SEE THE LORD

When the demigods heard Lord Viṣṇu's voice but did not "see" Him, they were actually seeing Him, because on the spiritual platform, there is no difference between seeing the Lord, offering prayers, and hearing transcendental sound. So when we worship the Deity, hear the holy names or the *Bhāgavatam*, or offer our prayers to Kṛṣṇa, He is always present.

Create a poster advertising the 25th anniversary of the installation of the Deities at your local temple. Add a beautiful picture of the Deities or the temple activities and mention the highlights that indicate how attendees will be "seeing" Kṛṣṇa. See example below:

25TH ANNIVERSARY CELEBRATIONS
COME SEE THE LORD!

Join us for this special event
Krishna Balarama temple
Vrindavan, India
6 July 2023
From 4:30 to 22:00

Highlights:
Pushpa Abhisekha (bathing the Deities with flower petals)
Kirtana and bhajanas
Spiritual discourses from the *Bhagavad-gita*
Offering of cards and gifts to the Deities
Drama: Krsna, our well-wishing friend
Prasadam feast

FROM HIRAṆYAKAŚIPU'S DIARY: ODE TO A DEMON

Read the following incomplete poem found scribbled in the pages of Hiranyakashipu's recently unearthed diary.

* An ode is a lyrical poem usually meant to be sung. The ode dates back to ancient Greece and praises people, places, things, and ideas. While the classical ode has strict requirements of form, contemporary odes have no restrictions.

Ode to Me

Night or day
Man or beast
Instrument of man
Cannot kill Me
So invincible am I
Death constantly cowers before Me

Indra's gone
Spat from his throne
A shadow of himself
And in his place is Me
So glorious am I
The demigods bow down to Me

The seven islands
Remain unploughed
Yet they still
Feed Me
So exceptional am I
The earth continues to fear Me

The oceans churn My jewels,
The valleys bear My flowers
Pouring water, drying and burning
Are directed all by Me
So formidable am I
Indra, Vayu, and Agni remain unneeded by Me

Questions:

1. Why is Hiraṇyakaśipu's ode unusual?
2. Give an example of an alliteration used in the poem. Hint: An alliteration is the occurrence of the same letter or sound, at the beginning of adjacent or nearby words.
3. Why does Hiraṇyakaśipu say that death cowers before him? Who is the God of Death?
4. Which two words used repeatedly in the poem shows Hiraṇyakaśipu's arrogance. Explain how.
5. What are the seven islands referring to in the second stanza?
6. How was Indra "spat from his throne"? What figure of speech is used here?
7. Why do Indra, Agni, and Vayu "remain unneeded"?
8. In this poem Hiraṇyakaśipu boasts about everything he controls. What was the one thing he couldn't control that every devotee strives to control? Why is it important to control this?
9. Hiraṇyakaśipu has many attributes in common with materialists today. Explain their similarities. Further explain why this will ultimately lead to their destruction.
10. The ode is incomplete. Write two lines to end the ode. You can choose to end the ode with Hiraṇyakaśipu gloating over his "immorality."

Optional: Now it's your turn. Choose one of the great devotees mentioned in this chapter (Prahlāda Mahārāja, Yudhiṣṭhira Mahārāja, or Nārada Muni) and write your own ode to them. Research their good qualities, both material and spiritual, so you can include them in your ode. What is the difference between your ode and Hiraṇyakaśipu's ode?

CHAPTER 4 ANSWERS

Śrīla Prabhupāda Acted for All *(Potential Answers)*

1. He took great inconvenience upon himself and went to America; he taught everyone the science of Kṛṣṇa consciousness without discrimination; he traveled and preached in all major continents to all types of people; he taught us to chant the holy name; he wrote books everyone could read; he opened temples with beautiful deities that everyone could see and thus advance in Kṛṣṇa consciousness; he engaged each person according to their inclination in Kṛṣṇa's service. Answers to 2, 3, and 4 are the learner's own and should be mentor-driven.

The Misery of Sense "Enjoyment"

1a. Deer being attracted to a hunter's flute; ears; hunter captures deer; 1b. Fish getting attracted to bait; tongue; fish gets caught by fisherman; 1c. Bumblebee getting trapped in a lotus flower; smell; bee dies inside the flower; 1d. Male elephant entering a pit to be with a female elephant; mind/touch; male elephant is captured by the hunter; 2a. body; 2b. sense objects; 2c. ability of the senses to enjoy only limitedly; 3a. uncontrolled or thoughtless eating; tongue; sickness; 3b. listening to loud music; ears; possible deafness; 3c. use of substances that could harm health; smell; sickness; 3d. attraction to skin-deep beauty; eyes; possible heartbreak; 4a. Hiraṇyakaśipu thought that a greater standard of enjoyment would bring him greater pleasure, but he didn't consider how his own senses are limited, only providing limited enjoyment. He failed to derive unlimited pleasure from a seemingly unlimited set of sources and remained dissatisfied. And finally, he failed to consider how uncontrolled senses lead to misery and destruction.; 4b. By controlling his senses, Prahlāda was able to avoid the misery and distraction they bring. He was able to focus his senses on the supreme source of pleasure and satisfaction, the Supreme Lord. By serving the Lord and His devotees, Prahlāda followed the correct method to derive unlimited pleasure, and therefore he remained satisfied.

Evaluating Sense Perfection

1. A Nobel Laureate is one who has won the Nobel Prize, which is widely regarded as the most prestigious award available in certain fields, such as Physics. He is implying that the study of the universe through the ascending process using telescopes is the same as perceiving a photo from a camera. Whatever we see, in whatever way, is limited because of our imperfect senses. Knowledge acquired through the senses (the ascending process) is also limited. 2. It is significant because ascending (modern) scientific knowledge is generally considered perfect (and scientists even get awarded for it), but here a scientist is pointing out that it is not perfect; 3. Śrīla Prabhupāda is commenting that the modern method of using a telescope cannot yield perfect knowledge because the senses are imperfect, and this is the reason scientists are not able to find life on higher planets. His statement is interesting because it agrees with Eugene Wigner's statement, but Śrīla Prabhupāda's source of knowledge is the descending process, unlike Wigner, who is speaking through experience of the ascending process; 4. One strong conclusion we can draw from this is that direct experience is not always needed to gain proper knowledge. Proper knowledge can be gained by hearing from perfect authorities and can be trusted even without direct personal experience. Vedic knowledge is therefore trustworthy. This is how Narayani evaluates the two statements.

Ode to a Demon

1. Usually odes are written to praise other people while in this poem Hiraṇyakaśipu praises himself.
2. "Constantly cowers."
3. In this chapter we learn that all the demigods were afraid of Hiraṇyakaśipu, and the God of Death (Yamarāja) is also a demigod who feared him. It is effective because usually people are afraid of death, but here Death personified is depicted as being afraid of him.
4. "Me" (in capitals) and "I." These words show he is always thinking of himself and how he is better than everyone else.
5. The earth.
6. He was overthrown by Hiraṇyakaśipu. Personification.
7. Their jobs of providing fire, rain, and wind are now

being controlled by Hiraṇyakaśipu, so he doesn't need them to do these services anymore.

8. He could not control his senses. Devotees try to control their senses because the material energy binds us to the material world by our senses. A devotee does not want to remain in the material world but wants to go back to Kṛṣṇa. The senses can be controlled by engaging them in Kṛṣṇa's service.

9. Just like Hiraṇyakaśipu, materialists try to control everything although on a smaller scale. They become unhappy because they become a slave to their senses. Thus greed and envy consume them because they always want more. They then enter the road to destruction because they have broken the laws of *śāstra*.

RESOURCES FOR ART ACTIVITY

5

PRAHLĀDA MAHĀRĀJA, THE SAINTLY SON OF HIRAṆYAKAŚIPU

Story Summary

After hearing Yudhiṣṭhira Mahārāja's enquiries, Nārada Muni decided to start from the beginning.

"It was time for five-year-old Prahlāda to go to school," he said. "He went to the school of Ṣaṇḍa and Amarka, who were sons of Hiraṇyakaśipu's priest, Śukrācārya."

Yudhiṣṭhira Mahārāja raised an eyebrow. He knew that Śukrācārya shouldn't have accepted such a post for a demon.

"His teachers taught him, along with other sons of the *asuras*, politics and economics. But understanding that politics involved distinguishing between friends and enemies, Prahlāda did not like it. He saw everyone equally."

Yudhiṣṭhira Mahārāja smiled, knowing well how politics can create friends and enemies even in one's own family. He wanted to hear more about this saintly boy, Prahlāda.

Nārada Muni explained that after some time, Prahlāda visited Hiraṇyakaśipu. The demon king sat Prahlāda on his lap and affectionately looked at his little boy.

"So, dear son, please tell me what's the best subject you've studied in school."

Prahlāda's eyes lit up as he gazed at his father and said, "O Pitā, King of the *asuras*, my spiritual master taught me that anyone who has a material body and leads a materialistic household life falls into a dark well where there is no water but only suffering. Instead, one should go to Vṛndāvana and take shelter of the Supreme Personality of Godhead there."

"Huh?" Hiraṇyakaśipu retorted, but then his eyes grew wider and he laughed so loudly that little Prahlāda almost fell off his lap.

"This child's intelligence has been spoiled by the enemy's words!" he exclaimed.

Handing Prahlāda to his servants, he said, "My dear demons, protect this boy at the *gurukula* from any Vaiṣṇavas who may go there in disguise."

Back at the *gurukula*, Ṣaṇḍa and Amarka were determined to find out who had polluted Prahlāda's intelligence. They smiled at Prahlāda and asked him in sweet voices, "Dear son, please tell us who has given you these instructions.

Please don't lie. Tell us who has spoiled your intelligence. Are you responsible, or the enemies?"

Prahlāda Mahārāja folded his palms and closed his eyes. He said, "I offer my respectful obeisances to the Supreme Personality of Godhead. His external energy has created this distinction of friend and enemy, deluding the intelligence of men." Looking at his teachers with his lotus-like eyes, he raised his voice and said, "Indeed, only now am I experiencing this although I've heard of it before from spiritual authorities."

Ṣaṇḍa and Amarka frowned and looked at each other. They knew they were right. Which authorities could have polluted his consciousness? they thought.

"When the Lord is pleased by your devotional service," Prahlāda continued, "you become a *paṇḍita* and don't distinguish between friends and enemies. You think, 'We are all servants of God, and so we are not different from one another.'

"You may think I've taken the side of the enemy, but the Lord has made me see He is the friend of everyone. Such is His mercy. He has given me the intelligence to take the side of your so-called enemy.

"O *brāhmaṇas*, as iron is attracted to a magnetic stone, my consciousness is naturally attracted to Lord Viṣṇu. Thus I have no independence."

Ṣaṇḍa and Amarka exploded in anger. "Bring me a stick!" shouted one of them. "This Prahlāda is destroying our name and fame. Now we have to treat him with the fourth method of political diplomacy!"

Threatening Prahlāda with a stick in hand, the other said, "This rascal Prahlāda is like a thorn tree in a sandalwood forest. To cut down sandalwood trees, an axe is needed, and the wood of the thorn tree is very suitable for the handle of such an axe. Lord Viṣṇu is the axe for cutting down the sandalwood forest of the family of demons, and this Prahlāda is the handle for that axe."

Prahlāda's teachers couldn't let Prahlāda destroy their dynasty. They forcibly educated Prahlāda in religion, economic development, and sense gratification. Months went by, and it seemed that Prahlāda had been absorbing all the knowledge about diplomatic affairs.

One day, after Prahlāda's mother had bathed her son and decorated him with fine clothes and ornaments, Ṣaṇḍa and Amarka presented him to his father.

Prahlāda respectfully bowed at Hiraṇyakaśipu's feet. Beaming, the demon king lifted Prahlāda and embraced him tightly. He smelled the child's head, and the tears that glided down his cheeks wet Prahlāda's smiling face.

With a gentle voice, Hiraṇyakaśipu said, "My dear son, for so long you've been hearing many things from your teachers. Now repeat to me what you think is the best of that knowledge."

Prahlāda Mahārāja's voice echoed through the hallways: "*Śravaṇaṁ kīrtanaṁ viṣṇoḥ*. . . Hearing and chanting about the transcendental holy

name, form, qualities, paraphernalia and pastimes of Lord Viṣṇu, remembering them, serving the Lord's lotus feet, offering Him respectful worship, offering Him prayers, becoming His servant, considering Him one's best friend, and surrendering everything unto Him (in other words, serving Him with the body, mind and words) – these nine processes are accepted as pure devotional service. One who has dedicated his life to the service of Kṛṣṇa through these nine methods is the most learned person."

Hiraṇyakaśipu's lips trembled, and his eyes became as red as coals. He turned toward Ṣaṇḍa and rebuked him: "What's this nonsense about devotional service you've taught this poor boy? You've disobeyed me and taken the side of the enemy!

"Deceptive people cannot hide for long. In time their enmity is revealed."

Ṣaṇḍa fell at the feet of Hiraṇyakaśipu, begging for mercy, "O my dear King, we didn't teach your son anything about what he spoke. He has spontaneous devotion to Viṣṇu. Please don't accuse us; we are not to blame. It's not good to insult a *brāhmaṇa* in this way."

Amarka also approached the King with folded hands and bowed his head, assuring the King that they were not responsible for Prahlāda's "contamination."

Hiraṇyakaśipu turned toward Prahlāda, trying to withhold his fury: "You rascal, most fallen in our family, if you didn't get this knowledge from your teachers, from where did you get it?"

Prahlāda calmly replied, "Materialistic people cannot control their senses. They repeatedly chew that which has already been chewed. So they go to hell. Their attraction to Kṛṣṇa is never aroused. These people accept as their *guru* a similar blind man addicted to sense enjoyment. They don't know that the goal of life is to go back to Godhead. These blind men following another blind man fall into a ditch and are bound by fruitive work. They therefore continue suffering life after life.

"Unless they smear their bodies with the dust of the lotus feet of a pure Vaiṣṇava, they cannot be attached to the lotus feet of the Lord. Only by taking shelter of the Lord's lotus feet can they become purified."

Hiraṇyakaśipu threw Prahlāda off his lap onto the ground in a rage.

His reddish eyes appeared like molten copper. He shouted, "Servants, take this boy away from me! Kill him at once!"

Some of the servants shrieked, fearing the King's wrath.

"This boy is the killer of my brother!" Hiraṇyakaśipu yelled, clenching his fists. "He has given up his family to be a servant of Lord Viṣṇu, our enemy. We can never trust him."

The servants caught hold of Prahlāda, and the boy peacefully submitted to them.

Hiraṇyakaśipu began to justify his rejection of his son: "If someone outside one's family is favorable, he should be given protection like a son. On the other hand, if a limb of one's body is poisoned by disease, it must be amputated so that the rest of the body may live happily. Similarly, even one's own son, if unfavorable, must be rejected, although born of one's own body."

Not able to look at Prahlāda, he said, "Therefore this enemy must be killed by all means!"

The *rākṣasas* took Prahlāda away. Just looking at them, you would be petrified by their ghastly faces, sharp teeth, and coppery beard and hair. With loud grunting noises, they pierced Prahlāda with their tridents – but Prahlāda remained calm and serene, silently meditating on the Supreme Lord. This seemed to agonize the demons more. "Chop him up!" they shouted, as they struck Prahlāda violently.

But the demons' weapons had no effect. The boy's lips constantly murmured the Lord's holy names. Thus he was unharmed and undisturbed because of his meditation on the Lord and His names.

"My dear King Yudhiṣṭhira," Nārada Muni said, "when Hiraṇyakaśipu heard how Prahlāda was unharmed, what to speak of being still alive, he contrived other means of killing his son.

"Hiraṇyakaśipu ordered his servants to throw Prahlāda beneath the feet of gigantic elephants; throw him among huge, fearful snakes; use

destructive spells; hurl him from the top of a hill; conjure up illusory tricks; administer poison; starve him; expose him to severe cold, winds, fire, and water; and throw heavy stones to crush him.

"Through it all, Prahlāda remained in trance, protected by the Lord's loving embrace.

"Imagine the King's anxiety when he found out that his son could not be killed in any way. He knew that Prahlāda was each time saved by the power of his devotional service.

"Hiraṇyakaśipu thought, 'This mere child is completely fearless. He's like a dog's curved tail that cannot be straightened because he can never forget his master, Lord Viṣṇu. He seems to be immortal. Perhaps I will die because of my enmity towards him.'

"Like this the King of the demons was plagued by worry and fear. Ṣaṇḍa and Amarka saw the King's morose and downcast face.

"They whispered to him in secrecy: 'O King, you have conquered all the three worlds. Simply by the movement of your eyebrows, the leaders of various planets are afraid. So there's no reason for you to be anxious. And Prahlāda is just a child. What harm can he do? Just arrest him so he won't flee. And by the time he grows up and learns from us more, he will change. So there's no reason to be anxious.'

"Becoming convinced by their plan, Hiraṇyakaśipu allowed them to teach Prahlāda about the occupational duties of royal householder families. Prahlāda appeared to be very submissive, but he did not like his teachers' instructions in material life, which marked the repetition of birth, death, old age, and disease.

"When the teachers were busy, Prahlāda's classmates wanted to play with Prahlāda. But Prahlāda instead instructed them about spiritual life. Attracted by this pure boy, they left their playthings and surrounded Prahlāda. Their hearts and eyes were fixed on him, eager to hear whatever he said. Prahlāda Mahārāja, although born in a family of demons, was an exalted devotee of the Lord, and thus he desired their welfare. He began instructing them about the uselessness of materialistic life."

Themes and Key Messages

Please go through this table of themes and key messages, with corresponding verses, and discuss each topic further.

THEMES	REFERENCES	KEY MESSAGES
A learned person does not make distinctions between friends and enemies.	7.5.3–4, 11–12	Prahlāda did not want to hear about politics because it involves distinguishing between friends and enemies. A devotee doesn't create friends and enemies because he sees that every living being is part and parcel of Kṛṣṇa (*mamaivāṁśo jīva-bhūtaḥ BG* 15.7) and are His servants. Therefore, they are not different from one another. In this way a devotee sees everyone equally and treats friends and enemies equally by trying to educate them both in Kṛṣṇa consciousness. Prahlāda Mahārāja tried to give his father spiritual knowledge, not considering his father's position as a demon.
One should eventually retire from household life and go to Vṛndāvana and take full shelter of the Lord. However, atheistic people never agree to surrender to the Lord.	7.5.5–6	Prahlāda Mahārāja advised his father to give up the attachments of household life, which he compares to a dark well, and go to Vṛndāvana, where he can worship and take full shelter of Kṛṣṇa. *Varṇāśrama* is meant to gradually elevate one's consciousness and help one break free from bodily attachments. Prahlada's demonic father, because of his envy and hatred for the Lord and His devotees, could never agree to do this.
We should see other devotees as our masters (*prabhus*) and should be friendly with one another for the service of the Lord.	7.5.11–12	Even though we are all servants of the Lord, Śrīla Prabhupāda advises us to be humble and see other devotees as our masters. As servants there is no question of enmity between servants. We should appreciate and praise one another's service and not be proud of our own. This is Vaikuṇṭha consciousness. In this way our relationships will be congenial and harmonious with Kṛṣṇa in the center.
It is natural for all living beings to be attracted toward Kṛṣṇa.	7.5.14	"Kṛṣṇa" means He who attracts everyone and everything. In Vṛndāvana all persons and creatures are attracted to Kṛṣṇa. The material world, where everyone is attracted to *māyā,* is contrary to Vṛndāvana. Hiraṇyakaśipu, who was in the material world, was attracted by women and money, whereas Prahlāda Mahārāja, being in his natural position, was attracted by Kṛṣṇa. As soon as we are purified of material contamination, we are again attracted by Kṛṣṇa. Devotional service purifies us of all unnatural attractions.

THEMES	REFERENCES	KEY MESSAGES
Materialists cannot understand or realize the Lord, but a devotee who has dedicated his life to the nine processes of devotional service, under the guidance of a pure devotee, is the most learned and becomes purified of all contamination.	7.5.23–24, 30–32	Prahlāda Mahārāja instructed his demonic father about the purpose of life: materialistic people who cannot control their senses are repeatedly chewing the chewed and going toward hell; they are blind led by other blind men (false *gurus*), their inclination toward Kṛṣṇa is never aroused, and they do not realize that the goal is to go back to Godhead. Only by taking shelter at the lotus feet of the Lord, smearing one's body with the dust of His pure devotees, and dedicating one's life to the nine processes of devotional service – hearing, chanting, remembering, serving the Lord's lotus feet, worshiping the Deity, offering prayers, becoming a servant, considering the Lord your best friend, and surrendering everything – one is considered learned and can be freed from material contamination.
The Lord always protects a pure and surrendered devotee because of the devotee's complete absorption in the Lord.	7.5.39–44	Prahlāda's constant meditation on the Lord made him immensely powerful, so much so that Hiraṇyakaśipu and his followers could not kill him by any means. This is because the Lord was always protecting him, reciprocating with His pure devotee's love and absorption in Him.

Higher-Thinking Questions

Now try to deepen your understanding of this chapter by delving into Śrīla Prabhupāda's purports and reflecting on the following questions:

1. Why shouldn't Śukrācārya have become the priest of Hiraṇyakaśipu? What should such a *brāhmaṇa* do instead? (Refer to verse 1 purport.)
2. According to verse 5 purport, how does following *varṇāśrama* help someone elevate their consciousness gradually and systematically?
3. What does verse 7 purport reflect about Śrīla Prabhupāda's preaching in the West? What advice does Śrīla Prabhupāda give to preachers with regards to those antagonistic towards Kṛṣṇa consciousness? What does this reveal about Śrīla Prabhupāda's mood?
4. In verses 8 to 10 it's interesting to see that demons view devotees as the enemy and with polluted intelligence. Why do they consider devotees like this?

5. Why does a devotee consider all other devotees as masters, or *prabhus*? (See verse 11 purport.)
6. How does Prahlāda Mahārāja try to convince his teachers that Lord Viṣṇu was not their enemy but their friend? (See verse 13 and purport.)
7. Why do you think Prahlāda instructed his demonic father in devotional service when he knew his father was an enemy of Lord Viṣṇu?
8. Briefly describe *bhakti* according to Śrīla Prabhupāda's analysis in the introduction to his purport on verses 23–24.
9. According to verse 32 purport, why don't highly educated persons not take to Kṛṣṇa consciousness?
10. In verses 37 and 38 how does Hiraṇyakaśipu justify the need to kill his own son. What analogies does he use?

ACTIVITIES

In this section you will find many exciting things to do. These activities will get you thinking, moving, drawing, and having loads of fun.

Analogy Activity

... to bring out the scholar in you

FURTHER EXPLORING SENSE ENJOYMENT

Let us try to understand two famous analogies from this chapter about sense enjoyment that Śrīla Prabhupāda often quotes:

"Because of their uncontrolled senses, persons too addicted to materialistic life make progress toward hellish conditions and repeatedly chew that which has already been chewed. Their inclinations toward Kṛṣṇa are never aroused, either by the instructions of others, by their own efforts, or by a combination of both." *SB* 7.5.30

"As blind men guided by another blind man miss the right path and fall into a ditch, materially attached men led by another materially attached man are bound by the ropes of fruitive labor, which are made of very strong cords, and they continue again and again in materialistic life, suffering the threefold miseries." *SB* 7.5.31

In the last chapter, we understood why sense enjoyment is not satisfying. These analogies further discuss the nature and effect of sense enjoyment. Let us look at them more closely.

First, let us understand the analogies themselves. Look at these illustrations of the above two analogies and write down your understanding of how they relate to sense gratification:

The men in the second and third columns realize that the sugarcane has no more juice but continue chewing on it. From this, what do you understand about a person who wants to gratify his senses?

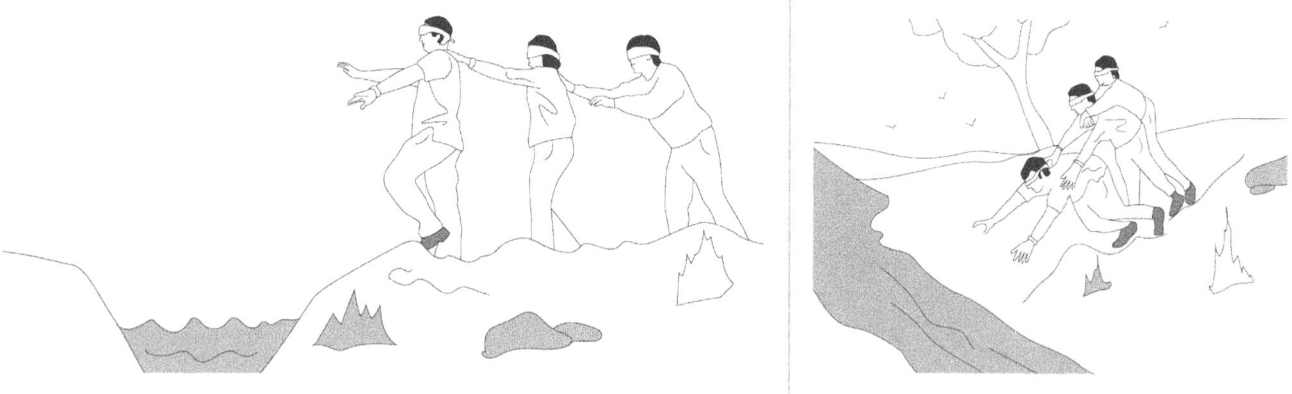

The two blind men who followed the first blind man were not aware that he too was blind. This resulted in disaster for all three. Who does the leading blind man represent, and who are the followers? What does the ditch represent?

Now, nominate one member of your study group to be Prahlāda Mahārāja, who will help all the above characters. Also, nominate some people to represent citizens who had the above experiences. Each of them takes turns to approach Prahlāda, narrating their dissatisfying experience, and Prahlāda guides them. Use verses 30 and 31 and their purports to determine how Prahlāda would speak.

Fill out the speech bubbles below with Prahlāda's guidance to each person mentioned.

Artistic Activity

... to reveal your creativity

PICHWAI ART: VṚNDĀVANA PAINTING

Prahlāda Mahārāja mentions that one should renounce material life and take shelter of Vṛndāvana, Lord Kṛṣṇa's holy *dhāma*.

In Vṛndāvana and in Kṛṣṇa temples Pichwai art is used to make backdrops, normally on cloth, for the deity altars ("Pichh" means back and "wais" means hanging). They are changed daily and are designed according to the season, festival, and rituals of that day. They can also be used as beautiful framed paintings.

Let us make a Vṛndāvana Pichwai painting.

Materials: Pencil, black sharpie, ruler, eraser, piece of cloth or a paper (rectangular), acrylic or watercolor paint or any other medium, paint brushes (only if you're using acrylic paints or watercolors)

Image 1

Steps:

1. Draw a rectangular and triangular border (Image 1).
2. Divide the top triangular lines into four equal sections (Image 2).
3. Make arches on those sections as depicted in Image 3.
4. Erase the inner lines (Image 4).

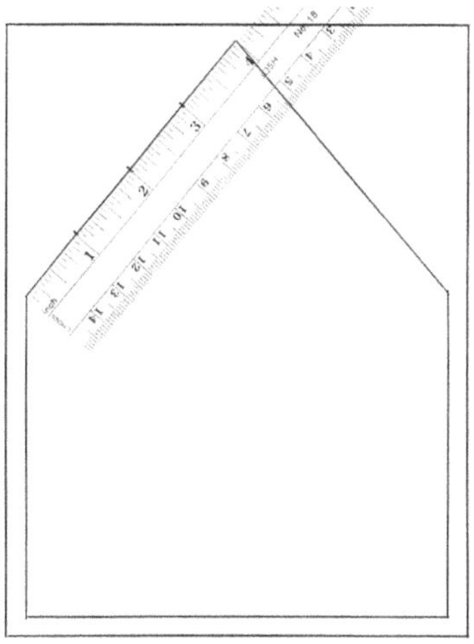

Image 2

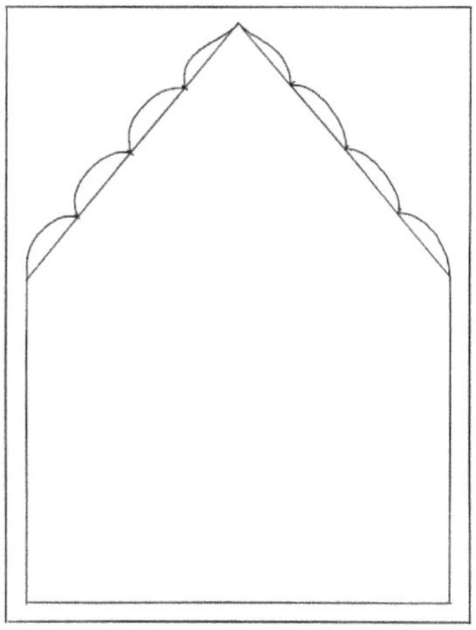

Image 3

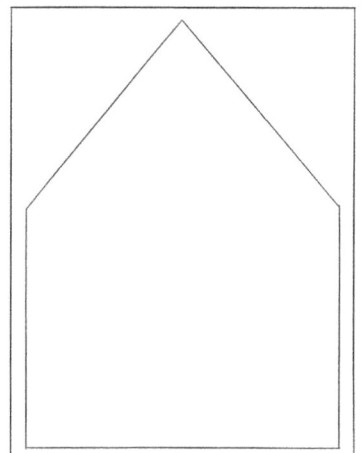

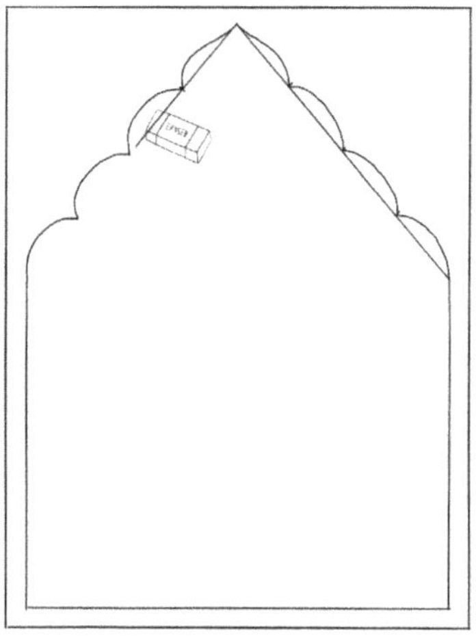

Image 4

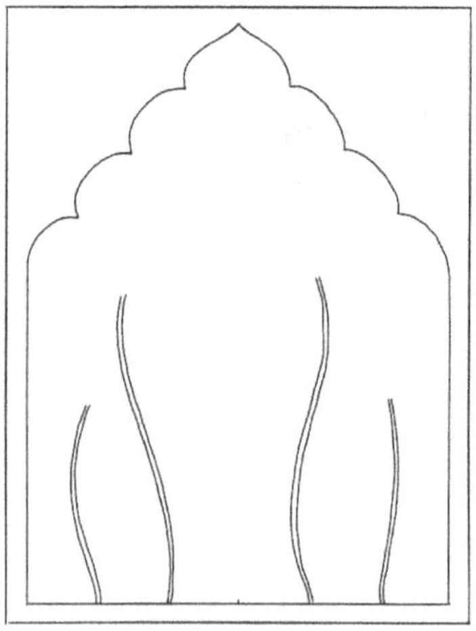

Image 5

Image 7

5. Divide the lower line into five equal sections and make lotus stems from four points (Image 5).
6. Use the cow template in the resources section to draw the cow (Image 6).
7. Draw lotus flowers and seed pods from each stem (Image 7).
8. Start coloring from one end of the flowers and stem using a darker shade to lighter shade. Also use red/ orange color to show henna on the cow (Image 8).
9. Complete the drawing with vibrant colors mentioned in Image 9. Let them dry well.
10. Then use it as a backdrop for your home deity altar or as a framed painting for your bedroom.

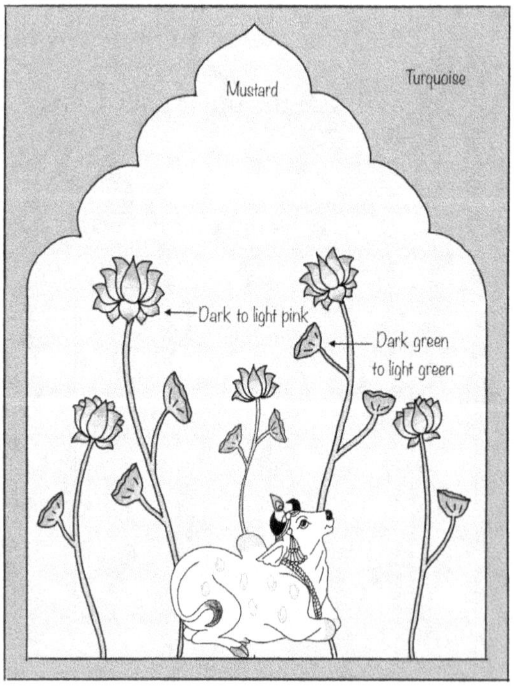

Image 9

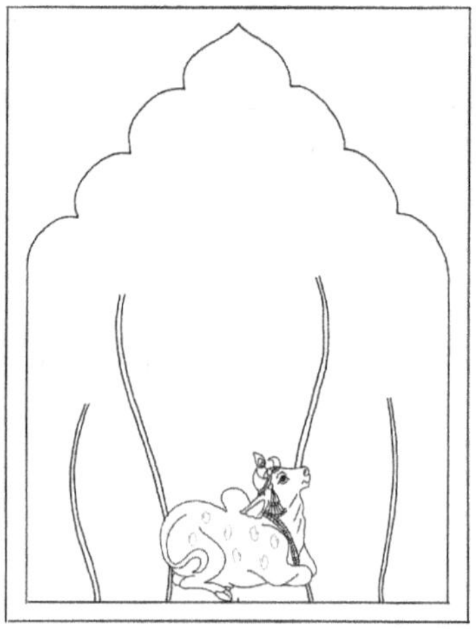

Image 6

Image 8

Action Activity

... to get you moving and learning

TEAM BUILDING

In this chapter Śrīla Prabhupāda encourages us to work cooperatively with one another since we are all servants of Kṛṣṇa with the same purpose of pleasing Him. Doing things together can be fun and can teach us how to work in a team.

Divide yourselves into groups. Using the objects below, make a structure that would hold a basketball or any large ball for at least five minutes.

Each group gets the following: five sheets of newspaper; cellotape; glue; stapler with staples; scissors; rubber bands

The group that works together and builds the tallest structure which does not fall for at least five minutes is the winner.

Learning outcomes:

1. You learn to work in groups.
2. You learn what healthy competition is.
3. Bonding develops with your friends because there is a common purpose.
4. You get a sense of achievement after finishing the project, and it boosts your confidence.
5. You come out of your narrow boundary of ego and low self-esteem as everybody contributes.
6. Immediate results increase the adrenaline, thus creating excitement.
7. Finally, who do you think gave you the intelligence to work together on this project?

Example

Critical-Thinking Activity

... to bring out the spiritual investigator in you

VAIKUṆṬHA CONSCIOUSNESS

In this chapter Prahlāda explains how considering a person or a group as a friend and another as an enemy in the material world is the root cause of many problems. Śrīla Prabhupāda points out that the concept of friend and enemy is absent in the spiritual world and that different groups trying to compete in the service of the Lord maintain a respectful attitude towards each other and try to improve their own service. He says that the material world could become Vaikuṇṭha if we adopt this mood.

Let us understand the mood of the spiritual world and how its mood can be brought down to the material world. Look at the Vaikuṇṭha Charter that has been created by the residents of Vaikuṇṭha. A charter is a document that details the goals, principles, and mutually agreed upon rules of a group of people working together.

Given below are a few issues (scenarios) that arise in the material world due to the "friend" and "enemy" mentality.

1. One person tries to cause some harm (physical or emotional) to another person, thinking him to be an enemy.
2. One country attacks another country when its security or peace is threatened or when it is trying to acquire resources.
3. Groups of people clash with each other and kill each other because they belong to different religions, races, communities, or other such groups.
4. Two businessmen decide to collaborate with each other to outdo another businessman whom they consider a common competitor.
5. Two leaders compete in a democratic election to become the President.

Divide the class into three to five separate groups, with each group taking up one scenario to work with. Each group role plays their respective scenario two times: the first time, role play as it is described in the prompt, clearly displaying the friend or enemy mentality; and the second time, role-play the same scenario, considering that the friend and enemy mentality is gone and that all parties have adopted the Vaikuṇṭha mood. (Refer to the Vaikuṇṭha Charter.) Finally, answer these prompts for your respective scenario in your notebook:

1. How did adopting the Vaikuṇṭha mentality affect the scenario?
2. Do you think such a change would be practical to execute for this scenario in today's world?

Vaikuṇṭha Charter

We, the residents of the spiritual world, agree to serve the Lord of Vaikuṇṭha by cooperating on all issues adhering to the following principles and rules.

MISSION

The goal of all residents and groups shall be to work towards the pleasure of the Lord.

IDENTITY

Each resident shall eternally identify himself or herself as a humble servant of the servant of the servant of Lord Kṛṣṇa.

SERVICES

All residents shall perform their designated services to the best of their ability for the satisfaction of the Lord.

MOOD

A mood of humility should be maintained by all residents. Everyone's contribution is valuable and praiseworthy but should not breed pride.

COMPETITIVE SPIRIT

Various groups may compete with each other to render the highest quality of service to the Lord but should remain appreciative of each other's efforts. They should also maintain a cooperative spirit to achieve the common goal of super excellent service to the Supreme Personality of Godhead.

Theatrical Activity

... to bring out the actor in you

PARODY: THE STUDENT BECOMES THE MASTER

A parody is a humorous piece of writing, drama, or music that imitates or represents a familiar situation or character in an exaggerated way.

Practice the following parody with your classmates and perform it for a special occasion or festival.

Scene: Classroom. Prahlāda is sitting on a desk cross legged chanting the Hare Kṛṣṇa *mahā- mantra.* Ṣaṇḍa and Amarka enter chatting.

Ṣaṇḍa: We must give the students more homework. You know what I always say.
Amarka: Yes, I know.
Ṣaṇḍa and Amarka: (in unison) Homework is the best invention since sliced bread.
(Ṣaṇḍa and Amarka laugh. Then they spot Prahlāda chanting and they stop laughing.)
Ṣaṇḍa: Oh no, he's doing it again. Chanting. Always chanting. Why are we so cursed?
Amarka: Let's stop him.

Amarka and Ṣaṇḍa do a series of funny things in front of Prahlāda to break his concentration, like a chicken impersonation, hopping on one leg, jazz hands, etc. (Improvise their humorous actions.) But as much as they try, they can't break Prahlāda's concentration.

Ṣaṇḍa: This is not working.

Ṣaṇḍa and Amarka look at each other and then at Prahlāda. They look back at each other and nod. They both walk towards Prahlāda and start to shake him. He finally awakens.

Prahlāda: Revered teachers, please accept my obeisances.
(Prahlāda bows down to them.)
Ṣaṇḍa: Prahlāda, why do you sit here and chant instead of playing outside with the other boys?
Prahlāda: Illustrious teachers, life is short. I must use every moment to advance spiritually.
Amarka: My dear boy, who taught you such hogwash? Such poppycock. Such balderdash. Every good demon knows life is meant for material advancement.
Ṣaṇḍa: And every good demon knows there are only three kinds of advancement that matter.
Amarka and Ṣaṇḍa: (in unison) Religion, economic development, and sense gratification!
Ṣaṇḍa: Because we must always have more.
Amarka: More gold.
Ṣaṇḍa: More houses.
Amarka: More chariots.
Ṣaṇḍa and Amarka: (in unison) More everything. Because you can never have enough.
Prahlāda: Most intelligent teachers, unless one is free from all material desires one cannot be attracted by Lord Viṣṇu.
Ṣaṇḍa: Prahlāda, you silly boy, you're batty. Befuddled. Brainwashed. Where did you learn this absolute dribble?
Prahlāda: Brilliant teachers, it was Nārada Muni who gave me this transcendental knowledge.
Amarka: Nārada Muni! But he is our enemy. Just like Viṣṇu.
Prahlāda: My dear teachers, you wrongly think Lord Viṣṇu is our enemy. People who think in terms of enemies and friends are unable to discover the Supersoul within themselves.
Ṣaṇḍa: This is blasphemy. Wait till your father hears this. He will throw you beneath the feet of elephants.
Amarka: Worse! He'll throw you in a snake pit.
Ṣaṇḍa: Or my personal favorite. He'll poison you and hurl you from a cliff.
Prahlāda: My esteemed teachers, let my father do as he wishes.
Amarka: Are you not afraid of dying?
Prahlāda: (with folded palms) Respected teachers, I will never be afraid, for I am the servant of Lord Viṣṇu. And either in this world or the next I will remain His servant.
Ṣaṇḍa: (blocking his ears) Our good demon names and fame will be ruined by this ungrateful child. He'll be the destroyer of us all.
Amarka: Let's leave this place at once, for surely our demoniac minds shall be contaminated by him.
Ṣaṇḍa: Yes, we shouldn't waste our time with him because soon he will perish.
(Ṣaṇḍa and Amarka leave.)
Prahlāda: My most venerated teachers, a devotee never perishes.

He begins to chant again. Scene ends.

Science Activity

... to bring out the spiritual scientist in you

AUTOMATIC ATTRACTION

In verse 14 Prahlāda says that his mind and consciousness is attracted to the Lord like an iron is attracted to a magnet. Do you know why iron gets attracted to a magnet?

A magnet is a piece of iron in which the atoms are all aligned in the same direction. This alignment creates a magnetic field, which is a force around the magnet that can attract objects, such as iron, to it.

Let us perform a simple experiment to detect this magnetic field. You will need:

1. A bar magnet
2. Iron filings
3. A plain white sheet of paper

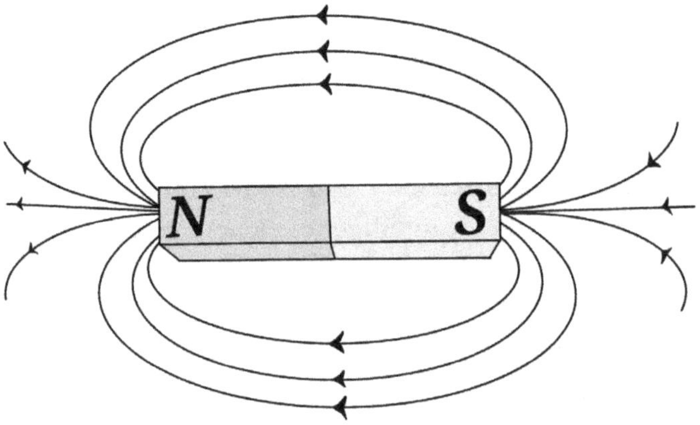

Place the bar magnet on the plain white sheet of paper. Sprinkle iron filings all around it. What do you notice?

The iron filings are attracted to the magnet, and they settle around it in a specific pattern. The pattern they form is called a magnetic field. In simple words, it is the space around the magnet where it can influence to attract iron towards it.

Magnets have many interesting properties, a couple of which are:

- They attract iron or some other metals towards them if these objects are placed within the magnetic field.
- Magnets have a north and a south pole. When similar poles of two magnets (North-North or South-South) are put next to each other, they repel. But when opposite poles (North-South) are put next to each other, they attract.

Prahlāda Mahārāja's statement can easily be understood from the perspective of these properties of magnets. Let us consider his analogy more deeply:

- The magnet can be compared to the Lord, who has the ability to attract His devotees.
- The devotees can be compared to the iron filings, which automatically get attracted to the magnet.
- The magnetic field can be compared to the process of *bhakti*.

Using the above statements, can you use the analogy and write a comment on why the devotee gets attracted to the Lord?

Writing and Language Activities

... to help you understand better

DIARY OF A DELUDED DEMON...CONTINUED.

Read the following excerpts from the recently unearthed diary of Hiraṇyakaśipu and then answer the questions that follow.

Excerpt 1: Today I entrusted my beloved son, Prahlāda, to the care of Ṣaṇḍa and Amarka. They will teach him the most important subject matters: politics, economics, and material activities. Soon he will learn to discern between friends and enemies. And one day he will rule my kingdom – although I wonder when that will ever happen since I will never die.

Excerpt 2: My son has failed me. Someone at his school has polluted him. Probably that miscreant Nārada Muni. Today I asked my son what was the best thing he had learned from his teachers. He said that a man engrossed in the material consciousness of duality, thinking, "This is mine and that belongs to my enemy," should give up his householder life and go to the forest to worship the Supreme Lord. I never heard such drivel in my life. To hear Prahlāda talk so frivolously sickens me. I warned his teachers to keep my son safe from the poisonous words of Nārada Muni. I hope for their sake they do their job.

Excerpt 3: My son has failed me for the last time. Today I again asked my son what he learned from his teachers. Prahlāda said that the best knowledge was accepting the nine processes of *bhakti* as pure devotional service. My wayward son said that one who has dedicated his life to the service of Viṣṇu through these nine methods is the most learned person. I was furious and I STILL AM. How dare he mention my enemy's name and speak of devotional service. What can one even gain from devotional service? Who wants to serve Viṣṇu? Anyway, I confronted his useless teachers, but they assured me that Prahlāda's predilections for devotional service were naturally developed in him. Prahlāda said that he learnt it from Nārada, ANOTHER enemy. Lord Viṣṇu is the axe for cutting down the sandalwood forest of the family of demons, and Prahlāda is the handle for that axe. This worshiper of Viṣṇu has no place in my household. Though he is born of my flesh, I shall get rid of Prahlāda.

Questions:

1. In excerpt 1, what is the most amazing thing in the world that Hiraṇyakaśipu (and the whole world) believes? (Hint: Yamarāja asked a similar question to Yudhiṣṭhira Mahārāja in the Mahābhārata.)
2. Explain both the denotation and connotation of "polluted" in excerpt 2. (Hint: Denotation is the literal meaning of the word. Connotation is the feeling or idea the word evokes.)
3. Are the words of Nārada Muni poisonous? Explain.
4. Compare and contrast Hiraṇyakaśipu's and Prahlāda's attitude to one's enemy.
5. Why does Hiraṇyakaśipu consider Prahlāda "the handle of the axe" in excerpt 3?
6. Do you have anyone in your life you consider an enemy? How has your opinion changed after understanding this pastime?

BOOKLET: NINE PROCESSES OF DEVOTIONAL SERVICE

Prahlāda Mahārāja lists nine processes that are accepted as pure devotional service:

- Śravaṇaṁ – Hearing about Kṛṣṇa
- Kīrtanaṁ – Chanting about Kṛṣṇa
- Viṣṇoḥ smaraṇaṁ – Remembering Kṛṣṇa or Lord Viṣṇu (not anyone else)
- Pāda-sevanam – Serving Kṛṣṇa
- Arcanaṁ – Worshiping Kṛṣṇa in the temple
- Vandanaṁ – Offering obeisances or prayers to Kṛṣṇa
- Dāsyaṁ – Assisting Kṛṣṇa as a servant
- Sakhyam – Seeing Kṛṣṇa as a friend and preaching to others about Him (requesting everyone to surrender to Him)
- Ātma-nivedanam – Surrendering to Kṛṣṇa

There are nine personalities or devotees who stand for or represent each of the nine processes. Research each of them.

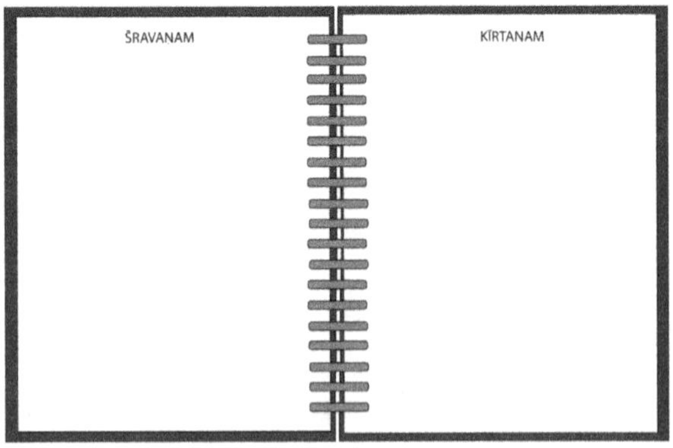

Make a booklet on the nine processes of devotional service by compiling pieces of paper together either by punching holes and binding them with string or paper pins, or stapling them.

The booklet should include:

1. A title page with a title and an illustration.
2. Individual pages that cover each of the nine processes.
3. Each page should include:
   a) The name and a small description of the process.
   b) An illustration.
   c) The name and small description about the personality representing the process.
   d) Your thoughts or realizations on the process (optional).

EQUALITY ON THE SPIRITUAL PLATFORM

In the 8,400,000 species of life, let us explore differences and similarities:

Group the given objects and write down in the box what category they belong to:

lily rose aster jasmine lotus		mango neem peepal (sacred fig) palm oak	
beetle butterfly moth ant bee		lobster crayfish starfish crab shrimp	
shark fish sea horse oyster sea otter		frog toad salamander newt tree frog	
lizards snake seaturtle crocodile alligator		crow eagle sparrow swan cuckoo	
dog cat horse elephant cow		Indian American Russian Chinese German	
brāhmaṇa kṣatriya vaiśya śūdra		Vipra Brāhmaṇa Vaiṣṇava Mahā-bhāgavata	

Considering all these categories of living entities, answer these questions:

1. Although each of these living entities are different, on what platform are they the same or equal?
2. What is spiritually common between an amphibian and a sea animal? What is spiritually common between an American and an Indian? What is common between all the different living entities above?
3. Color the drawing on the right and guess which *śloka* of the *Bhagavad-gītā* it depicts. Write the verse and translation in your notebooks. Then explain the meaning in your own words.

PODCAST INTERVIEW: ATTRACTIVE KṚṢṆA

"Kṛṣṇa" means He who attracts everyone and everything. In our material way of life, however, we find ourselves more attracted to things of this world. We are only occasionally attracted to Kṛṣṇa or anything or anybody related to Him.

Think about that one personality or character from the scriptures whom you find (even if occasionally) attracted most to. Why do you find him/her most attractive?

Now, imagine that you are a successful Youtuber and podcaster and you've invited this personality for a podcast interview.

Write down all the questions you would have for this personality. You would want to frame questions in such a way that your attraction to this personality is revealed to your audience. You would want your audience to be attracted to this personality as much as you are.

Also, write down tentative answers to a couple of your questions that you would expect from the personality.

We know that smearing one's body with the dust of Kṛṣṇa's pure devotees or taking complete shelter of the guidance from His pure devotees purifies us and increases our attraction to Kṛṣṇa.

Conclude the podcast by sharing with your audience how you intend to follow the guidance of the personality you've interviewed.

Can you see how the Lord's devotees are also attractive?

Here is a sample:

Personality: Hanumān

Question: If there was one message you could give to all the young boys and girls in my audience today, what would that be?

Answer: Never underestimate the power of taking the Lord's holy names.

Your Conclusion: I am so thankful to you, dear Hanumānjī, for your deep, thoughtful insights on devotion to the Lord, which you shared with me and my audience. I would love to imbibe your spirit of service to all parts and parcels of the Supreme Lord.

DIPLOMACY AND SIMPLICITY

Hiraṇyakaśipu and Prahlāda's teachers used diplomacy to persuade Prahlāda to learn about material subjects in school. Verse 19 talks of the diplomatic principles (*upāyas*) used by kings in those days.

When a citizen agitates the public against the king, the king uses these four methods:

a) Sāma: The king tries to pacify him with sweet words.
b) Dāna: The king offers him a lucrative post as a governor or minister.
c) Bheda: He tries to create dissension in the enemy camp.
d) Daṇḍa: He employs *argumentum ad baculum* – severe punishment.

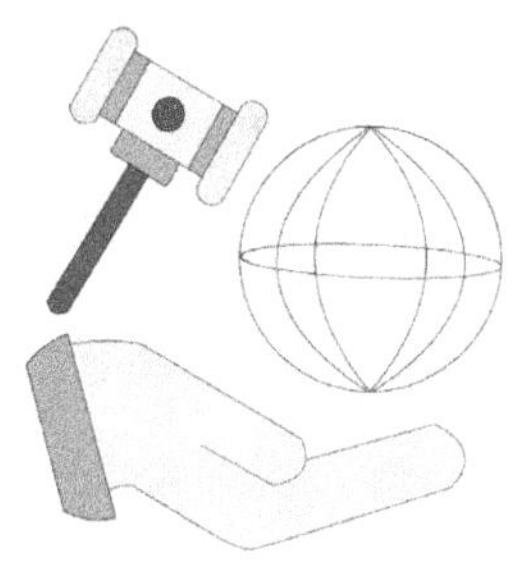

Let us analyze some examples:

1. In the Rāmāyaṇa, Lord Rāma used these principles as follows:
   a) Through Hanumān, He advised Rāvaṇa to free Sītādevī.
   b) To win Rāvaṇa over, He even offered him the kingdom of Ayodhyā in ret was not told directly to Rāvaṇa. Rāma mentioned it in His talks with Sugrīva.)
   c) Rāma weaned away Rāvaṇa's brother, Vibhīṣaṇa, and crowned him king of Laṅkā even when Rāvaṇa was alive.
   d) Rāma destroyed the *rākṣasa* Rāvaṇa and his race.

2. Lord Kṛṣṇa used these four principles in His role as the peacemaker in the *Mahābhārata*:
   a) When Kṛṣṇa came to Duryodhana's court, He came in a conciliatory mood, saying that the Kauravas and Pāṇḍavas were part of the same family. The Pāṇḍavas had already done their part by living in the forest for years and living incognito, so to live in harmony they should be given a part of the kingdom.
   b) He begged Duryodhana to give the Pāṇḍavas just five villages.
   c) Kṛṣṇa said that if it is only because of one person's (Duryodhana's) obstinacy the whole Kuru race will be destroyed, then it is better that Duryodhana be rejected.
   d) Kṛṣṇa declared that if the Kauravas decided to go for war then they would be destroyed. Kṛṣṇa sided with the Pāṇḍavas to destroy the Kauravas.

Now explain how Hiraṇyakaśipu used these principles against Prahlāda.

Prahlāda, in all his simplicity, was completely surrendered to the Supreme Personality of Godhead. He was not at all worried about his bodily comforts and was ready for any consequence. The Lord understood this and saved Prahlāda by incarnating as Nṛsiṁhadeva.

Now try to answer these questions:

1. Which of the following do you find easier to comprehend and practice? Explain your answer.
   a) Hiraṇyakaśipu's diplomacy which backfired on him?
   b) Prahlāda's devotion and simplicity that protected him?

2. Is Hiraṇyakaśipu's diplomacy or Prahlāda's simplicity better for us as devotees? Why? (Discuss in class.)

ORAL: SAY NO TO BULLYING

Hiraṇyakaśipu was the worst bully. Using what you've learned from this chapter about equality, not making enemies, and inculcating a community of Vaikuṇṭha consciousness, prepare an oral presentation about the negative impact of bullying in schools and cyberbullying (on the internet). Research different perspectives on the issue, present the pitfalls of bullying, and give solid and effective solutions, including the spiritual perspective. Present your findings orally in front of your class or teacher.

CHAPTER 5 ANSWERS

Further Exploring Sense Enjoyment

1. Engage them in the service of the Lord, because He is called Govinda, which means "one who gives pleasure to the senses." 2. Accept a bona fide spiritual master whom you can follow. Then you will be able to lead others on the right path. 3. Will strictly follow in the footsteps of his own spiritual master so he can guide you on the right path.

Automatic Attraction

The process of *bhakti* is so powerful that it can make anyone within its influence to become attracted to the Lord, just like a magnet can attract anything within its magnetic field.

Diary of a Deluded Demon

1. Living entities die at every moment, but a foolish being still thinks he will never die and does not prepare for death.
2. The denotation of polluted is contaminated, harmful, or a poisonous substance. Here the connotation is to influence someone with immoral thoughts and spoil their character.
3. No. Nārada Muni is simply preaching and chanting, but someone who is poisonous is envious of Kṛṣṇa and His devotees and will criticize them.
4. Prahlāda did not discriminate between enemy and friend as he was equal to everyone, seeing them as spirit soul, whereas Hiraṇyakaśipu saw Lord Viṣṇu and the demigods as his enemies, judging them externally. Prahlāda understood that people who distinguish between enemy and friend are unable to ascertain the Supersoul within themselves, while Hiraṇyakaśipu identified with just the body and how to enjoy with the body and senses. He therefore considered anyone who hindered his enjoyment or success to be his enemy.
5. Lord Viṣṇu is compared to the axe. An axe cannot cut a tree by itself. It needs a handle. The tree of demoniac civilization can be cut to pieces by the axe of devotional service to the Lord. Prahlāda Mahārāja is like the handle of the axe, who assists Lord Viṣṇu to chop down the forest of demoniac civilization.

Equality on the Spiritual Platform

Groups: flowers; trees; insects; crustaceans; sea animals; amphibians; reptiles; birds; mammals; people of different nationalities; people belonging to different *varṇas*; spiritually elevated human beings

1. On the spiritual platform as spirit souls.
2. The Lord as the Paramātmā lives within them. They are all part and parcel of God. They are all God's children and equal in His eyes.
3. *BG* 5.18:

vidyā-vinaya-sampanne brāhmaṇe gavi hastini
śuni caiva śva-pāke ca paṇḍitāḥ sama-darśinaḥ

"The humble sages, by virtue of true knowledge, see

with equal vision a learned and gentle *brāhmaṇa*, a cow, an elephant, a dog and a dog-eater [outcaste]."

On the spiritual platform, as spirit souls, there is no difference among these living beings; therefore spiritually learned persons with divine vision sees them as equal.

Diplomacy Versus Simplicity

Hiraṇyakaśipu's use of the four principles:

a. Ṣaṇḍa and Amarka tried to persuade Prahlāda with sweet words to find out the source of his Vaiṣṇava beliefs.

b. Then they gave Prahlāda the incentive of teaching him material knowledge, which would make him a great king.

c. They tried to separate Prahlāda from his friends.

d. When nothing worked, Hiraṇyakaśipu decided to kill Prahlāda using various cruel methods.

1. a. Any tool can be used for the good of mankind. However, Hiraṇyakaśipu tried to use these principles against the Lord and His devotee, which was his downfall.

b. To be a simple and uncomplicated keeps everything in perspective. The chances of getting confused or getting bogged down by one's ego is very less. Furthermore, one's implicit faith in the Lord gives one hope and strength even in difficult circumstances.

2. A devotee does not want to get involved in complicated diplomatic discussions. His business is with Kṛṣṇa and Kṛṣṇa's devotees. Thoughts of the Lord and His devotees keep one fixed toward one's spiritual goals.

RESOURCE FOR ART ACTIVITY

6

PRAHLĀDA INSTRUCTS HIS DEMONIAC SCHOOLMATES

Story Summary

Dozens of gleaming eyes stared at Prahlāda, enraptured by his charisma, sweet smile, and gentle voice. Prahlāda's school friends could not get enough of him; whenever their teachers were away, they would sit in a circle around Prahlāda, taking in his every word. His instructions and advice fascinated them, innocent young boys from demon families. They had never heard anything other than materialistic topics regarding mundane religion, economics, and sense gratification.

Today, while one of the boys guarded the doorway to make sure that Ṣaṇḍa and Amarka were nowhere in sight, the boys wanted to hear more from Prahlāda Mahārāja.

Prahlāda's face glowed as his soft eyes scanned the boys' eager faces.

Pointing at his chest and looking down at his body, he said, "To get this human body is very rare. It is temporary, but it is meaningful because only in human life can you perform devotional service to the Lord."

"True!" exclaimed a bright-faced boy in front. "I don't see the dogs at our school doing anything besides eating and sleeping."

The other

boys laughed as Prahlāda continued, "So an intelligent person doesn't waste time. He uses this human body from the tender age of childhood to practice devotional service. You see, even a slight amount of devotional service can perfect your lives."

"But we want to play and have fun!" shouted a boy from the back. Some of the other boys nodded.

Prahlāda grinned and said, "My dear friends, happiness that comes from the senses can be experienced in any form of life. You don't have to endeavor for happiness because it comes on its own, according to the actions of your past life, just as your distress. So why bother with this!"

Gesturing with his hands, he continued, "The human form of life gives you a chance to return home, back to Godhead, where happiness is far greater than what you experience here. Therefore, every human being, you all, must engage in devotional service to the lotus feet of Lord Viṣṇu. It's a natural thing to do because Lord Viṣṇu is the most beloved and intimate master of the soul. He is your true well-wisher!

"Besides, your bodies are stout and strong, and you can distinguish right from wrong. Can't you?"

The boys looked at each other and then nodded.

"So use your young mind and intelligence to know and achieve the goal of life.

"As you know, every human being lives at most a hundred years. And for those who can't control the senses, half of those years are lost in sleeping. So, such a person only lives for fifty years. Then you spend ten years in childhood and ten years in boyhood, sporting and playing, so twenty years are wasted. And finally, when you are too old, unable to do anything, you pass another twenty years. That's almost an entire lifetime gone! And then you have a few more years to spend in household life."

"Yes, it is a waste of time," said another boy. "Then we just die. What's the use of it all?"

"Yes," agreed Prahlāda. "Especially in materialistic married life you are unable to control the senses and liberate yourself. You are strongly bound by ropes of affection for your wife, children, and other relatives. You waste all these years because you don't engage in devotional service.

"It's hard to give up the association of family members. How can a husband give up the affectionate and kind service of his wife or the pleasing sweet baby talk of his children? How can such an attached householder give up the association of such family members? A daughter is especially dear to a father and is in his mind even when she gets married. And what about one's elderly parents? How can he give up their company? And he's attached to household comforts, furniture, animals, and servants. Who would give up such comforts?

"The attached householder is like a silkworm that weaves its own cocoon and then becomes a prisoner in it. Simply to satisfy the genitals and the tongue, the attached family man is bound to this world. How can he escape?"

Some of Prahlāda's friends shook their heads. They knew too well what this meant, thinking of their materialistic, demoniac parents.

"And it's not just family attachment that

binds one to this material world – it's also one's attachment to money. For a materialist, money is sweeter than honey!"

The boys giggled.

"Thieves, soldiers, and merchants try to get money even risking their own lives. Even though they know they will be punished by the law or by Yamarāja, they continue cheating others to accumulate money. They don't understand that they are wasting their lives trying to maintain their families and material lifestyles. They don't understand that the purpose of human life is God realization; rather they are most attentive to seeing that not a farthing of theirs is lost. Such persons suffer from the threefold miseries, but still they don't develop a distaste for material life. Just like cats and dogs they are busy only providing for their families. They are only addicted to sense gratification and becomes playthings in the hands of attractive women. They are bereft of spiritual knowledge and overcome by ignorance.

"No one bereft of spiritual knowledge has been able to liberate himself from material bondage. Those who are addicted to this kind of life are called demons."

"We are the sons of demons," one boy blurted out. "Does this make us demons?"

Prahlāda Mahārāja looked at him with compassionate eyes, "Although you are the sons of demons, you don't have to be demons. Keep aloof from demonic persons and take shelter of the Supreme Personality of Godhead, Nārāyaṇa."

"Jaya Nārāyaṇa!" another boy called out, and the others chimed in response.

"Shhh," said the boy guarding the door. "It will be the end of us if we are heard."

Unaffected by the warning, Prahlāda continued, "Dear sons of demons, the Supreme Lord Nārāyaṇa is the Supersoul, the silent witness in the core of your hearts, and the father of all beings. Anyone can please Him, be it a child or an old man. Please know this fact and there'll be no difficulty in pleasing Him.

"The Lord is present in all forms of life, in the material creation and elements and even the modes of material nature. Although He is one, He is present everywhere. He is *sac-cid-ānanda* and the cause of all causes. But He appears nonexistent to the atheist who is covered by the Lord's external energy."

Folding his palms, Prahlāda appealed to his friends: "Therefore, my dear friends born of demons, please act in a way to satisfy the

Supreme Lord. Give up your demonic nature and act without enmity. Show mercy to all living beings by enlightening them in devotional service. Become their well-wishers."

The boys smiled from ear to ear, feeling

enlightened by Prahlāda's compassion. They felt he was certainly their well-wisher.

"If you become the Lord's devotee and please Him, you will obtain everything. The Lord is unlimited, the original source of everything. So what's the use of following the principles of religion, economic development, and sense gratification which we can all obtain under the modes of material nature? We devotees are only interested in glorifying the Lord, so we don't need to ask for anything regarding *dharma*, *artha*, *kāma*, and *mokṣa*.

"Religion, economic development, and sense gratification are described in the *Vedas* as *tri-varga*, or three ways to become liberated. But these are only the external subject matters of the *Vedas*; they are material. However, surrender to Lord Viṣṇu's lotus feet is transcendental to everything."

"I want to become a devotee!" exclaimed one boy, his face beaming with excitement. "And me too!" chimed another, and another, and another.

Prahlāda raised his hands and said, "You surely can. You can understand this confidential knowledge by the mercy of a saintly person like Nārada."

"Did you learn this knowledge from him?" asked one boy.

Prahlāda nodded and continued, "I've received this knowledge from the great saint Nārada Muni, who is always engaged in devotional service. This knowledge is called *bhāgavata-dharma* and is fully scientific. It is based on logic and philosophy and is completely pure. So, anyone who has taken shelter of Nārada Muni's disciplic succession can understand this knowledge."

"Jaya!" shouted the boys. They understood that they had already received spiritual knowledge from Nārada Muni's disciplic succession through Prahlāda.

Another boy put his hand up and said, "Dear Prahlāda, we all don't know of anyone else as our teachers besides Ṣaṇḍa and Amarka. And you remain within the palace, so it's very difficult for you to associate with a great personality. So how was it possible for you to hear from Nārada? Kindly remove our doubts."

Themes and Key Messages

Please go through this table of themes and key messages, with corresponding verses, and discuss each topic further.

THEMES	REFERENCES	KEY MESSAGES
Human life is very rare, so we should use the human form of body from childhood to practice devotional service.	7.6.1–2	The human body is rarely achieved, and although temporary like other bodies, only in human life can one perform devotional service. Therefore, according to the Vedic system, from the beginning of life, from five years of age, one follows the *brahmacarya* system to engage in the activities of devotional service to perfect one's life. This should be the goal of education.
Instead of endeavoring for the happiness of the senses that is automatically obtained, we should endeavor for the highest goal.	7.6.3–5	Material happiness, just like distress, happens of its own accord in any body or species. Therefore, human beings shouldn't waste their time and energy fighting against distress or working very hard for happiness but should use their human life for the highest goal – to revive their relationship with the Supreme Lord and engage in His devotional service. Only the human form of life gives us the chance to go back to Godhead. We should therefore live in such a way that we keep ourselves always healthy and strong in mind and intelligence so that we can distinguish the goal of life from a life full of problems.
Persons too attached to household life misuse the human form of life and become strongly bound to the material world, whereas devotees strive to become liberated from material existence.	7.6.6–18	Seventy out of the one hundred years of human life are spent in sleep and in youth, and twenty more years in old age are wasted by a person who doesn't know the aim of life and how to utilize this human form. The remaining years are spent in family life. One who is excessively affectionate and attached to one's spouse and family cannot give up their association. Just to satisfy the genitals and the tongue, they are like silkworms trapped in a cocoon. They are immersed in collecting money, even if it means cheating to get it. They are unable to take to spiritual life and are overcome by ignorance. They are addicted to sense gratification, especially the association of the opposite sex, and are therefore bound to material life. One should avoid such persons and take shelter of the Supreme Lord, for a devotee wants to become liberated from material life.

THEMES	REFERENCES	KEY MESSAGES
It is not difficult to please the Lord because He is the Supersoul and father of all beings. He is easily pleased by our devotional service and by our sharing of Kṛṣṇa consciousness with others.	7.5.19–24	Prahlāda's friends, who were from demon families, thought that it was very difficult to please the Lord. So Prahlāda assured them that pleasing Nārāyaṇa does not require as much endeavor as pleasing one's family, community, and nation. The Lord is easily pleased since He is the Supersoul of all beings, He pervades everything, and He is everyone's father and well-wisher. Just as there is no difficulty in establishing the intimate relationship between a father and son, there is no difficulty in reestablishing the natural, intimate relationship between Nārāyaṇa and the living entities. If one performs even very slight devotional service, the Lord is always ready to save one from the greatest danger, as in the case of Ajāmila. Prahlāda advises his friends to please the Lord by devotional service and by preaching His glories to others.
Surrender to the Lord's lotus feet is transcendental to the external subject of the *Vedas* – religion (*dharma*), economic development (*artha*), and sense gratification (*kāma*) – which are the three ways to salvation (*mokṣa*) but are material.	7.6.25–26	If one satisfies the Lord and surrenders to Him in love, nothing is unobtainable, since He is the cause of all causes. Therefore devotees do not strive for *dharma*, *artha*, *kāma*, and *mokṣa* as prescribed in the *Vedas,* because one can automatically obtain these things under the three modes of material nature and are therefore considered material. Devotional service is greater and transcendental to these material subjects of the *Vedas*. Devotees only glorify the Lord and do not ask for anything material. They are simply satisfied by rendering transcendental loving service at the lotus feet of the Lord and glorifying Him everywhere by preaching, which is their life and soul. Vedic ritualistic ceremonies and injunctions are meant to elevate one to the spiritual platform, and if they don't, it's simply a waste of time.

Higher-Thinking Questions

Now try to deepen your understanding of this chapter by delving into Śrīla Prabhupāda's purports and reflecting on the following questions:

1. In verse 1 purport, why does Śrīla Prabhupāda suggest that "in all the schools, colleges and universities, and at home, all children and youths should be taught to hear about the Supreme Personality of Godhead"?

2. Why is devotional service natural as mentioned in verse 2? Refer to purport.

3. According to verse 2 purport, what is the root cause of suffering? Śrīla Prabhupāda

gives the formula to be happy and peaceful. Refer to the *Bhagavad-gītā* verse quoted and summarize in your own words the peace and happiness formula.

4. According to verses 4 and 5 and their purports, what's the true benefit of human life that is not available in the animal species?
5. In verse 8 purport what is the process that Śrīla Prabhupāda suggests so we don't become trapped wasting the years of our life only in sense gratification?
6. In verse 19 purport Prabhupāda proposes an argument that what is the point if one gives up family life for the service of the Lord but still undergoes the same effort and trouble. Prabhupāda says that this is not a valid objection. Why is this so?
7. According to verse 24 purport, what are the three truths a preacher should know and preach to everyone? Why do you think this is important?
8. Refer to verse 26 purport and explain the difference between the material and spiritual platforms. Why do you think that Vedic ritualistic ceremonies are a waste of time if they do not bring one to the spiritual platform?

ACTIVITIES

In this section you will find many exciting things to do. These activities will get you thinking, moving, drawing, and having loads of fun.

Analogy Activity

... to bring out the scholar in you

THE HOUSEHOLDER'S COCOON

Verses 11 and 13 compare the position of a householder to that of a silkworm who gets trapped in its own cocoon: "The attached householder is like a silkworm, which weaves a cocoon in which it becomes imprisoned, unable to get out. Simply for the satisfaction of two important senses – the genitals and the tongue – one is bound by material conditions. How can one escape?"

Let us try to understand why the householder is like a silkworm, what his "cocoon" is, how he gets trapped in it, and why he needs to get out.

Look at the illustration of the analogy. Label the different parts of the diagram appropriately to reflect the analogy accurately. Refer to the translation of verses 11 and 13.

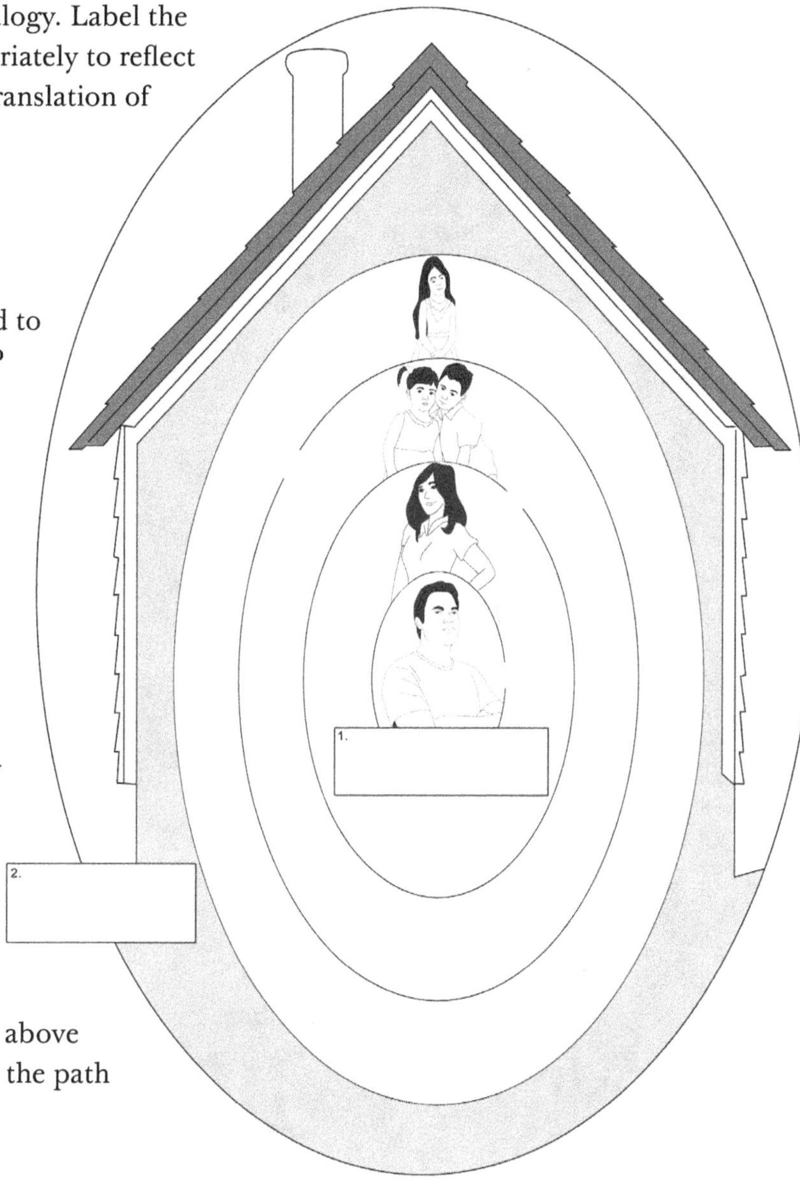

Look at the diagram and discuss the following:

1. Why is the householder compared to a silkworm trapped in its cocoon?
2. Is it not harsh and negative to consider a "happy" and "satisfying" household life a trap that destroys a person? Substantiate your answer.
3. Devotees also have families, friends, and household wealth. Then, could this analogy also be applied to devotees? Why, or why not?
4. Is there a way for the householder to break the cocoon and come out? Read the purport to verses 11 and 13 to find out. Finally, change the above illustration appropriately to show the path out for all of them.

Artistic Activity

... to reveal your creativity

FRIENDSHIP BAND

We learn from Prahlāda Mahārāja's example that friendship with devotees is a special blessing and nourishes our devotional lives. It is built on the foundation of an eternal relationship with Kṛṣṇa and His parts and parcels. Prahlāda also teaches us to be friends and well-wishers to everyone by giving them Kṛṣṇa consciousness. Let's make a friendship band for a friend, reminding us of ideal friendship.

Materials: Yarn of 3 colors, about 1 yard each (1 yard = 3 feet = 36 inches = almost 1 meter!); scissors; ribbons of 4 colors, about 10 inches each; small brush/pencil; glue; black ink pen

Image 1

Steps:

1. Roll a ribbon tightly over the pencil/brush into a cylinder or tube shape (Image 1).

2. Secure the end with glue. Gently slide it out and keep it aside. Similarly, make three other ribbon tubes (Image 2).

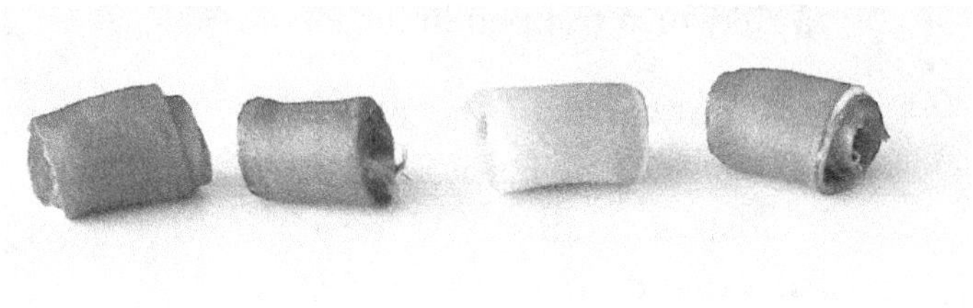

Image 2

3. Cut each yarn into three pieces of 12 inches each. Take the nine strings together. Leave about a centimeter at one end and tie a knot (Image 3).

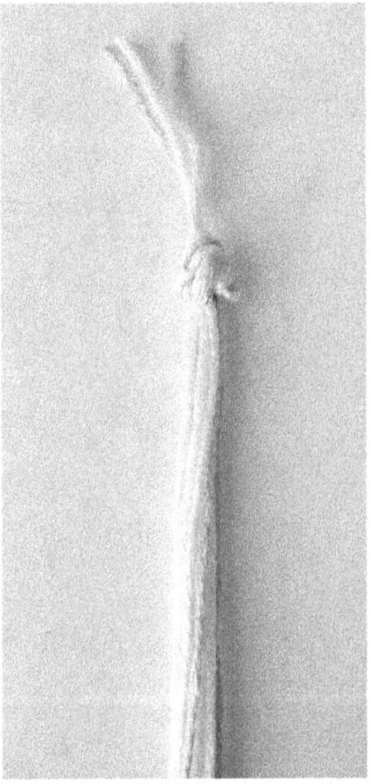

Image 3

4. Now braid the yarn till you have about 6 inches of braid. Slide the four ribbon tubes through the braid (Image 4).

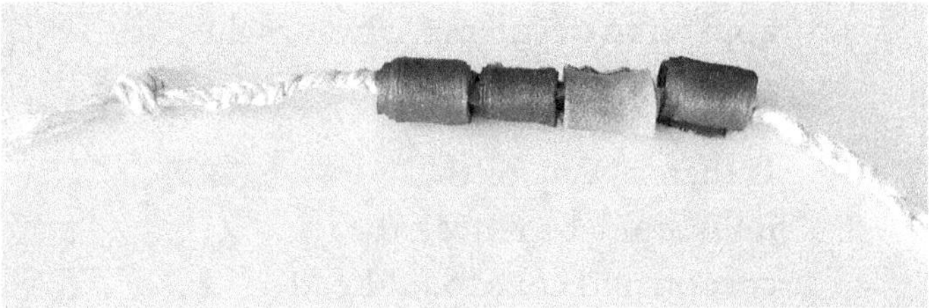

Image 4

5. Secure the tubes with knots at both ends. Leave a centimeter and cut the yarn (Image 5).

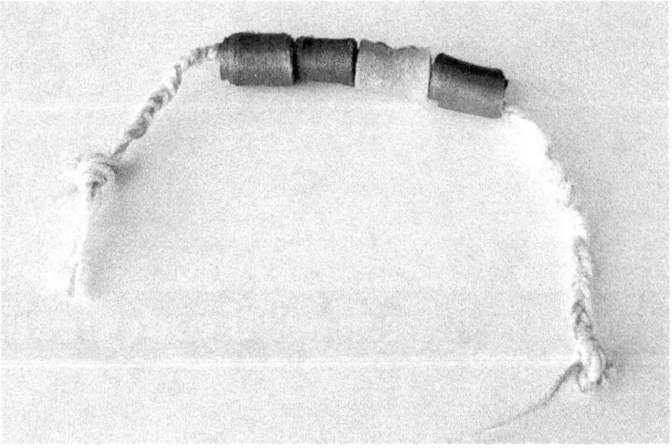

Image 5

6. With the black ink pen, write the letters L, O, V, and E on each tube (Image 6).

7. Present your friendship band to a dear friend.

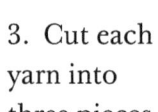

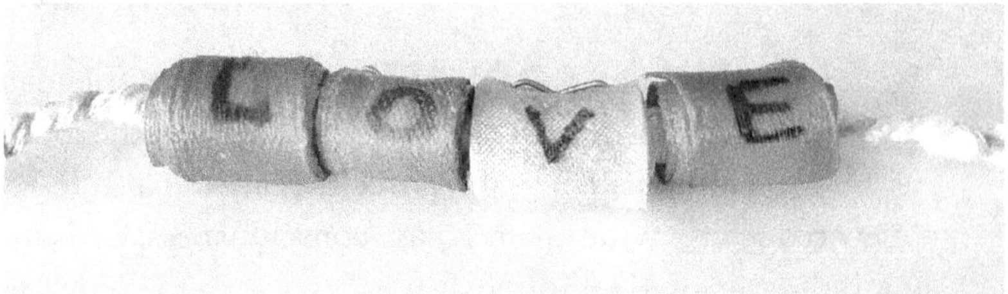

Image 6

Theatrical Activity

. . . to bring out the actor in you

A LIFE WASTED OR USED: YOU CHOOSE

Write a narrated skit that can be performed by one or two actors. This skit will have no dialogue, only narration. You may include directions for the actor too. The skit should show how a living entity's time is lost by sleep, bewilderment, sporting, playing, family life, and old age. Refer to verses 6 to 8 for more details.

The second part of the skit should show how one's life changes if one chooses to use one's life and time as a devotee. End with the lines "You get to choose. What will it be?"

You may begin the skit by using the prompt below or writing your own beginning:

You are born. You choose where based on your past. You are given one hundred years. It seems like a lot. You have plenty of time – all the time in the world. But you spend fifty years of your life sleeping. After all, sleep is invigorating. You need it. Now you have only fifty years left. What are you going to do? The first ten years . . .

Critical-Thinking Activity

... to bring out the spiritual investigator in you

PRAVṚTTI-MĀRGA VS NIVṚTTI-MĀRGA

Over the last few chapters we've been studying how sense gratification causes more harm than good. For this reason, Prahlāda Mahārāja advised his friends not to get too attached to sense gratification, but to train in *bhāgavata-dharma* from the beginning of childhood.

It is interesting to note that Ṣaṇḍa and Amarka, the teachers of the *gurukula*, trained the children on the path of sense gratification. In Vedic terms, this path is called *pravṛtti-mārga*, and it involves four activities:

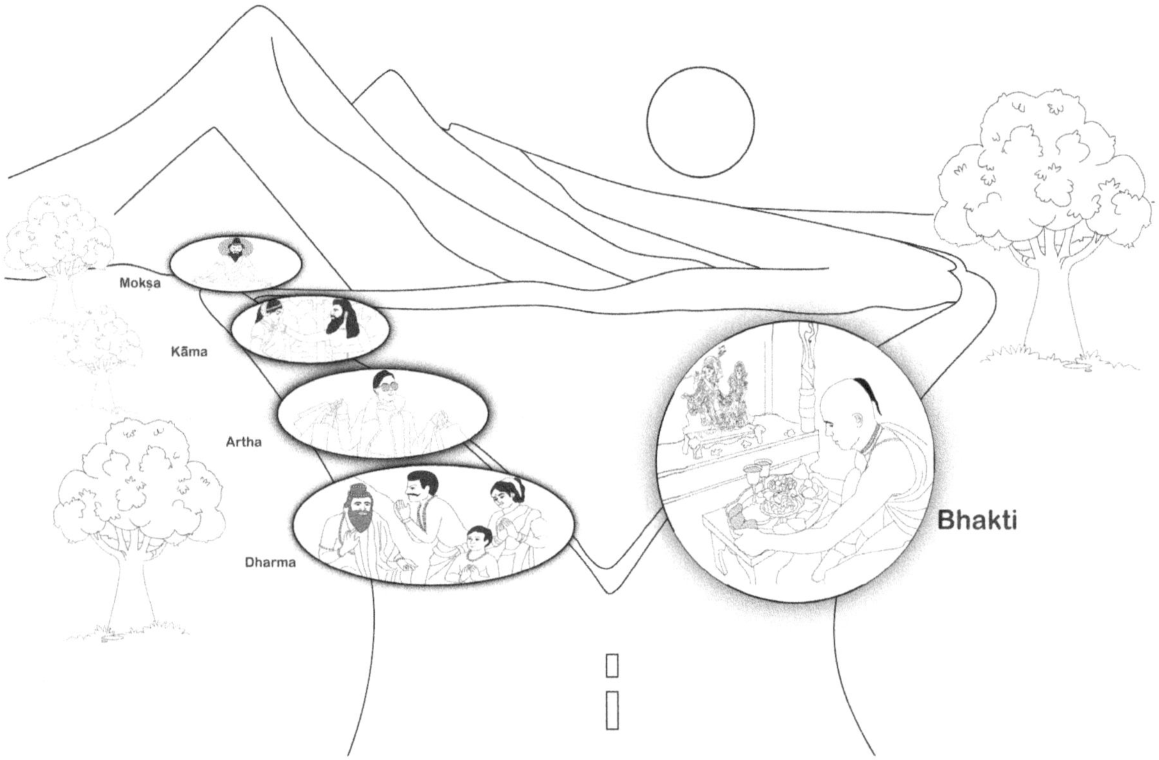

1. **Dharma,** or performance of one's duty, to obtain a certain desired result.

2. **Artha,** the means to enjoy – through wealth, elevation to higher planets, better birth, or other worldly facilities, etc.

3. **Kāma,** or sense enjoyment, which is acquired as a result of performing *dharma* and acquiring *artha*.

4. **Mokṣa,** or liberation, in which one gets interested after becoming tired of sense gratification.

Prahlāda Mahārāja, however, chose to engage in the nine processes of devotional service rather than these four activities, and encouraged his friends to do the same. In Vedic terms, Prahlāda chose to tread the *nivṛtti-mārga*, or the path of detachment from matter. By adding devotional service under a bona fide spiritual master to this path, one can make quick progress towards Kṛṣṇa.

Even in today's world, both *pravṛtti-mārga* and *nivṛtti-mārga* are taught in institutions that uphold sense gratification and sense control as their respective values. For example, *pravṛtti-mārga* is taught in modern-day universities, and *nivṛtti-mārga* with devotional service is taught in ISKCON.

Look at the two classrooms of the two institutions in the table below. Evaluate each statement under each of the institutions, stating whether you believe it to be true or false, and provide your reasoning.

	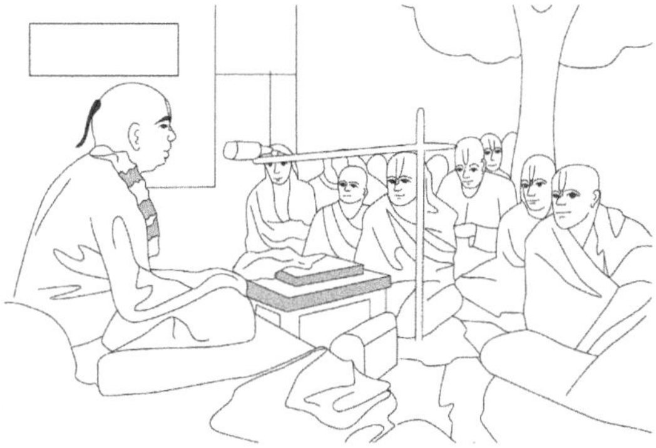
1. The mood of today's university is similar to the mood of Ṣaṇḍa and Amarka's institute.	6. Prahlāda's nine processes of devotional service to Kṛṣṇa are taught in ISKCON.
2. *Dharma*, *artha*, and *kāma* are taught in today's universities, albeit in a different way.	7. Practicing devotional service in ISKCON helps one progress on the path of *nivṛtti*, or detachment from the world and attachment to the Lord.
3. A person who graduates from university is well trained in sense control and can easily resist worldly pleasures that may cause him long-term harm.	8. ISKCON devotees are often unable to resist sense pleasures since devotional service without university education cannot help in sense control.
4. Faith in the presence of a higher power and one's subordination to that power comes naturally to a university graduate.	9. ISKCON devotees tend to attribute everything as Kṛṣṇa's creation, but because they are detached from it, they do not give much importance to the creator.
5. University graduates are trained to achieve higher goals.	10. ISKCON devotees are trained to achieve higher goals.

Based on your evaluation, write down in one sentence your conclusion about the different results obtained from following the *pravṛtti-mārga* and *nivṛtti-mārga*.

Introspective Activity

... to bring out the reflective devotee in you

USING TIME WISELY

In verses 6 and 7, Prahlāda Mahārāja gives a breakdown of how a person utilizes his life if he is a nondevotee and how one's life is wasted if disconnected from the Lord's service.

As a devotee and a student of the *Bhāgavatam*, you are trying to follow in the footsteps of young devotees like Prahlāda and Dhruva. The way you utilize your life would likely be different from the description in verses 6 and 7.

Now reflect how your life is different from those who do not practice spiritual life. In your notebook, make a one-page journal entry to include the following:

- Why Kṛṣṇa consciousness is important to you.
- A diagrammatic timeline of how you have so far spent your life, with the timeline also indicating how you plan to continue serving in the future.
- Which devotees from the *Bhāgavatam* inspire you and why.
- How you have benefited from being a devotee, and what you think you would have missed out on, especially in childhood, if you had not been given a chance to cultivate devotional service.
- What you could do to help others reap the same benefits.

DIALOGUE: HELP, DOCTOR FRIEND!

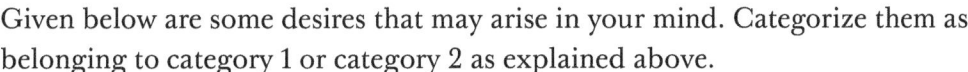

Śrīla Prabhupāda mentions that we should live in such a way that we keep ourselves always healthy and strong in mind and intelligence so we can attain our spiritual goals.

We all have our value system in which we put our faith and which helps us distinguish between right and wrong. A devotee's value system is defined as follows: whatever is favorable for increasing our devotion to Lord Kṛṣṇa is right, and whatever is unfavorable for our devotion is wrong.

Along with our value system, we have our conditioning. Our conditioning determines our likes and dislikes.

So, to keep ourselves always healthy and strong in mind and intelligence, it is necessary to categorize our desires into two:

1. Desires borne out of our value system; e.g., the desire to chant the holy names of the Lord with attention.

2. Desires borne out of our conditioning; e.g., lusty desire for the opposite sex.

Given below are some desires that may arise in your mind. Categorize them as belonging to category 1 or category 2 as explained above.

a) The desire to sleep early and thus feel fresh to chant early the next morning.
b) The desire to save time in the morning by skipping breakfast.
c) The desire to meet with friends who may take us to Kṛṣṇa conscious programs.
d) The desire to visit holy places that are relevant to our Kṛṣṇa consciousness.
e) The desire to go shopping to get rid of our boredom or have the latest gadget.
f) The desire to please senior devotees who are guiding us in our Kṛṣṇa consciousness.
g) The desire to eat food without offering it to Kṛṣṇa.
h) The desire to binge watch movies.

Given below is a scenario of a 16-year-old girl. Read through it and identify places where she succumbs to desires borne out of conditioning.

"Isn't it too late to be ordering pizza now, Shriya?" asked Shriya's younger sister Priya.

"Be quiet and mind your own business! You are only 11 and I am 16! You'll know the stress of high school and unfinished assignments when you are my age. Go and sleep! I have to stay awake now to do this assignment. I will definitely need those pizzas and chips."

"Well, then, you shouldn't have spent the whole afternoon binge watching Netflix," Priya thought to herself.

So you can imagine how Shriya woke up the next morning after sleeping late with a tummy full of pizza. Her head hurt, but she was in too much of a frenzy to notice because she was late for school. Mother insisted that she have breakfast, but she refused. Mother tried putting her lunch box into her bag so at least she could have some homemade, healthy *prasāda*, but the already frustrated Shriya got completely mad. Clenching her teeth and looking right into mother's eyes, she said under her breath (she couldn't shout because father was still home), "Mamma, keep this food to yourself and let me leave. I hate it when you try to mother me when I'm already late!"

Mother had a blank expression on her face. "If I were mamma, I would have given her a slap," thought Priya. She knew mamma had woken up early to cook healthy, homemade, offered-to-the-Lord food for Shriya. Now Shriya would again eat some junk food from the canteen.

"Shriya, did you do your chanting and meditation this morning?" asked father from the other room. "Yes, Papa, I did," lied Shriya. Priya rolled her eyes at her sister who ignored her. She was already on the phone with her bestie who was also rushing to school. "Gossip friend" was what Priya called her.

"Shriya needs a doctor," Priya thought. "She needs a doctor who can help her get healthy in body, mind, and intelligence just as the *Śrīmad-Bhāgavatam* recommends."

Now, imagine you are Shriya's doctor of body, mind, and intelligence. In a dialogue format write the conversation that Shriya would have with you regarding her problems. What would she tell you? What would your suggestions be? Remember to empathically listen to Shriya's frustrations first before giving advice on how she can become healthier in body, mind, and intelligence. Make her aware of the consequences of her actions while assuring her that you care.

Science Activity

... to bring out the spiritual scientist in you

A SILKWORM IN A COCOON

Silk is derived from cocoons built by silkworms. Research the internet and find out:

- Why does a silkworm weave a cocoon around itself?
- Can a silkworm come out of its cocoon alive?
- Are there any other species that also weave cocoons?
- What other kinds of interesting shells do different animals have in nature?

You can look for websites or videos that give you this information and share it with your group. Relate your learning from this activity with the analogy activity of this chapter.

Writing and Language Activities

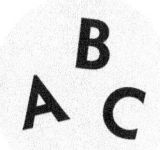

... to help you understand better

WRITING A PROPOSAL

Since this human birth is extremely rare, isn't it best to start training ourselves on the path of self-realization when we are young? It's certainly more fun and impactful when we start at a young age.

Prahlāda also instructed his class friends to practice spirituality from the very beginning of life.

Write a proposal to your temple community leader, explaining the need to ignite interest about spirituality in young lives from as early in life as possible:

1. You can start by explaining the need for children to be trained in spiritual values, like compassion, sacrifice, and service to God, which equip them to deal with real life problems as they grow into adults.
2. Propose a two-week residential program in the temple for children between 10 and 18 during the summer vacation.
3. Propose the events and schedule of the programs; for example, morning *āratis* and *japa*, discussions with scholarly devotees, *kīrtana saṅgas*, and some fun activities, like *harināma*, book distribution, cooking, evening bonfires, hiking, swimming, etc. You may include a day's schedule in a timetable format.
4. Conclude by reiterating the advantages of the training program in nurturing young lives as they grow into adolescents and then adults; for example, inculcating discipline, learning to live within a community, making friends for life, and creating wonderful memories of life in Kṛṣṇa consciousness.

ESSAY: MONEY IS SWEETER THAN HONEY

Verse 10 mentions that to a materialist money is sweeter than honey, and they try to accumulate money at all costs, even by risking their lives.

Referring to the purport, write a persuasive essay explaining why the proverb "money is sweeter than honey" may not be true. Explain the pitfalls of living with only material goals in mind without considering spiritual aspirations (use examples). Then describe how ideal *varṇāśrama* trains one to enter household life with greater understanding on how to control the senses, which eventually

leads to the renounced stage of life. You may also conclude by discussing how money can be sweeter than honey when used in the service of the Lord with the intention of pleasing Him.

A FIVE-POINT TRAINING AGENDA

Over the past few chapters, we have been studying how sense gratification causes more harm than good. In this chapter Prahlāda says that the best way to save ourselves from getting too attached to sense gratification is to train in *bhāgavata-dharma* from the beginning of childhood. In *brahmacarya*, student life, one is trained to control the senses and focus on the Lord.

Let us understand how *brahmacarya* could help us with sense control. The following Quote Card has been created with Śrīla Prabhupāda's statements about the subject in this chapter. Photocopy this Quote Card. Find a senior *gṛhastha* devotee in your community to discuss

CANTO 7, CHAPTER 6
QUOTE CARD: BENEFITS OF *BRAHMACARYA* TRAINING

1. According to the Vedic system, therefore, from the very beginning of life the *brahmacarya* system is introduced so that from one's very childhood – from the age of five years – one can practice modifying one's human activities so as to engage perfectly in devotional service. (Purport, verse 1)

2. And [in modern civilization] if by chance a child is saved, he is educated only for sense gratification. (Purport, Verse 1)

3. In all the schools, colleges and universities, and at home, all children and youths should be taught to hear about the Supreme Personality of Godhead. (Purport, verse 1)

4. A *brahmacārī* learns how to control his senses and sacrifice everything for the *guru*. When he is fully trained, if he likes he is allowed to marry. Thus he is not an ordinary *gṛhastha* who has learned only how to satisfy his senses. (Purport, verse 9)

5. Although they [devotee kings in Vedic culture] were extremely opulent and were the masters of kingdoms, they could give up all their possessions because they were trained early as *brahmacārīs*. (Purport, verse 10)

its contents with. If possible, find a devotee who may have been trained in ISKCON as a *brahmacārī* and who later entered *gṛhastha* life and has raised devotee children in the movement.

1. Write down five questions to ask this devotee based on the contents of the Quote Card. Your questions should be open ended and should try to bring out the advantages of *brahmacārī* training/childhood Kṛṣṇa conscious training in contrast to those who have not had such training.

2. Request a meeting with this devotee, give him the Quote Card, and interview him. With permission, you may record the interview or take notes to help you later.

3. Remember to ask for anecdotes, personal experiences, and interesting information.

4. Use the information on the Quote Card and the interview to create a leaflet endorsing a Sunday Children's program run by your local temple. The leaflet should list the top five ways training in *bhāgavata-dharma* from a young age would benefit children.

LETTER TO A PRISONER

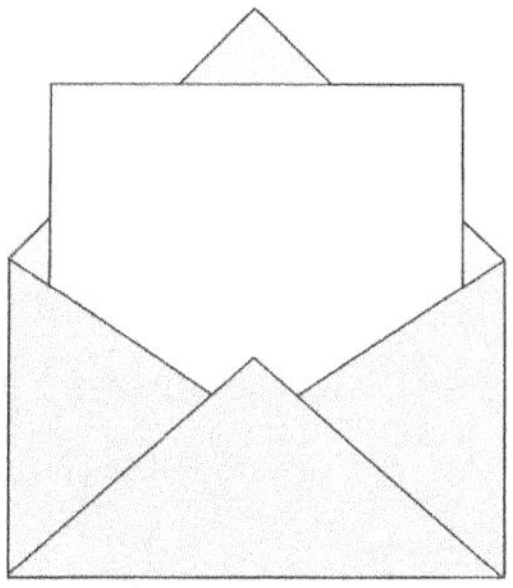

Your old school friend, whom you lost contact with years ago, is now in juvenile prison. Write a letter to him or her expressing your empathy. Explain how we are all essentially trapped in this material prison. Include the analogy of the silkworm trapped in its own cocoon. Use the purports of verse 16 to explain how humans are different from animals and why in this human form we should pursue spiritual life. You can use the opening below or begin another way.

Dear Nyle,

I know we haven't been in contact for years, ever since you moved to the city. I wish we had kept in touch. Your mother wrote to me and told me of your plight, and I am so sorry to hear you are in prison.

Recently I was reading *Śrīmad-Bhāgavatam* and realized that we are all trapped in this material prison.

A COMPARATIVE STUDY OF EDUCATION

Let us compare education in Vedic times to modern-day education, and let's see how Prahlāda's teachings (of Vedic times) compare to Hiraṇyakaśipu's ideals (of modern times):

First read the following points and sort them in the table (note down the corresponding numbers next to each category).

1. There was no talk about Kṛṣṇa, the Supreme Personality of Godhead.

2. Prahlāda explained about the uselessness of materialistic life.

3. Education in modern times is mostly about sense gratification.

4. The human form of life should be used in the devotional service of the Supreme Lord.
5. Emphasis was on religion (devoid of the Supreme Lord), economic development, and sense gratification.
6. One should practice devotional service from the tender age of childhood.
7. Vedic education emphasized *gurukula* education, staying with the *guru* and being away from parents.
8. *Brahmacārya*, which is one of the most important stages of the Vedic education system, is neglected.
9. Education was related to diplomatic affairs of pacifying public leaders, appeasing them with lucrative posts, dividing and ruling over them, and punishing them in cases of disobedience.
10. Emphasis was on *brahmacarya* and reading the Vedic texts.
11. There is no talk of holy scriptures, leave alone the chanting of the holy name.
12. *Bhāgavata-dharma*, consisting of the nine processes of devotional service, was taught in *gurukula*.
13. In any form of life, we are related with Viṣṇu, who is the most beloved, the Supersoul, son, friend, and guru. Our eternal relationship with God can be revived in the human form of life, and that should be the goal of education.
14. Material education is contaminated by the three modes of material nature, but spiritual education is transcendental.
15. One gets educated for earning money and using it to gratify the senses.

a. Teachings in Hiraṇyakaśipu's school	
b. Teachings of Prahlāda	
c. Teachings in *gurukula* in the Vedic era	
d. Teachings in modern-day schools	

Now, with the help of the above information, write an article of about 600 words on the following topic, using your own arguments and what you've learned thus far in this canto. Remember to make your ideas flow, introducing the two kinds of education in the first paragraph and then giving your views:

"My idea of education in today's age and how it can be balanced with spiritual education."

CHAPTER 6 ANSWERS

The Householder's Cocoon

Labels: 1. The materialistic householder; 2. The "trap" of material life.

Questions: 1. The householder who hasn't been trained in spiritual life is already in a disadvantageous position, and he further gets absorbed in material life when he gets attracted to family and household affairs. Since family and household affairs absorb him so much that he loses any trace of interest in his main business of human life, it is compared to a trap; 2. No; while pious household life may be somewhat satisfying, there are multiple challenges one goes through to face it. So while materialistic householders think they will be happy in household life, they have to put a lot of effort to maintain their status and comforts. Such family life, even if satisfying, does not guarantee lasting happiness, a better destination after death, or the development of love for the Lord. In the sense that it does not provide lasting positive benefits, it is considered undesirable; 3. No; devotees do not just have families, friends, and wealth, but they also try to acquire devotion to the Lord. Therefore, they are not considered attached householders. Moreover, when their family members are devotees and their wealth is used in the service of the Lord, they are always associating with and serving the Lord, which leads to their ultimate liberation from the material world. Therefore, they are not trapped; 4. By meeting and sincerely following a bona fide spiritual master, a householder can break the trap of material life and free himself and his family members. Therefore, the diagram may be modified by adding a spiritual master on top, and the cocoon may have an opening on the top from where everyone can get out and surrender to the spiritual master.

Pravṛtti-mārga Vs. Nivṛtti-mārga

Answers: 1. True; because both teach sense gratification but not God consciousness; 2. True; university education encourages one to work hard (a kind of *dharma*), to become qualified to earn money (*artha*), and to enjoy oneself (*kāma*); 3. False; many university students fall victim to inappropriate activities and may even risk dropping out because of this; 4. False; the concept of a higher power is not formally taught in university, except maybe in religious study subjects; 5. True; they are trained to achieve only higher material success but do not know about spiritual success; 6. True; Śrīla Prabhupāda included as many of the nine processes as possible in the daily program he left us; 7. True; this is a natural byproduct of practicing devotional service; 8. False; devotees are generally better at controlling their senses and are not involved in illicit activities, gambling, meat-eating, or intoxication – even a small child like Prahlāda became fully sense controlled by the practice of devotional service; 9. False; devotees respect both the creator and the creation, but they don't want to enjoy it independent of Kṛṣṇa; 10. True; they are trained to achieve higher, spiritual goals.

A Comparative Study of Education

1-a; 2-b; 3-d; 4-b; 5-a; 6-b; 7-c; 8-d; 9-a; 10-c; 11-d; 12-c; 13-c; 14-b; 15-d

7

WHAT PRAHLĀDA LEARNED IN THE WOMB

Story Summary

Prahlāda pondered for a moment. Certainly, he wanted to give credit to his *guru*, Nārada Muni, who had given him the knowledge he had just shared with his class friends. The words of his *guru* still resonated in his heart. Those wonderful instructions had made all anxiety and fear dissipate just as they were doing now.

"My dear friends," said Prahlāda, "when my father went to Mandarācala Mountain to perform his severe austerities, the demigods feared the worst. They took advantage of my father's absence and tried to subdue the demons and fought with them, showing them no mercy. They killed the demon leaders one by one, making the rest flee from their homes. They plundered the King's palace and arrested my mother, the Queen."

"Oh no! Then what happened?" asked a wide-eyed classmate, while the others leaned forward to hear more.

"Nārada Muni heard the pitiful cries of my mother and appeared on the scene. He tried to persuade Indra to release the sinless lady because I was in her womb. 'Let her stay with me until the child is delivered,' he told Indra. But Indra had already known that I was the seed of that great demon. He wanted to kill me as soon as I was born."

Some of the boys gasped, while others just gawked at Prahlāda.

"Nārada Muni told Indra, 'Within this woman's womb is a faultless and sinless child. He is a great, powerful servant of the Supreme Personality of Godhead, so you will not be able to kill him.'

"Believe it or not, Indra immediately listened to Nārada and released my mother. And not only that, but the demigods also circumambulated her because they understood me to be a devotee within her womb.

"After the demigods returned to heaven, kind Nārada took my mother to his *āśrama* and gave her shelter, assuring her of protection until her husband's return. My mother then stayed in his care, unafraid of anything. Being pregnant, she wanted to give birth only after my father's arrival; in the meantime she served Nārada Muni with great devotion.

"Because of his kindness to the fallen souls, Nārada instructed my mother and me, while I was in her womb, in religion and transcendental knowledge. I remembered his pure instructions although my mother forgot them in time."

Prahlāda gazed at the sincere faces of the boys one by one. With love-laden eyes, he said, "My dear friends, if you have faith in my words, which come directly from Nārada Muni, you will also be able to understand transcendental knowledge even though you are small children. Similarly, a woman, who is sometimes considered less intelligent because of her attachment to material enjoyment, can also understand spiritual knowledge and know what is spirit and what is matter. You see, my friends, receiving spiritual knowledge can never be checked by any material condition."

One of the boys sitting in front of Prahlāda put his palms together and said, "Dear Prahlāda, please give us more of this spiritual knowledge. We are thirsting to hear more from you."

Prahlāda smiled and then pointed at the branches of a tree out of the window. "The fruits and flowers of this tree will go through six changes," he said. "They are born, they exist then grow, transform, wither, and then die. Your material body also goes through such changes. But the spirit soul within the tree and within your body doesn't go through any of these changes."

Now looking at each of the boys intently, Prahlāda continued, "You are the *ātmā*. And the Lord is also referred to as the *ātmā*. Both *ātmās* are completely spiritual, individual, the knowers of the external body, and are free from birth and death. So a person who knows this gives up the conception that 'I am this material body and everything related with this body is mine.'

"In fact, a spiritually advanced person knows that the spiritual particle exists within the body just as a geologist knows where there is gold and how to extract it from stone. But one without such knowledge cannot understand how the spirit exists within the body."

"If it's that simple, why don't most of us understand this?" asked one bright-eyed boy.

"That's because the individual soul is conditioned by the Lord's material energy, the three modes of material nature, and the material elements," answered Prahlāda.

"You see, each soul has two kinds of bodies – a gross body made of five gross elements and a subtle body made of three subtle elements. However, the soul is none of these, and one should find the soul by analyzing and separating spirit from matter."

One boy put his hand up and asked, "So, revered Prahlāda, can we understand all this just by using our intelligence?"

Prahlāda shook his hand and said, "Not really. Our intelligence is also covered and only perceives what it thinks is reality. It perceives the consciousness or the soul in three states of activity – wakefulness, dreaming, and deep sleep. But the soul is aloof from this. The intelligence observes these states, thinking that this is reality."

Looking at the confused look on the boys' faces, Prahlāda said, "Just think of this. You can understand that there is air because of the aromas it carries, right?"

The boys nodded.

"Similarly, you can understand that the soul exists through the three states of consciousness. The intelligence perceives when you are awake, you dream, and you go into deep sleep. Still, these states are distinct from the soul, just as aromas are distinct from the air. But the intelligence only perceives this differently because it is influenced by the three modes of material nature and material activities."

"But we still need intelligence," interrupted another boy, "to understand these things. Isn't this what we are trying to do now?"

"True," answered Prahlāda, "but we cannot truly understand these spiritual subject matters through the polluted intelligence. Only when the intelligence is purified, we can realize that this material condition of life is full of misery and is temporary."

"And how do we purify our intelligence?" chipped another enthusiastic friend.

"Aha! That's an excellent question," said Prahlāda, beaming from ear to ear. "We have to know who is the source of this intelligence. The Supreme Personality of Godhead, as the Paramātmā, is the original master, the ruler, and the origin of the intelligence and the states of consciousness. So we have to revive our consciousness of the Lord. When you are Kṛṣṇa conscious, you realize that material existence, whether you are awake or dreaming, is nothing but a dream and has no real value.

"Therefore, my dear friends, your duty is to take up to Kṛṣṇa consciousness, which destroys this material intelligence and burns the seed of fruitive work. When you become a devotee of Kṛṣṇa, your ignorance is immediately removed.

"Devotional service, as explained directly by the Lord, is the best way to become free from material life and develop love for the Lord."

"Wh . . . what exactly is devotional service?" asked another boy, not sure if his question sounded foolish.

Prahlāda smiled at him reassuringly and replied, "You should take shelter of a bona fide spiritual master and serve him with great faith and devotion; offer all your possessions to *guru* and Kṛṣṇa; associate with saintly persons; worship the Lord and hear His glories with great faith; glorify Him and always meditate on His lotus feet. You should also worship the Lord's Deity form, remember Him as Paramātmā in everyone's heart, and respect all living beings according to their position.

"By these activities you will be able to cut down the enemies of lust, anger, greed, illusion, madness, and jealousy and serve the Lord with pure love."

"And how do we know if we are experiencing pure love?" asked another boy.

"Such a devotee naturally controls his senses; therefore he is liberated. When such a liberated devotee hears about the Lord's divine qualities and pastimes, his hair stands on end, his voice falters, and tears fall from his eyes in ecstasy. Sometimes he sings and dances in jubilation and sometimes he loudly chants like a madman, 'Hare Kṛṣṇa, Hare Kṛṣṇa!'

"As a result, his material desires and material consciousness are burnt to ashes. By such *bhakti* you can get the Lord's shelter and directly contact Him. And when you are in direct touch with the Lord, do you know what happens?"

The boys looked at one another speechless.

"The wheel of repeated birth and death completely stops!"

"We want to become the Lord's devotees," one boy muttered, trying to look away, "but it's very hard."

"It's not hard, O dear sons of the *asuras*!" said Prahlāda, raising his voice. "In fact, it is harder to go to hell!"

A hush of whispers broke out in the room.

"Listen, my dear friends!" exclaimed Prahlāda, getting the boys' attention once again. "The Lord is within your heart; He is the closest to each of us. He is our well-wisher and best friend. So why is there difficulty in connecting with Him and worshiping Him? Why should you find difficulty in engaging in His devotional service? Why are you so addicted to sense gratification?"

The boys looked down sheepishly, realizing the truth in Prahlāda's words.

"All your possessions and riches, a beautiful wife, children, your residence, your pets, all your money and sense enjoyment do not last. They are all flickering. A sensible person knows he is eternal – so what is the benefit of all these temporary things?

"Even the pleasure of the heavenly planets is fleeting. A materialistic person seeking wealth and comforts just ends up frustrated. Indeed, the results he gets are the opposite of those he desires."

"Forgive us for our foolishness," said a boy softly, "but what do you mean?"

"Everyone in this world wants happiness, right? No one wants distress. And so we act just so we can be happy. However, we become happy when we don't endeavor for happiness. As soon as we act to get material happiness, we have to go through much distress."

The boys nodded, agreeing with Prahlāda's reasoning.

"This temporary material body is meant to become stool or earth when it dies, so what's the use of all the false temporary relationships and material possessions related to the body? Everything related to the body is also finished when the body is destroyed. Because of ignorance, you just consider all these things valuable, but compared to the ocean of eternal happiness in Kṛṣṇa consciousness, they are most insignificant. So how can the living being be interested in fruitive activities, which bring these material bodies one after another, birth after birth, resulting in hardship and misery?"

The boys looked at one another, dumbfounded, yet Prahlāda's words were making sense.

"The four principles of advancement in spiritual life – *dharma*, *artha*, *kāma*, and *mokṣa* – depend on the Supreme Personality of Godhead. Therefore, my dear friends, don't be distracted by this but follow in the footsteps of great devotees. Without material desire, fully depend on the Lord and worship Him with devotion.

"The Supreme Lord, Hari, is the soul and Supersoul of all living beings. We all are manifestations of His energy. So He is the most dear to us, and He is the supreme controller. Anyone within this universe – from a demigod to a demon – who serves Mukunda's lotus feet becomes liberated and is situated in the most auspicious condition of life, exactly like us [the *mahājanas*].

"O my friends, even you, the sons of Yakṣas and Rākṣasas, unintelligent women, *śūdras* and cowherd men, the birds and lower animals, and all sinful entities can revive their original, eternal spiritual life and live forever by accepting the principles of *bhakti-yoga*.

"To serve the lotus feet of Govinda and to see Him everywhere is the goal of life as explained by the revealed scriptures. Only this pleases Him. You cannot please Him by becoming *brāhmaṇas*, demigods, great saints, or learned scholars, neither can you please Him by charity, austerity, sacrifice, cleanliness, or vows. The Lord is pleased only by unflinching, unalloyed devotion to Him. Without devotion everything is a show.

"So, my dear friends, in the same way that you see yourself and take care of yourself, take to devotional service to please the Supreme Personality of Godhead. Make your lives perfect and happy by becoming Kṛṣṇa conscious."

Themes and Key Messages

Please go through this table of themes and key messages, with corresponding verses, and discuss each topic further.

THEMES	REFERENCES	KEY MESSAGES
Progress in spiritual life cannot be obstructed by any material condition.	7.7.1, 38, 50, 54–55	Even though Prahlāda was in the womb he was able to hear the instructions of Nārada and become elevated on the spiritual platform. Similarly, Prahlāda Mahārāja was able to instruct his classmates who were children and from families of demons. His mother was also able to serve the pure devotee Nārada. Yakṣas, Rākṣasas, *śūdras*, cowherd men, and even birds and animals can get the benefits of *bhakti-yoga*. There is no difficulty in connecting with Kṛṣṇa because He is the well-wisher of all beings and the Supersoul in everyone's hearts. Therefore no material impediment can come in the way of devotional service to Govinda, which is the ultimate goal of life.
The *ācārya* in disciplic succession is not an ordinary human being, and anyone who serves him and hears from him becomes enlightened in transcendental knowledge.	7.7.14–17	When one has complete faith in the spiritual master, who is a direct representative of the Supreme Lord and who is especially empowered to broadcast the glories of the Lord, real knowledge of matter and spirit are revealed to that person. Therefore Prahlāda emphasizes that anyone, even a woman, like his mother, or children, like himself and his friends, can become elevated by hearing spiritual subjects from a pure devotee who has received knowledge in *paramparā*.
An advanced person who understands spiritual knowledge attains perfection in spiritual life.	7.7.18–28	Spiritual knowledge is understanding that the soul is spiritual and transcendental, separate from the material body. Just as a geologist understands how to detect gold in stone, a spiritualist can understand how the spirit particle, the soul, exists within the body. Such an intelligent person can analyze and separate spirit from matter. He also understands that the soul is conditioned by the material elements and polluted material intelligence, which consists of wakefulness, dreaming, and deep sleep. One should reject these three states of intelligence, composed of the three material modes, to understand the pure soul. Only by Kṛṣṇa consciousness all ignorance is dissipated.

THEMES	REFERENCES	KEY MESSAGES
Bhakti is the best of all paths to become disentangled from matter. It is directly explained by the Lord and is the easiest way of developing love for God.	7.7.29–33	The process of *bhakti* includes serving a bona fide *guru* with faith and devotion, offering one's possessions to *guru* and Kṛṣṇa, associating with saintly persons, worshiping the Supreme Lord, hearing the glories of the Lord with faith, glorifying the Lord's activities and qualities, meditating on His lotus feet, worshiping the Deity, remembering the Lord as Paramātmā in the hearts of everyone, and respecting all living beings. These activities cut down the influence of lust, anger, greed, illusion, madness, and jealousy. Thus, the secondary result of *bhakti* is being able to control the senses, and the primary result is experiencing love for God.
In the perfectional stage of devotional service, one experiences the symptoms of love of God and one's material desires are burnt to ashes. As a result, the wheel of *saṁsāra* stops.	7.7.34–37	When one develops pure love for Kṛṣṇa, one experiences ecstatic symptoms. One loudly chants the qualities of the Lord and offers respects to all living beings, seeing them as devotees. One constantly thinks of the Lord's pastimes, and thus one's material desires are burnt to ashes. In this way, achieving the shelter of the Lord's lotus feet, one becomes liberated from the wheel of repeated birth and death (*saṁsāra*) and goes back to Godhead. Therefore, Prahlāda encourages his friends to become devotees and meditate upon and worship the Lord.
The struggle for material things is unworthy, so better to worship the Supreme Lord with devotion – nothing pleases Him more.	7.7.39–42, 48, 51–52	Material opulence, even on the heavenly planets, is temporary. A materialist gets frustrated trying to enjoy more because he often gets opposite results. The material body, its possessions, and family relations are also temporary. One should perform one's duties but depend on Kṛṣṇa for the results. It is better to depend on the Supreme Lord with devotion and without material desires because nothing pleases the Lord more than unflinching, unalloyed devotion to Him.

Higher-Thinking Questions

Now try to deepen your understanding of this chapter by delving into Śrīla Prabhupāda's purports and reflecting on the following questions:

1. Why did King Indra immediately accept Nārada's instructions to release Prahlāda's mother even though he suspected that the child in her womb could be a demon? (See verse 11 purport.)

2. It is said that one shouldn't stay with a woman in a secluded place. Does this mean that Nārada transgressed the Vedic injunctions when he gave shelter to Kayādhu? Refer to verse 14 purport and explain your answer.

3. Śrīla Prabhupāda comments in verse 16 purport that sometimes women may forget devotional instructions, like that of Kayādhu, and are therefore regarded as less intelligent. Why are women sometimes considered less intelligent? Does this apply to all women? Explain.

4. Prahlāda Mahārāja advises his friends in verse 17 that, like him, his friends can also understand transcendental knowledge. How can transcendental knowledge be received and understood as described by Śrīla Prabhupāda in the purport?

5. What does Prahlāda Mahārāja imply when he says that his friends should have faith in his words?

6. This chapter emphasizes the importance of distinguishing matter from spirit. Why do you think one should first understand this to advance spiritually? (Refer to verse 22 purport.)

7. What is self-realization as explained by Śrīla Prabhupāda in verse 23 purport?

8. If one does not take shelter of the Lord's lotus feet, one's intelligence is polluted, even though one can use the three divisions of intelligence to understand the soul. Why is this so? (See verse 26 and purport.) What is the best way to purify one's intelligence?

9. Why is *bhakti-yoga* described as the best by the Lord in the *Bhagavad-gītā*? (See verse 29 purport.) Why shouldn't we be worried about the reactions of our past sinful reactions as explained by Śrīla Prabhupāda in the purport?

10. Why is it more difficult to go to hell than to go back to Godhead as described in verse 38 purport?

ACTIVITIES

In this section you will find many exciting things to do. These activities will get you thinking, moving, drawing, and having loads of fun.

Analogy Activity

... to bring out the scholar in you

EXPERT PERCEPTION

Verse 21 compares a spiritually advanced person who can separate the material body from the spiritual soul to a geologist who can separate gold from its ore. Let us understand this analogy more thoroughly.

Look at the pictures below. The first one shows a geologist working to determine if a piece of ore she is studying contains any gold in it, and the second one is a Vedic scholar studying to see if he can separate the body from the soul.

Both experts must refer to the following task cards and pick the appropriate information to complete their respective tasks. Can you help them by putting "G" against each geologist appropriate task, and "S" against every Vedic scholar's task?

The Materials

minerals
air fire
grit earth stone
water ether sand
gold particles ego
mind mud
intelligence

The Treasure

photogeology
sāṅkhya study
geosampling
drilling
negating material elements

The Method

gold
soul

The Risk

An untrained

____

may fail to detect the right treasure.

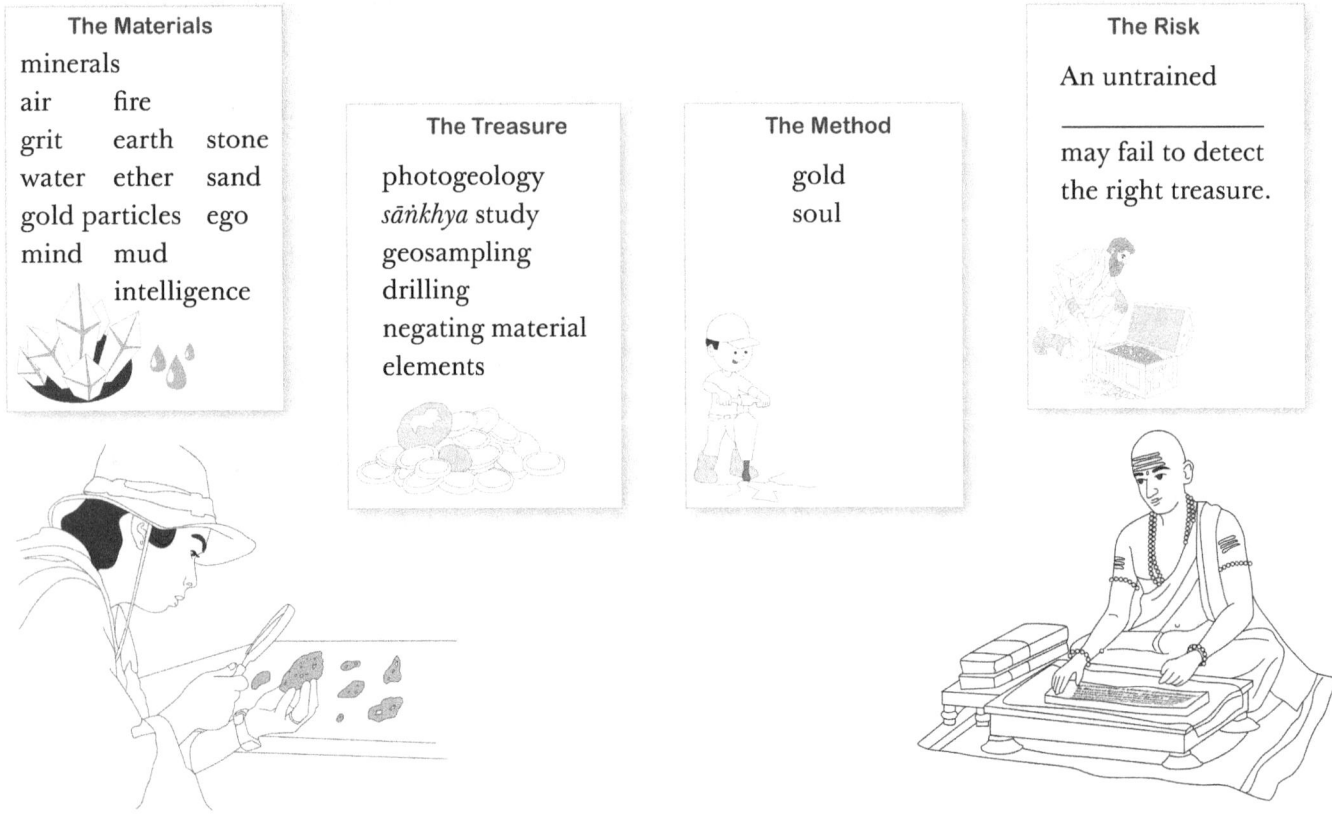

Now that each expert has completed his task, consider and discuss the following:

1. What is common to the methodology each expert employs?
2. What is common to the nature of the results each expert obtains?
3. Why is the result important in each case?
4. Can they swap roles? Why or why not?
5. What can we conclude about the process of acquiring knowledge about the soul from this analogy?

Artistic Activity

... to reveal your creativity

PAPER CRAFT: FLOWER BOUQUET

Deity worship is a unique and special way to develop our relationship with Kṛṣṇa and personally serve Him with love. Let's make a paper flower bouquet for your home Deities or altar.

Materials: scissors; colored paper: pink, purple or blue, yellow, and brown (or choose as per your preference); glue; ruler

Steps:

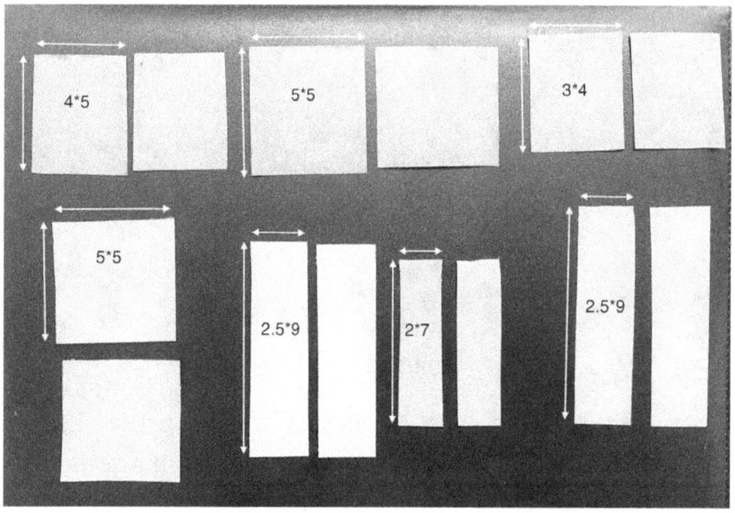

Image 1

1. Cut the papers of different colors in the size shown in Image 1. (Top row in brown, bottom left squares in pink, next two rectangular strips in yellow, next two in pink, and last two in blue or purple. Measurements in centimeters.)
2. Cut a rectangular brown paper from the top (Image 2) and fold in triangles. Roll the other two brown papers and glue together to make two sticks (Image 2).
3. Fold the first pink square from one edge and roll it to make a rose (Image 3). Wrap the brown paper with triangles around the rolled pink rose (Image 3).
4. Fold the narrow rectangular pink paper and roll it around one of the sticks (Image 4). Fold the yellow paper and make cuts on one side as shown and wrap it around the pink part on the stick (Image 4).

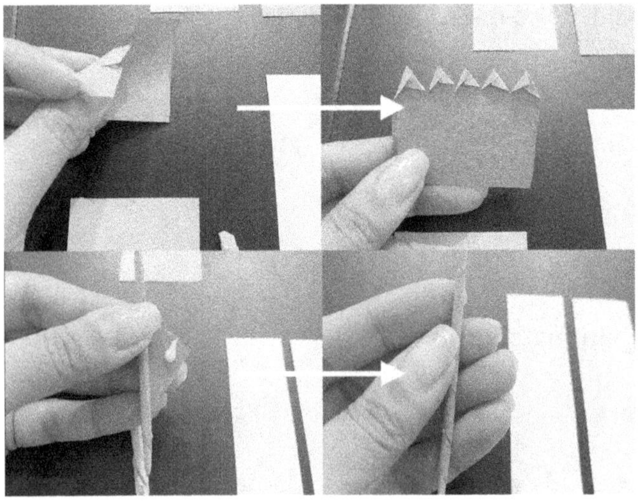

Image 2

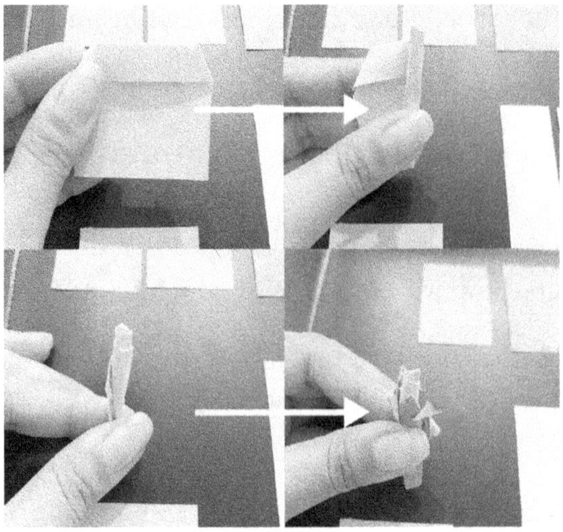

Image 3

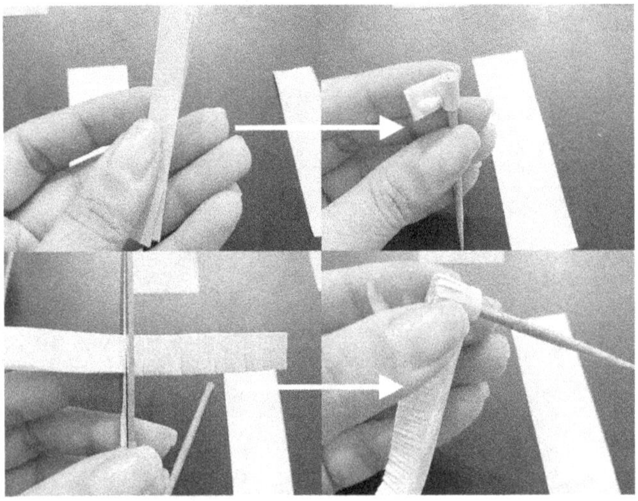

Image 4

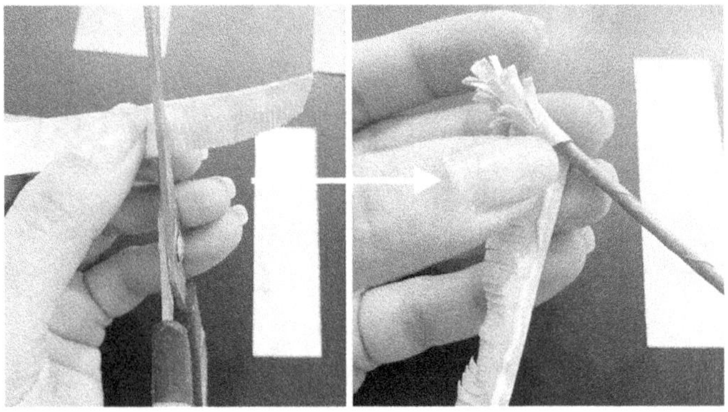

Image 5

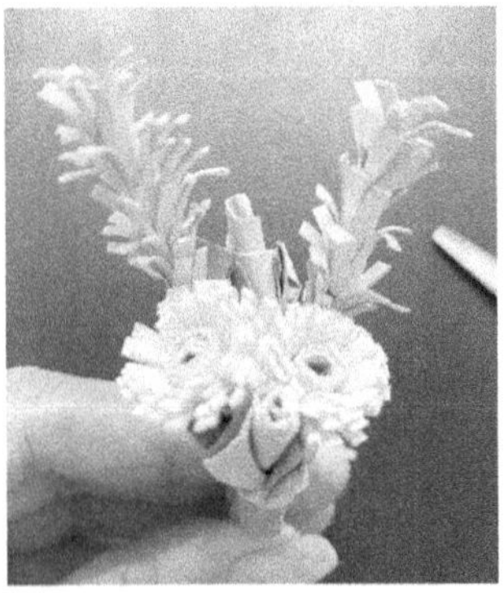

Image 6

5. Next, fold the purple paper and make cuts on one side as shown in Image 5. Wrap it diagonally with glue around the other brown stick to make a lavender flower.
6. Using the same measurements and paper pieces in Image 1, make multiple flowers and put them together in a bouquet.
7. Then offer them to your Deities or offer to Śrīmatī Rādhārāṇī as a hand bouquet (Image 7).

Image 7

Action Activity

... to get you moving and learning

SĀDHANA BOARD

Devotional service pleases Kṛṣṇa. Our *sādhana* (basic practices of hearing and chanting) is an essential part of our devotional practices. Sharing Kṛṣṇa consciousness with others also pleases the Lord, and we can do this effectively when we have a good *sādhana*.

A *sādhana* board can be a wonderful tool to organize and enhance your spiritual practices. Here's a step-by-step guide on how to create it:

Materials: bulletin board, whiteboard, or a sheet of paper; colorful markers or sticky notes; pins, magnets, or adhesive tape; four category labels (C, H, A, T); devotional quotes, images, or illustrations for decoration (optional).

Steps:

- Select a location: Choose a suitable location for your *sādhana* board. It should be easily visible and accessible so that you can interact with it daily.
- Set up the board: If you are using a bulletin board or whiteboard, hang it on the wall. If you are using a sheet of paper, attach it to the wall with adhesive tape. Check with an elder before hanging or taping the paper to the wall.
- Divide into categories: Use colorful markers to create four sections on the board, each corresponding to one of the categories: C, H, A, T. Label these sections accordingly (see illustration below).
- Chant a *Śloka* (C): In the Chanting section, you can pin or tape special prayers by great devotees that resonate with you. This could include verses from the *Bhagavad-gītā*, prayers from saints, or your personal favorite devotional chants. You can write the *śloka* itself or use sticky notes to change it every week. This will be the verse you chant daily and strive to remember.
- Holy Name (H): Here, track your daily count (rounds) of chanting the holy names. You can set a goal for a minimum number of repetitions per day and update this count regularly.
- Association (A): In the Association section, you can add reminders to seek the company of senior devotees, join *satsangas*, or engage in devotional discussions. You can also jot down insights or teachings from these interactions.
- Tribute (T): In the Tribute section, express your gratitude to the Lord for whatever you have received. You can add thanksgiving notes, prayers of gratitude, or simply write down things you are thankful for.
- Decorate (Optional): To make your *sādhana* board more inspiring, decorate it with devotional images, quotes, or illustrations that resonate with your practice.
- Daily engagement: Make it a daily routine to interact with your *sādhana* board. Chant the *śloka*, update your holy name count, reflect on your association with senior devotees, and offer thanks to the Lord.

- Weekly refresh: Every week, change the *śloka* in each category to keep your practice fresh and engaging.
- Review and reflect: Periodically, step back and review your *sādhana* board. Reflect on your progress, adjust your goals if needed, and continue to cultivate your devotion.

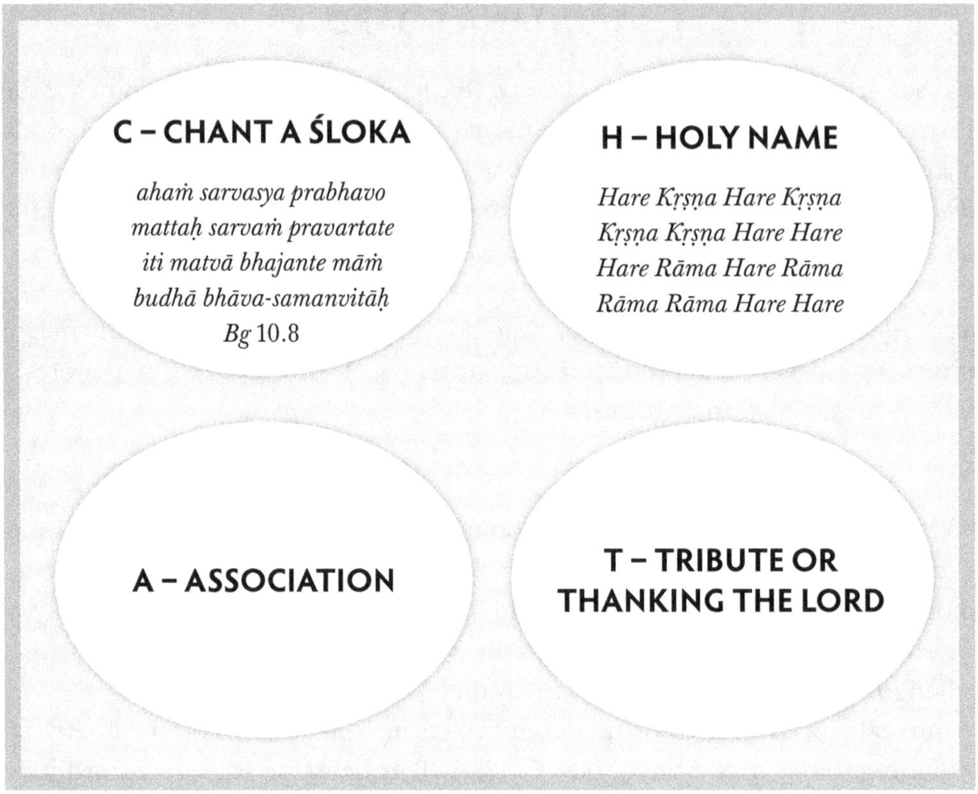

Critical-Thinking Activity

... to bring out the spiritual investigator in you

TWO WAYS TO HAPPINESS

In this chapter, Prahlāda Mahārāja continues to discourage his friends from the path of sense gratification and encourages them on the path of *bhakti*.

Pravṛtti: The Materialist's "Happiness"

Commenting on *pravṛtti-mārga*, Prahlāda says, "One is happy as long as one does not endeavor for happiness; as soon as one begins his activities for happiness, his conditions of distress begin." (*SB* 7.7.42)

Look at the path of sense enjoyment on the next page. It shows the materialist's path to happiness and the possible obstacles on the path. Study this path carefully and understand the milestones, the possible obstacles, and the results.

Now consider:

1. Is the statement of Prahlāda Mahārāja from verse 42 accurate? Why?
2. What is the role of the Lord's will in this whole scheme?
3. How can Prahlāda explain this to his friends in an easily understandable way?
4. How could you, in today's scenario, explain this to a friend?

NIVṚTTI/BHAKTI MĀRGA – PATH OF DEVOTIONAL SERVICE

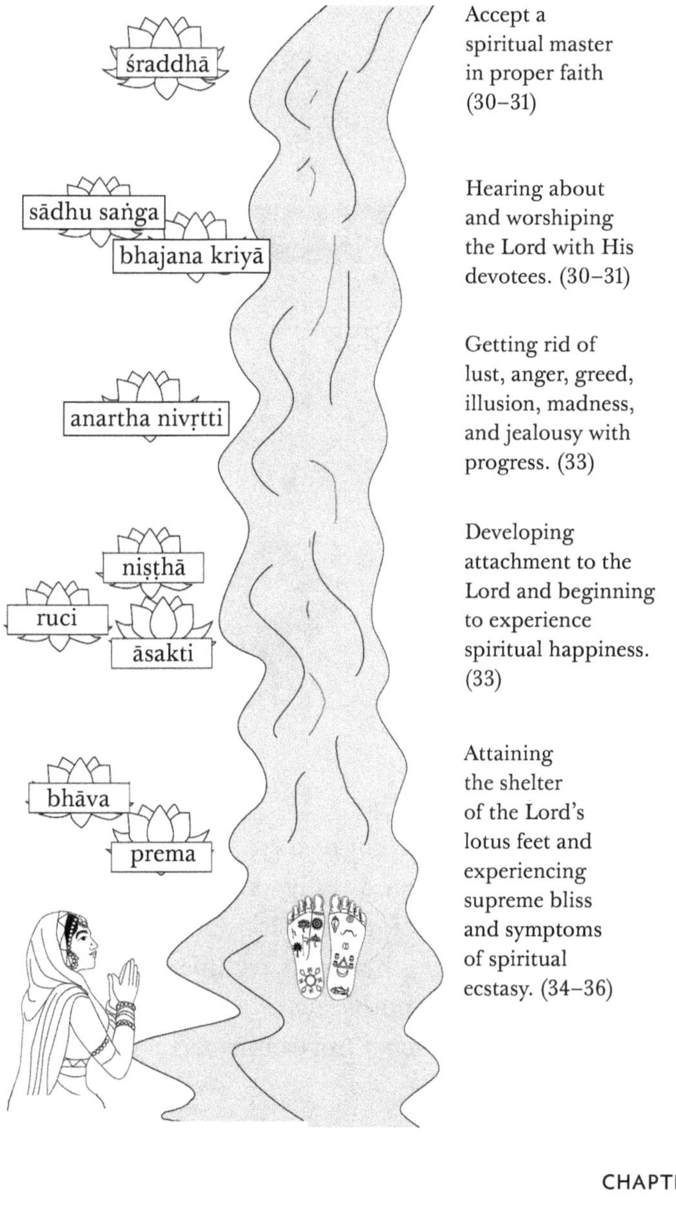

śraddhā
Accept a spiritual master in proper faith (30–31)
sādhu saṅga
bhajana kriyā
Hearing about and worshiping the Lord with His devotees. (30–31)
anartha nivṛtti
Getting rid of lust, anger, greed, illusion, madness, and jealousy with progress. (33)
niṣṭhā
ruci
āsakti
Developing attachment to the Lord and beginning to experience spiritual happiness. (33)
bhāva
prema
Attaining the shelter of the Lord's lotus feet and experiencing supreme bliss and symptoms of spiritual ecstasy. (34–36)

PRAVṚTTI MĀRGA – PATH OF SENSE ENJOYMENT

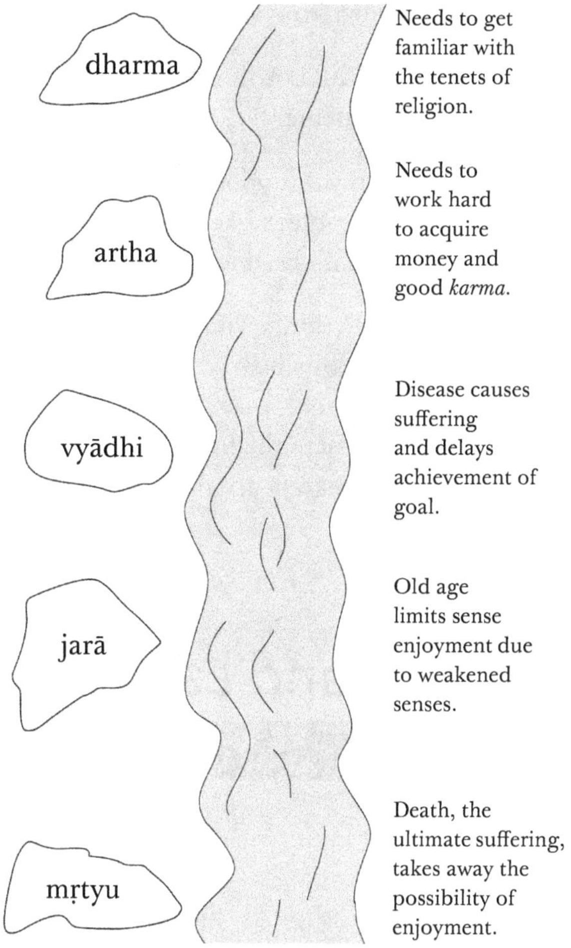

dharma
Needs to get familiar with the tenets of religion.
artha
Needs to work hard to acquire money and good *karma*.
vyādhi
Disease causes suffering and delays achievement of goal.
jarā
Old age limits sense enjoyment due to weakened senses.
mṛtyu
Death, the ultimate suffering, takes away the possibility of enjoyment.

Nivṛtti: The Spiritualist's Happiness
Explaining how real happiness can be obtained by devotional service in verses 29 to 37, Prahlāda concludes: "By the transcendental bliss realized from constant engagement in devotional service, one is completely liberated from material existence." (*SB* 7.7.37).

Look at the path of *bhakti* as explained by Prahlāda in the diagram on the left. Understand the nine stages of progress, and the result of following it.

Now consider:

1. How do we understand the statement from verse 37?
2. What is the Lord's will in this whole scheme?
3. What do you understand about trying to obtain happiness from Prahlāda's instruction?
4. List three things you could do to follow this instruction.

The world and the living beings are the Lord's property and depend on His plan, despite their having certain desires.

Finally, complete the following statement:
Prahlāda Mahārāja approves the ____________ path because ____________________________

Writing and Language Activities

... to help you understand better

ESSAY: THE PURSUIT OF HAPPINESS

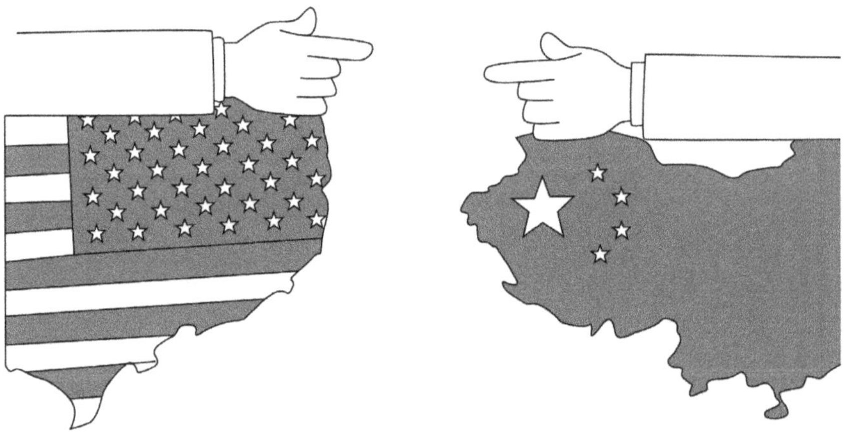

The Roman, Mughal, and British empires have all fallen and new superpowers have emerged. Using one or more of these vanished empires as examples, briefly explain how they fell and comment on their impermanence. In your essay describe how the latest superpowers (for example, USA, China, Russia) are stuck in the same cycle of pursuing economic development to the detriment of their citizens. Give recommendations to the superpowers, discussing why one is happy as long as one does not pursue happiness and explaining what is the best welfare activity for their citizens. Refer to verses 39 to 42 as well as verses 51 and 52 of this chapter to strengthen your argument. You may begin your essay with the following prompt or choose to begin another way.

In *Bhagavad-gītā* the world is described as *duḥkhālayam aśāśvatam* (miserable and temporary). . . .

EXPERT PREACHING

Kṛṣṇa is pleased when we share Kṛṣṇa consciousness with others. Prahlāda Mahārāja expertly preached to his classmates, citing examples that his friends could relate to. Śrīla Prabhupāda was similarly adept at conveying the essence of Kṛṣṇa consciousness.

Once Śrīla Prabhupāda was walking with his disciples through a park in Oakland, California. They passed a small zoo with a large sign in front that read, "Children's fairyland." Śrutakīrti Dāsa, in his book *What is the Difficulty*, writes the following in the 21st chapter:

"Pointing over to the horizon, at the skyscrapers in the distance, he added, 'Adults' fairyland.'

Śrīla Prabhupāda would often explain philosophical points in a simple way that would immediately illustrate deep truths. Here in two words, he exposed the folly of modern civilization."

In this fun activity, write a short paragraph or a poem using common objects like a seesaw, a ferris wheel, etc., to explain the endless wanderings of the living entity in this material world. You can also choose to address any other teaching of Prahlāda Mahārāja. The idea is to creatively inspire others to think deeply about issues that would normally not get much attention.

This is also good practice to enhance your preaching skills.

LETTER: BHAKTI-YOGA IS EASY

One of your friends is struggling to follow the path of *bhakti*. He finds it difficult. Write an encouraging letter to him explaining why and how *bhakti* is easy to practice compared to material life. As Śrīla Prabhupāda explains in verse 38 purport that it is more difficult to go to hell than practicing *bhakti-yoga*. Read the verse and use some of the arguments in the purport to convince your friend why he should continue with his devotional practices. Use your personal experiences as well.

You could also explain, according to this chapter, how devotional service cannot be hindered by any material circumstance.

You may begin as follows:

Dear Nimai,

I am sorry to hear that you are finding it difficult to practice devotional service. But today I read in the seventh canto of the *Bhāgavatam* how easy it can be according to Prahlāda Mahārāja. . . .

ĀCĀRYAS IN PARAMPARĀ

This chapter teaches us the importance of receiving knowledge in *paramparā* (disciplic succession), as Prahlāda's classmates heard from Prahlāda, and as Prahlāda heard from Nārada Muni. Our Brahma-Madhva-Gauḍīya-Vaiṣṇava *sampradaya* consists of illustrious *ācāryas* who dedicated their lives in practicing and spreading Kṛṣṇa consciousness in *paramparā*.

Below are names of some *ācāryas* in the Gauḍīya-Vaiṣṇava *paramparā*:

a. Śrīla Sanātana Gosvāmī
b. Śrīla Rūpa Gosvāmī
c. Śrīla Jīva Gosvāmī
d. Śrīla Gopāla Bhaṭṭa Gosvāmī
e. Śrīla Narottama dāsa Ṭhākura
f. Śrīla Kṛṣṇadāsa Kavirāja Gosvāmī
g. Śrīla Jagannātha dāsa Bābājī
h. Śrīla Bhaktivinoda Ṭhākura
i. Śrīla Gaurakiśora dāsa Bābājī
j. Śrīla Bhaktisiddhānta Sarasvatī Ṭhākura

Below are brief descriptions of these *ācāryas* in a jumbled manner. Match the *ācārya* with the descriptions. Then, from your research, give an additional, specific description for each *ācārya*.

1. Established the Gauḍīya Maṭha, which aimed to promote Kṛṣṇa consciousness and spiritual awareness in India and all over the world.
2. Exemplified scholarship and devotion and wrote books that gave the origins of the Gauḍīya Vaiṣṇava tradition, particularly the *Ṣaṭ-sandarbhas*, which elucidate the philosophy of *bhakti* (devotion) in service to Kṛṣṇa.
3. Composed the monumental scripture *Śrī Caitanya-caritāmṛta*, which chronicles the life and teachings of Lord Caitanya Mahāprabhu.
4. Demonstrated profound devotion and selfless renunciation and authored essential texts, like the *Hari-bhakti-vilāsa*, to elucidate the principles of devotional service within the Gauḍīya Vaiṣṇava tradition.
5. A son of a *brāhmaṇa* in South India from the Śrī *sampradāya*. Out of his devotion, his *śālagrām-śilā* manifested into a beautiful deity called Rādhā-ramaṇa.
6. The *guru* of Śrīla Bhaktisiddhānta Sarasvatī Ṭhākura, who exemplified deep devotion, solitary meditation, and spiritual detachment.
7. Famous for his devotional poetry and songs that inspired countless followers to embrace the path of devotion and love for Lord Kṛṣṇa.
8. Considered to be the leader of the Six Gosvāmīs of Vṛndāvana and who wrote extensive philosophical and devotional literature, including *Bhakti-rasāmṛta-sindhu*, or *Nectar of Devotion*.
9. An exemplary *gṛhastha* who served as a high court judge and was instrumental in reviving and propagating the teachings of Lord Caitanya in the late 19th century.

10. Considered a topmost Vaiṣṇava of his time, he lived as a humble mendicant and was deeply immersed in chanting the holy names of Kṛṣṇa. He was instrumental in discovering the birthplace of Lord Caitanya.

Optional: Are you curious to find out more about any of these *ācāryas*? Choose one personality from the list that you want to know more about. Do some research and then time travel to his time as a curious spectator. Be a witness to one of his pastimes and describe it in your journal. Then share your notes in your time travel journal with your friends.

POEM: THE SUPREME PATH OF BHAKTI-YOGA

Read and study the following poem that describes the practices and goals of the different spiritual paths that help a *jīva* become disentangled from material life. Notice the different levels of *yogis* of which *bhakti-yoga* is the superior path. Then in the diagram briefly describe each *yogi* – their goals, practices, and the results they achieve.

A *sakāma-karma yogī*
Uses the Vedic way to live his life
Practicing his *varṇāśrama* duties
For material enjoyment, he strives
Rituals and rules define his way
His sincerity gains him piety
Celestial planets are where he may
Reach, lest he sins with notoriety

As a *sakāma-karma yogī* advances spiritually
He may progress into a *niṣkāma-karma yogī*
No more goals he yearns for materially
Mokṣa is all that he seeks, beyond everything foggy
Diligent performance of *varṇāśrama* duties
Purifies his heart of vices and follies
And not performing those duties
Is sinful and he suffers lowly reactions to these

By performing his duties with diligence
with the aim of purifying his heart,
A *niṣkāma-karma yogī* with confidence
may become a *jñāna yogī*, playing his part
He gains nothing by performing his *varṇāśrama* duties
He loses nothing by neglecting his *varṇāśrama* duties
He performs only the limbs of *jñāna-yoga* or *sannyāsa*
He aims only to attain the ultimate goal of impersonal *mokṣa*

Similar to the journey of a *jñāna-yogī*
is that of an *aṣṭāṅga-yogī*
Giving up of *varṇāśrama* duties eventually
and aiming at *mokṣa* impersonally
But our *ācāryas* have always taught
That the path of *bhakti* is where the Lord is bought
By the love of the devotee and the personal touch
is the best amongst all of the paths, no doubt as such.

The practice of *bhakti* involves the nine limbs
With devotion and love, chant the holy hymns
Varṇāśrama duties, no longer mandatory
Pure love of Godhead is what one aims for passionately
Bhakti purifies the heart of vices and follies
Coverings of *karma* or *jñāna*, the only obstacles are these

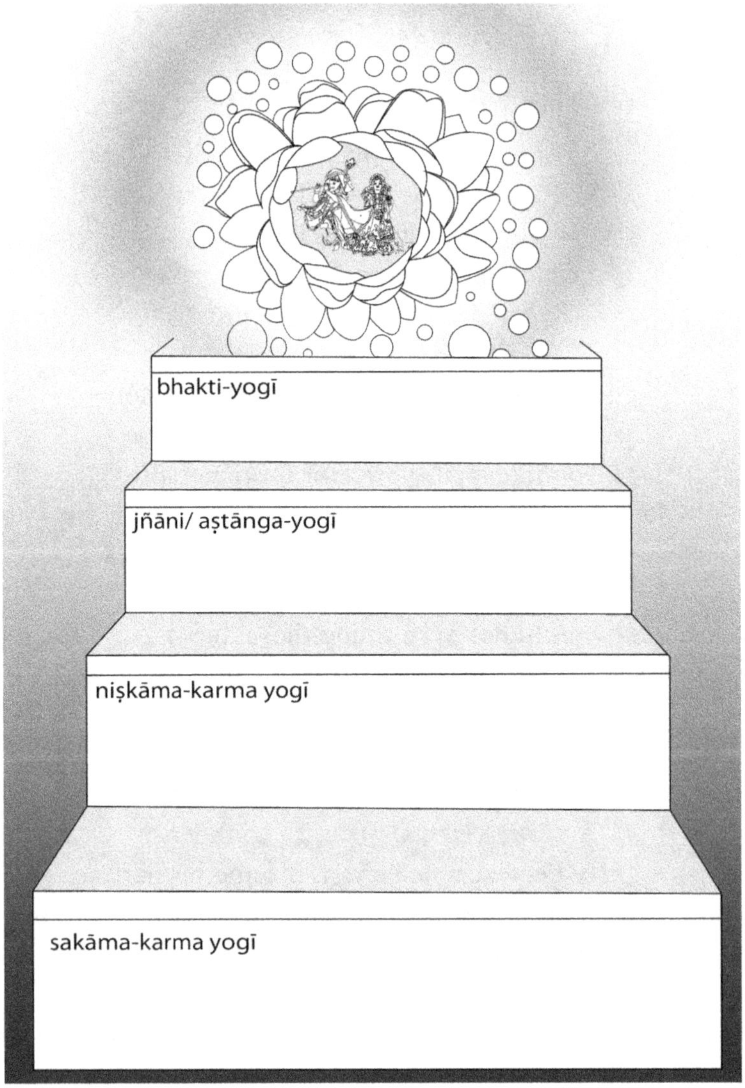

CHAPTER 7 ANSWERS

Expert Perceptions

1. Each expert has a mixed set of items that they need to separate with their expertise to find the thing they are looking for. They do this by negation, i.e., by separating and removing the elements they don't need till they are left with the thing they need; 2. In both cases, the "precious" object is of a different, superior nature compared to everything else it seems to be mixed with; 3. In the first case, they end up with a precious metal. In the second case, they are left with the soul. In both cases, the nature of the end product is different from the things it is mixed with and needs to be studied separately; 4. They cannot swap roles, because the extraction of gold from ore and the understanding of the presence of the spiritual soul in the material body are both specialized studies that can only be done by experts in their respective fields; 5. We can conclude that just as a geologist is expert in his field to distinguish gold from other materials, a spiritualist needs to be expert by training under a spiritual master to understand the distinction between spirit and matter – we cannot make the distinction unless we become experts ourselves through the process of training.

Two Ways to Happiness

Pravṛtti: 1. Yes – as is evident from the picture, the path of *pravṛtti* is full of obstacles and hard work – Prahlāda explains that we have to undergo so much difficulty to get a little enjoyment, and the possible sufferings are more than the final enjoyment; 2. Obtaining sense enjoyment depends not just on working hard or overcoming obstacles but on whether the Lord sanctions the result or not. Śrīla Prabhupāda quotes *BG* 2.47 to explain this; 3. He could use an example – to become the ruler of the universe, one has to undergo so much austerity, like his father did. Yet, his father (at this point in the pastime) could be removed at any time – it was only by the will of the Lord he could continue; 4. You could also explain it using the visual diagram and an example relevant to your times (learner's answers).

Nivṛtti: 1. We can attain the happiness we are looking for by practicing devotional service to Kṛṣṇa; 2. The Lord, by His own mercy and by the mercy of the spiritual master, will always try to help a devotee progress on this path, unlike on the *pravṛtti* path, where he exercises some consideration; 3. Prahlāda Mahārāja is clearly stating that *bhakti* is the way to attain the happiness we seek. This happiness is lasting and enables service to the Lord; 4. Learner's own answers.

Ācāryas in Paramparā

1 (j); 2 (c); 3 (f); 4 (a); 5 (d); 6 (i); 7 (e); 8 (b); 9 (h); 10 (g)

8

THE LORD SLAYS THE KING OF THE DEMONS

Story Summary

Prahlāda Mahārāja stood in front of Hiraṇyakaśipu with folded palms. The boy's serene face and gentle eyes met the crooked and cunning gaze of his father. Hiraṇyakaśipu hissed like a snake. His body trembled in anger remembering how Ṣaṇḍa and Amarka, Prahlāda's teachers, had come complaining about Prahlāda's influence on his classmates. They had observed that all the sons of the demons were becoming devotees of the Lord.

"How dare he!" Hiraṇyakaśipu thought, his lips quivering and eyes burning like coals. He yelled, "O most impudent boy, foolish disruptor of this family, O lowest of mankind, how dare you disobey me! You are an obstinate fool. Today I will send you to the abode of Yamarāja!"

Prahlāda didn't even flinch, which made the king of the demons even angrier: "You know that when I am angry all the three worlds tremble. You rascal, by whose power have you become so fearless that you think you can overstep my power to control you?"

Prahlāda Mahārāja looked at his father in the

eyes and said, "My dear king, the source of my strength is also the source of yours. Indeed, the source of all kinds of strength is one. He is not only the strength of you or me but the strength of everyone. Every moving or nonmoving being, whether superior or inferior, including Lord Brahmā, is controlled by the strength of the Supreme Personality of Godhead.

"The Supreme Lord is the supreme controller and time factor. He is the power of the senses, mind, and body. He has unlimited influence. He creates, maintains, and destroys this world by His power."

Hiraṇyakaśipu was dumbstruck, his face turning different shades of red and purple.

"My dear father," Prahlāda continued, in a voice as calm as a summer breeze, "please give up your demoniac mentality. Don't discriminate between friends and enemies. Be equal to everyone. There is no enemy in this world except for the uncontrolled mind. When you come to the platform of equality, you can worship the Lord perfectly.

"There have been fools like you who did not conquer the six enemies, beginning with lust, greed, and anger. They proudly thought that they had conquered all the enemies in the ten directions, but they were mistaken. However, if someone is victorious over the six internal enemies and is equal to everyone, he has no enemies. Only an ignorant person imagines enemies."

Hiraṇyakaśipu looked as if he would burst. He howled, "You rascal, you think you are greater than me in controlling the senses. You think you are too smart. It seems like you would like to die at my hands!"

Prahlāda glanced at the pillar in front of him and his father.

Breathing heavily, the demon king flung his hands in the air and said, "O most unfortunate Prahlāda, you've always described a supreme being other than me who is above everything, who is the controller of everyone, who is all-pervading. So, where is your God now?"

Glancing at the pillar again, Prahlāda said, "He is everywhere."

Noticing Prahlāda's eyes on the pillar, Hiraṇyakaśipu remarked, "If He is everywhere, then why is He not in this pillar before me?

"You think your God will protect you when I sever your head?" Hiraṇyakaśipu cynical laugh echoed through the hallways. His muscular shoulders heaved as he laughed, and then he suddenly stopped. His deadly gaze sent shivers through everyone, except Prahlāda.

The king of the demons lifted his sword and cursed Prahlāda again and again. He walked toward the pillar and said, "I want to see it. I want to see your God come to protect you!" He struck his fist against the column.

From the pillar came a terrifying sound, which seemed to crack the covering of the universe. Even Lord Brahmā and the demigods heard it

from their abodes and thought that the end of the world was near.

Hiraṇyakaśipu stepped back, his face turning pale. Everyone frantically looked around but couldn't find the source of the sound.

Then, to prove that the words of Prahlāda were true – that the Supreme Lord is present everywhere, even within the pillar of an assembly hall – the Supreme Personality of Godhead, Hari, burst out from the pillar in a wondrous form never seen before.

Hiraṇyakaśipu's eyes widened. "What is this creature that is half man and half lion?" he thought.

This was Lord Nṛsiṁhadeva, who was so enraged that His devotee was put into danger that He had come in this fearsome form. His angry eyes resembled molten gold, His shining mane expanded the dimensions of His fearful face, His parted jaws exposed His deadly teeth, and His razor-sharp tongue moved about like a dueling sword. His ears were erect, and His nostrils and gaping mouth appeared like mountain caves. His short, thick neck, broad chest, thin waist, and His many long arms holding His divine weapons made everyone gape in awe. The hairs on His body were as white as the moonrays. His entire form touched the sky.

Hiraṇyakaśipu murmured to himself, "Lord Viṣṇu, who has great mystic power, has made this plan to kill me, but what's the use? Who can fight with me?"

Taking up his club, Hiraṇyakaśipu attacked the Lord like an elephant. But in the Lord's blinding effulgence, the king of the demons became invisible, just as a small insect falls into a fire and is not seen. This wasn't astonishing, for the Lord's effulgence illuminates the entire universe during creation.

Hiraṇyakaśipu was not deterred. He beat the Lord with his club. But Lord Nṛsiṁhadeva held him up just as Garuḍa captures a snake. Then the Lord let the demon slip from His hands.

Mahārāja Yudhiṣṭhira, who had been hearing the story from Nārada Muni all this time, sat up erect with his eyes opened wide and his hand to his chest.

Nārada Muni said, "O Yudhiṣṭhira, the demigods, who had been watching from behind the clouds, were anxious. They knew that if Hiraṇyakaśipu escaped, he would take revenge on them.

"But the Lord cannot be fooled, O son of Bharata. Hiraṇyakaśipu was the foolish one. He thought that the Lord was afraid of him and had let him go. So he relaxed for a few moments, and then took up his sword and shield to attack the Lord again.

"Lord Nṛsiṁhadeva's loud and shrill

laughter pierced the universe. The Lord captured Hiraṇyakaśipu again, but the demon managed to free himself and move with the speed of a hawk, sometimes in the sky and sometimes on the ground. The demon king closed his eyes, fearing the Lord's laughter, and defended himself with his sword and shield, leaving no exposure to the Lord.

"Then, just as a snake captures a mouse or as Garuḍa captures a venomous snake, Lord Nṛsiṁhadeva captured Hiraṇyakaśipu, who could not be pierced even by Indra's thunderbolt. Hiraṇyakaśipu struggled to set himself free, waving his arms and legs, but Lord Nṛsiṁhadeva placed the demon on His lap. Supporting Hiraṇyakaśipu with His thighs, and in the doorway of the assembly hall, when it was neither day nor night, the Lord tore the demon's abdomen open with His sharp nails."

"The Lord kept all of Lord Brahmā's benedictions intact!" exclaimed Yudhiṣṭhira Mahārāja.

Nodding, Nārada Muni continued, "Lord Nṛsiṁhadeva's mouth and mane were sprinkled with blood, and it was impossible to look at His fierce eyes. He licked the edge of His mouth with His tongue and made a garland for Himself with Hiraṇyakaśipu's intestines. He looked like a lion who had just killed an elephant.

"The Supreme Personality of Godhead, with His many arms, first uprooted Hiraṇyakaśipu's heart, and then with His nails He killed Hiraṇyakaśipu's demon soldiers and followers who were trying to attack Him with their weapons.

"The demigods' airplanes were thrown into outer space by the hair on Nṛsiṁhadeva's head, the earth appeared to slip from its position because of the pressure of the Lord's lotus feet, and the hills and mountains sprang up because of His intolerable force. The Lord's bodily effulgence diminished the light of the sky and all surroundings.

"Lord Nṛsiṁhadeva growled, His eyes still burning in fury. Finding no contestant to face Him, He sat on the king's throne. No one was brave enough to approach the Lord and serve Him directly. The demigods' wives showered flowers from heaven upon the Lord, and the demigods' airplanes crowded the sky. They beat drums and kettledrums and sang the Lord's glories, celebrating His victory."

Nārada then described all the demigods and celestial beings who had come to see this unique form of the Lord. They approached Lord Nṛsiṁhadeva, who glowed brilliantly.

One by one, they offered their obeisances and prayers, their hands folded at their heads:

Lord Brahmā prayed:
O unlimited, omnipotent Lord, obeisances to You
With the material energy You always interact
The universe You create, maintain, and destroy
But You remain pure and the same, that is a fact

Lord Śiva prayed:
The time for Your anger is not now
Here's Prahlāda, Your surrendered devotee by far
Now that his father has been killed
Protect him, affectionate as You naturally are

King Indra said:
O Supreme deliverer and protector,
You've reclaimed our share of sacrifice
You've dissipated the gloom in our hearts
For Your devotees, material opulence will never suffice

One by one, the saints and celestials approached the Lord with heartfelt prayers: the *sādhus*, the Pitṛs, the Siddhas, the Vidyādharas, the Nāgas, the Manus, the prajāpatis, the Gandharvas, the Cāraṇas, the Yakṣas, the Kimpuruṣas, the Vaitālikas, and the Kinnaras.

Finally, Lord Viṣṇu's associates from Vaikuṇṭha came forward and prayed:

O Lord Nṛsiṁha, our supreme shelter,
Your wondrous form good fortune brings
To the whole world, even a demon
Who was filled with envy and despicable things

He was Jaya in Vaikuṇṭha
Cursed by *brāhmaṇas* and down he fell
Come to fight You by Your desire
To act as Your enemy, now we know well
Jaya and Vijaya had a choice
To take seven births as Your friend or three as Your enemy
But the latter they did choose
So they got Your special mercy

Themes and Key Messages

Please go through this table of themes and key messages, with corresponding verses, and discuss each topic further.

THEMES	REFERENCES	KEY MESSAGES
One's preaching is effective when one follows the instructions of a bona fide spiritual master and is serious and sincere in Kṛṣṇa consciousness.	7.8.1–2	If you try to sincerely understand the discourses given by pure devotees, you will find them very pleasing. In this way, Prahlāda's friends became convinced of Prahlāda's instructions. And Prahlāda's preaching was effective because he heard his *guru's* instructions and followed them perfectly. So the preacher and the hearer have to be sincere and serious to progress spiritually.
When one mistreats great souls, one's lifespan, possessions, and good fortune are all destroyed.	7.8.3–4	Because of Hiraṇyakaśipu's mistreatment of a pure devotee, he was destroyed and lost everything. So we should be careful to always treat Vaiṣṇavas with love and respect and see them as very dear to the Supreme Personality of Godhead.
A devotee is never afraid because he fully surrenders to Kṛṣṇa's lotus feet and is thus always protected by the Lord.	7.8.6–8	Prahlāda did not claim to be powerful as Hiraṇyakaśipu did, and yet he was fearless of Hiraṇyakaśipu, whose anger made the three worlds tremble. This is because Prahlāda was fully surrendered to and dependent on Kṛṣṇa and was confident of the Lord's protection in all dangerous conditions. All power and strength come from the Lord just as all kinds of fire emit heat and light, which come from the sun, so Prahlāda's strength and power came from His faith in the Lord.
One who conquers the six internal enemies and is equal to all does not have enemies.	7.8.9–10	Prahlāda advised his father that if he controlled his mind, including conquering the six enemies – lust, anger, greed, illusion, madness, and jealousy – he would not have enemies. Only a person in ignorance imagines that he has enemies, whereas a Kṛṣṇa conscious person knows there are no external enemies but only those within himself, the uncontrolled mind and senses.
In all circumstances the devotee can see the Lord whereas nondevotees cannot.	7.8.12–13	The Lord is never manifest to the foolish and unintelligent, for He is covered by *yogamāyā*, His internal energy. Only the devotees can see Kṛṣṇa because they have genuine love for Him and can thus see Him everywhere. Therefore, Prahlāda was able to see the Lord everywhere, even in a pillar, and was unafraid of his father's threats.

THEMES	REFERENCES	KEY MESSAGES
Lord Nṛsiṁhadeva appears on earth to protect His devotees and annihilate the demons because of His love for His devotees.	7.8.40–54	The demigods and the inhabitants of the various heavenly planets praised the Lord and thanked Him for protecting them and relieving them of their distress. Demons like Hiraṇyakaśipu can be powerful only for a certain time, but the obedient servants of the Lord remain powerful and are always victorious over the influence of the demons by the grace of the Supreme Lord. The Lord appears on earth to protect His devotees and destroy the demons who harass His devotees. In this way, He shows love for His devotees and at the same time awakens their appreciation and love for Him.

Higher-Thinking Questions

Now try to deepen your understanding of this chapter by delving into Śrīla Prabhupāda's purports and reflecting on the following questions:

1. In verse 5 Hiraṇyakaśipu insults Prahlāda with harsh words. Summarize, according to the purport, how his words could've meant the opposite.
2. Why did Kṛṣṇa ask Arjuna to declare that His devotee never perishes? (See verse 6 purport.)
3. Although Hiraṇyakaśipu was a demon, why was he fortunate? (Refer to verse 11 purport.)
4. Demons declare that they cannot accept the existence of God because they cannot see Him. Why doesn't the Lord manifest Himself to such people? Who can see the Lord, and why?
5. In verse 12 Hiraṇyakaśipu calls Prahlāda "unfortunate." Why did he consider his son unfortunate, and why was Prahlāda actually fortunate?
6. What did the Lord prove to the demons and the world when He appeared from the pillar? (See verse 17 purport.)
7. Lord Nṛsiṁhadeva let Hiraṇyakaśipu slip from His hands and made him think he had won. In the same way, why does the Lord sometimes let a sinful man enjoy as if he were not under the clutches of material nature, as mentioned by Śrīla Prabhupāda in verse 27 purport?
8. In verse 31 purport, what warning does Śrīla Prabhupāda give to the godless civilization in which we exist?
9. According to verse 34 purport, why did Lord Nṛsiṁhadeva sit upon Hiraṇyakaśipu's throne, even though he was a demon?

10. Why was Lord Śiva, unlike the other demigods, unafraid of the Lord's anger? (Refer to verse 41 purport.)

11. The Lord could've protected His devotees and destroyed the demons by His external energy. Why do you think the Lord appeared Himself to do this? [Hint: What did the Lord instill in His devotees when they themselves saw His prowess, divine form, and His act of saving them?]

ACTIVITIES

In this section you will find many exciting things to do. These activities will get you thinking, moving, drawing, and having loads of fun.

Analogy Activity

... to bring out the scholar in you

CURING THE UNIVERSAL MENINGITIS

Verse 35 describes Hiraṇyakaśipu as the "meningitis" of the universe. Meningitis is a disease that causes fever, cold palms and feet, and confusion, among other symptoms. It cripples the functioning of the body. Let us study the ways in which Hiraṇyakaśipu crippled the inhabitants of the universe and understand how the Lord restored them.

Look at verses 36 to 55 and fill out the speech bubbles from each of the demigods. The first blank indicates the problem ("fever") Hiraṇyakaśipu created, and the second blank indicates the solution ("medicine") brought about by the Lord.

Dear Lord, I faced a problem of ___________, and Your killing Hiraṇyakaśipu has made it easy for me to ___________.

Lord Brahmā (40)

Lord Śiva (41)

Indra (42)

Sages (43)

Pitṛs (44)

Siddhas (45)

Kinnaras (55)

Based on the above statements, what do you think the analogy tries to teach us about how we should react (what "medicine" to take) during calamities ("fever")?

Artistic Activity

... to reveal your creativity

POINTILLISM ART: SEEING THE LORD EVERYWHERE

Prahlāda saw the Lord everywhere, even in a pillar. The pure devotees perceive the presence of the Lord everywhere; they do not see anything separate from the Lord. Lord Kṛṣṇa says in *Bhagavad-gītā* 9.4, "By Me, in My unmanifested form, this entire universe is pervaded."

In this activity, we will use the pointillism style of painting to illustrate the above-stated principle. In this technique, small strokes or dots of color are applied to a surface such that from a distance they visually blend to reveal the subject of the painting.

Materials: Small canvas or card stock paper; pencil; few acrylic or watercolor paints; 3 small brushes, sizes 1, 2, 4; water; rag to clean the brush; thick paper to practice the art sample.

Steps:

1. On the thick paper draw the throne and pillar in Hiraṇyakaśipu's assembly hall lightly with a pencil (image 1).

Image 1

2. Start adding the lighter colors by applying the paint in small dots or strokes with the tip of the brush (image 2).

3. Add the darker colors once the light colors have dried (image 3).

4. Once you are comfortable with the color application, follow the above steps to illustrate Lord Nṛsiṁhadeva's appearance from the pillar. You can trace the picture from the story summary or draw your own composition.

Image 2

Image 3

Action Activity

... to get you moving and learning

OVERCOMING THE FEAR OF DEATH

Prahlāda did not fear death because he had fully realized that he was a spirit soul that could not be harmed by anything material.

The following is a song by George Harrison, from the famous Beatles, about death, our worst fear. George was a serious follower of Śrīla Prabhupāda and his teachings. You can play the song from the internet and sing along with it. You can also learn it and give a performance at a school function or temple program. Discuss the main points of this song. Use the questions to guide your discussion.

THE ART OF DYING

by George Harrison

There'll come a time when all of us must leave here
Then nothing sister Mary can do
Will keep me here with you
As nothing in this life that I've been trying
Could equal or surpass the art of dying
Do you believe me?

There'll come a time when all your hopes are fading
When things that seemed so very plain
Become an awful pain
Searching for the truth among the lying
And answered when you've learned the art of dying

But you're still with me
But if you want it
Then you must find it
But when you have it
There'll be no need for it

There'll come a time when most of us return here
Brought back by our desire to be
A perfect entity
Living through a million years of crying
Until you've realized the art of dying
Do you believe me?

1. Why do you think George and even Śrīla Prabhupāda referred to death as an art?
2. Why is there nothing more important than learning this art as mentioned in the first stanza?
3. How can you learn the art of dying? (Hint: Refer to second stanza.)
4. What were George's personal thoughts about dying?
5. The last paragraph gives us the gist of Kṛṣṇa consciousness. Can you explain how?
6. How does the art of dying involve overcoming our fear of death?

Introspective Activity

... to bring out the reflective devotee in you

CIRCLE OF CONTROL

Let's learn practically how to alleviate our fears and anxieties by focusing on our circle of influence, or control, rather on things that we have little or no control over.

1. List the things, people, incidents, etc., that you are afraid of. Think of when you were really scared and when someone helped you overcome your fear.
2. The circle below is your **circle of control**. Outside the circle is the area over which you have no or little control. To the circle add all the things that are within your control and outside the circle add those that are out of your control. Usually, we are more scared of things which we have no control over. Some examples are given to guide you. Try to add more such items to understand what you fear and what you don't.
3. Then discuss with your class how ultimately dependence on Kṛṣṇa and taking shelter of Him can help eliminate all kinds of fear and anxiety, within and out of your control.

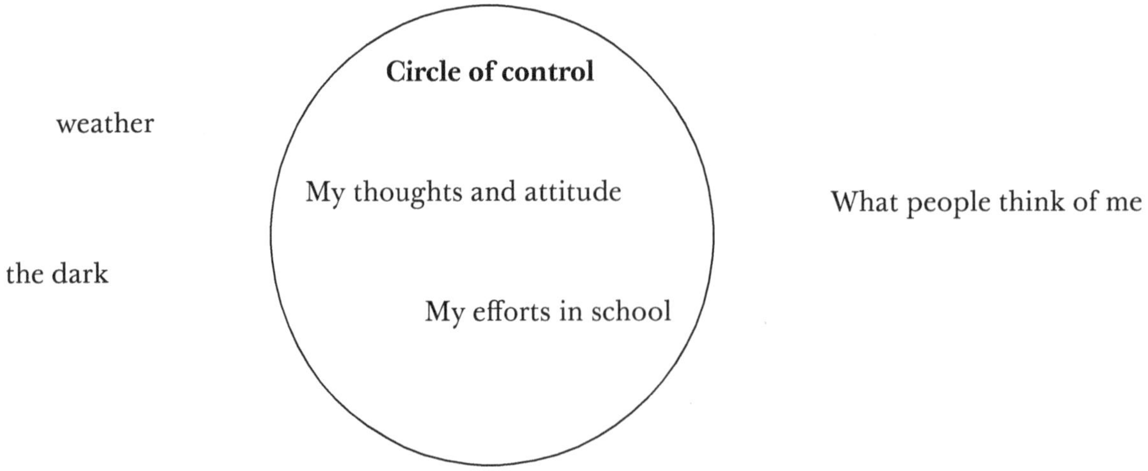

Critical-Thinking Activity

... to bring out the spiritual investigator in you

THE LORD PROTECTS, PUTS DOWN, AND PRESERVES

Let us analyze the Lord's killing of Hiraṇyakaśipu a little more in this chapter. In the *Bhagavad-gītā*, the Lord states three purposes for His descent in every millennium (*BG* 4.8): *paritrāṇāya sādhūnāṁ* (to deliver the pious), *vināśāya ca duṣkṛtām* (to annihilate the miscreants), *dharma-saṁsthāpanārthāya* (to re-establish the principles of religion). Lord Nṛsiṁhadeva accomplished all three goals by killing Hiraṇyakaśipu.

In the resources is a Mission Model diagram that demonstrates how this one act achieved these three missions and what were their impact on the world.

Directions:

- Photocopy the Mission Model in the Resource section and paste it on a cardboard. Attach the needle (pointer) in the middle using a pin. Make sure the needle is moving freely around the wheel when spun.
- Sit around the spinner, keeping it in the center of the table. Take turns to spin the needle. Wherever the needle stops, read the label on the outer circle. Then go inwards, reading the inner labels, till you reach the innermost label. Explain how all the tags are related, and comment how it changed the world at that time. For example, if the spinner stops on "Prahlāda," you could say: By killing the demon Hiraṇyakaśipu (label of the inner circle), Nṛsiṁhadeva delivered the pious Prahlāda (label of middle circle). This shows that the Lord never fails to protect His devotee.
- Spin the spinner till all the outer blocks have been covered once.
- Finally, answer the following questions: How does this Mission Model demonstrate the fair and compassionate nature of the Lord towards all?
- Do you think there are other reasons, besides the ones discussed in this activity, for the Lord's descent? [Hint: The Lord could've used His external energy to protect His devotees and kill the demons.]

Science Activity

... to bring out the spiritual scientist in you

ANCIENT FLYING MACHINES

Verse 33 states that airplanes were thrown into outer space by the hair on Nṛsiṁhadeva's head. In ancient Vedic texts, airplanes called *vimānas* are mentioned. Here are some of the *vimānas* you may have come across:

Puṣpaka-*vimāna*: the airplane made of flowers that brought Rāma back to Ayodhya after exile

Vaikuṇṭha-*vimāna*: the airplane that was sent to bring Dhruva back to Viṣṇu's abode

Kardama's *vimāna*: Kardama Muni created a flying city to please his wife

Śālva's *vimāna*: Śālva attacked the city of Dvārakā on a wonderful disappearing airplane

There are many other *vimānas* mentioned in Vedic texts. Vimāna-*śāstra* is a Vedic text that describes the detailed science behind how these *vimānas* are constructed, much like aerospace technology describes how modern airplanes are constructed.

Browse the internet for information about *vimānas*. Make five small flash cards of what you learned. Present it to the class.

Note to facilitator: The above activity is kept simple and generic to facilitate different types of learners who can go to different depths in their research.

Writing and Language Activities

... to help you understand better

PREACHING LIKE PRAHLĀDA

For knowledge to be transmitted effectively, the preacher must be sincere and serious in Kṛṣṇa consciousness and the hearer also should be sincere and serious to hear.

As preachers, think of three to five individuals whom you know are interested in Kṛṣṇa consciousness but are not following the path strictly yet. Consider which aspects of Kṛṣṇa consciousness they would appreciate depending on their natures. By liking or appreciating

something in Kṛṣṇa consciousness – be it *kīrtana*, *prasādam*, philosophy, the Deities, the temples, the Lord's pastimes, etc., – they gain *sukṛti*, pious credits. Only when they attain enough *sukṛti* will they gain faith and thus take up the process.

For each individual, devise a strategy that would help them appreciate and like some aspect of Kṛṣṇa consciousness. Describe the strategy briefly for each of the three to five individuals.

For example:

1. My school friend: He plays the drums and he loves percussion instruments. I will bring him to the temple whenever talented *kīrtaniyas* visit so that he will appreciate the *kīrtanas*. I will also introduce him to my devotee friends who play the *mṛdaṅga* well. He will love them too.

Once you've devised your plan, now carry it out.

If they become devotees, you should know that your strategy of helping them appreciate Kṛṣṇa consciousness was the first step in making them follow the path. You should also know that they had some sincerity and seriousness to pursue spiritual life in the first place. Śrīla Prabhupāda always encouraged his preachers to fan the spark of Kṛṣṇa consciousness in a sincere seeker.

RAP: YOUR ONE TRUE ENEMY

Below is an incomplete rap battle between Hiraṇyakaśipu and Prahlāda Mahārāja consisting of five stanzas.

Complete a modern retelling of this pastime by writing three more stanzas using verses 10, 12, 13, and 17. The first two lines of stanza six have been written for you, or you can choose to write your own version of the pastime. Your lyrics must end with the appearance of Lord Nṛsiṁhadeva.

Directions:

- Hiraṇyakaśipu is described as cruel while Prahlāda was peaceful, mild, gentle, and in control of his senses. Your rap lyrics should reflect this.
- There are a few persuasive techniques you can use to construct rap battle lyrics, such as exaggeration, rhetorical questions, repetition, alliteration, and the rule of three. Include at least two of these methods in your work (see hints at the end of this activity). Remember in a rap not every line needs to rhyme.

- You can practice your rap aloud expressively and rhythmically using body movement, clapping, and costumes. A Sunday program performance of the rap may be a good idea.

Boy, you're a fool, uncool, an absolute clown
Listen up, I'll tell you how it's going down
You messed with the wrong dad
'Cos all three worlds know I'm bad
I rule you, control you
Wouldn't wanna be you
Whose power allows this
Blatant defiance?

Oh, father, now hear me
The source of your strength is the source of mine
For everyone it's Viṣṇu. That nobody can deny
He powers the body, the mind, the senses, and time
He's unlimited, unstoppable, and controls the modes
He creates, preserves, and destroys these abodes

Boy, do you think you're all that?
No, hear me, obey me or I'll lay you down flat

I beg you, father, the time is late
So please, please give up this fate
Enemies and friends, see them as one or you'll fall behind
Your one true enemy is your mind.
Control it, enslave it, tell it who's boss
And maybe, just maybe, you can avoid a loss.

Boy, you're not better than me at all
Now my time has come 'cos I'm gonna make you fall

Father, I told you, I told you, and I'll tell you again
You must beat the six enemies within . . .

Hints:

Exaggeration: Giving information that is over the top or slightly untrue. For example, in line one Hiraṇyakaśipu calls Prahlāda "an absolute clown."

Rhetorical question: A question that doesn't require a response from the reader/listener. It engages the reader quickly, because as readers/listeners we like to feel involved, and allows us to think more personally about the topic. In stanza three Hiraṇyakaśipu says, "Boy, do you think you're all that?" not needing a response from Prahlāda or the listener.

Repetition: When words or phrases are repeated so they stick in one's mind.

In stanza six Prahlāda says, "I told you, I told you."

The rule of three: It's a storytelling principle that suggests a group of three words, phrases, or ideas that are more engaging, effective, and memorable. Things presented to us in clusters of three seem to stick in our minds better. For example, in stanza four Prahlāda says "control it, enslave it, tell it who's boss," reminding us how important it is to control the mind.

Alliteration: Repeating the consonant sounds at the beginning of words to make them stand out. In the first stanza Hiraṇyakaśipu says, "Wouldn't wanna."

THE SIX INTERNAL ENEMIES

Prahlāda Mahārāja advised Hiraṇyakaśipu to conquer the six internal enemies: lust, anger, greed, pride, illusion, and envy, and to control the mind and senses. When one does not control the mind and conquer these internal enemies, one is less likely to be equipoised and thus more likely to create external enemies. Let us see more in detail how they are related.

Materials: 4 glass jars or containers of any kind, plain paper sheets cut into 30 strips for writing, pencil, scissors, black marker, timer

Directions:

1. On the strips of paper, write at least five examples of the different internal enemies of Hiraṇyakaśipu and five instances of his external vision. For example, Hiraṇyakaśipu was in illusion because he forgot he was a servant of Kṛṣṇa and acted as a master. He thought he was the proprietor, controller, and enjoyer of the three worlds, and therefore wanted to subjugate all celestial beings, stop the worship of Viṣṇu, and so on. (See more examples in the answer section if needed.)

2. For Prahlāda Mahārāja, write about six examples of his transcendental knowledge, service, and purified mind. For example, he was aware of his real identity as a servant of Kṛṣṇa, his madness was reflected in his preaching without fear for his life, he was greedy to remember and hear the qualities of the Lord, he was intolerant of ignorance in others and thus loved broadcasting the glories of the Lord and his spiritual master, etc.

3. Lastly, write about six instances of Prahlāda Mahārāja's external vision. For example, he saw the Lord's presence and control everywhere, he had no enemies seeing the Supersoul in everyone's heart, he respected his demoniac father, he saw the futility of material endeavors, etc.

4. Mix all the paper strips.

5. Mark two jars representing Prahlāda Mahārāja's internal mind and the other as his external vision. Similarly, mark the other two for Hiraṇyakaśipu's mind and his vision.

6. Set the timer to five minutes.

7. Now put each strip in the proper jar before the time runs out.

8. In your notebook write two sentences on the correlation between the internal enemies and the external enemies. What does Prahlāda suggest to conquer the internal enemies, the root cause of external enemies, suffering, and dissatisfaction?

PRAYERS BY CELESTIAL BEINGS

After Lord Narahari killed Hiraṇyakaśipu, the demigods and celestial beings approached the Supreme Personality of Godhead with prayers.

The prayers of the primary demigods have already been summarized for you. Now go through the prayers of the rest of the demigods and celestial beings in this chapter.

Select three of your favorite prayers and summarize them in the form of poetic couplets as done in the story summary.

For example:

The sadhus prayed,
Austerity is a part of life
for humans and higher beings
You reestablished this principle
destroyed by the demon king of kings

CHAPTER 8 ANSWERS

Curing the Universal Meningitis

Brahmā: upsetting maintenance of the universe; maintain it peacefully again; Śiva: Prahlāda; protection; Indra: Hiraṇyakaśipu; You; Sages: austerity and penance; approved; Pitṛs: offerings of sesame seeds and water offered during *śrāddha*; stolen property; Siddhas: mystic power; restored it; Kinnaras: Your service; serve You.

Lesson: Calamities or disturbances can disrupt our devotional service due to many reasons (here due to a bad leader), but we should always remain surrendered to the Lord and expect His mercy to tide over it.

Overcoming the Fear of Death

1. Just as one learns how to create or do art, one can learn how to die in the proper way with the ideal consciousness.
2. Whatever we think of at the time of death determines our next destination. If we learn the art of dying, we will die with our minds fixed on Kṛṣṇa and go back to Him instead of returning to the miserable material world.
3. From someone who has realized the art of dying and who will not cheat you – in other words, from a pure devotee.

4. He was waiting with anticipation for death because he knew that the soul was forever and Kṛṣṇa would protect him.
5. The living entity comes back to this material world again and again, living through the 8,400,000 species because of material desires and trying to be "perfect" in material life. In this miserable impermanent world, he finally realizes that he is the spirit soul and not the body. Then he learns the art of dying.
6. When we live a life of full Kṛṣṇa consciousness, we will realize that we are not these temporary material bodies but an eternal spirit soul, which can never be harmed. Fully realizing our spiritual identity and learning to die in full Kṛṣṇa consciousness – in other words, learning the art of dying – we will not fear death because we know that we will reach Kṛṣṇa's lotus feet in the spiritual world.

The Lord Protects, Puts Down, and Preserves

Prahlāda: answer given; Brahmā: By killing Hiraṇyakaśipu, the Lord upheld the words of His devotee Brahmā, even to a demon. This shows that the Lord goes to great lengths to protect His devotees' promises; sages/devotees: By killing Hiraṇyakaśipu, the Lord protected the devotional service of His devotees; demigods: By killing Hiraṇyakaśipu, the Lord delivered His administrative assistants from distress and showed how He protects His devotees; Jaya: By killing Hiraṇyakaśipu, the Lord bestowed special mercy on His devotee, who went to great lengths to serve Him in the mood of chivalry, by liberating him and ultimately returning him to Vaikuṇṭha. This shows that the Lord is kind even to His "enemies"; Hiraṇyakaśipu: By killing Hiraṇyakaśipu, the Lord showed that He does not tolerate offenses against a pure devotee, and one loses one's lifespan, opulence, reputation, religion, possessions, and good fortune when one offends a pure devotee; demons: By killing Hiraṇyakaśipu, the Lord showed that even a person who directly or indirectly supports an offender at the lotus feet of a pure devotee loses one lifespan, opulence, reputation, religion, possessions, and good fortune; pious king: By killing Hiraṇyakaśipu, the Lord helped the kings to uphold and preach devotional principles; Vedic scriptures: By killing Hiraṇyakaśipu, the Lord protected people from going astray from the scriptures, which are meant to elevate themselves from material life; *yajña*: By killing Hiraṇyakaśipu, the Lord reinstated the practice of performing sacrifice, which is meant to please Him; penance: By killing Hiraṇyakaśipu, penance, process of self-purification to attain the Supreme Lord, was practiced again; *varṇāśrama*: By killing Hiraṇyakaśipu, the Lord reestablished the system of division of society, which is meant to please Him and liberate the participants; devotional service: By killing Hiraṇyakaśipu, the Lord showed through His devotee the process by which we can please Him.

Question about the Lord's nature: He naturally protects His devotees, liberates the demons He personally kills, and establishes a system by which common living beings can take to the path of pure devotion and come back to Him. He is therefore kind and compassionate to all.

Question about the internal reason for the Lord's descent: Yes; He desires to protect His devotees Himself just as a father personally protects a child out of love. He also wants to have loving exchanges with His devotees and reciprocate their love. He performs such pastimes to attract conditioned souls to Him.

The Six Internal Enemies

Examples:

Illusion: One forgets that they are servants of Kṛṣṇa but acts as a master. Hiraṇyakaśipu thought he was the proprietor, controller, and enjoyer of the three worlds and therefore wanted to subjugate all celestial beings, stop the worship of Viṣṇu, and so on.

Madness/pride: One forgets that Kṛṣṇa is the source of all opulence and strength and feels oneself as an independent entity possessing great strength and opulence. Hiraṇyakaśipu became mad after sensual pleasure and having power over people.

Envy: Hiraṇyakaśipu was envious of the Lord and all living entities. He did not accept the supreme position of Lord Viṣṇu and he did not see the living beings as parts and parcel of Kṛṣṇa and worthy of his respect and service. Rather he blasphemed the Lord and exploited and mistreated all kinds of living entities, including his own son Prahlāda Mahārāja.

Lust: Desire of anything to satisfy one's own senses. It is the opposite of love where the spirit soul desires to please the senses of Lord Kṛṣṇa. Hiraṇyakaśipu desired longevity, unrivaled rulership, and opulence, and even wanted to be worshiped as God. Anyone who didn't support his desires became his enemy.

Anger: When desires are unfulfilled, it leads to anger. Hiraṇyakaśipu was cruel to those who interfered with his enjoyment. The demigods, Gandharvas, Siddhas, etc., all experienced his wrath.

Greed: When lust is fulfilled, greed develops. Hiraṇyakaśipu was never satiated and hankered for more. He thus took over the throne of Indra and created enemies with the demigods.

RESOURCE FOR CRITICAL-THINKING ACTIVITY

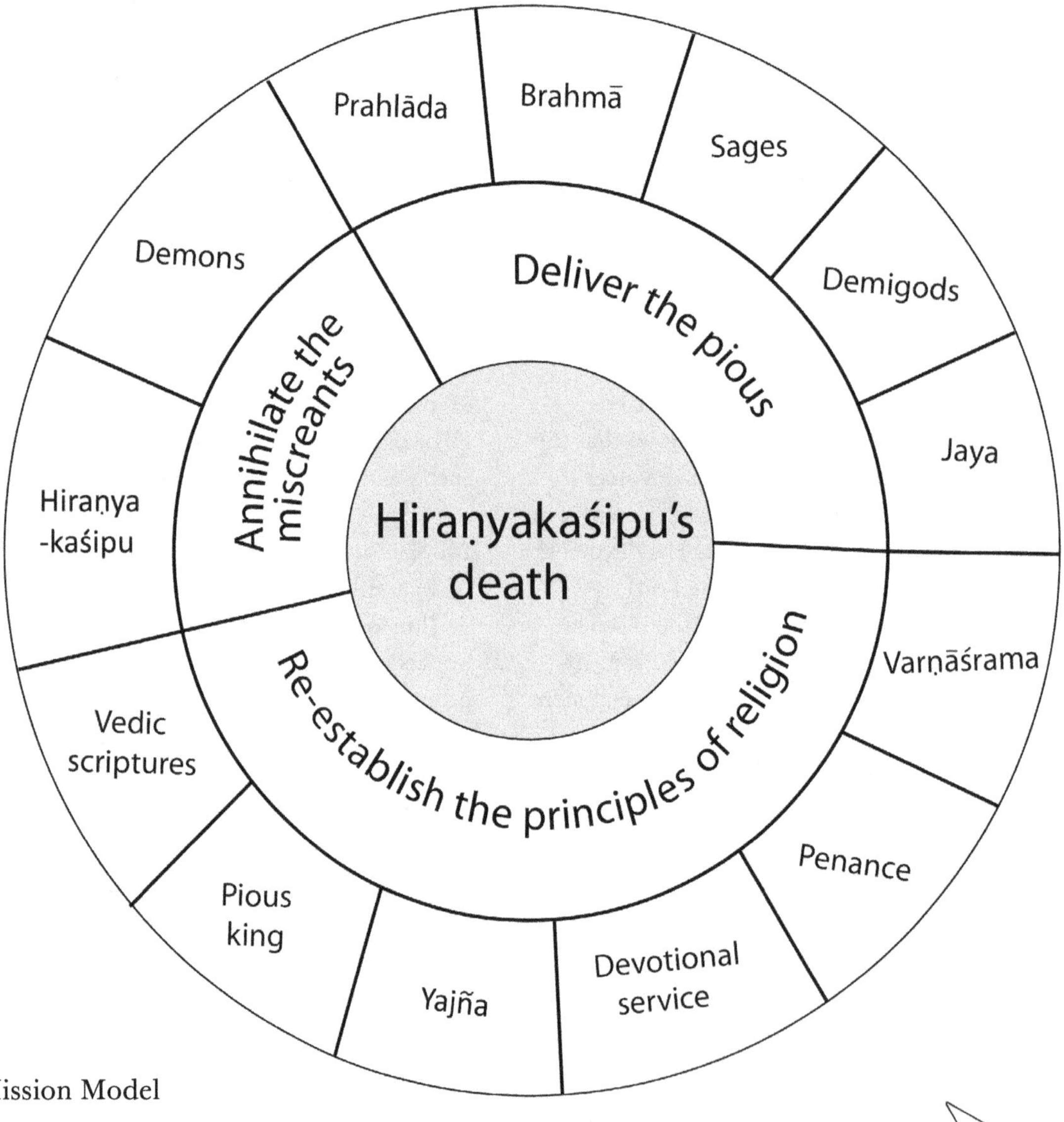

Mission Model

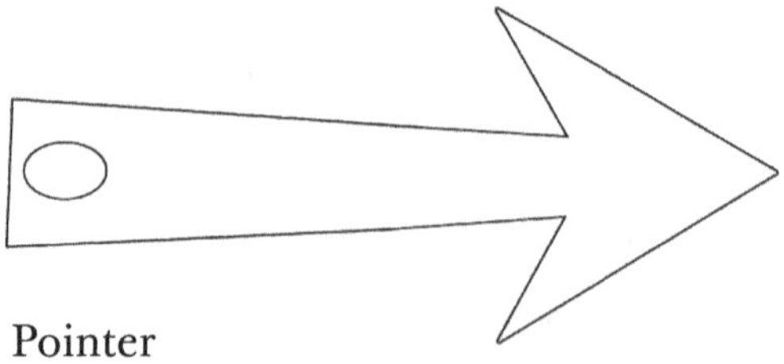

Pointer

9

PRAHLĀDA PACIFIES THE LORD WITH PRAYERS

Story Summary

Lord Nṛsiṁhadeva bared His teeth and roared. Clearly, the demigods' prayers had not pacified His anger. Lord Brahmā signaled to Lakṣmīdevī to go forward and pacify the Lord, but she just shrugged. She couldn't understand this extraordinary form of her Lord.

"My dear boy," Lord Brahmā told Prahlāda, "Lord Nṛsiṁhadeva is still furious at your demoniac father. Please go and appease Him."

Prahlāda slowly inched forward and then fell flat at the Lord's lotus feet. Lord Nṛsiṁhadeva's growl turned to a gentle purring. He raised Prahlāda and placed His hand on the boy's head. That lotus hand always takes away all fear in His devotees. And when that hand touched Prahlāda's head, the boy could not contain his love for the Lord anymore. Tears poured from his eyes and his heart fluttered in divine madness. He felt as if he had had an internal bath – his heart was cleansed of any last specks of material contamination. Glancing at the Lord's lotus feet, Prahlāda embraced them in the core of his heart.

Then, Prahlāda stared at Lord Nṛsiṁhadeva,

transfixed by His beauty, while the Lord stroked his head. With a faltering voice, Prahlāda began offering beautiful prayers: "How can someone like me, born in an *asura* family, offer suitable prayers to please You? Even all the highly qualified demigods, who are in the mode of goodness, couldn't satisfy You with their excellent words. So what can You expect of me? I am most unqualified."

The Lord purred again, appreciating His devotee's humility and meekness.

"No one can satisfy You by any material means, even if one possesses the greatest wealth, education, beauty, intelligence, strength, austerity, and mystic powers," Prahlāda continued. "You are only pleased by devotional service; this is for certain. Even the mighty elephant Gajendra could only satisfy the Lord by pure devotion.

"A *brāhmaṇa* who is not Your devotee is lower than a devotee who is a dog-eater. Such a devotee is better than any so-called *brāhmaṇa* because the devotee can purify his entire family, whereas a proud *brāhmaṇa* cannot even purify himself."

The demigods looked at each other, speechless. They could not believe the bold words coming from this young boy.

"O my Lord, You are fully satisfied in Yourself. You don't need service from anyone. But You accept our offerings just for our benefit. Such is Your mercy. But unfortunately, those who are grossly foolish do not surrender to You. Then how can human society benefit?

"Therefore, although I was born in a demoniac family, I will offer prayers to You with all my heart and as much as my intelligence would allow. Anyone in this material world can become purified just by offering prayers to You and hearing Your glories."

Glancing at Lord Brahmā, Prahlāda continued, "The demigods, headed by Lord Brahmā, are not like me or my father. They are Your sincere servants. You've come in this fearsome form just to protect devotees like them and vanquish the demons who disrupt the universe. This is Your pastime for Your own pleasure.

"So, my dear Lord Nṛsiṁhadeva, please give up your anger, now that You've killed my father. All the worlds are rejoicing the death of this demon, for even saintly persons take pleasure in the killing of a scorpion or snake. Now everyone is confident about their happiness, and they will always remember Your auspicious incarnation that has freed them from all fear."

Lovingly glancing at the Lord's face, Prahlāda continued, "O my Lord, I'm not afraid of Your ferocious mouth and tongue, Your bright eyes, frowning eyebrows, or sharp nails. I don't fear Your sharp teeth, Your garland of intestines, or Your blood-soaked mane, nor do I fear Your tumultuous roaring, which makes even elephants flee. O insurmountable, compassionate Lord, I'm only afraid of my condition of life in this material world. When will You call me to the shelter of Your lotus feet, the goal of liberation?"

Wiping away his tears, Prahlāda continued, "People are suffering in this world, within heavenly or hellish planets. They try many remedies to remove their miseries, but alas, such remedies in the material world are more miserable than the miseries themselves, for one has to accept so many miseries to come to a 'better' situation.

The only remedy is to engage in Your service. Please instruct me in such service."

Lord Nṛsiṁhadeva purred again and gazed at Prahlāda, urging him to continue.

"O my Lord Nṛsiṁhadeva, I can become completely purified from the three modes of nature just by serving You in the association of Your swanlike, liberated devotees. In their association I will be able to chant Your glories, following in the footsteps of Lord Brahmā and his disciplic succession. Certainly, in this way I shall cross over this ocean of darkness.

"My Lord Nṛsiṁhadeva, anyone who is not cared for by You cannot do anything for their improvement. Their remedies are only temporary. For example, parents cannot protect their children, a doctor and medicine cannot relieve a suffering patient, and a boat cannot protect a drowning man. Everyone, from Lord Brahmā down to the small ant, is controlled by Your energy. Everything that we do is under Your control. So the best remedy for suffering humanity is to remember You and receive Your mercy.

"My Lord, people are entrapped by your external energy. They try to fulfill their material desires by following the *karma-kāṇḍa* section of the *Vedas*. But this is mere entanglement. Unless one takes shelter of Your lotus feet, there is no possibility of getting free of this entanglement.

"O Supreme transcendent Lord, time represents You. No one can conquer You. However, I am being crushed by the wheel of time, so I surrender fully to You. Now kindly take me under the protection of Your lotus feet."

Lord Nṛsiṁhadeva seemed to smile. The demigods were beaming, proud of this little boy's surrender, humility, and love for the Lord.

With tear-stained eyes, Prahlāda continued, "My dear Lord, people want to be elevated to the higher planetary systems to gain opulence, a long life, and increased enjoyment, but I've seen all this through the life of my father. When he was angry and laughed sarcastically at the demigods, they were immediately vanquished just by seeing the movements of his eyebrows. Yet, my powerful father has now been vanquished by You in a moment!"

"Jaya!" shouted some of the demigods. They felt elated hearing the Lord's glories from the lips of this elevated boy.

"My dear Lord, I have complete experience of worldly opulence and material pleasures. But as powerful time You destroy them all. So I don't wish for these things. I only wish that You put me in touch with Your pure devotee and make me serve him as a sincere servant.

"Everyone in this material world wants happiness, but it's like a mirage in a desert. Where is water in a desert, or should I say, where is there happiness in this material world? Moreover, what is the value of this body? It's just a source of various diseases. But still, everyone aspires for temporary happiness. Even though this happiness is hard to get, they still run after it unable to control their senses, and so they never come to the right conclusion."

Prahlāda looked around at the demigods whose eyes were glued to him and

Lord Nṛsiṁhadeva. He bowed his head to them and then to the Lord and said, "O Supreme Lord, because I was born in a family of demons, what is my position? And what is to be said of Your mercy to me? You didn't put Your lotus hand upon the heads of the demigods, yet You've put it upon mine.

"For You there is no such thing as higher and lower; You offer benedictions according to the level of Your devotee's service. O my Lord, because of my association of material desires one after another, I was gradually falling into a blind well of snakes, just like everyone else. But Your servant Nārada Muni kindly accepted me as his disciple and instructed me in devotional service. My first duty is to serve him. How can I leave his service?

"O my Lord, You've saved me from my father's sword. He challenged me that if there is a supreme controller as I had mentioned, let Him save me. So I think that just to prove true the words of Your devotee, You've saved me and killed him."

Prahlāda continued to glorify the Lord with poetic prayers, describing how the Lord is the source of the entire cosmos and how everything exists through His energies. He described the Lord's role as Kāraṇodakaśāyī Viṣṇu and how as Garbhodakaśāyī Viṣṇu He created Lord Brahmā from the lotus of His abdomen. Lord Brahmā achieved divine bliss just by finally seeing the Lord's form. Prahlāda then glorified the Lord's various incarnations, which are meant to protect His devotees and destroy the demons who destroy religious principles.

Finally, Prahlāda said, "O best of great personalities, I'm not afraid of this material existence because wherever I am, I am fully absorbed in You. I am only concerned for the fools and rascals who are making elaborate plans to enjoy. I am concerned out of love for them.

"My dear Lord Nṛsiṁhadeva, I see that there are many saintly persons, but they are only concerned with their own deliverance. They go to the Himālayas and the forest to meditate with vows of silence. They are not interested in delivering others. But I do not want to be liberated alone. I know that without Kṛṣṇa consciousness no one can be happy, so I want to bring them back to Your lotus feet.

"*Gṛhamedhis* want to just enjoy sex life, so they repeatedly suffer, while those who are *dhīra*, or sober, tolerate material desires and do not suffer like these fools and rascals. Wise men do not bother themselves with Vedic study; they just engage in practical devotional service. Therefore, my Lord, I offer my respectful obeisances to You. By rendering six kinds of devotional service to

You – offering prayers, dedicating the results of activities to You, worshiping You, working on Your behalf, always remembering You, and hearing Your glories – we can achieve the stage of the *paramahaṁsa*, the most exalted soul."

Again Prahlāda offered his prostrated obeisances and then kneeled with folded palms before the Lord.

Lord Nṛsiṁhadeva had given up His anger. He laid His gentle eyes on Prahlāda and spoke:

"My dear Prahlāda, most gentle one, best of the family of *asuras*, I am very pleased with you. No one can understand Me without pleasing Me. And one who pleases Me no longer has to lament for his material condition.

"My dear boy, My pastime is to fulfill the desires of every living being, so ask from Me any benediction and I shall fulfill it."

Prahlāda smiled as he stared at the Lord. Seeing the Lord face to face was the fulfillment of all his desires. How could he want anything else?

Themes and Key Messages

Please go through this table of themes and key messages, with corresponding verses, and discuss each topic further.

THEMES	REFERENCES	KEY MESSAGES
One becomes fearless when one is in Kṛṣṇa consciousness – absorbed in Lord Nṛsiṁhadeva.	7.9.1–5	No one could approach Lord Nṛsiṁhadeva, fearing His angry form. But Prahlāda was unafraid because he had obtained the special mercy of Lord Nṛsiṁhadeva. The Lord touched his head, manifesting symptoms of ecstasy in Prahlāda's body. The hand of Lord Nṛsiṁhadeva creates fearlessness in all His devotees, because He assures them of His protection. Therefore, a devotee's hope of becoming fearless is to chant the names of Lord Nṛsiṁhadeva and to always think of Him.
The Lord is not pleased by any material qualification. He is only pleased by pure devotion.	7.9.6–10	Although Prahlāda was born in a demoniac family, he was cleansed of all bodily contamination because of his exalted position as a devotee. Prahlāda Mahārāja realized that one cannot satisfy the Lord by any material qualification but only by devotional service. Even a devotee born in a low family of dog-eaters is greater than a *brāhmaṇa* who has all brahminical qualifications but is not a devotee. Prahlāda was also very humble and considered himself unqualified to offer prayers to the Lord. In this way he pleased the Lord. (Gajendra was another example of surrender and devotion who pleased the Lord despite his bodily disqualifications.)

THEMES	REFERENCES	KEY MESSAGES
Devotional service is meant for the devotee's benefit.	7.9.11–12	The Lord is full in Himself; He doesn't need any service from us. But the more we engage in devotional service, the more we benefit. Kṛṣṇa appears in the material world out of His compassion, to demand our surrender for our benefit. This demand is for the benefit of all human society. By hearing the Lord's glories and offering prayers to Him we are purified of material life.
The devotee takes pleasure in worshiping and glorifying the Lord in any form, whether pleasing or fierce.	7.9.15–16, 37–38	The lion is fearful for all other animals except its own cubs, and the fish in the ocean are unafraid of the mighty ocean although all other land creatures are afraid of it. This is because the small fish have taken shelter of the big ocean. Similarly, the devotee is unafraid of the Lord's fierce form and takes pleasure in glorifying the Lord in such a form because of the greatness of the Lord and His protection. A devotee like Prahlāda Mahārāja is only afraid of conditioned life.
The best remedy to get out of miserable life is to engage in the Lord's service. All protection, temporary or otherwise, is due to the potencies of the Supreme Lord.	7.9.17–20	The remedies in the material world are more miserable than the miseries themselves, because so much endeavor goes into becoming materially happy. In material life, whether one is happy or miserable, both conditions are miserable. If one wants a truly blissful life, one must constantly engage in the Lord's loving service and chant His holy names in the association of advanced devotees. Material remedies are temporarily beneficial, just as parents cannot protect their child, a physician cannot relieve a suffering patient, and a boat cannot protect a drowning man. Even if one thinks himself protected by one's parents or any other cause, everything is due to the Lord's potencies.
Only surrender to the Lord's lotus feet awards protection from the wheel of time and the desires for material enjoyment.	7.9.21–25, 28	The Lord has created this material world to fulfill our desires to enjoy separately from Him. In this way we are crushed by the wheel of time, in repeated birth and death. Powerful time doesn't allow us to enjoy forever. Therefore, Prahlāda didn't wish to possess opulence and power, which are all temporary and illusory, like a mirage in the desert. He prayed rather to be in touch with a pure devotee, who can show him the way to become truly happy in devotional service. Prahlāda also prays to be protected from material entanglement, from the desire to enjoy the material world. Only surrender to the lotus feet of the Lord can protect us from and destroy material desires.

THEMES	REFERENCES	KEY MESSAGES
A pure Vaiṣṇava prays not only for himself but for the deliverance of all living beings suffering in the material world.	39–50	A Vaiṣṇava, like Prahlāda, is extremely compassionate and prays for the benefit of all conditioned souls who are trying to enjoy in the material world. He understands that bhakti is the only refuge, and therefore feels great unhappiness for the fools, the *gṛhamedhis,* who make elaborate plans to be happy in this world. He prays for their deliverance and admits that he doesn't want to be liberated alone.

Higher-Thinking Questions

Now try to deepen your understanding of this chapter by delving into Śrīla Prabhupāda's purports and reflecting on the following questions:

1. Although one should try to get rid of the six internal enemies, as explained in the last chapter, Narottama dāsa Ṭhākura says that they all have their proper use. Referring to verse 1 purport, explain how anger should be used, as done by Lord Nṛsiṁhadeva Himself.
2. Why wasn't Lord Nṛsiṁhadeva's form extraordinary for Prahlāda Mahārāja? (See verse 2 purport.)
3. In his purport to verse 10, Śrīla Prabhupāda mentions that this verse applies to the European and American devotees in Kṛṣṇa consciousness. Explain, according to Śrīla Prabhupāda, how these devotees are more exalted than caste *brāhmaṇas* born in *brāhmaṇa* families.
4. Although saintly persons never desire the killing of any living being, why is a devotee happy when an envious person, like Hiraṇyakaśipu, is killed? How is this considered not bad to feel this way? (See verse 14 and purport and use the analogy of scorpions and snakes to explain your answer.)
5. Prahlāda wasn't afraid of any dangers in the material world, nor was he afraid of the Lord's fearsome form. What was he afraid of, according to verse 16 and purport, and why?
6. In verse 18 purport Śrīla Prabhupāda mentions that one may say that advancing in spiritual life involves *tapasyā*, voluntarily accepting inconvenience, just as those who work hard to mitigate miseries. However, how do you think that such *tapasyā* is not as dangerous as trying to mitigate all miseries?
7. Prahlāda asks the Lord to protect him in verse 22. Although he was already protected when Hiraṇyakaśipu was killed, from what does he ask for protection here?

8. Why should we stop repeatedly making plans for attaining material happiness as mentioned by Śrīla Prabhupāda in his purport to verse 25? What plans should we make that will satisfy us?
9. Prahlāda humbly admits in verse 26 that his body was born from a demon, and yet the Lord was merciful to him by placing His hand upon his head. What did the Lord prove, besides being merciful, by doing this?
10. The Lord saved Prahlāda in response to whose prayers? What does this prove about the Lord? (See verse 29 and purport.)
11. Why do you think Prahlāda explained the process of creation in verses 32 to 36 besides trying to glorify the supremacy of the Lord? (Refer to verse 36 and purport.)
12. In verse 38 why is the Lord described as Triyuga? What does this indicate about the incarnation in Kali-yuga?

ACTIVITIES

In this section you will find many exciting things to do. These activities will get you thinking, moving, drawing, and having loads of fun.

Analogy Activity

. . . to bring out the scholar in you

THE DEPENDENCE SOLUTION

In verse 19, Prahlāda Mahārāja gives three examples to prove that one who is not protected by the Lord cannot be protected in any other way in the material world. Here is the verse in simpler words:

"My Lord Nṛsiṁhadeva, O Supreme, because of a bodily conception of life, those not cared for by You cannot actually do anything for themselves. They may try to solve the problems they face in different ways (parents protecting their child; a doctor and medicine relieving a sick patient; and a boat saving a drowning man), but the solutions they find are both temporary and impermanent and ultimately depend on the Lord. Taking shelter of Your lotus feet is the only possible permanent solution."

Prahlāda Mahārāja brings out two points using the three examples:

1. We may come up with different solutions to the problems we face. But for the solutions to work nicely, the Lord's sanction is required.
2. Normally, it's easy to understand how material solutions/remedies help overcome material problems. But we need spiritual intelligence to understand that we also need the mercy of the Lord for the material solutions to work.

Let us use the analogy examples Prahlāda Mahārāja quotes to understand these two points.

Look at each of the pictures below. They each illustrate one of the three examples Prahlāda Mahārāja mentions. The Helping Hand represents the material solutions available to the distressed person to overcome the situation, while the Invisible Hand on top represents the hand of the Lord. (Notice that the Helping Hand has a shadow of the Lord's Invisible Hand, showing that the Lord's hand is there in every situation.)

	1	2	3
The Lord's Invisible Hand helps a person in this situation by...	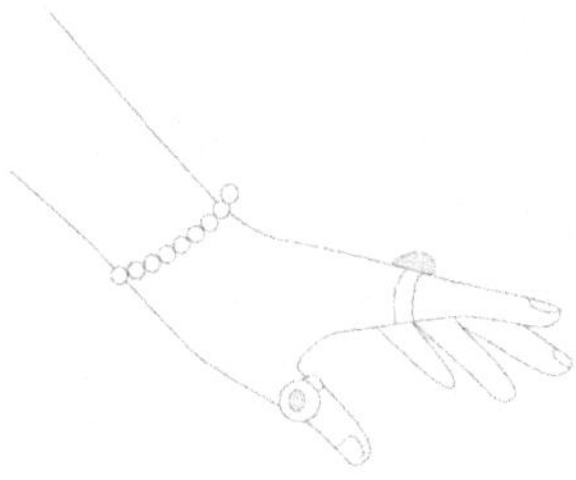	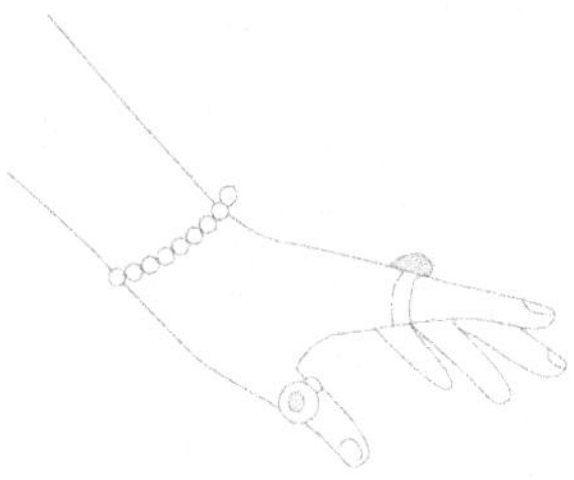	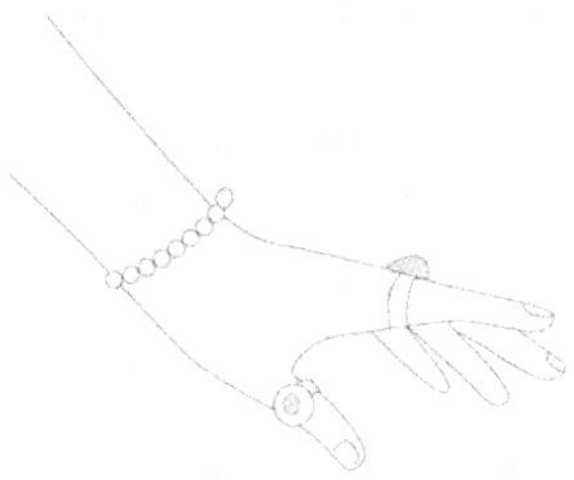
The distressful situation mentioned by Prahlāda Mahārāja in this verse is...	 Sick man	 Child in danger	 Drowning man

The material solutions or remedies available to overcome this situation are...

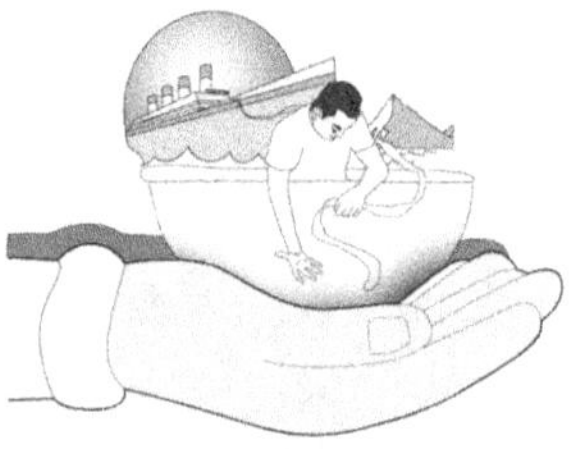

Divide your study circle into three groups. Each group can evaluate one of the above examples. Consider the following prompts for each case:

1. Does the Helping Hand have all the necessary remedies to help the person in the distressful situation?
2. Is the Helping Hand always successful in getting the person out of the distressful situation? Remember to research and provide examples/case studies/statistics to support your answer.
3. Does the Lord's Invisible Hand have any role to play? Again, think deeply about how you can substantiate your answer with appropriate research or evidence.
4. Is there any way to "see" or prove the existence of the Lord's Invisible Hand?

After discussing within your groups, present your example and conclusions to the class. Finally, in one sentence, write in your notebooks what you understood about the Lord's Invisible Hand.

Artistic Activity

... to reveal your creativity

LORD NṚSIṀHADEVA MASK

The Lord's fearsome form appears beautiful to His devotees, because it reminds them of His love and protection. Create a 3-D Lord Nṛsiṁhadeva mask, which you can use to enact a skit of the Prahlāda-Nṛsiṁhadeva pastime, or just to remind you of the Lord.

Materials: Paper plate (preferably in yellow or orange); black marker/color pen; scissors; paper (yellow, brown, and orange colored, or colored with crayons or color pencils); paper glue

Steps:

1. At the back of a paper plate, make the marking for eyes and nose as shown in Image 1.
2. Make holes for the eyes (size of the holes as the user's eyes) and cut the nose section as marked. Give nose cutting a little lift as shown in Image 2.

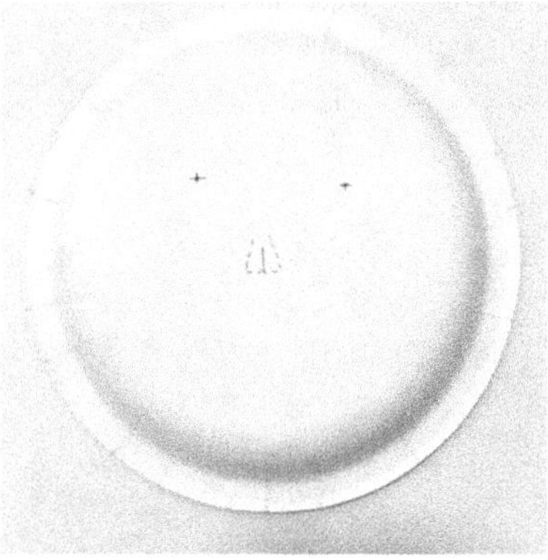

Image 1

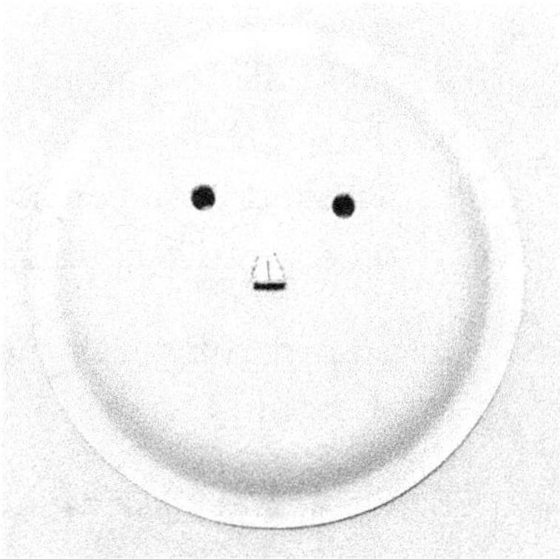

Image 2

3. Make the following four cut-outs as shown in Image 3:
   - For beard-
     Cut out a rectangular piece of yellow paper. Size should be in reference to the eyes as shown in top left image of Image 4.
     Fold the paper in half and draw the shape of the beard.
   - For cheeks-
     Cut a rectangular piece of yellow paper. Length should be at least equal to the diameter of the plate.
     Fold the paper in half and draw the shape of the cheeks as shown in top right image of Image 3.

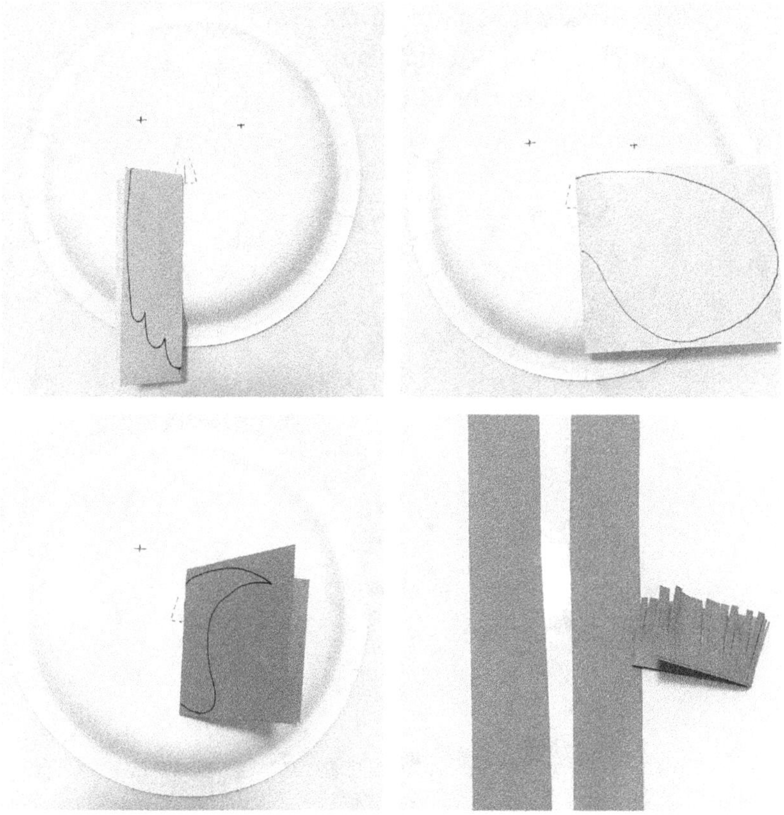

Image 3

   - For eyebrow and nose-
     Cut a square piece of brown or orange paper. Width should be more than the distance between eyes.
     Fold the paper in half and draw the shape for nose and eyebrows as shown in left bottom image of Image 3.
   - For frills (mane)

Cut out long strips of brown or orange paper. Make small cuts on one side as shown in right bottom image of Image 3.

4. Make all the cuttings as drawn. Draw nose and whiskers as shown in Image 4 on respective cuttings.

5. Start pasting each cut-out as shown in Image 4.

6. Complete mask as shown in Image 5. You can add two holes on each side if you wish to attach an elastic to wear the mask. Or you can paste a stick at the bottom if you wish to make a hand-held mask.

Image 4

Image 5

Introspective Activity

... to bring out the reflective devotee in you

HOW TO BECOME FEARLESS

Here are certain statements or riddles that relate to certain devotees who had to face their fears. Connect these statements with devotees who overcame their fear as described, and briefly explain how it is related to them.

There can be more than one answer to the statements. Think of other devotees who would fit in and discuss with a partner. Reflect whether any of these statements apply to you and then discuss with your partner.

STATEMENT	DEVOTEE
1. Fear paralyzes, faith energizes. Having faith in God energizes you to overcome the fear.	
2. Don't think about how to drive the problems away. Think of driving the fear of the problem away by invoking the Lord through prayer, meditation, and *mantra* chanting.	
3. Don't fight directly with your inner demons. Fight them with inner energies – healthy habits and virtues – which come by practicing Kṛṣṇa consciousness.	
4. Don't think that Kṛṣṇa is there to solve all your problems and you don't have to do anything. You need to face your problems and your fears. Then Kṛṣṇa will guide you.	
5. Fear looks backwards and forward. Faith looks upward and forward.	
6. When you are gripped by fear because of an imminent danger, think of all the dangers that you went through in the past, how you survived, and what was God's role in that. He did not abandon you then. He will not abandon you now.	
7. Fear is a natural response to danger, and it makes you think how you will get out of it. Fear can also occur when there's no immediate danger.	

*The above statements are from lectures by Chaitanya Charan Dāsa and Gaurāṅga Dāsa

Critical-Thinking Activity

... to bring out the spiritual investigator in you

THE IMPORTANCE OF MAHAT-SEVĀ

Prahlāda Mahārāja saw Lord Nṛsiṁhadeva, the Supreme Lord Himself, directly and was blessed to serve Him directly. Yet, in verses 24 and 28 he prayed to Lord Nṛsiṁhadeva to allow him to serve Nārada Muni, the Lord's pure devotee. Why did Prahlāda find Nārada's service so important?

Prahlāda Mahārāja's friends asked him the same question. In response, Prahlāda, in this activity, sends some cryptic messages to his friends, and each of these messages contains one intimate reason for his desiring to serve Nārada Muni. Can you decode these messages and understand his reasons?

1
guru-kṛṣṇa-prasāde
pāya bhakti-latā-bīja
(*Cc Madhya* 19.151)

2
tāṅdera caraṇa sevi
bhakta-sane vāsa
janame janame
haya, ei abhilāṣa
(Narottama Dasa Ṭhākura *bhajana*)

3
gopī-bhartuḥ pada-
kamalayor dāsa-
dāsānudāsaḥ
(*Cc Madhya* 13.80)

4
yasya prasādād
bhagavat-prasādo
(Gurvastakam,
verse 8)

5
ahaṁ bhakta-
parādhīno
(*SB* 9.4.63)

6
naṣṭa-prāyeṣv
abhadreṣu nityaṁ
bhāgavata-sevāyā
(*SB* 1.2.18)

7
syān mahat-sevāyā
viprāḥ puṇya-
tīrtha-niṣevaṇāt
(*SB* 1.2.16)

Each of Prahlāda's friends received only one of these messages. They decided to meet and understand this important subject matter by putting the messages together. They wrote down their combined understanding in one sentence, which they adopted as the motto of their now Kṛṣṇa conscious school, which they renamed as Bhakta Prahlāda Pāṭhaśālā. After discussing with a group of your friends, can you come up with what they may have written?

Finally, they wrote a heartfelt letter to Prahlāda, expressing their understanding of the futility of material enjoyment and pouring out their gratitude to Prahlāda for teaching them the importance of service to a pure devotee.

Their letter is printed here, but just when they were about to seal it and send it, ink accidentally spilled on portions of the palm leaf. Can you rewrite the portions covered by the ink blots, so Prahlāda can get the full message?

Dear Prahlāda,

Thank you for your messages regarding why you prayed to Nṛsiṁhadeva to serve 1. ______ than the Lord Himself directly. We are amazed at your answers and are convinced that we, too, should follow in your footsteps. Based on your messages, we've made a new school motto: 2. ______. Do you like it?

Prahlāda, we cannot thank you enough for making us Kṛṣṇa conscious and for teaching us the importance of serving the devotees. We've been saved by you, and *guru* Nārada, from adopting the ways of our fathers, the demons. At Ṣaṇḍa-Amarka Pāṭhaśālā, we were often taught different ways to enjoy ourselves in this material world, and we were going to live our lives like that. Your father's death has shown us how the 3. ______ is the most powerful and can take away everything we may acquire in a moment. And today, we are thinking – how would we have taken the shock of Hiraṇyakaśipu's death had you not taught us about the Lord?

We would have been lost, Prahlāda. Our faith in the world would have been shattered, but we would've not had anywhere else to place that faith in. We would've lived our lives thinking of the most wonderful Nṛsiṁhadeva as our enemy. Thank you for changing this understanding.

You also showed us that no matter what we try, only the 4. ______ can protect us. Your father couldn't protect himself despite being so powerful because he was a non-believer. On the other hand, he could not hurt you either, because although you were apparently small and powerless you had faith in the 5. ______. These are powerful lessons for us.

By your example, you have taught us that just like we can approach a big man by first approaching and pleasing 6. ______, we can please the Supreme Lord by pleasing 7. ______. We understand this so nicely now and wish to serve pure devotees rather than our selfish desires.

Mahāprabhu taught us that we are servants of 8. ______ – what a wonderful concept, and how different from what we learned at Ṣaṇḍa-Amarka school! To understand this properly, we need to serve 9. ______ in the association of 10. ______. And now that you are the King, it will be easy!

We miss you at school, Prahlāda, but we are so happy to have you as our King. We'll soon pay you a visit.

Love,

Your friends from the
Bhakta Prahlāda Pāṭhaśālā

Writing and Language Activities

... to help you understand better

FUTILITY OF MATERIAL HAPPINESS

This meme aptly represents the difficulty in pursuing material happiness. Our material dreams and goals are like running after mirages in the desert. As we get closer to our goals, we realize the misery associated with it.

Prahlāda Mahārāja teaches and shows us that material opulence can perish at any moment.

Write a paragraph describing a personal journey or journey of a friend who pursued a material goal that ultimately did not end up as expected. Your writing can be a funny narrative or a deep reflective article.

Example pointers:

1. Dream vacation that goes against your expectations: weather changed unexpectedly or you were cheated by locals, etc.
2. Dream dinner at an expensive restaurant that you've been saving up for months, but you fall sick right before the dinner.
3. Dream date with the most popular girl or boy in your class, but as soon as the conversation starts, they turn out to be not what you expected.
4. Dream ideology as an activist for which you have sacrificed a lot, but when you come closer to your goals, you have to deal with shrewd authorities who are just after power and money.
5. Health issues, relationship issues, legal matters, feuds, etc., which can enter your life at any time while you are pursuing any material goal.
6. Does this mean we should not pursue any material goals? Discuss with a partner or your teacher.

DIALOGUE: CONVERSATIONS WITH PRAHLĀDA

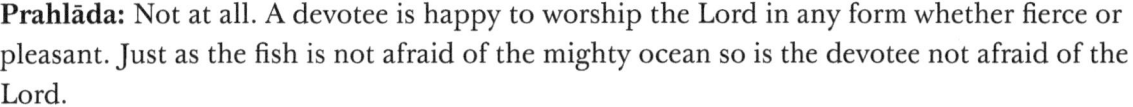

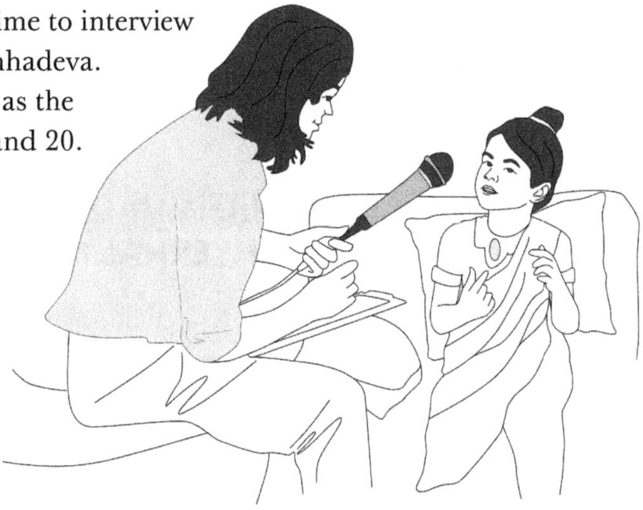

A modern reporter has been transported back in time to interview Prahlāda Mahārāja after his prayers to Lord Nṛsiṁhadeva. Write responses to the questions, in a similar style as the interviewer, referring to verses 9, 10, 11, 12, 16, 17, and 20.

Reporter: Today we are excited to have Prahlāda Mahārāja on our show. Welcome, Prahlāda! Thank you for joining us today.

Prahlāda: Thanks for having me.

Reporter: So I heard you met God in a very fearful form. Were you scared? Tell us all about it.

Prahlāda: Not at all. A devotee is happy to worship the Lord in any form whether fierce or pleasant. Just as the fish is not afraid of the mighty ocean so is the devotee not afraid of the Lord.

Reporter: So you are saying you are not afraid of anything?

Prahlāda: There is one thing I'm afraid of. . . . (complete the dialogue here)

Reporter: Right, right. But not anyone can approach the Lord. You have to be born in a high-class family. Like me.

Prahlāda:

Reporter: So the Lord must be very happy that everyone is worshiping Him. After all, He gets the benefit.

Prahlāda:

Reporter: So, Prahlāda, tell me, do you know the secret to happiness?

Prahlāda:

Reporter: It all seems so easy. But let me ask you this. Your father tormented you and even tried to have you killed. How do you feel now, knowing that he's dead?

Prahlāda:

Reporter: I'm surprised you feel that way. What are you planning to do now? Our viewers would love to know what's the next big thing for Prahlāda.

Prahlāda:

LORD NṚSIṀHADEVA KILLS OUR INTERNAL ENEMIES

What should we ask Lord Nṛsiṁhadeva to protect us from? Just material calamities and dangers?

In 1967 in New York Śrīla Prabhupāda had a stroke. He then taught his disciples the Nṛsiṁha prayers for the first time. He said the words one by one, and Jadurāṇī dāsī wrote them down. She then called the temples in San Fransisco and Montreal and told them the prayer. Prabhupāda said, "You should pray to Kṛṣṇa that my spiritual master has not yet completed his work, so please let him finish."

In another instance, in 1970 in Los Angeles, Śrīla Prabhupāda taught his disciples to recite the Nṛsiṁha prayers before he could leave for Japan and said, "Nṛsiṁhadeva will give you protection in my absence."

Although Lord Nṛsiṁhadeva protects His devotees from external disturbances, in these cases Prabhupāda was considering spiritual protection, or approaching Lord Nṛsiṁhadeva to help them in their service and progress in their spiritual lives.

Thus, Lord Nṛsiṁhadeva not only protects us physically but protects our spiritual progress, eliminating obstacles that slow our journey. The six internal enemies within us – lust, envy, greed, pride, anger, and illusion are the most common obstacles.

How do you think Lord Nṛsiṁha can help us diminish the effect of these internal enemies in our hearts? By simply approaching Him in a humble, devotional attitude, we can pray to Him to help us remove these impediments.

Let's prepare some prayers to offer Him in this regard. First refer to the six internal enemies in the last chapter. Then complete the following prayers to Lord Nṛsiṁhadeva and then read them out to Him (in the form of the Deity or picture) in a prayerful mood.

Example: 1. Lust: O Lord Nṛsiṁhadeva, You are the all-powerful and merciful Lord. I am full of lust, and with your help I can see this lust as my internal enemy. Please help me. I am always wanting to satisfy my own senses. Please destroy this enemy within me and help me engage my senses in serving you, O Lord, rather than gratifying my senses.

2. Envy: O Lord __________, You are __________________________. I am full of ______ ______________________________. Please help me. I often mistreat others and disrespect them. Please ____.
3. Greed:

4. Pride:
5. Anger:
6. Illusion:

REFLECTIVE ESSAY: BENEFITS OF DEVOTIONAL SERVICE

With the help of a mind map, list all the benefits mentioned in this chapter a devotee gets from serving the Lord. Then, from this list see all the ways you've benefited from devotional service. Choose one benefit and elaborate on it in a reflective essay. For example, if you felt you were protected by the Lord, either externally or internally, share a story of the incident in a way that would inspire your reader and convince them of the benefits of devotional service.

* A reflective essay is often written as a personal narrative. You look back at something in your past and provide insights that may entertain or help the reader.

NO MATERIAL QUALIFICATION

List the personalities in the *Bhāgavatam*, and of any other personalities you know, who became devotees irrespective of their material backgrounds. You may use modern examples or those from scripture. Analyze the common spiritual qualities they have and discuss in a paragraph why material qualifications don't matter to progress in spiritual life.

SHOWING THE HIGHEST COMPASSION

A pure Vaiṣṇava like Prahlāda is *para-dukha-dukhī*. He is completely satisfied in his connection with Kṛṣṇa and does not have any personal need or suffering, but he is distressed to see people forgetting Kṛṣṇa and enjoying separately from Him.

The compassion exhibited by exalted devotees is transcendental. It is beyond the material compassion shown for the needs of the body, mind, intelligence, and ego. A pure devotee tastes great spiritual happiness and desires that all living entities come to their constitutional position and relish this endless happiness.

Study the mind map on compassion as a resource at the end of this chapter. The mind map has prompts on various aspects of the topic. Compare the attributes of transcendental compassion with compassion for the temporary body and its possessions.

Then complete the following real-life scenarios to make these cases of compassion transcendental (be creative in your answers):

1. Jahnavi is having lunch with her friends. She notices that one of them doesn't have anything to eat and offers her friend her lunch. But again, the girl comes hungry to school

the next day. Jahnavi feels compassion for her friend and acts kindly, which is good, but how can she help her friend more by using transcendental compassion?

Example answer: She can get more help for her friend by approaching a welfare organization, but apart from that, she can see that the girl's suffering is a result of her bad *karma*. By engaging the hungry girl in devotional service, she can give a permanent solution, so the results of her past *karma* are eventually extinguished and she no longer accumulates *karma*. Jahnavi could give the girl *prasāda*, invite her to the temple to have *prasāda*, slowly introduce her to Kṛṣṇa consciousness, and also pray to Kṛṣṇa for the girl's spiritual welfare.

2. Nimai's football team player has just lost his pet dog. Nimai feels sorry for him. He is thinking of getting his friend a new pet. But how can he help his friend with transcendental compassion?

3. Madhuri's uncle is diagnosed with cancer. She starts researching all about it so she can help her uncle find a solution, which is very considerate. But how can she show transcendental compassion to him?

4. Gaura's friend loves reading books of all kinds and scrolling the internet. One day the friend is in a serious accident and ends up in the hospital with many fractures. He cannot move, so Gaura feels bad for his friend. He feeds his friend with a spoon and gives him his medicine. He thinks of reading to his friend his favorite book to pass the time. But how can he show his injured friend transcendental compassion?

5. Arjun wants to help his friend study because his friend is slow at learning. This is a wonderful, selfless act of compassion, but how could he also show transcendental compassion to his friend?

CHAPTER 9 ANSWERS

The Dependence Solution

The Lord's Invisible Hand helps a person in this situation by 1. Curing him of the illness; 2. Protecting him in ways that is beyond a parent's capacity; 3. Providing the ability to hold the rope or to swim to safety.

In each case 1. the Helping Hand has the necessary remedies to help the person in the distressful situation; 2. These are not always successful in helping a person in the distressful situation. From common everyday examples, or from any local news snippets/anecdotes/historical events/statistics of how many people are dying of certain diseases or from sinking ships, etc., it would be easy to prove that the same remedies sometimes work and sometimes don't; 3. The fact that the same solutions sometimes work and fail at other times proves that there is another factor involved that determines success or failure. Prahlāda Mahārāja here establishes that the Hand of the Lord is that invisible factor. Again, using often published examples or anecdotes of devotees who have experiences of miraculous "escapes," one can establish that someone may indeed be saved against all odds, while others may perish with the best of facilities; 4. The existence of the Lord's Invisible Hand can be established both by accepting the statements of authorities, such as Prahlāda Mahārāja, and by understanding the truth in them through studying various examples.

How to Become Fearless

1. Arjuna: Arjuna was paralyzed by fear when he had to fight his family on the battleground. Then Kṛṣṇa gave him the knowledge of *Bhagavad-gītā* that helped dispel his fears. Arjuna's faith in Kṛṣṇa and His words spiritually invigorated him to fight the battle.
2. Dhruva: Being insulted by his stepmother, Dhruva was filled with grief. His desire to become greater than even Lord Brahmā consumed him. He feared that his desire would not be fulfilled, so he was determined to become the greatest ruler in the world. Eventually, he invoked Kṛṣṇa by constant meditation and chanting of the Lord's name for many months. Thus he overcame his material desires and fears.
3. Parīkṣit Mahārāja: After being cursed to die in seven days, Parīkṣit Mahārāja did not lament or fear for his death but repented for his mistake. He went to the banks of the Ganges where he heard the *Śrīmad-Bhagavatam* from Śukadeva Gosvāmī in seven days. Parīkṣit Mahārāja converted this curse into an opportunity for devotional service to the Lord. His Kṛṣṇa consciousness drove away all fears and lamentation.
4. Arjuna: Arjuna knew that Kṛṣṇa was there as a charioteer to guide him. But the battles that he fought were his own. He had to take his bow and arrow and decide on strategies to fight his enemy. Kṛṣṇa was there only to guide him.
5. Draupadī: Initially, when Draupadī was disgraced in the assembly hall, she panicked and called for her husbands all around, then the elders of the assembly, but when she did not get help from anybody, she lifted her hands up and asked help from Kṛṣṇa. Then He appeared and provided her unlimited cloth to save herself.
6. Kuntīdevī: In her prayers to the Lord she thanks Him for being there each time she and the Pāṇḍavas were in trouble. She looks back and thinks of how many times the Lord had saved them, and she desires that these calamities come again and again so that she could see the Lord again and again, and thus there will be no more birth and death. She did not fear calamities but feared not seeing the Lord.
7. Fear in danger: Pāṇḍavas in the house of lac – The Pāṇḍavas were afraid of the palace of lac that was set on fire by their cousins, but with Vidura's help and their own intelligence, they escaped.

   Fear in absence of danger: Kaṁsa – He was always afraid of death, which would come in the form of Kṛṣṇa. He therefore never had a moment of peace.

The Importance of Mahat-sevā

Cryptic messages: 1. By the mercy of *guru* and Kṛṣṇa we receive the seed of devotional service; 2. One must worship the lotus feet of the *ācārya* and live within the society of devotees; 3. I identify myself only as the servant of the servant of the servant of the lotus feet of Lord Śrī Kṛṣṇa, the maintainer of the *gopīs*; 4. By satisfaction of the spiritual master, the Supreme Personality of Godhead becomes satisfied; 5. Kṛṣṇa: I am under the control of My devotees; 6. All that is troublesome in the heart is destroyed by regularly serving a pure devotee, and pure devotional service is established in the heart; 7. By such service, one gains affinity for hearing the messages of Vāsudeva.

Sample motto statements: Serve the devotee, clean your heart; Serving great souls eternally; Serve the devotee, satisfy the Lord.

Ink blots: 1. Nārada Muni rather; 2. *Students' own message*; 3. the Lord; 4. the mercy of the Lord/ protection of the Lord; 6. his dear child or pet; 7. His devotee; 8. servants of the servants of the Lord; 9. Nārada and yourself; 10. devotees

RESOURCE: MIND MAP ON COMPASSION

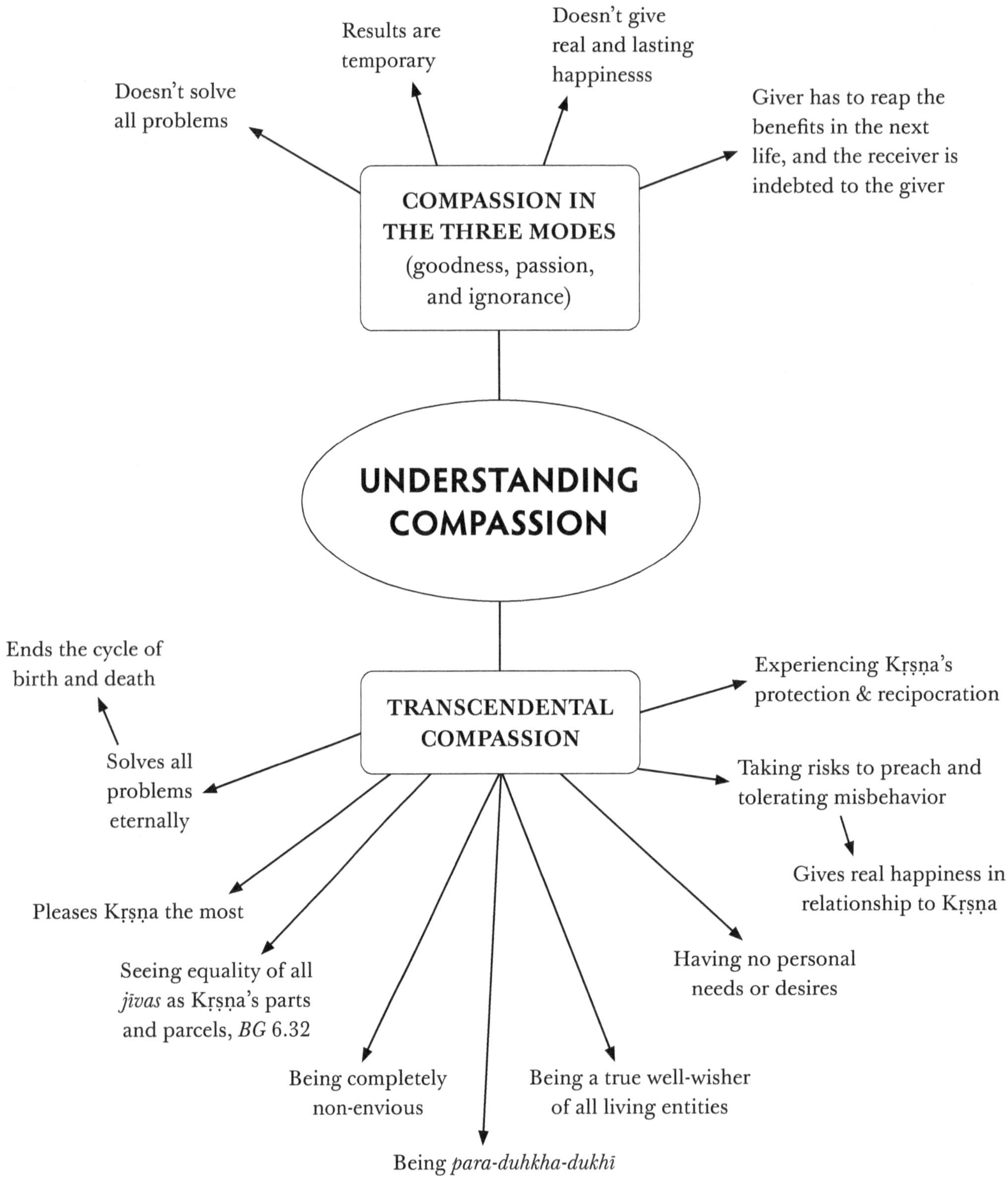

10

PRAHLĀDA, THE BEST AMONG EXALTED DEVOTEES

Story Summary

What did Prahlāda Mahārāja want? Everyone was waiting to hear. But Prahlāda simply smiled and said, "I was born in an atheistic family, so I'm naturally attached to material pleasures. So, please, my dear Lord, don't tempt me. I don't want such materialistic life. This is why I have taken shelter of You.

"O my worshipable Lord, because of our lusty desires we are in this material world. The seed of lust is within everyone's hearts. But You've sent me to this material world to show people the nature of a pure devotee.

"So I don't want any material benediction. And You are so kind to Your devotee that You won't induce him to ask for unbeneficial things. Someone who wants some material benefit in exchange for Your service cannot be Your pure devotee. He is like a merchant who wants profit in exchange for service."

Lord Brahmā, Lord Śiva, and the other demigods smiled and nodded, proud of the little boy who just wanted to serve the Lord out of love.

"How can a servant who wants material profits from his master be a qualified servant? And similarly, how can a master be pure if he bestows benedictions upon his servant just to maintain his prestigious position?"

Kneeling and looking at the Lord with tear-stained eyes, Prahlāda Mahārāja continued, "O my Lord, You are my eternal master and I am your unmotivated servant. There is no need for our being anything else. You are naturally my master, and I am naturally Your servant. We have no other relationship."

Lord Nṛsiṁhadeva growled softly as if to confirm the statements of His pure servant.

"But if You want to give me a benediction, my Lord, then I pray that there be no material desires within the core of my heart."

The Lord nodded in approval, smiling and lifting His hand in a blessing pose.

"O my Lord, because of lusty desires everything is destroyed from the beginning of life – our mind, senses, life, body, intelligence, opulence, strength, truthfulness, and so on. But if we give up all material desires, we become eligible to possess wealth and opulence like Yours. O Supreme Person in the form of a wonderful lion and man, I offer my respectful obeisances to You."

Lord Nṛsiṁhadeva's kind voice resonated like thunder: "My dear Prahlāda, even though you don't want to enjoy anything material, I order you to enjoy the opulence of the demons. You should act as their king till the end of the *manvantara*."

"That's around 71 *yuga* cycles . . ." whispered someone to another. More whispers filled the hall.

Prahlāda bowed his head in obedience, as his Lord continued, "It doesn't matter that you are in the material world, my dear boy; just simply hear My instructions and always be absorbed in Me, give up all mundane work, and just worship Me. In this way, you will exhaust all the reactions of past *karma* and in time give up your body and go back home to My spiritual abode. But, my dear Prahlāda, you will never be forgotten. Your glorious activities will be sung in all the worlds. Not only that, anyone who remembers you and Me, and chants your prayers to Me, will also become free from the reactions of material activities."

Prahlāda got up and stepped closer to the Lord. Looking straight into Lord Nṛsiṁha's gentle eyes, he said, "O Supreme Lord, I just have one wish . . ."

Again, murmurs broke out, and Lord Brahmā lifted his hand to silence everyone.

"What is it?" asked Nṛsiṁhadeva, moving closer and stroking Prahlāda's head.

"You are most merciful to the conditioned souls," said Prahlāda in a choked voice, "and I know that my father has been purified just by Your touch and Your glance. Still, I wish that You excuse him for all his sinful activities, including blaspheming You and committing heavy sinful acts against me."

Nṛsiṁhadeva looked lovingly at Prahlāda, just as a lioness looks at her cubs, and said, "Don't worry, O most pure Prahlāda, not only has your father been purified, but also 21 forefathers in your family. Because of you, your entire dynasty and country have been purified – even from previous lifetimes.

"My dear Prahlāda, King of the Daityas, My devotees are naturally non-envious and are decorated with all good qualities. You are the best example of My devotee, and others should follow in your footsteps. Whoever follows you will also become My pure devotee.

"My dear child, even though your father has been purified by dying at My hands, it's the duty of a son to perform the *śrāddha* ritualistic ceremony so that his dead father can be promoted to the higher planetary system and become a good citizen and devotee. After you perform these rituals, take charge of your father's kingdom. Sit on the throne but don't become distracted by materialistic activities. Keep your mind fixed on Me, and at the same time don't transgress the Vedic injunctions. As a formality perform your duties."

Prahlāda bowed again to the Lord while Nṛsiṁhadeva purred softly. Seeing that the Lord was pleased, Lord Brahmā came forward, his faces as bright as autumn moons. "O *ādi-puruṣa*," he addressed the Lord, "we've been most fortunate that You've killed this sinful demon, Hiraṇyakaśipu. He became excessively proud from the strength of his powers and austerities and therefore transgressed all Vedic injunctions." He lowered his head and voice, and avoiding the Lord's eyes, he continued, "I gave him the benediction that no living being in my creation would be able to kill him.

"O my Lord, You've saved this little boy from the hands of death. What great fortune he's received in the form of Your full protection. Although he's just a boy, he's Your exalted devotee. He's shown us that anyone who meditates upon You is never afraid of anything, including death."

The Lord's eyes moved from Prahlāda to Lord Brahmā. In a grave voice, He said, "My dear Lord Brahmā, just as it is dangerous to feed milk to a snake, it is dangerous to give benedictions to demons. I warn you never to do this again!"

Lord Brahmā nodded and bowed his head. He worshiped the Lord, and then Lord Nṛsiṁha, who had appeared from a pillar in this unusual form to protect His dearmost devotee, vanished as quickly as He had appeared.

Nārada Muni continued his narration to Yudhiṣṭhira Mahārāja, "Prahlāda Mahārāja then worshiped and offered prayers to Lord Brahmā, Śiva, and the Prajāpatis, seeing them as part of the Lord. Then Lord Brahmā, along with Śukrācārya and other priests, inaugurated Prahlāda as the king of all the demons and giants in the

universe – a king that would be greater than his father, Hiraṇyakaśipu."

"Jaya!" exclaimed Yudhiṣṭhira Mahārāja.

"So, my dear King Yudhiṣṭhira, coming back to your original question about how Śiśupāla and others achieved salvation," said Nārada, "the two associates of Lord Viṣṇu who had become Hiraṇyākṣa and Hiraṇyakaśipu, the sons of Diti, were both killed by the Lord. Out of illusion they thought that the Lord was their enemy."

"Then what happened to them?" asked the King. "As you mentioned, they were to take three lives."

"Yes, they then took birth as Kumbhakarṇa and the ten-headed demon, Rāvaṇa. These two *rākṣasas* were killed by the arrows of Lord Rāma. They left their bodies, fully absorbed in thoughts of the Lord, just as they had done as Hiraṇyākṣa and Hiraṇyakaśipu. Finally, they were born in human society as Śiśupāla and Dantavakra, again as the Lord's enemies and again killed by the hands of the Lord. As you've seen, they merged into Lord Kṛṣṇa's body.

"Not only them, but many other enemy kings were liberated at the hands of the Lord. They achieved *sārūpya-mukti*, the same spiritual body as the Lord's."

"That is amazing!" exclaimed Mahārāja Yudhiṣṭhira. "How is this possible? Only pure devotees immersed in thoughts of the Lord achieve a divine form as the Lord's in the spiritual world."

Nārada smiled and answered, "That may be so, my dear King, but even those who constantly think of the Lord as their enemies attain the same position. This is the Lord's mercy. Just imagine, if enemies can achieve this result, what is to be said of pure devotees who always serve the Lord and think of nothing but Him in every activity?

"Anyone who hears and chants this narration of Lord Nṛsiṁhadeva and Prahlāda is certainly liberated from material bondage and reaches the spiritual world, where there is no anxiety."

Yudhiṣṭhira Mahārāja thought, "Oh how fortunate is Prahlāda Mahārāja to have received such mercy. I am most unfortunate."

Nārada Muni read his mind and said, "How extremely fortunate are you and your brothers, my dear King! The Supreme Personality of Godhead, Kṛṣṇa, lives in your palace just like a human being. That is why great saintly people who know this visit your house. He, the Supreme Person, sought by great saintly persons, is your relative, your dearmost friend, and constant well-wisher. Indeed, He is like your body and soul. He acts sometimes as your servant and sometimes as your spiritual master."

Yudhiṣṭhira Mahārāja's eyes filled with tears, reminded of his rare, great fortune.

Nārada bowed his head and prayed, "May the Lord, the source of Brahman, who is worshiped as the protector of His devotees by great saints, *yogīs*, *jñānīs*, and other transcendentalists, be pleased with us."

Yudhiṣṭhira Mahārāja asked, "But why would the Supreme Person, the source of Brahman, become servants of ordinary souls like us?"

"Oh, the Lord's activities, especially with regards to His devotees and how He reciprocates with their love, is inconceivable. Even exalted persons like Lord Śiva and Lord Brahmā could not describe or know fully the truth about Kṛṣṇa. However, if anyone should know about His greatness it is Lord Śiva. Can I tell you a story?"

"Yes, please!" exclaimed the King, his eyes dazzling with excitement.

"My dear King Yudhiṣṭhira, once, a long, long time ago, the demon Maya Dānava, the mystic architect of the heavens, spoilt Lord Śiva's reputation, and who besides Lord Kṛṣṇa Himself could save him?"

"Oh, please tell me how Lord Śiva's reputation was ruined and how Lord Kṛṣṇa saved it."

Nārada continued, "Once, the demigods fought with the *asuras* and defeated them. The demons then took shelter of Maya Dānava, who constructed three invisible airplane residences made of gold, silver, and iron. The demon commanders resided there and were thus invisible to the demigods. Taking advantage of this, the demons began to vanquish the three worlds – the upper, middle, and lower planetary systems.

"When the demons began destroying the upper planets, the rulers went to Lord Śiva for help. Lord Śiva reassured them and then aimed his arrows toward the three residences occupied by the demons. His deadly arrows, which were like fiery beams coming from the sun, scorched the three dwellings, killing all the inhabitants.

"But Maya Dānava thought of a plan. He dropped the demons into a well filled with nectar, which could bring their dead bodies to life. Their bodies were thus rejuvenated and became invincible like thunderbolts. They got up like lightning penetrating the clouds.

"Lord Viṣṇu could see Lord Śiva's disappointment. 'How to stop this nuisance created by Maya Dānava?' He thought. 'How can I save My devotee's name?'

"Aha! Lord Viṣṇu became a cow and Lord Brahmā a calf. They entered the demon residences and drank all the nectar in the well. Even though the demons and Maya Dānava could see what was happening, by the Lord's illusory power, they could not do anything in retaliation.

"Giving up, Maya Dānava told the demons, 'Whatever is destined by the Supreme Lord cannot be undone by anyone, whether one be a demigod, a demon, a human being, or anyone else.'

"But it wasn't over. The Lord wanted to make sure Lord Śiva was victorious. He gifted Lord Śiva a chariot, a charioteer, a flag, horses, elephants, a bow, a shield, and arrows. Equipped in this way, Lord Śiva sat on his chariot ready to fight with the demons. He set fire to all three demon residences and burnt them to ashes. The demigods celebrated Lord Śiva's victory.

"O King Yudhiṣṭhira, thus Lord Śiva is known as Tripurāri, the annihilator of the three demon dwellings."

"Oh, how merciful is the Lord to His devotees!" exclaimed Yudhiṣṭhira Mahārāja.

"Yes," said Nārada, nodding in approval. "What more can be said about Lord Kṛṣṇa's extraordinary activities? He appeared as a human being, yet he performed uncommon and wonderful pastimes by His own potency. We all can be purified by hearing about His activities from the right source."

Themes and Key Messages

Please go through this table of themes and key messages, with corresponding verses, and discuss each topic further.

THEMES	REFERENCES	KEY MESSAGES
The ultimate goal of devotional service is love of Godhead; therefore, devotees do not ask for any material benedictions from the Lord.	7.10.1–5	Prahlāda did not desire anything material from the Lord. He recognized that lusty desires are the root cause of our existence in this material world, so he didn't want material opulence, which would distract him from the goal of life, pure devotional service and reawakening one's pure love for God. One who seeks benefits from the Lord is like a merchant who wants something in exchange for his service. People also approach the Lord to mitigate their distress. Even though such persons are pious because they approach the Lord directly, they cannot be pure devotees because they are interested in material benefits. But a pure devotee, like Prahlāda, only wants to serve the Lord unconditionally.
Every living being is an eternal servant of the Supreme Lord, Kṛṣṇa. Only in this constitutional relationship can we find real happiness.	7.10.6	The natural position of the Lord is to be the supreme proprietor and enjoyer, and the natural position of the living being is to be a servant of Him and surrender unto Him. In this relationship we can be truly happy. If we want to enjoy separately from Kṛṣṇa and think that He, the master, is our order supplier, we cannot be happy. The master should also not simply attend to the desires of the servant, as Lord Brahmā had done with Hiraṇyakaśipu. Lord Śiva tells his wife, Pārvatī, that the highest goal of life is to satisfy Lord Viṣṇu, and Caitanya Mahāprabhu emphasized that we should become the servant of the servant. Prahlāda Mahārāja also prayed to become the servant of the Lord's servant. Unless we come to this position of being an unmotivated servant, we cannot go back to Godhead.
By giving up all material desires, the devotee becomes liberated and can possess opulence as great as the Lord's.	7.10.7–9	The only benediction Prahlāda wanted from Nṛsiṁhadeva is that he should not have any material desires. Lusty desires destroy all good qualities, like patience, intelligence, strength, shyness, memory, and truthfulness, which can be used to satisfy the Lord. It also makes us accept repeated birth and death. However, when we give up material desires and have the spiritual desire to serve and please the Lord, we become liberated and stop repeated birth and death. Moreover, we become eligible to possess wealth and opulence like that of the Lord's. This doesn't mean that we become one with the Lord or equal to Him; we get the opportunity to become a servant, friend, parent, or lover, who are all equally opulent as the Lord. The master and servant are different yet equal in opulence (*acintya-bedābheda-tattva*).

THEMES	REFERENCES	KEY MESSAGES
A devotee without material desires can enjoy opulence and still not be affected by it because he is fully absorbed in devotional service.	7.10.11–14	The Lord ordered Prahlāda to rule the kingdom and enjoy material opulence for 71 *yuga* cycles. The Lord considered that it did not matter whether Prahlāda was in the material world; He instructed Prahlāda to continue hearing His instructions and messages and be absorbed in thoughts of Him. As a result of pure devotional service, Prahlāda would become free from the results of all pious and impious activity and will return home, back to Godhead. Anyone who remembers Prahlāda's activities and glories, in his relationship with Nṛsiṁhadeva, would also become free from the reactions of material activities and become liberated.
The Lord's peaceful, equipoised devotees, decorated with all good qualities, purify all places and even their condemned dynasties.	7.10.15–22	Prahlāda asked for the benediction that his father be excused for his sins. The Lord confirmed that because of Prahlāda's pure devotion, his father had become purified along with 21 forefathers. Prahlāda had purified both his father's and mother's lineage, including the families of his previous births. He had also purified the entire country. Such is the glory of pure devotees. Those who follow Prahlāda Mahārāja's example will naturally become devotees.
One should somehow become attached to the Supreme Personality of Godhead and incessantly think of Him; in this way, at the time of death, one will receive a body similar to the Lord's.	7.10.35–40, 46–47	In the three births of Jaya and Vijaya, they were killed by the hands of the Lord and therefore were liberated. Many kings, including Śiśupāla and Dantavakra, attained salvation and attained spiritual bodies (like that of the Lord – *sārūpya mukti*) because they thought of the Lord at the time of death. They constantly remembered the Lord either through fear, envy, or anger. So what to speak of a devotee of the Lord who is related to Him as a servant, friend, parent, or lover? By constantly engaging in the Lord's service and remembering Him favorably, the devotee goes back to the spiritual world and associates with the Lord. Anyone who attentively hears this narration of Prahlāda and Lord Nṛsiṁha will also reach the spiritual world.

Higher-Thinking Questions

Now try to deepen your understanding of this chapter by delving into Śrīla Prabhupāda's purports and reflecting on the following questions:

1. What is a *nitya-siddha* devotee? How do you know that Prahlāda is such a devotee? (Refer to verse 3 purport.) In verse 13 purport, Srila Prabhupada also describes him as *sādhana-siddha*. So how do you think that he, as well as Nārada Muni, is a mixed *siddha*?
2. The Lord never encourages His devotee to do something that is not beneficial. So, why did the Lord tell Prahlāda to ask for a benediction when He knew that Prahlāda did not desire anything material? (See verse 3 and purport.)
3. How does Prahlāda distinguish between a pure servant and pure master in verse 5? (Refer to purport.)
4. According to verses 7 and 8 and their purports, does not having material desires mean that we shouldn't have any desires? Explain.
5. If a devotee is materially opulent, does it mean that he has material desires and is therefore impure? (Hint: What does he do with his opulence as mentioned in verse 12 purport?)
6. Why did the Lord instruct Prahlāda to perform the *śrāddha* ceremony for his father if he had already been purified by the Lord's touch at the time of his death? (See verse 22 and purport.)
7. Similarly, even though a pure devotee is not obligated to follow the injunctions of the *Vedas* or perform any duties because of his devotion to the Lord, why did Lord Nṛsiṁhadeva instruct Prahlāda to formally perform his kingly duties? (See verse 23 purport.)
8. How can a devotee's life be extended, even bypassing his death or destiny (*karma*)? (Refer to verse 29 purport.)
9. Do you think Yudhiṣṭhira Mahārāja is as fortunate as Prahlāda Mahārāja? Refer to verses 48 and 49 and purports?
10. In verse 50, Nārada is trying to make a distinction between different transcendentalists and pure devotees. What is the distinction, and what does his prayer reveal about his innermost desire?

ACTIVITIES

In this section you will find many exciting things to do. These activities will get you thinking, moving, drawing, and having loads of fun.

Analogy Activity

... to bring out the scholar in you

PURIFYING THE MERCHANT MENTALITY

In verse 4 Prahlāda Mahārāja compares a person approaching the Lord for material gain to a merchant who serves not out of a pure service attitude, but with a desire for personal profit.

Through his statement, Prahlāda Mahārāja teaches us that the highest standard of devotional service is to serve the Lord without desire for anything in return. Yet, the *Bhāgavatam* itself, in 2.3.10, says that anyone, with any type of desire, can approach the Lord. In *BG* 7.16, Lord Kṛṣṇa also confirms that not just pure devotees (*premīs*) approach Him but also four kinds of pious people with material desires: the *ārta* (wanting solutions to overcome distress), *arthārthī* (wanting wealth), *jijñāsu* (wanting knowledge to satisfy their curiosity), and *jñānī* (wanting knowledge to know the Absolute Truth).

So what happens to these people who approach Him with material desires? And although pure devotees, like Prahlāda, call them merchants and refuse to be like them, why does the Lord accept them? Let us explore these questions through the merchant analogy.

Look at the following "store" in the illustration. The storekeeper is Kṛṣṇa, who has five kinds of goods to sell. Five varieties of devotees visit the store, hoping to receive a

different item from Him. They "pay" for their goods by rendering some service, either by giving Him money or doing some menial service. Complete Columns 2 and 3 of the table below by understanding who received which item from the storekeeper? Then, think about the benefits each received (including ones apart from the obvious) and fill them out in Column 4.

DEVOTEE	ITEM RECEIVED	TYPE OF DEVOTEE	BENEFITS
Dhruva			
Gajendra			
Four Kumāras			
Śaunaka Ṛṣi and sages of Naimiṣāraṇya			
Prahlāda			

Based on what you've filled in column 4, answer the following:

1. What common benefit did all these devotees receive from the Lord, apart from what they approached Him for?
2. Do you think everyone ends up getting this additional benefit from the Lord? Why, or why not?
3. What should a person do to get this kind of benefit from the Lord?
4. What special feature, which you've learned in this chapter, can one notice in devotees who've received this benefit?

Artistic Activity

... to reveal your creativity

PRAHLĀDA-NṚSIṀHA GLASS ART

Materials: Glass sheet or firm transparent plastic sheet; glass color paints (sold in a set with outliner); 3D outliner (usually comes with the paint set); fine paint brush; soft cloth to clean; water to clean brush; color mixing tray

Directions:

1. First choose one of the Prahlāda-Nṛsiṁha images from Resources. Place your glass sheet or plastic on the image (Image 1). You may fasten your sheet with tape to the image so that it will not move while tracing.

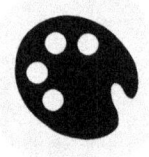

Image 1

2. Start tracing the image on the glass sheet or plastic with the 3D black outliner (Image 2).

3. Trace your image slowly and carefully, and after finishing an area, wait for a few minutes till the liner dries so you don't end up smudging your design (Image 3).

4. Once you've completed your tracing, color the image within your outline, using the brush. First, add a little paint in the color tray and mix any colors if necessary (Image 4 and Coloring Tips below).

Image 2

Image 3

Image 4

Image 5

Image 6

5. Then let your sheet dry completely and remove the tape. You can now see your transparent glass image (Image 5).

6. Glue or tape your plastic sheet to a window or glass cabinet so that everyone can view your beautiful Prahlāda-Nṛsiṁha art (Image 6).

7. If you are using a glass sheet, turn the painted side around (resulting in an inverted image) and frame it.

Some Coloring Tips:

- To color the hair brown, mix colors red and green.
- Color the body of Prahlāda Mahārāja with yellow mixed with water, so it's a lighter shade.
- Color the body of Lord Nṛsiṁhadeva with light brown (mix red + green + yellow).
- Color the Lord's head effulgence with orange (mix yellow + tinge of red).
- Coloring suggestions as in example images: jewelry with yellow, and stones with red or green; the Lord's *dhotī* in red with blue border; Prahlāda's *dhotī* in pink; the Lord's shawl in blue; Prahlāda's shawl in green; lips in red; flower garlands as you like.

Note:

In case your color or outliner gets mixed or there are some mistakes, don't worry. Once the outliner dries, you can remove it with a damp cloth. And when the paint color is still wet you can clean it with a dry cloth.

Introspective Activity

... to bring out the reflective devotee in you

OUR TREASURE OF FORTUNES

It is natural for a pure devotee, like Yudhiṣṭhira Mahārāja, to be humble and think of himself as unqualified and unfortunate. In this chapter, Nārada Muni encourages Yudhiṣṭhira Mahārāja by reminding him that he is greatly fortunate. Just as Prahlāda was fortunate that Lord Nṛsiṁhadeva appeared to him, the Pāṇḍavas were greatly fortunate because Kṛṣṇa was their close friend and relative and had intimate dealings with them.

Sometimes when we see others as more fortunate than us, we can feel unqualified and discouraged. Our feelings may be different from that of a pure devotee's and can arise from our conditionings and insecurities. Even so, we should always remind ourselves of our various great fortunes and be grateful for them so that we are happy and satisfied with the gifts Śrīla Prabhupāda has given us.

Fill in the blanks about our fortunes from what we've learned so far:

1. The Lord always ___________ the devotee: Lord Śiva was protected by _____________ in his battle against the demons led by __________.

2. The Lord offers the devotees liberation greater than that of demons: It is true that the enemies of the Lord also achieve _________ by constantly ______________-__________, but the devotees are offered much more. They are given a ______________________ with opportunities to constantly ____________________.

3. A devotee is not under __________. The Lord can __________ a devotee's *karma* too. Even a devotee's death can be nullified by the ___________________ of the Lord.

4. A devotee becomes decorated with all auspicious __________ and purifies not just himself but his entire ______________.

In this chapter, as throughout the *Bhāgavatam*, Śrīla Prabhupāda has given many Sanskrit verses for us to contemplate on. Taking time to relish and meditate on the teachings in these verses will remind us of our immense good fortune.

In the table below are some Sanskrit verses/phrases used by Prabhupāda in the purports of this chapter. Match them to their corresponding meanings (only provide the corresponding letters in your answer).

1.	*patraṁ puṣpaṁ phalaṁ toyaṁ* *yo me bhaktyā prayacchati* *tad ahaṁ bhakty-upahṛtam* *aśnāmi prayatātmanaḥ* (*BG* 9.26)	a.	Whether one desires everything or nothing, or whether he desires to merge into the existence of the Lord, he is intelligent only if he worships Lord Kṛṣṇa, the Supreme Personality of Godhead, by rendering transcendental loving service.
2.	*sarvopādhi-vinirmuktaṁ* *tat-paratvena nirmalam* *hṛṣīkeṇa hṛṣīkeśa-* *sevanaṁ bhaktir ucyate* (*Cc. Madhya* 19.170)	b.	If one is too materialistic but at the same time wants to be a servant of the Supreme Lord, the Lord, because of His supreme compassion for the devotee, takes away all his material opulence and obliges him to be a pure devotee of the Lord.
3.	*yasyāham anugṛhṇāmi* *hariṣye tad-dhanaṁ śanaiḥ* (*SB* 10.88.8)	c.	When a devotee needs something, the Supreme Personality of Godhead supplies it.
4.	*ye yathā māṁ prapadyante* *tāṁs tathaiva bhajāmy aham* (*BG* 4.11)	d.	If one offers Me with love and devotion a leaf, a flower, fruit or water, I will accept it.
5.	*akāmaḥ sarva-kāmo vā* *mokṣa-kāma udāra-dhīḥ* *tīvreṇa bhakti-yogena* *yajeta puruṣaṁ param* (*SB* 2.3.10)	e.	As one surrenders unto Me, I reward him accordingly.
6.	*yoga-kṣemaṁ vahāmy aham* (*BG* 9.22)	f.	Kṛṣṇa is everything.

7.	*vāsudevaḥ sarvam iti* (*BG* 7.19)	g.	Bhakti, or devotional service, means engaging all our senses in the service of the Lord, the Supreme Personality of Godhead, the master of all the senses. When the spirit soul renders service unto the Supreme, there are two side effects. One is freed from all material designations, and, simply by being employed in the service of the Lord, one's senses are purified.

Memorize any or all the above verses along with their meanings. Reflect upon how any of the above verses have brought good fortune into your life or could bring greater fortune into your life. Choose two verses and write down your reflection in a few sentences.

Example:

There are many different paths of spirituality in this world. They all promise different goals, and they all have their own prescribed paths. Kṛṣṇa prescribes the path of *bhakti* in the *Bhagavad-gītā* (4.11), *ye yathā māṁ prapadyante tāṁs tathaiva bhajāmy aham*: "As one surrenders unto Me, I reward him accordingly." The practice of *bhakti* is purest, without contaminations of fruitive activities (*karma*) or speculative activities (*jñāna*), and gives the highest goal, love of Kṛṣṇa. So, I feel fortunate that because I'm trying to surrender to Kṛṣṇa, He will give me the greatest reward, love for Him.

Action Activity

... to get you moving and learning

GAME: BORN TO SERVE

We cannot escape service. Whatever role we have, we are constantly serving and being served. Sometimes we find happiness in serving, but this pleasure doesn't last forever. Our tendency to serve comes from the soul, whose inherent nature is to serve Kṛṣṇa. Only in our service relationship with Him can we experience lasting happiness.

In this game let us explore our service roles in this world and meditate on reviving our relationship with Kṛṣṇa as His eternal servant.

How to Play:

- Players are to sit in a circle.
- Make chits (slips of paper) with names of different roles we find in this world, like friend, mother, sibling, etc. Include anyone who is serving another in any capacity, like nurse, doctor, teacher, etc.

- Each player then picks one chit to determine who they are. They should not tell anyone their role. One of the chits will contain the role of "Central Character."
- All players have to make eye contact with one another while observing the rest, to identify the Central Character. The Central Character player has to blink at each player without anybody else coming to know about it.
- If the Central Character blinks at a person, the player has to count five and say, "I serve the Central Character" without saying who the Central Character is.
- Then the player comes into the center of the circle and enacts how he is serving the Central Character in the role that his chit mentions. For example, if the player is a friend of the Central Character, he may act out lending notes, or getting a birthday cake, and so on. If he is the grandfather of the Central Character, he could enact going on a walk with the Central Character, etc. If he is a bus driver he could enact driving a bus. The other players have to guess the role of the player and how he is serving the Central Character.
- If any other player catches the Central Character blinking at someone else, the player gives a shout out. After the Central Character is identified for at least three times, the game begins again with everyone choosing new chits.

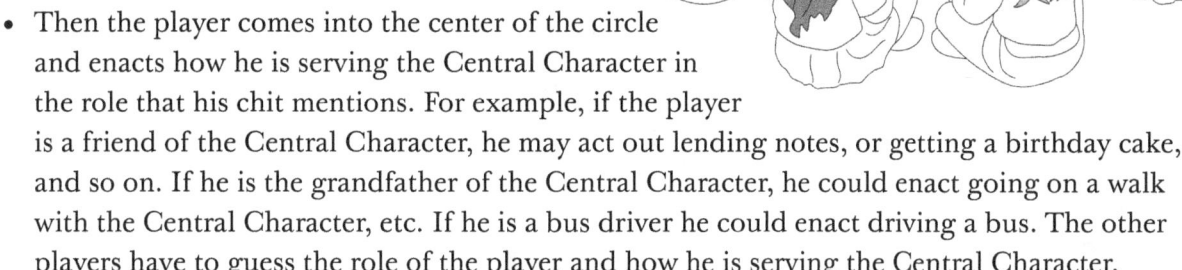

At the end, when all the roles are enacted, players can discuss the following:

- How they are serving others around them and getting served by them.
- How each of the service roles are temporary. Discuss a few examples.
- How their service to Kṛṣṇa is eternal and doesn't change.
- How serving Kṛṣṇa can strengthen their service to others.

Critical-Thinking Activity

... to bring out the spiritual investigator in you

MATERIAL VERSUS SPIRITUAL OUTLOOK

In verse 7 Prahlāda requests Nṛsiṁhadeva to remove all the material desires from the core of his heart. We also saw in the analogy how sincere devotees become cleansed of the desire to receive material benefits from the Lord. Why do pure devotees reject material opulences, and why does the Lord sometimes award them these opulences?

Pure devotees constantly experience spiritual pleasure by serving the Lord in nine different ways. Their pleasure also comes from the Lord's pleasure. Spiritual pleasure is far greater than material pleasure, and therefore they find no need to take shelter of material opulence to become happy. They use any material opulence simply to serve the Lord as He desires, just as Prahlāda Mahārāja agreed to accept material opulence in this chapter.

We've already come across several other devotees in the *Bhāgavatam* who've shown us this truth, and we will come across more in our studies. Let us see what we can learn from the lives of some of these devotees (verses paraphrased).

How does the example of each of these devotees illustrate that spiritual pleasure is far superior to material pleasure?

O my Lord, I pray that within the core of my heart there be no material desires, and that you engage me in the service of Nārada Muni. (*SB* 7.10.7)

Prahlāda

O Lord, since I have now got You, I am so satisfied that I do not wish to ask any benediction from You. (*CC. Madhya* 22.42)

Dhruva

O Lord of Madhu, as the Ganges forever flows to the sea without hindrance, let my attraction be constantly drawn unto You without being diverted to anyone else. (*SB* 1.8.42)

Queen Kunti

O Lord, I do not desire to enjoy or rule any of the planets, nor do I desire mystic power or liberation. I always yearn for the opportunity to serve you. (*SB* 6.11.25)

Vṛtrāsura

Now, based on what you have understood, help the following people (who belong to the four categories of pious people who approach the Lord) understand the spiritual pleasure principle by giving them an appropriate response for their situations.

These are tweets, and you need to respond in tweets, within a word limit of 300 characters. You need not explain but simply give a pointer to help them think properly.

← Tweet

1

Prayers are not always answered. Maybe the Lord sometimes sleeps at work these days.

Respond

2

Didn't get my visa despite offering 1,001 rupees to the famous Balaji Deity. Disappointed.

Respond

3

Dear Anand, happy birthday! Praying to the Lord to give you health, wealth, and happiness the whole year.

Respond

4

Just donated $100,000 to Gokuleshvara temple. Hope the Lord reciprocates by helping our business, so we can give him more next time!

Respond

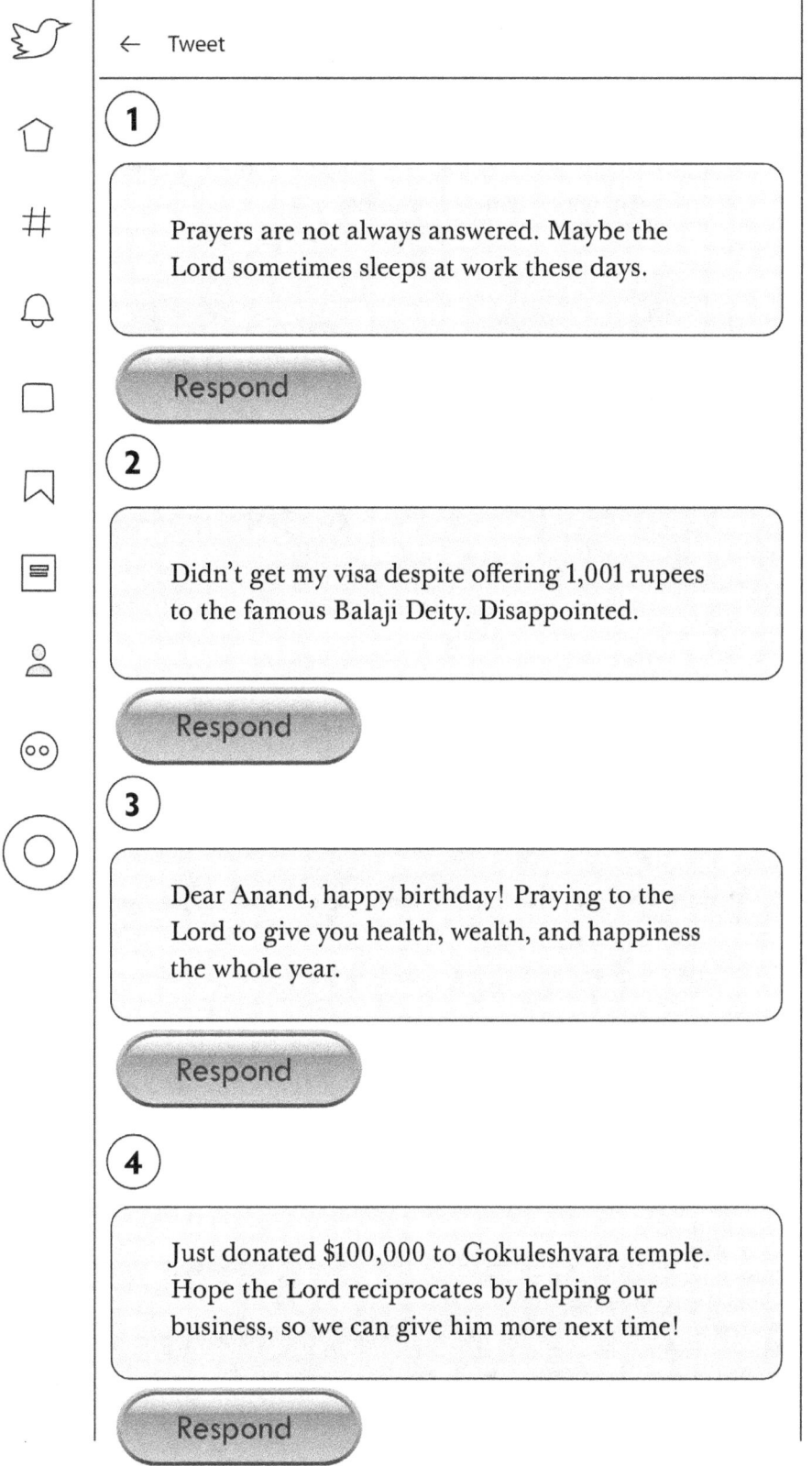

Writing and Language Activities

... to help you understand better

ARE YOU A GIVER, TAKER, OR MATCHER?

Let us explore how each of us may be a Giver, Taker, or Matcher.

Look at the pictures below and see if you are a Giver, a Taker, or a Matcher. Take a small test to see in which category you belong.

There is a dance-drama in school. You badly want the lead part and so does your friend. You will

a) Let him have it.
b) Not tell him about the lead part. You quietly go to the drama teacher and enroll yourself in the lead role.
c) Tell him to take the lead role but ask him to drop out of the basketball team so you can take his place.

Result: Congratulations if you ticked a) You are a giver.
b) You are a taker.
c) You are a matcher.

Although the soul's nature is to be a giver, a selfless servant, because we are covered by the modes of nature, most of us are matchers in life. We rarely give anything without expecting something in return.

However, the pleasure one gets from trying to do selfless service is something to be experienced. Try helping an old lady cross the road or feed the fish in a nearby pond and you will know.

Now think of an incident that gave you a chance to do some selfless service. How did you feel that day?

If such joy can come from serving others selflessly, imagine what it must be like to serve the Supreme Lord selflessly, in our constitutional position, without expecting anything in return, just as Prahlāda experienced.

Here are various scenarios from our scriptures. Try to classify each of these characters as Givers, Takers, or Matchers:

1. Before the Kurukṣetra war, Duryodhana and Arjuna come to Kṛṣṇa for help. Kṛṣṇa gives them the choice of His army or Himself. Arjuna chooses Kṛṣṇa, and Duryodhana heaves a sigh of relief because he wanted the army.
   Duryodhana is a ______________
2. Hiraṇyakaśipu prays to Brahmā for eternal life.
   Hiraṇyakaśipu is a ______________
3. Hanumān is told to get the *sañjīvanī* from the Himālayas. He immediately travels to the Himālayas and brings the whole *sañjīvanī* hill.
   Hanumān is a ______________
4. Indra does not want to give the *pārijāta* tree to Kṛṣṇa.
   Indra is a ______________
5. In *Bhagavad-gītā* (3.11), the Lord says that the demigods, being pleased by your sacrifices, will also please you, and thus, by cooperation between men and demigods, prosperity will reign for all.
   Men are ______________
   Demigods are ______________

BECOMING GENUINE GIVERS BY SERVING KṚṢṆA

As shown in the above activity, it is best to be givers, because it is the natural propensity of the soul. But because we are covered by material desire, even if we seem to be "Givers," we may have some subtle desire for gaining recognition or pious credits. To purify ourselves so that we can become real givers, we need to give ourselves to Kṛṣṇa first.

jīvera 'svarūpa' haya - kṛṣṇera 'nitya-dāsa' (*Cc. Madhya* 20.108)
The constitutional nature of the living entity is to serve Kṛṣṇa always.

Śrīla Prabhupāda often commented that if we don't bow down to Kṛṣṇa, we bow down to *māyā*. We bow down to old age, disease, and death.

Let's see how serving Kṛṣṇa, through the examples of the following unalloyed devotees, is the greatest. In the table below, match the devotee with their service to Kṛṣṇa.

DEVOTEE		SERVICE TO KṚṢṆA
1. Kuntīdevī	a.	Surrendered everything, including his own body, to the Lord who came as Vāmanadeva.
2. Hanumān	b.	Lived for spreading Kṛṣṇa consciousness because his spiritual master had asked him to do so. He established ISKCON temples all over the world.

	DEVOTEE		SERVICE TO KṚṢṆA
3.	Bali Mahārāja	c.	She wanted the calamities that she had suffered to occur again and again so that Lord Kṛṣṇa would stay with her forever and she could serve Him.
4.	Nārada Muni	d.	She was one of the Ālvārs from South India. She saw herself as a *gopī* and her village as Vṛndāvana. She wrote the famous Tiruppavai in Tamil, which is recited till today in India.
5.	Śrīla Prabhupāda	e.	Seventeenth century saint who constantly sang the praises of Lord Viṭṭhala (Lord Kṛṣṇa). He composed nearly five thousand songs, which are called *abhangas*.
6.	Āṇḍāl	f.	When Lakṣmaṇa was saved by the *sañjīvanī*, Lord Rāma embraced this devotee and said, "You are my brother, like Bharata." But he just wanted to be the Lord's servant forever.
7.	Saint Tukārām	g.	The transcendental interplanetary traveller whose only business is to turn everyone to the transcendental service of the Lord. His disciples include Dhruva Mahārāja, Prahlāda Mahārāja, Vyāsadeva, among others.

1. All the above devotees were surrendered servants of the Lord. Did they want anything in return?
2. Can you see the correlation between their service to Kṛṣṇa and their service to others? In other words, did their service to Kṛṣṇa make them better givers overall? Discuss.
3. From the above list of devotees or from anyone else you know, who inspires you the most in selfless service? How would you like to serve Kṛṣṇa unconditionally (not wanting anything in return)? Write a few sentences in your notebook.

ARGUMENTATIVE ESSAY OR DEBATE: IS WORSHIP TO MAN WORSHIP TO GOD?

Refer to what you've studied so far in this chapter about the superiority of serving the Lord and write an argumentative essay on "Is worship to man worship to God?"

You may also divide your class into two debate teams, one for the topic and one against, to come to the *Bhāgavatam's* conclusion.

Essay guidelines:

- Take a position on your topic and form a thesis statement. (A thesis statement is a sentence that sums up the central point of your paper or essay and usually comes near the end of your introduction.)
- Consider your audience.

- Present clear and convincing evidence from your source of reference.
- Draft your essay and then edit your draft.

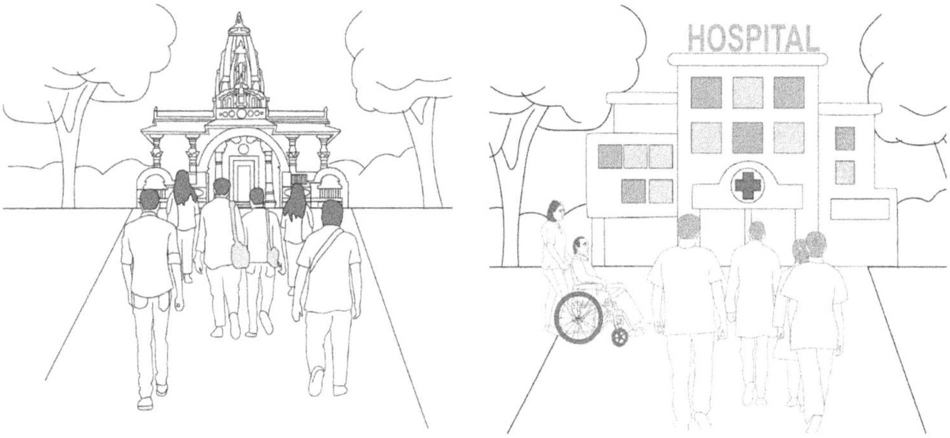

Debate guidelines:

- A formal debate usually involves three groups: one supporting a resolution (affirmative/motion team), one opposing the resolution (opposing team), and those who are judging the quality of the evidence and arguments and the performance in the debate.
- Each member of the motion and opposing teams speaks for five minutes, alternating sides.
- The team supporting the motion must not shift its point of view.
- Provide evidence or reasons to support your statements. Facts presented must be accurate.
- Have a ten-minute discussion session, with each side taking turns to counteract the arguments of the other team.
- Always be respectful to opposing team members, listen, and don't interrupt.

LETTER TO KṚṢṆA: WHY I CHOOSE TO SERVE YOU

As you've learned in this chapter, first list all the material benefits one achieves from serving the Supreme Lord exclusively. Then list the spiritual benefits. You may use the help of a mind map.

Then, based on your evaluation, explain in a letter to Kṛṣṇa why you would choose worshiping Him, even with material desire, than approaching anyone else.

WHEN A DEMON PRAYS

In this chapter Lord Nṛsiṁhadeva chastises Lord Brahmā for fulfilling Hiraṇyakaśipu's wishes.

The Tenth Canto of *Śrīmad-Bhāgavatam* tells a similar story of Lord Śiva fulfilling the desires of the demon Vṛkāsura. He wanted a benediction, so he approached Nārada Muni for advice. Nārada advised him to worship Lord Śiva as he awards benedictions easily. Vṛkāsura journeyed to Kedārnāth, to the temple of Lord Śiva. He built a fire and cut off his flesh and offered it to the fire to please Lord Śiva. His offering was made in the mode of ignorance. He continued his sacrifice for six days but was unable to achieve his desire to see Lord Śiva. On the seventh day he decided to cut off his own head and offer it to Lord Śiva. While he was about to cut off his head, Lord Śiva felt compassion for him and appeared.

"Stop," he said, "There is no need for you to cut off your head. What benediction do you want?"

"When I touch someone's head it must crack open and die."

With a heavy heart Lord Śiva granted his benediction, but the demon decided to kill Lord Śiva and steal Pārvatī. Śiva fled and the demon chased him. Śiva escaped to other planets but none of the demigods could help him. Finally, he ran to Lord Viṣṇu. Viṣṇu had known he was in danger and appeared before Śiva and Vṛkāsura as a *brahmacārī*.

The Lord said, "Why have you come here?"

The demon explained his benediction.

The Lord said, "I don't believe it. Śiva was cursed to wander the earth as a ghost. I have no faith in his words. Why don't you test if the benediction works."

"How?"

"Place your hand on your own head. If the benediction is false you can kill the liar, Śiva."

Vṛkāsura placed his hand on his own head and immediately his head cracked open.

Questions:

1. Why did Nārada recommend the worship of Lord Śiva instead of Lord Viṣṇu to the demon?
2. The line "but was unable to achieve his desire to see Lord Śiva" highlights an important difference between a devotee and a demon. Explain the difference.
3. Give two reasons why the worship of demigods is a waste of time.
4. Explain the figurative expression "heavy heart."

CHAPTER 10 ANSWERS

Purifying the Merchant Mentality

Table: (in the order of Columns 2, 3, and 4):

Dhruva: money bag (kingdom); *arthārthī*; he received a kingdom greater than that of Brahmājī but also became cleansed of material desire and desired only to serve the Lord.

Gajendra: solution; *ārta*; he got saved from the crocodile but was also cleansed and developed a desire to serve the Lord.

Four Kumāras: Vedic tree; *jñānī*; they received knowledge of the personal form of the Lord and became pure devotees.

Śaunaka Ṛṣi: thinking brain; *jijñāsu*; they received adequate knowledge about the Lord to satisfy their curiosity and also developed a strong desire to serve Him in pure love.

Prahlāda: Rādhā Kṛṣṇa pendant; *premī*; he desired to serve the Lord with no material desires, and he received the benediction to do so.

1. The common result each received due to their sincerity was the opportunity to overcome material desires and develop pure devotional service; 2. Depends on the mentality of the devotee. The Lord provides this opportunity to all those who approach Him with a sincere heart, even if they have material desires – He fulfills the material desires and blesses them with a chance to further progress in relation to Him. If, however, one only wants fulfillment of material desires and has no desire to spiritually progress, the Lord limits Himself to granting just that also; 3. One should sincerely approach the Lord and serve Him through the spiritual master and the devotees, just like the examples of the devotees in this activity. One should not simply desire to become materially opulent by the Lord's blessing and enjoy in this world independent of the Lord and service to His devotees; 4. Devotees also become as opulent as the Lord in some aspect, even after they become purified of the material desire to possess opulence of any kind (e.g., Dhruva and Prahlāda were opulent in wealth; the Kumaras became opulent in knowledge). But devotees use all their opulence in the Lord's service, not for their personal enjoyment.

Treasure of Fortunes

1. protects; Lord Viṣṇu; Maya Dānava
2. liberation; salvation; thinking of the Lord; a place in the Lord's abode; serve Him
3. *karma*; nullify; causeless mercy
4. qualities; dynasty

1. d; 2. g; 3. b; 4. e; 5. a; 6. c; 7. f

Material Versus Spiritual Outlook

Part 1: 1. Prahlāda: Knowing that the Lord vanquished his father's opulence in a moment, he preferred to serve the Lord and his *guru* with everything he had; 2. Dhruva: He realized that the love the Lord offered him was greater than any kingdom he could receive, and so he was bound by the Lord's love to serve Him; 3. Vṛtrāsura: Knowing the permanent nature of the Lord's relationship with the soul, he realized that neither defeat to Indra nor destruction of the body could hinder the relationship. Defeat and death therefore didn't bother him since it would not stop the spiritual pleasure of serving the Lord; 4. Kunti: She realized that everything belongs to the Lord and everything He gives is only by His mercy, so she preferred to be attracted to the Lord and His care than to the material gifts he could offer.

Part 2 (*Potential Answers*): 1. No, the Lord does not. Unanswered prayers are a sign that you need to look for the right answer, and not just for the answer you expected; 2. Well, maybe the Lord too was disappointed that you didn't ask Him for anything more than a visa to a foreign country. Try offering 1,001 rupees while asking for a visa to Vaikuṇṭha next time. Trust me, He won't disappoint you; 3. The Lord can also give love, liberation, and service that lasts forever. Happy birthday!; 4. If He needs to give you wealth, the wealth is His in the first place. So how are you going to give something that doesn't belong to you in the first place – and that is His – back to Him next time?

Are you a Giver, Taker, or Matcher?

1. Taker; 2. Taker; 3. Giver; 4. Taker; 5. Both are Matchers

Becoming Genuine Givers by Serving Kṛṣṇa

Did they want anything in return? No

1.(c); 2.(f); 3.(a); 4.(g); 5.(b); 6.(d); 7.(e)

When a Demon Prays

1. Lord Śiva is easily satisfied, and people in the mode of ignorance, like Vṛtrāsura, cannot stick to the worship of Viṣṇu.
2. A devotee is confident that whatever he offers to the Lord in full devotional service is accepted by the Lord, but a demon wants to see his worshipable deity face to face so that he can directly take the benediction. A devotee does not worship Viṣṇu or Lord Kṛṣṇa for any material benediction.
3. The process of worshiping demigods is very difficult, and the result obtained is flickering and temporary and may not be for your ultimate benefit, as illustrated in this story.
4. To have a heavy heart means to be sad, depressed, or regretful, usually about something that is happening or something one has to do.

Opulences from Serving the Lord (*Potential Answers*)

Material: material desires being fulfilled, obtaining all good qualities and character, gaining various opulences to serve the Lord, all ancestors (even condemned) being liberated.

Spiritual: becoming free of material desires, becoming detached from sense pleasure, becoming attracted to hearing and chanting the glories of the Lord, coming closer to the Lord, growing in one's love for the Lord, being endowed with saintly qualities, purifying every place and making it a place of pilgrimage, going back to Godhead and possessing a form similar to the Lord's.

RESOURCE FOR ART ACTIVITY

RESOURCE FOR ART ACTIVITY

11

THE PERFECT SOCIETY: FOUR SOCIAL CLASSES

Story Summary

Mahārāja Yudhiṣṭhira's face glowed with bliss. Who wouldn't be joyful after hearing the enlivening life story of Prahlāda Mahārāja?

He again inquired from Nārada Muni: "O best of *brāhmaṇas*, best of the sons of Lord Brahmā, no one is more merciful than you, neither is anyone better than you in executing devotional service. So I want to hear from you about religious principles that lead to the ultimate goal of life – devotional service. I want to hear about the occupational duties of human society, the system of social and spiritual advancement known as *varṇāśrama-dharma*."

Nārada folded his palms and closed his eyes and said, "I offer my obeisances to Lord Kṛṣṇa, the protector of religious principles. I will explain this eternal religious system as I heard it from the mouth of Lord Nara-Nārāyaṇa Himself, who even now resides at Badarikāśrama.

"The Supreme Lord is the essence of all Vedic knowledge and the root of all religious principles. All knowledge and principles are meant to know Him and follow His laws. No one can manufacture one's own religion. Religious principles, including following *varṇāśrama-dharma*, are meant to please Kṛṣṇa. They are meant to teach us how to serve Kṛṣṇa without any motivation. Human society can only be happy if they do this."

"Please tell me more about these religious principles," said Yudhiṣṭhira Mahārāja.

"We have to cultivate thirty qualities to satisfy the Lord. Among them are truthfulness, mercy, austerity, tolerance, control of the mind and senses, nonviolence, charity, simplicity, satisfaction, serving saintly persons, seeing every soul as part of the Lord, hearing the Lord's activities and instructions, serving and worshiping the Lord, and surrendering one's whole life. These are some of the basic principles that should be followed by any human being."

After giving a general list for one's behavior, Nārada Muni began to describe the principles of the four *varṇas* and *āśramas*. He explained that human beings must first be trained in these thirty qualifications, and among these qualified people the *varṇāśrama* process can be introduced. This would ensure that people execute their work and activities as purely as possible.

The first three *varṇas* –*brāhmaṇas*, the priestly class; *kṣatriyas*, the administrative class; and *vaiśyas*, the mercantile class – who are purified by their family traditions and behavior, should worship the Lord, study the *Vedas*, and give in charity. They should follow the four *āśramas* – *brahmacarya*, *gṛhastha*, *vānaprastha*, and *sannyāsa*.

"What are the duties of each of these three *varṇas*," asked Yudhiṣṭhira Mahārāja.

"O King," replied Nārada Muni, "the *brāhmaṇas* have six occupational duties, of which the first three are most important: to worship the Deity, to study the *Vedas*, to give in charity, to accept charity or gifts (only for one's livelihood), to teach spiritual knowledge, and to induce others to worship the Deity.

"A *brāhmaṇa* can never engage in the service of others; otherwise he becomes a *śūdra*."

"And what about the *kṣatriyas* and *vaiśyas*?" asked Mahārāja Yudhiṣṭhira.

"A *kṣatriya* should never accept charity. Besides this, he can engage in the other five activities of the *brāhmaṇas*. However, a *kṣatriya* should not take taxes from *brāhmaṇas* or Vaiṣṇavas although he can do that with his other subjects.

"The *vaiśyas* should always follow the directions of the *brāhmaṇas* and should engage in agriculture, trade, and cow protection."

"And isn't there a fourth class, the *śūdras*?" asked Mahārāja Yudhiṣṭhira.

"Oh yes, they have only one duty – to accept and serve a master from a higher social order."

"Can any of the social orders take on the duties of another?" asked the King, trying to analyze this from every angle.

"Hmm . . ." muttered the sage, furrowing his eyebrows in thought. "A *brāhmaṇa* may take the duty of a *vaiśya*, doing agriculture, cow protection, and trade for his livelihood. This is because he is often offered land and cows in charity. But better than this is if he picks up grains from a field or from a shop without begging, or just depend on what he has received without begging."

"Are there any other cases where one social order can do the work of another?" asked Yudhiṣṭhira Mahārāja.

"Well, those in the lower orders should not accept the duties of those in the higher orders – except in an emergency. But under no circumstances should *kṣatriyas* accept the livelihood of others."

Being a *kṣatriya* himself, Yudhiṣṭhira Mahārāja understood why this was so. The four divisions of human society were created by the Supreme Lord according to the three modes of material nature and the work that each should follow. Each of the *varṇas* have specific qualities and characteristics that make them most suited for that *varṇa*. One with particular symptoms wouldn't be suited to act in another role.

To confirm what he was thinking, Yudhiṣṭhira Mahārāja asked, "So what are the symptoms of each of the *varṇas* that make them most suited to act in that *varṇa*?"

Nārada Muni answered, "The *brāhmaṇas* control the mind and senses; they perform penance and austerity; they are clean, satisfied, simple, merciful, and truthful; they forgive easily and have knowledge; and they completely surrender to the Supreme Lord."

Then, smiling at the King, knowing that he exemplified a perfect *kṣatriya*, Nārada Muni continued, "The *kṣatriyas* are influential in battle; they are unconquerable, patient, challenging, and charitable. They also control the bodily needs; they are forgiving, attached to the brahminical nature, and always jolly and truthful.

"As for the *vaiśyas*, they are devoted to the demigods, the spiritual master, and the Supreme Lord. They try to advance in religious principles, economic development, and sense gratification (*dharma*, *artha*, and *kāma*), and they always expertly endeavor to earn money."

"And what about the *śūdras*?" asked the King, knowing that they also play an important part in society.

"Oh, they are always respectful and loyal to the higher social orders; they are always clean, free from duplicity; they serve their master, performing sacrifices without uttering *mantras*; they don't steal and always speak the truth, giving all protection to the cows and *brāhmaṇas*."

Nārada Muni continued to explain that for peace and happiness to prevail in the material world the *varṇāśrama* institution must be introduced and followed, otherwise there would be a *varṇa-saṅkara* society. A *varṇa-saṅkara* society is one of mixed classes, in which no one can distinguish between any of the *varṇas*, and therefore society cannot function properly. The chastity and devotion of women is essential to create good population eligible for participating in the *varṇāśrama* system. The classes become mixed when unchaste women and irresponsible men provoke adultery in society, leading to unwanted population. Therefore it is imperative that a woman remain chaste and faithful to her husband.

"A chaste woman follows four principles," continued Nārada. "She should not be greedy but satisfied in all situations; she should be expert in her household duties and educated in religious principles; she should speak pleasingly but truthfully; and should always be clean and pure. In this way a chaste woman should serve her

qualified husband with affection. A woman who does this, following the example of the goddess of fortune, will surely go back to Godhead with her devotee husband and live happily in the Vaikuṇṭha planets."

Yudhiṣṭhira Mahārāja smiled and nodded. He knew from his experience in family life what Nārada Muni meant.

"My dear King," Nārada continued, "learned *brāhmaṇas* have concluded that in every age it is auspicious when people discharge their own prescribed duties, according to their nature and influence of the material modes of nature. And if one gradually gives up these activities, he attains the *niṣkāma* stage, freedom from material desires.

"And very importantly, dear King, one's class or *varṇa* is determined not by birth but by qualification. In other words, if someone is born in one class but displays the symptoms of another class, he should be accepted as the other class according to his symptoms."

Themes and Key Messages

Please go through this table of themes and key messages, with corresponding verses, and discuss each topic further.

THEMES	REFERENCES	KEY MESSAGES
Our supreme occupational duty, *sanātana-dharma*, is to be a servant of Kṛṣṇa, which can be realized through the institution of *varṇāśrama*.	7.11.2	Everyone remains a servant because this is their eternal position, but they usually serve *māyā*, the illusory energy, in the material world. However, *sanātana-dharma* is our real and eternal occupational duty, which is to serve the Supreme Lord. This occupational duty can be organized and realized through *varṇāśrama-dharma*, in which there are four *varṇas* and four *āśramas*.

THEMES	REFERENCES	KEY MESSAGES
We should follow religious principles prescribed in the scriptures, which are meant to please the Supreme Lord, who is the essence of all religious principles.	7.11.7–12	Kṛṣṇa is the root of all religious principles (*dharma*) and the essence of all Vedic knowledge. One must follow the principles laid down in the *śruti* (the *Vedas*) and *smṛti* (the scriptures following the Vedic principles) and not concoct one's own ideas of how to please the Lord. However, following the *śruti* and *smṛti* without devotional service cannot lead to the perfection of life. In other words, any *dharma,* including *varṇāśrama-dharma*, cannot succeed without devotion to Kṛṣṇa. Similarly, anyone from any background should develop all the thirty principles of a human being, such as truthfulness, cleanliness, nonviolence, tolerance, simplicity, etc. These are non-sectarian principles, which please the Lord and promote peace and goodwill in the world. However, by becoming a devotee, one automatically acquires these good qualities. (*SB* 5.18.12)
The four *varṇas* for a perfect society have certain occupational duties and qualities, which bring happiness in this life and the next, and only in times of emergency may they accept the occupational duty of another.	7.11.13–20, 31	The *brāhmaṇas*, *kṣatriyas*, and *vaiśyas* should become purified by their family traditions and behavior and worship the Lord, study the *Vedas*, and give in charity. The *śūdras* should accept a master from the higher social order and serve him. Each of the orders should perform their duties and occupation diligently. "It is better to engage in one's own occupation, even though one may perform it imperfectly, than to accept another's occupation and perform it perfectly." (*BG* 18.47 & 3.35) Except in emergency, those in the lower orders shouldn't accept the occupational duties of the higher orders.
When women are polluted, society becomes *varṇa-saṅkara*, population with unwanted children.	7.11.25–29	Women should be chaste and serve their devotee husband. A man should be an ideal servant of the Lord, and the woman should be an ideal wife like the goddess of fortune. In this way, society would be protected from unwanted population. In a *varṇa-saṅkara* society, no one can distinguish between the different *varṇas.*
One should not be accepted as a *brāhmaṇa*, *kṣatriya*, *vaiśya*, or *śūdra* according to birth, but by qualification.	7.11.35	The *śāstras* reject classification as a *brāhmaṇa*, *kṣatriya*, *vaiśya*, or *śūdra* based on one's birth. Even if one is born in a particular social order but does not have the symptoms or qualifications of that order, he cannot be considered a *brāhmaṇa* or any of the other classes. Therefore, the four divisions of society should be ascertained according to qualities and activities – not birth.

Higher-Thinking Questions

Now try to deepen your understanding of this chapter by delving into Śrīla Prabhupāda's purports and reflecting on the following questions:

1. Verse 7 purport explains that to become a devotee one must follow the principles of the scriptures, yet following the scriptures without devotional service is not recommended. So what is the most important factor in following religious principles?

2. How are so-called religious principles without devotional service only cheating, as mentioned by Śrīla Prabhupāda in his purport to verse 7.

3. The thirty qualifications of a civilized human being are mentioned in verses 8 to 12, which can be acquired by performing devotional service. However, do you think you should still try to cultivate these qualities on your own as well? Read the purport and the purport to verse 13 and explain.

4. Explain the universal, non-sectarian nature of Kṛṣṇa consciousness described in the purport to verses 8 to 12.

5. Why shouldn't *kṣatriyas* accept charity as described in verse 14 purport? Who can accept charity and why?

6. As mentioned in verse 14, why do you think that a king or *kṣatriya* should not levy taxes on *brāhmaṇas* [or Vaiṣṇavas] but may levy minimal taxes on his other subjects?

7. According to verse 14 purport, why were Rūpa and Sanātana Gosvāmīs, even though born in *brāhmaṇa* families, ostracized from brahminical society?

8. Why do you think that only a *kṣatriya* shouldn't accept the occupational duty or livelihood of another even in an emergency?

9. How are the *brāhmaṇas* from degraded backgrounds in the Kṛṣṇa consciousness movement supported by Nārada in verse 17? Refer to purport.

10. According to Śrīla Prabhupāda in verse 20 purport, practically everyone in Kali-yuga is a *śūdra*. Why is this so, and why is it important to reestablish the divine *varṇāśrama* institution which has been lost?

11. Why do you think the role and qualities of chaste women are described in detail in this chapter? Refer to verse 25 purport. [Hint: How does *varṇa-saṅkara* society occur?]

12. Do you think that a woman should indiscriminately serve any kind of husband? (See verse 28 and purport.) What is the ideal situation described in this purport and the purport to verse 29?

ACTIVITIES

In this section you will find many exciting things to do. These activities will get you thinking, moving, drawing, and having loads of fun.

Analogy Activity

... to bring out the scholar in you

DRESS THE INTERDEPENDENT VARṆA TYPES

Materials: craft paper (different colors or white); scissors; double-sided tape; pencil/pen to draw; coloring pens or pencils

Directions:

1. Trace or draw the templates provided in Resources on colored paper or white craft paper, or photocopy the drawings provided.
2. Make four drawings/copies of the man and the *dhoti*.
3. Cut the images and figures. Color them.
4. Using double-sided tape, stick the right props and objects to each *varṇa* figure. See example image of a *kṣatriya*.

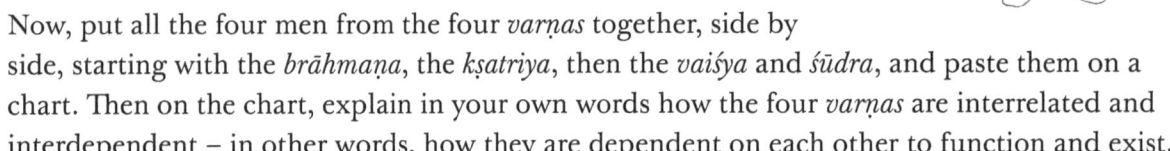

Now, put all the four men from the four *varṇas* together, side by side, starting with the *brāhmaṇa*, the *kṣatriya*, then the *vaiśya* and *śūdra*, and paste them on a chart. Then on the chart, explain in your own words how the four *varṇas* are interrelated and interdependent – in other words, how they are dependent on each other to function and exist.

Introspective Activity

... to bring out the reflective devotee in you

CAREER DHARMA*

The career we choose plays an important role in our devotional lives. If we have a field of work that we like and that matches our nature, we can happily perform our work as an

* Based on the book by Urmila Edith Best and Ruchira S. Datta

offering to the Supreme Lord and progress in our spiritual path. Unfortunately, people are often not aware of their nature and get stuck in the wrong career. Then they spend their lives in frustration and are unable to find the happiness in service.

The following four fields of work are described in *Career Dharma – The Natural Art of Work* by Urmila Edith Best and Ruchira S. Datta. Analyze each and see which one resembles you best. See also the corresponding career choices; these are only some suggestions. You would need to do more research and discuss with your parents and teachers to choose a career path that fits you. For more information and a thorough analysis and overview of the subject, refer to the book *Career Dharma*.

Field of Artistry

People in this field like to work to provide all the functionalities of society. Their work provides pleasure and beauty to the world. Without their services, this world would be a dry place. People belonging to this field like to please others by serving them.

They ask themselves the following questions: Is my work beautiful? Is it supportive to my clients/customers? Is it pleasing to them?

They are usually not super-ambitious people. If basic comforts are provided to them, they are satisfied.

Career choices: Visual and performing artists; architects; those in the entertainment industry; fashion and interior designers; engineers; secretaries; cashiers; athletes; nurses; plumbers; technicians; caregivers; cooks; etc.

Field of Resources

People in this field work to provide resources to society. They provide raw materials for food, clothing, construction, etc. They look at systems of resources, channel them, expand and increase them, and then distribute the resources back to society. They like to create profits. All the entrepreneurs and those who are primary employers come under this field. Most of the charity work in society is done by those in this field.

They ask the following questions: Is what I am doing sustainable? Is it regenerative? Am I creating profit?

They are ambitious and always in the mode of expansion.

Career choices: Industrialists; farm owners; entrepreneurs; human resources managers; stock analysts; bankers; miners; etc.

Field of Government

People in this field provide organization, security, roads, schools, hospitals, etc., to protect and care for as many people as possible in society.

The ask themselves the following: Is my work just and ethical? Is it honorable? Am I providing protection for people?

Unlike those in the field of artistry where they serve others as servants, in this field they serve others like a parent.

Career choices: Law makers; lawyers; members of parliament; military; security personnel; police; governors; diplomats; presidents; mayors; firefighters; etc.

Field of Ideas

Those in this field work to provide truth, wisdom, guidance, and education to society. All intellectuals fall in this field where sharing of ideas takes place. They are not particularly concerned with pleasing others. Some try to find the truth within themselves, and others love sharing truth. Often, they share their truth through language, mathematics, statistics, and sometimes through art. Unlike those in artistry, people in the field of ideas use language, art, etc., not to beautify society but to convey their ideas of wisdom and truth.

They ask the following questions: Is my work true and is it for the ultimate good of others, even if it may not please others? Is it wise?

They are usually not ambitious people. They find their joy in the mental and intellectual stimulation that their work provides.

Career choices: Doctors; teachers; researchers; authors; painters, musicians, or journalists who focus not on providing entertainment but in sharing philosophies, truth, wisdom, and education.

Theatrical Activity

... to bring out the actor in you

SKIT: FOUR VARṆAS FOR FOUR FRIENDS

Four friends are together and are discussing their future careers. (You may rename the characters as you like.)

Emily: Priya, do you know this year we will need to choose subjects for a career?

Priya: Yes, I know, Emily. I'm getting worried because I don't know what career path to choose. It's not so easy.

Ravi: Well, yesterday in class we were learning about society in Vedic times. Do you know that society was divided into four parts, each according to the work done by a person? They followed *varṇāśrama-dharma*.

Emily: Huh? Tell me more about it, Ravi.

Ravi: There were broadly four classes of people, four *varṇas*, and each of them did their work which was suitable to their nature.

Emily: How can my nature decide what work I have to do?

Veer: (interrupting) Our nature shows us what we like and are inclined to do. You see, in the *Bhagavad-gītā*, Chapter 4, verse 13, Lord Kṛṣṇa says that He Himself has created these *varṇas*. What's the verse, Ravi?

Ravi: (imitating Kṛṣṇa speaking)

cātur-varṇyaṁ mayā sṛṣṭaṁ
guṇa-karma-vibhāgaśaḥ
tasya kartāram api māṁ
viddhy akartāram avyayam

"According to the three modes of material nature (*guṇas*) and the work associated with them (*karma*), the four divisions of human society are created by Me. And although I am the creator of this system, you should know that I am yet the nondoer, being unchangeable."

Priya: What is *guṇa* and *karma*?

Ravi: *Guṇa* are the three modes of material nature: goodness, passion, and ignorance. We are driven by these modes according to our *karma* in our previous births. Depending on the dominance of any one of these modes, we choose our field of work, *karma*.

Priya: That's interesting! That means I don't have to choose; the modes will guide me to do whatever work I want to do?

Ravi: Something like that!

Veer: (stands before everyone and waves his hand) Attention, everyone! Now I am going to show you some magic (grins). As I snap my finger, we will be transported to Vedic times.

(He snaps his fingers. The inner curtain opens. It's a busy marketplace, where people are buying and selling things. Some laborers are carrying loads. A merchant is transporting loads of grain in a cart to sell. A *brāhmaṇa* with some Vedic texts is walking through hurriedly.

Suddenly, some soldiers march towards the entrance of the marketplace.)

Emily: (to her friends, surprised) Am I dreaming, or what? (rushes to the *brāhmaṇa*) Who are you, and why are you dressed like this? What do you do?

Brāhmaṇa: (looks at Emily with amusement) I am a *brāhmaṇa*.

Lord Kṛṣṇa describes the qualities of *brāhmaṇas* in *Bhagavad-gītā* (18.42) as follows:

śamo damas tapaḥ śaucaṁ kṣāntir ārjavam eva ca
jñānaṁ vijñānam āstikyaṁ brahma-karma svabhāva-jam

"Peacefulness, self-control, austerity, purity, tolerance, honesty, wisdom, knowledge, and religiousness – these are the natural qualities by which the *brāhmaṇas* work."

These are all qualities in the mode of goodness.

I must be a good scholar of the scriptures, and I must teach others. I must also preach and cultivate other *brāhmaṇas*. I must do *yajñas*, sacrifice. Since I don't earn anything, I am allowed to take charity from others.

Emily: I like your ponytail! What is that thread you are wearing around your chest?

Brāhmaṇa: (showing the tuft of hair on the back of his head and smiling) This is called a *śikhā*. It is a sign of renunciation and devotion to God. The thread signifies that a person is twice-born, or a *dvija*, so he is qualified to learn the *Vedas*.

Emily: I would like to do a *brāhmaṇa*'s work. I love reading and learning, and even teaching. You know everyone in school asks me questions and I'm able to answer them.

Veer: Hey, there is the leader of the soldiers! Let me go and talk to him. (rushes to the soldier) Who are you?

Soldier: I am a *kṣatriya*. My job is to protect the other three *varṇas* of society. As Lord Kṛṣṇa says in *Bhagavad-gītā* (18.43):

śauryaṁ tejo dhṛtir dākṣyaṁ
yuddhe cāpy apalāyanam
dānam īśvara-bhāvaś ca
kṣātraṁ karma svabhāva-jam

"Heroism, power, determination, resourcefulness, courage in battle, generosity and leadership are the natural qualities of work for the *kṣatriyas*." These qualities are in the mode of passion.

Veer: You have real muscles, and you are so strong! I love to have muscles like that, and I do love to lead people. I'm the school ambassador, you know. (Soldier smiles and pats Veer's shoulder.)

Ravi: There's a rich merchant with a bag of money! Let us talk to him! (The children rush to him.) Who are you? You look very rich! Is that money in your bag? How did you get so much money?

Merchant (looks at the children and smiles): Yes! I am a *vaiśya*. People like me do different kinds of work. As Lord Kṛṣṇa says in *Bhagavad-gītā* (18.44):

kṛṣi-go-rakṣya-vāṇijyaṁ
vaiśya-karma svabhāva-jam

"Farming, cattle raising, and business are the qualities of work for the *vaiśyas*." These work qualities are in the mode of passion and ignorance.

Ravi: That's great! I too would like to become a big businessman and the richest person in the world, like Bill Gates. But I will use this money for making more and more people God conscious.

Veer: Oh! We forgot the most hardworking member of our society! The laborer who serves all others. Let us go and talk to him. (They all go towards the laborer who is helping the merchant.)

Priya: Sir! Can you tell us about yourself?

Laborer: I help every other class of people by serving them.

paricaryātmakaṁ karma
śūdrasyāpi svabhāva-jam

We do labor and service to others.

Priya: It is such a difficult job to please everybody. Where would *varṇāśrama* be if you were not there to serve the *vaiśyas*, *kṣatriyas*, and *brāhmaṇas*! (thoughtful) I love to serve others. People always tell me how caring and supportive I am.

Ravi (to audience): Do you know that each of the *varṇas* are like parts of Lord Kṛṣṇa's body?

Emily: The *brāhmaṇas* are His head.

Veer: The *kṣatriyas* are His arms.

Ravi: The *vaiśyas* are His thighs.

Priya: And the *śūdras* are His legs.

All together: Just as every part of our body is important for our functioning, every *varṇa* is important for the proper functioning of a God conscious society. Everyone works for Kṛṣṇa. Everyone works for each other's salvation.

Varṇāśrama-dharma ki jaya!
Hare Kṛṣṇa Hare Kṛṣṇa Kṛṣṇa Kṛṣṇa Hare Hare
Hare Rāma Hare Rāma Rāma Rāma Hare Hare.

Critical-Thinking Activity

... to bring out the spiritual investigator in you

THE DANGERS OF PARA-DHARMA

In the purport to verse 31, Śrīla Prabhupāda quotes *Bhagavad-gītā* (3.35), wherein Lord Kṛṣṇa states that it is better to perform one's duty (*sva-dharma*), according to one's *varṇa*, imperfectly than try to perform the duties of someone else (*para-dharma*) perfectly. Kṛṣṇa says it is dangerous to follow another's path. Let us try to understand this statement in perspective.

Vraja, a young and inspired devotee girl, is waiting at the office of Gaura Kṛpā Prabhu, who is a career counsellor. She is looking through a catalogue in his office that has different caricatures related to career choice. As she contemplates on them, she realizes that these are not meant for mere amusement but have a strong message: one should not choose a career that is against one's nature and interest.

The cartoons have been reproduced below. Analyze each of them using the questions at the end as a guide.

1

"Sir, after much thought, I've decided that my principles ask me to 'teach-her' than be her 'prince-see-pal'. Sorry, I have to decline your offer!"

2

"Sir, it is not possible to continue running this prison for the government. Our company will have a financial 'cell-out'!"

3

"Yup, that's the latest version of the alphabet: $ € Rs. With profit being the only motive of schools, As and Bs have become useless."

4

"Yes, my desk job provides ample opportunity to display artistic talents. I get to make square graph charts, rectangular tables, and round pie charts on digital paper all day."

For each case, answer the following:

a) Identify the original *varṇa* in which the job was happening or was supposed to happen.
b) Which *varṇa* mixed with or replaced this *varṇa*?
c) What was the result of this?

Writing and Language Activities

... to help you understand better

"CASTE"ING BY QUALITY AND WORK

Verse 35 mentions that the classification of men (casting) into different *varṇas* should be done by personal qualities (*guṇa*) and work (*karma*), and not by birth. In the purport Śrīla Prabhupāda quotes *Bhagavad-gītā* (4.13), in which Kṛṣṇa also confirms this.

In fact, great sages have always determined *varṇa* by *guṇa* and *karma*. Look at the timeline on the next page. It depicts some great personalities who were accepted as a certain *varṇa* despite not being born in that *varṇa*. Can you identify their birth ancestry and the *varṇa* they were finally accepted into and write it in the table?

	PERSONALITY	BIRTH ANCESTRY	ACCEPTED AS...
1	Nārada (former life)		
2	Viśvāmitra		
3	Paraśurāma		
4	Vena		
5	Aśvatthāmā		
6	Haridāsa Ṭhākura		
7	Rūpa and Sanātana Gosvāmīs		
8	Narottama dāsa Ṭhākura		
9	Prabhupāda's western disciples		

Based on what you learn from the chart above, what conclusion can you draw about ISKCON's preaching mission, in which everyone is invited to participate?

ESSAY: CASTE SYSTEM VERSUS THE VARṆĀŚRAMA SYSTEM

From the last activity, let us continue discussing and finding out more about how "caste" doesn't determine your *varṇa*.

Often the caste system in ancient India and even modern-day India gets confused with the *varṇāśrama* system. In this essay, you will discuss how the caste system is different.

First research about the caste system in India – its roots, ideologies, negative impact in society, etc., and then contrast this with the *varṇāśrama* system.

You may also research Śrīla Bhaktisiddhānta Sarasvatī's role in establishing *varṇāśrama* and defeating the caste system propagated by the *smarta brāhmaṇas.*

In your introduction write your thesis statement, which introduces your topic and expresses one main idea/point of your essay. Then in different paragraphs discuss each of the conclusions and findings from your research and contrast each point with *varṇāśrama*. You may include some of the arguments or story from Śrīla Bhaktisiddhānta Sarasvatī. Your conclusion should tie up with your thesis statement about what was deduced.

ESSAY: CHASTITY – OVERRATED OR UNDERESTIMATED?

Usually we think of *varṇāśrama-dharma* in relation to the four *varṇas*: *brāhmaṇa*, *kṣatriya*, *vaiśya,* and *śūdra*. But in this chapter we learn that women have an important role to play to keep the *varṇas* intact. Let us delve into this topic a bit more, especially in relation to the modern world. Is chastity in women overrated or underestimated today?

Write an essay on the topic. Try to cover the following points:

- Explain how *varṇāśrama-dharma* distinguishes between male and female duties. Clarify why this distinction does not oppress women.
- Define chasteness according to the *Bhāgavatam*.
- Explain why the *Bhāgavatam* emphasizes chasteness in women.
- Discuss how the breakdown of Vedic principles has led to the exploitation of women and a loss of chastity in the modern world.

You may use the following references, or any other, from the Vedabase:

Śrīla Prabhupāda room conversation, Philadelphia, July 13, 1975
Morning walk, December 10, 1975
SB 7.11.25–29
SB 3.30. 41
SB 6.6.1

After writing your essay, discuss it with your devotee friends or teacher and try to discover how material biases may have initially influenced your understanding of the topic. What has changed in your understanding?

INTERVIEW: THE AIM OF OCCUPATION

In this activity you will interview people in different fields of work. They should have at least 10 to 15 years of experience in their field. Try to interview a minimum of four people, two devotees and two nondevotees.

The goal is to encourage them to reflect on their nature, duties, characteristics of the work they belong to, the ultimate goal of performing their duties, *dharma* in general, personal character development, detachment from material desires, and ultimately service of the Absolute Truth.

Please present your findings in a short write-up, focusing on the difference between the understanding and conduct of a devotee and a nondevotee regarding the aim of their occupational duties.

There are two resources provided: 1. Sample questions to guide the interviews (to be adapted according to your interviewee); 2. Chart showing different stages of progress in occupational duties.

Resource 1:

1. What are the general characteristics of people who do the same work as you?
2. What are your strengths that are critical to your success in this field?
3. Describe your nature. (For devotees: Is it predominantly in the mode of goodness, or passion, or a mix?)
4. Is there anything you would like to change in your nature?
5. Can you recollect an experience that added integrity and depth to your character?
6. How has your experience changed your perspective of an ultimate goal in life?
7. What are your objectives or goals regarding your career?
8. What do you think is the supreme motivation for any work?
9. Are you happy in your chosen field? Why, or why not?
10. As you grow older, do you notice a reduction in material aspirations and an interest in pursuing a higher or "spiritual" path?

Resource 2:

The *varṇāśrama* system is a cooperative system perfectly created by Lord Kṛṣṇa to help us become purified from the material modes and to gradually develop higher consciousness. By acting piously under the laws of the Lord, everyone ultimately comes to the stage of service to the Supreme Personality of Godhead. The ultimate aim is *acyutātmatvam* – to think always of the Supreme Personality of Godhead, Kṛṣṇa, or Viṣṇu (*SB* 7.11.21).

The following chart presents the above information for easy reference:

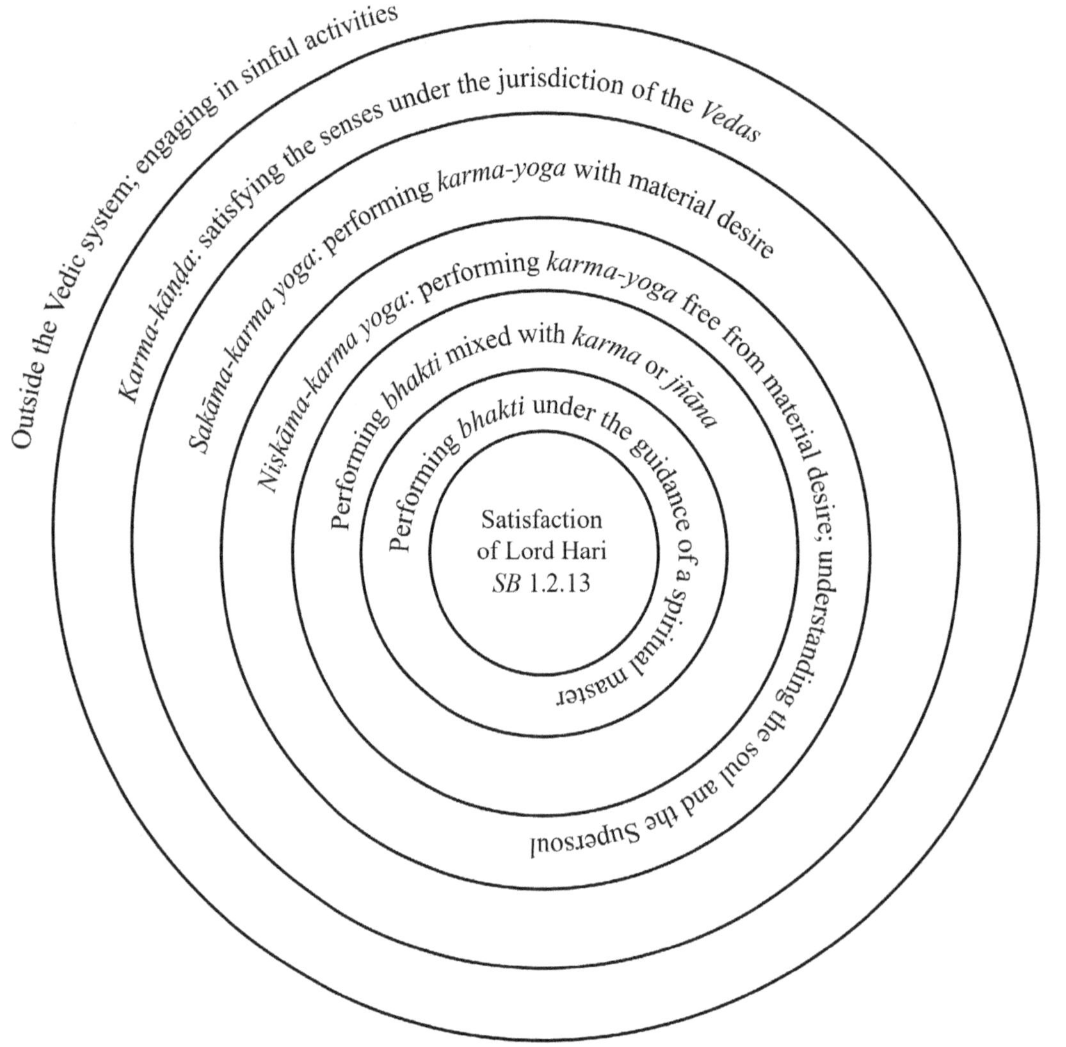

DEVOTIONAL POETRY

Satisfaction of the Supreme Lord Hari is the essence of all religious principles, including *varṇāśrama-dharma*. Without devotion to the Lord one cannot be successful in executing occupational duties. *Śrīmad-Bhāgavatam* (1.2.8) expounds this in beautiful poetry:

dharmaḥ svanuṣṭhitaḥ puṁsāṁ
viṣvaksena kathāsu yaḥ

notpādayed yadi ratiṁ
śrama eva hi kevalam

"The occupational activities a man performs according to his own position are only so much useless labor if they do not provoke attraction for the message of the Personality of Godhead."

Another example of glorifying Lord Kṛṣṇa as the ultimate goal of life is presented by Raghupati Upādhyāya and much appreciated by Caitanya Mahāprabhu in the following verse from *CC Madhya* 19.96:

śrutim apare smṛtim itare bhāratam anye bhajantu bhava-bhītāḥ
aham iha nandaṁ vande yasyālinde paraṁ brahma

"Those who are afraid of material existence worship the Vedic literature. Some worship *smṛti*, the corollaries to the Vedic literature, and others worship the *Mahābhārata*. As far as I am concerned, I worship Kṛṣṇa's father, Mahārāja Nanda, in whose courtyard the Supreme Personality of Godhead, the Absolute Truth, is playing."

Now, based on this theme that Lord Kṛṣṇa is the goal and essence of all religious principles, compose a short verse in your choice of language to extol the glories of *bhakti-yoga*. It can be in any style or meter, but the idea is to present the subject in the choicest poetry. You can also refer to Resource 2 from the previous activity.

Example:

Who will be happy by gaining
name, fame, and wealth
Who could be happy with
knowledge and renunciation
Who might be happy in heaven or
in Brahman's light
For they have found only a few pebbles
but lost the blue sapphire of Vraja

CHAPTER 11 ANSWERS

The Dangers of Para-Dharma

1. *Brāhmaṇa* (teacher) being asked to take over as principal or administrator, which is a *kṣatriya* service. He could lack skills, motivation, or both, for this work; as a result, the school could suffer in various ways, financially or managerially, and the individual may not feel satisfied with his profession anymore; 2. *Vaiśya* (company) being asked to financially manage a prison, which is a governmental correctional facility for criminals, in the *kṣatriya* realm. The company's focus is profit, not correction. So the government's purpose is defeated when they allow people of profit mentality to run a correctional facility; 3. School's motive is education – brahminical. But when schools are run as a business, the motive becomes to make money. This compromises the quality of the education, even if schools offer more attractive material facilities, since the proper motivation is not the focus; 4. Artist working as a data scientist. While both are salaried professions, choosing one that does not suit one's nature causes dissatisfaction and could eventually lead to the person quitting despite apparent success. The artist would end up doing a poor job because his focus is not on the figures but on finding some artistic expression in it as depicted in the example.

"Caste"ing By Quality And Work

1. Maidservant's son (*śūdra*); Vaiṣṇava *brāhmaṇa*; 2. King's son (*kṣatriya*); *brāhmaṇa*; 3. *Brāhmaṇa*'s son; *kṣatriya*; 4. King; was deemed an unfit *kṣatriya*; 5. *Brāhmaṇa*'s son; was considered a fallen *brāhmaṇa*; 6. Muslim; *ācārya* of the holy name (Vaiṣṇava *brāhmaṇa*); 7. Ostracised by Hindus for converting to Islam; Vaiṣṇava *brāhmaṇas*; 8. King's son; *brāhmaṇa*; 9. Non-Vedic/sinful backgrounds; Vaiṣṇava *brāhmaṇas*

ISKCON's teachings, as demonstrated in the scriptures, are meant to make everyone a devotee. From a *varṇāśrama* perspective, anyone from any *varṇa* can become a devotee. ISKCON also demonstrates by example how *brāhmaṇas* and *sannyāsīs* can be born in any part of the world and get accepted based on their quality and work.

RESOURCE: ARTISTIC ACTIVITY

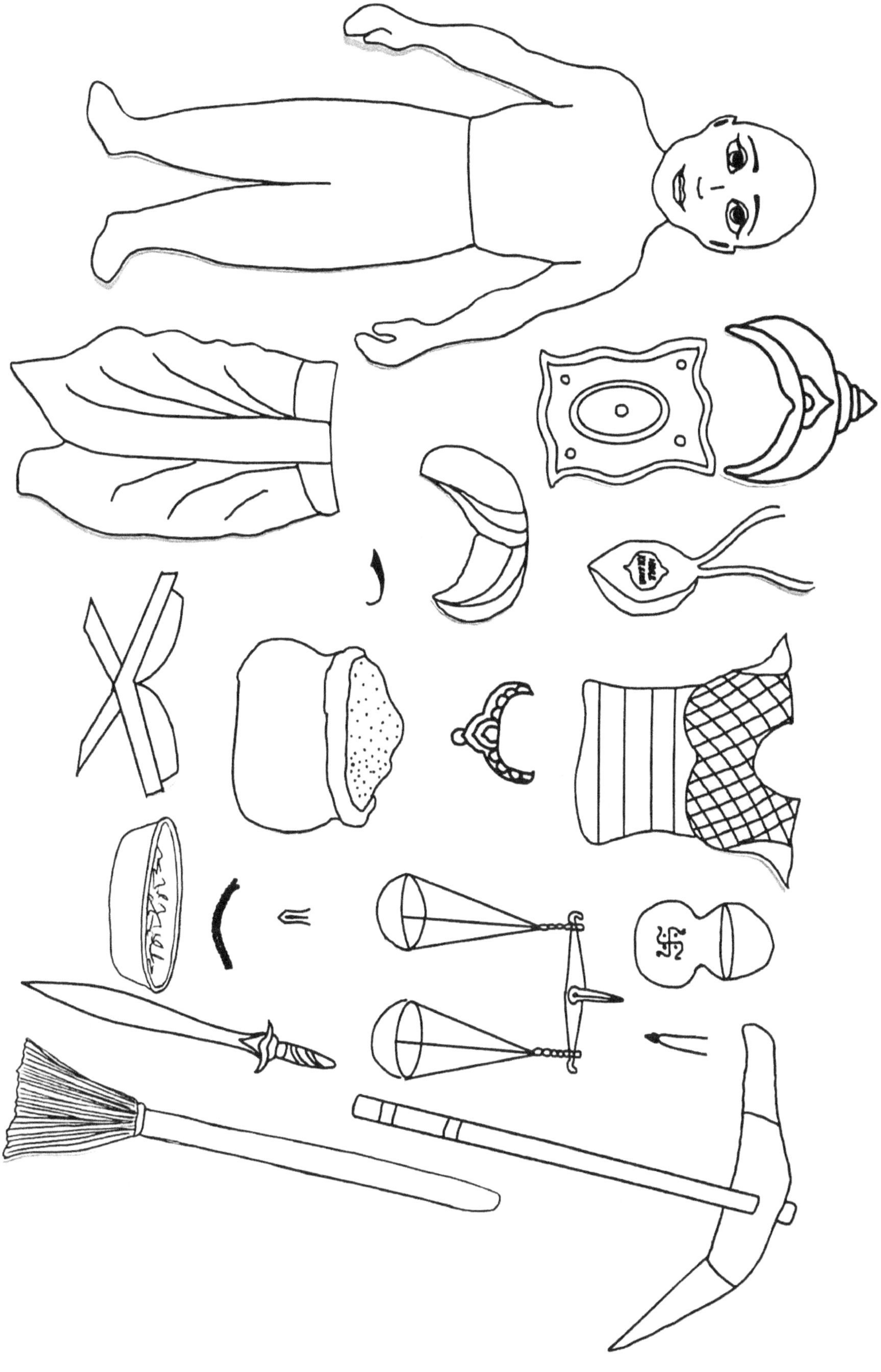

12

FOUR SPIRITUAL CLASSES

Story Summary

Having described the four *varṇas*, the social classes, Nārada Muni began describing the four spiritual classes, the *āśramas*: "The first class is the student, or the *brahmacārī*, who practices celibacy. He lives in his *guru*'s *āśrama*, the *gurukula*, where he learns the scriptures, Vedic *mantras*, and worship of the Supreme Lord. He also learns complete control of his senses. This is not easy, but by being submissive to his *guru* and having a solid friendship with him, serving him, and offering obeisances to him at the beginning and end of his studies, he receives the *guru*'s blessings.

"The student must perform certain duties so that from a young age he grows with ideal character. He must begin and end his day by worshiping and remembering the spiritual master, fire, the sun-god, and Lord Viṣṇu with the chanting of the Gāyatrī *mantra*. The *brahmacārī* should dress very simply with deerskin garments and a belt of straw and wear the sacred thread. He should carry a rod and waterpot and beg for alms, giving all his collections to his *guru*. Only when the *guru* orders him to eat can he do so."

Yudhiṣṭhira Mahārāja remembered his *gurukula* days and smiled. Even though he was brought up in a palace, he had to follow the duties of a *brahmacārī*. His training had helped him be a responsible *gṛhastha*, an ideal king, and a loving devotee of the Lord.

Nārada continued, "A *brahmacārī* should be well behaved and gentle, active and expert, and have full faith in the instructions of the *guru* and the *śāstra*. Most importantly, because he is practicing celibacy, he should not associate with

or talk unnecessarily to women or those who are attached to women."

"Why is this so important?" asked Mahārāja Yudhiṣṭhira.

"Oh, dear King, the senses are so powerful that they can agitate even the mind of a *sannyāsī*, a complete renunciate, who is in the fourth spiritual class. For this reason, the *brahmacārī* should not even associate with his *guru*'s young wife.

"You see, my dear King, women are compared to fire and men are compared to butter or a butter pot. Butter melts in the presence of fire. In other words, however advanced one may be in restraining the senses, it is almost impossible for a man to control himself in a woman's presence, even if she is his own daughter, mother, or sister. Therefore, a man should never be with any woman in a secluded place and should only associate with them for important business.

"As long as we are not self-realized, as long as we misidentify with the body, we cannot be free from duality, which is epitomized by the duality between man and woman. Conditioned souls have every chance to fall down when their intelligence is bewildered."

"But what about *gṛhasthas*, those who are married? Is it okay for them to have a bit more freedom with women?" asked the King.

"Oh no!" exclaimed Nārada Muni. "All the rules and regulations of associating with the opposite sex apply to all *āśramas*, to the *gṛhastha* and *sannyāsī*, alike. The *gṛhastha*, however, is given permission by his spiritual master to have sex only for the purpose of having children, so he still has to practice celibacy in one sense.

"A student from the *brāhmaṇa*, *kṣatriya*, or *vaiśya* classes should get trained in this way under the care of the *guru* in the *gurukula*. There he should study the Vedic literature and should give the *guru* some *dakṣiṇā*, remuneration. Then when the spiritual master orders, the disciple should leave and accept one of the other *āśramas* – the *gṛhastha*-, *vānaprastha*-, or *sannyāsa-āśrama* – as he desires."

"So it's not compulsory for the *brahmacārī* to become a *gṛhastha*?" asked the King.

"No. Because the ultimate aim is to understand the Absolute Truth, there's no need of going through all the *āśramas*. One can proceed directly from the *brahmacārī-āśrama* to the *sannyāsa-āśrama*."

"Oh, but that's rare," muttered the King.

Nārada Muni nodded. He said, "The goal of all the *āśramas* is to realize the all-pervading presence of the Supreme Lord, who has simultaneously entered the material world and is aloof from it, situated in His own abode."

Yudhiṣṭhira Mahārāja pondered for a moment and said, "So except for the *gṛhastha-āśrama* which allows regulated sense enjoyment, all the *āśramas* encourage complete detachment and sense control."

"Yes," said Nārada Muni. "When one retires from family life, one must follow the strict rules and regulations in the *vānaprastha-āśrama*. A *vānaprastha* should live simply and be austere. He should not eat grains from tilling the fields and cooked on the fire. Indeed, he should eat only fruit ripened by the sunshine.

"He should live in a thatched cottage in the forest or take shelter of a mountain cave, enduring all kinds of turbulent weather. He should not shave and should wear deerskin and tree bark as clothes, carrying only a waterpot. He should remain in the forest for as long as twelve years or at least one year, performing austerities that would not disturb his consciousness. All these duties and rules are meant to elevate his consciousness and gradually help him become detached from material life. Finally, when the *vānaprastha* is too old to perform his duties to further progress spiritually, he should fast from food. He should prepare to leave his body by merging the gross and subtle bodies into the five physical elements of the earth.

"The object of speech should be offered to the fire; craftmanship and the two hands should be given to Indra; the power of movement and the legs should be given to Lord Viṣṇu; sensual enjoyment should be given to Prajāpati . . . Like this, each of the senses should be offered to the presiding deity of each of the elements.

"The mind, along with material desires, should be merged in the moon demigod, the intelligence

should be placed in Lord Brahmā, and the false ego, which makes us think 'I am this body, and everything connected to this body is mine,' should be merged in Rudra, the predominating deity of false ego.

"In this way, after all one's material designations have merged into the respective elements, the spiritual soul, which is one in quality with the Supreme Lord, should completely detach from material existence like fire whose wood has been burned away. In the end only the spiritual being remains, which is Brahman, equal in quality with Parabrahman."

Themes and Key Messages

Please go through this table of themes and key messages, with corresponding verses, and discuss each topic further.

THEMES	REFERENCES	KEY MESSAGES
The duties of a *brahmacārī* shape one's life at a young age so that one grows with ideal character.	7.12.1–6	A student should practice controlling the senses, serving the *guru* in submission, worshiping the Lord under the *guru*'s guidance, studying the scriptures with faith, dressing simply, and offering whatever he has to the *guru*. He should be well behaved and gentle, active and expert, and minimize his association with women. A female student (*brahmacāriṇī*) should do the same with regards to men. The student *āśrama* trains one to have ideal character, behavior, and values, and most importantly, to nurture one's relationship with *guru* and Kṛṣṇa.
The Vedic system restricts association between men and women so that one can gradually progress in the different *āśramas* and then eventually give up material enjoyment altogether.	7.12.7–8	*Brahmacarya* means the vow to not marry and to observe strict celibacy. A *brahmacārī* or *brahmacāriṇī* should therefore restrict association with the opposite sex because the senses are so powerful that they can even agitate the mind of a *sannyāsī*, a renunciate. Therefore, one practicing celibacy should avoid talking unnecessarily to the opposite sex or reading literature on talks between man and woman. This injunction of restricting association with the opposite sex is the basic principle of spiritual life. The Vedic system teaches one to avoid sex life so that one may gradually progress from stages of *brahmacarya* to *gṛhastha* to *vānaprastha* and then to *sannyāsa* and give up material enjoyment, which is the original cause of bondage to the material world.
As long as one is not self-realized, a man should avoid associating even with his own daughter in a secluded place, for women are like fire and men are like butter.	7.12.9–11	If a butter pot and fire are kept together, the butter in the pot will melt. Women are compared to fire and men to butter or a butter pot. However advanced one may be in controlling the senses, it is difficult for a man to control himself in the presence of a woman, even if she is his own daughter, mother, or sister. Therefore, as long as one is not completely self-realized and is affected by the dualities of this world, one is advised to restrict one's association with the opposite sex. Even a *gṛhastha* should restrict sex life and use it only for having children, fulfilling the order of the *guru* and performing the *garbhādhāna-saṁskāra*.

THEMES	REFERENCES	KEY MESSAGES
The goal of following the regulative principles of all the *āśramas* is to realize the all-pervading presence of the Supreme Lord.	7.12.15–16	By strictly following the principles of one's *āśrama* one can realize that the Lord is pervading the entire universe, including every atom, and simultaneously is in His own abode. In any *āśrama* one must always try to understand the pervasive presence of the Lord and how He is acting.
When one retires from *gṛhastha-āśrama* (family life), one enters *vānaprastha-āśrama* (retired life) in which one performs various austerities and eventually leaves one's body, fully giving up material existence.	7.12.17–31	Various duties and austerities are described for a practicing *vānaprastha*, which are supposed to elevate one's consciousness and gradually detach one from material life. Some of these duties include eating very simply, having very simple lodging, dressing very simply, living in solitude without bodily comforts, and fasting. A *vānaprastha* should give up bodily identification and leave his body, merging the gross and subtle bodies into the various physical elements of the earth. In this way, only the indestructible soul remains. He gives up material existence like fire whose wood has been burned away.

Higher-Thinking Questions

Now try to deepen your understanding of this chapter by delving into Śrīla Prabhupāda's purports and reflecting on the following questions:

1. According to verse 7 purport, why is restricted association between man and woman a basic principle in spiritual life?

2. Verse 8 explains that one should restrict intimate association with the *guru*'s young wife. Why is this so as explained in the purport?

3. Why do you think that a *brahmacārī* or a *gṛhastha* who is trying to remain celibate should not indulge in the items mentioned in verse 12?

4. Why is it important for only the *brāhmaṇas*, *kṣatriyas*, and *vaiśyas* to study the scriptures and not the *śūdras* as explained in verse 14 and purport? However, the purport describes everyone in this age as *śūdra*. Does this mean they should not study the scriptures? [Hint: Refer to the previous chapter about how one can advance by qualification, not birth.]

5. What can one realize by following the regulative principles of the *āśrama* system as described in verse 15 purport?

6. After reading the descriptions of the duties of a *vānaprastha* in this chapter, do you think they are possible and easy to do in this Kali-yuga? What do you suggest that the *vānaprastha* of this age practice, which would give the same results, in conjunction with living simply and following the general rules? [Hint: *Varṇāśrama-dharma* in general wouldn't be effective without this.]

ACTIVITIES

In this section you will find many exciting things to do. These activities will get you thinking, moving, drawing, and having loads of fun.

Analogy Activity

... to bring out the scholar in you

FIRE MELTS BUTTER

Verse 9 discusses the dangers of unrestricted gender-mixing with the following analogy: "Woman is compared to fire, and man is compared to a butter pot. Therefore, a man should avoid associating even with his own daughter in a secluded place."

One should understand and apply the principle behind this statement. Butter melts in the presence of fire. Similarly, a man's senses are difficult to control in the presence of a woman. Śrīla Prabhupāda further explains in the purport that we should never think that we can perfectly control the senses and therefore mix freely. How do we do this in our everyday lives when we need to interact with the other gender?

Let's see how Ishaan and his younger sister, Ishvari, learn to resolve this dilemma. Ishaan and Isvari are from a devotee family and attend the local school and temple. Here are some scenarios they face in their everyday lives. Read each scenario, and as a group, discuss what would be best for Ishaan and Ishvari to do in each of the situations. Then provide a potential answer next to each scenario.

1. Being siblings of the opposite gender, they live in the same home and are around each other most of the time. Ishaan is also sometimes alone with his mother and Ishvari alone with her dad.

   Should they not speak or interact with each other because the analogy strongly warns against any interaction between genders?

2. They need to interact with classmates and friends of the opposite gender in school.

Should they try to avoid associating with the opposite gender, constantly fearing they may get attracted to the opposite gender they talk to?

3. When they visit the temple, Ishvari sometimes is assigned some service by a *brahmacārī*.

Should she reject that service because it is best for her not to speak to a *brahmacārī*?

4. Ishaan often goes out on *harināma* with the *brahmacārīs*.

If a young lady interested in spirituality approaches them, should they refuse to talk to her because they are strictly following the rules of *brahmacarya*?

Isha, I've been thinking . . . it's not just the boy-girl mixing thing . . . the senses need to be controlled – like when eating or drinking – isn't it?

Yes, Ish, that's true. We need to follow the basic etiquette, but I think we can control the senses just by practicing devotional service nicely.

5. What is your opinion of Ishaan's thoughts and Isvari's response to it? Can you add anything else to Ishvari's points?

Finally, present your understanding of what gender mixing is, what its dangers are, and how to behave properly with the opposite gender in everyday situations.

Artistic Activity

... to reveal your creativity

FLOWER OF SUBMISSION

This chapter teaches us about the submissive nature of a bona fide disciple, which is reflected in the external behavior and internal conviction of the disciple.

Internal submission: Goodwill for the *guru*; surrender to his orders; deep faith in *guru*; sincere desire to serve *guru* and Kṛṣṇa; purified senses and mind; free from *anarthas*

External submission: Offering obeisances; following orders; engaging in *sādhana-bhakti*; being clean; acting as a menial servant; restraining the senses

When one cultivates the internal qualities, the external qualities naturally manifest. Let us show this through a flower activity – when the core is solid, the petals appear strong and beautiful.

Materials: Card stock in four colors; scissors; glue; black pen; pencil; color pen

Steps:

1. Draw a six-petalled flower on one of the cards (Image 1). This should be on the brightest color paper.
2. Cut it along the outline (Image 2) and trace it on another color paper. Cut the second traced drawing along the outline and glue it on another card. Add a stem and a few leaves (Image 3), which makes the flower seem to be bending in submission.
3. Write the six internal submission characteristics on each of the petals of the traced flower (Image 4).
4. Cut out the petals of the bright original flower and place it on the traced flower (Image 5).
5. Add the six external qualities on the top flower and add the honeybee (representing Kṛṣṇa attracted by the qualities) and other details (Image 6). Color the honeybee and the leaves.
6. Glue the petals of the top flower to the bottom flower just at the base of the petals. Fold the petals up slightly to give a 3D effect (Image 7). This also gives access to the internal qualities in the heart of a surrendered disciple.

Image 1

Image 2

This is a fun and inspiring way to remember and cultivate wonderful qualities that attract the mercy of Lord Kṛṣṇa.

Image 3

Image 4

Image 5

Image 6

Image 7

Introspective Activity

... to bring out the reflective devotee in you

UNDERSTANDING CELIBACY

The great *ācāryas* in our *sampradāya* always taught us by example how to respectfully deal with the opposite sex. Their senses were so intensely engaged in the service of the Supreme Lord that impure consciousness with respect to the opposite sex could never touch them.

Here are some examples:

Haridāsa Ṭhākura:
A prostitute was sent by Rāmacandra Khān to distract the great *nāmācārya* Haridāsa Ṭhākura from his celibacy and thereby destroy his reputation. She was sent to seduce him, but Haridāsa Ṭhākura was always engaged in chanting the holy names. Haridāsa Ṭhākura was not only unaffected by her advances, but he converted her into a chaste devotee of the Lord by the power of the holy names.

Viśvanātha Cakravartī Ṭhākura:
The *guru* of young Viśvanātha Cakravartī Ṭhākura wanted to make sure his disciple was ready for the austere life of a celibate. As a test, he asked Viśvanātha Cakravartī Ṭhākura to spend a night with his beautiful, young wife. The *guru* was happy to learn that all through the night Viśvanātha Cakravartī had only narrated nectarine pastimes from the *Bhāgavatam* to his young wife. His *guru* proudly gave him permission to dedicate his life to the service of the Lord as a renunciate. His taste for the *Bhāgavatam* would protect him from mundane allurements, especially from the opposite sex.

Bhaktisiddhānta Sarasvatī Ṭhākura:
When Śrīla Bhaktisiddhānta Sarasvatī's spiritual master, Śrīla Gaurakiśora dāsa Bābājī Mahārāja disappeared from this world, some of his disciples wanted to drag his body through the sands of Vraja, as Bābājī Mahārāja had once humbly requested. Bhaktisiddhānta could not stand to see this happen, so he challenged them that only if there was one disciple present who had not had intimate relations with a woman in the past 24 hours, could the disciple touch the deceased body of Gaurakiśora dāsa Bābājī. Nobody was qualified except Bhaktisiddhānta Sarasvatī himself! He then took the body of his *guru* and placed it in *samādhi* in Māyāpur. He was known as a staunch *naistika-brahmacārī*, a celibate throughout his life.

In the modern age these examples are very rare. In today's ISKCON, can you think of inspiring personalities who have lived/or are living as celibates. (For example, Jananivāsa Prabhu and Pankajāṅghri Prabhu from Māyāpur.) Learn more about these devotees and explore what kind of feelings and thoughts they awaken within you. For example, you may feel inspired by their life of sacrifices, curious as to what made them choose this path of life, respect for their focus and determination, etc.

1. Now, write down certain basic etiquettes you would want to follow (as a girl or as a boy) to show respect to a *brahmacārī* or a *sannyāsī*, considering the austerities they have taken up to serve and benefit others.

2. On the other hand, we also know that sometimes those donning the robes of a celibate are unable to maintain the purity of that role. We may have encountered or heard of others being harassed or molested by these pretenders. (When a celibate does wrong, it destroys people's faith in that society or institution, which is unfortunate.) How do you think you, as a girl or a boy, can protect yourself from such miscreants?
3. What do you think would be the red flags (warning signs) from such individuals?
4. If, unfortunately, one does become a victim of some form of harassment, what would you suggest the victim do?

Theatrical Activity

... to bring out the actor in you

A spiritual master requests his two students to read the twelfth chapter of the Seventh Canto of the *Śrīmad Bhāgavatam*. The students raise their doubts after the reading.

Gopal: Śrīla Gurudeva, we've finished reading the instructions of Nārada Muni on the *brahmacārī* and *vānaprastha āśramas*.

Hari: I have some questions, Śrīla Gurudeva.

Gurudeva: Please go ahead.

Hari: The instructions given by Nārada Muni seem difficult to follow in today's times. Do they seem more suitable for *jñāna-yogīs*? Can you please help us understand them in the light of *bhakti-yoga*, Gurudeva?

Gurudeva: Yes. The ultimate purpose of all bona fide *yoga* processes is Lord Kṛṣṇa. *Yoga* is for realizing Vāsudeva. All severe austerities are performed to know Him. Which verse am I thinking of?

Gopal & Hari: *vāsudeva-parā vedā vāsudeva-parā makhāḥ*. . . (*SB* 1.2.28–29)

Gurudeva: Right! The supreme goal of life is Vāsudeva. *Varṇāśrama-dharma* is designed to gradually elevate the living entity to the point of full absorption in the Lord, *samādhi*. One could be attached to the impersonal effulgence of the Lord, to His Paramatma feature, or to His beautiful personal form.

Gopal: *vāsudeva paro dharmaḥ* . . . but the supreme *dharma* is rendering loving service unto Vāsudeva.

Gurudeva: Yes, certainly! The practice of scriptural study under the guidance of a spiritual master, offering menial service, restraining the senses, observing the rules and regulations, practicing austerity, and following duties, etc., are common principles.

Hari: Oh, now I understand; Nārada Muni has given us the general principles. The *ācārya* gives us the details of how to follow such principles according to time and circumstance. Śrīla Prabhupāda gave us the rules and regulations we need to follow to love Kṛṣṇa!

Gurudeva: There you go! In essence, the only rule is to remember Kṛṣṇa always, by engaging in the nine limbs of *bhakti*, and never forget Him.

Gopal: The *varṇāśrama* system raises one to the platform of *samādhi* through purifying the consciousness.

Hari: Alternatively, if one is continuously serving Kṛṣṇa, then one has already achieved perfection!

Gurudeva: Because Kṛṣṇa is supremely pure, one who is always associating with Him is also pure and is understood to have performed all duties and injunctions.

Gopal: Thank you, Śrīla Gurudeva, for wonderfully summing up!

Hari: Hare Kṛṣṇa!

Critical-Thinking Activity

... to bring out the spiritual investigator in you

REDEFINING EDUCATION

The Vedic *gurukula* system, as described in this chapter, trains students in important values, etiquette, and spiritual principles. Let's see how we can incorporate these elements in the modern educational system.

The government of your country plans to revamp its education system. They invite ISKCON's Education Minister to join their planning committee and make recommendations for improving the modern education system, especially regarding strengthening values among students. ISKCON's Education Minister in turn invites students of the *Bhāgavatam*, specifically those who have studied Canto 7, to make some recommendations. He starts an online discussion board on the Ministry's website. See the discussion board on the next page.

Start a class discussion board based on this. You could create either an online or offline discussion board and add some ideas to each section from what you have read in this chapter. Also include any other ideas from a previous canto or from other teachings of Prabhupāda that you know. Display your offline board or send out links of the completed online board to your seniors and ask them what they think.

Note: Learners should provide their own answers. From this chapter they may refer to verses 1 to 7 to understand values, ethics, and social interactions. They may discuss other ideas from their knowledge of previous cantos. The discussion will need to be carefully moderated.

Bhāgavatam Values

Hare Kṛṣṇa dear students of the Bhāgavatam,

With great pleasure, I wish to share with you that the Education Board of the country has invited suggestions from ISKCON to improve our schooling system. I invite you to post your suggestions in the discussion board below. I have already created some threads for you to respond to. You could create new threads to open new discussions or post comments on existing threads.

Your servant, Vidyānidhi Dāsa

1 Spirituality

What impact can the inclusion of spirituality create in schools? How do you think Kṛṣṇa consciousness can be presented as a non-sectarian, spiritual science to create this impact?

2 Mood

What changes can we bring about in the mood of students toward teachers, peers, and the process of learning itself?

3 Values and Ethics

Which values do you think students of today lack most? How can we cultivate them?

4 Social Interactions

In what ways do current peer interactions negatively impact students? What can we learn from the Bhāgavatam about changing this?

5 Personal Development

Which personal development strategies or habits from the Bhāgavatam would you recommend be taught in today's schools?

Writing and Language Activities

... to help you understand better

COMIC STRIP: BRAHMACĀRĪ BLUES

Study the cartoon on the next page and answer the following questions:

1. Why is the cartoon named *Brahmacārī Blues*?
2. Is Vidura's name appropriate for his character? Justify your answer.
3. What does the word *confluence* mean?
4. What is Neil's view on women? Explain it in context of the phrase "bane of my existence." How should a *brahmacārī* view women?
5. *No sweat* is an example of what figure of speech?

6. How does Vidura feel in the last frame? Support your answer.

7. At the end of the cartoon what was Neil's decision? Give two reasons why Neil is not ready to be a *brahmacārī*.

THE FOUR ĀŚRAMAS OF LIFE

Taking the lifespan of a human being to be one hundred years, the following diagram depicts a timeline divided into the four *āśramas* of life. Write the salient points of each *āśrama* in the boxes below.

1–25 years

Up to 50 years

Up to 75 years

Up to 100 years

VĀNAPRASTHA ĀŚRAMA TODAY

Here is a list of dos and don'ts for a *vānaprastha*. In the table below, write how feasible it is in today's age to follow each rule and what you think can be the alternative.

VĀNAPRASTHA RULES	FEASIBLE (YES/NO)	FEASIBLE WITH CHANGES
1. A *vānaprastha* should not eat grains grown by tilling of the fields. He should also not eat unripe grains that have grown without tilling of the field. Nor should a *vānaprastha* eat grains cooked in fire. He should eat only fruit ripened by the sunshine.		
2. When he obtains some new grains, he should give up his old stock of grains.		
3. A *vānaprastha* should live in a thatched cottage or a mountain cave only to keep the sacred fire, and he should endure snowfall, wind, fire, rain, and the sunshine.		
4. The *vānaprastha* should wear matted locks of hair on his head and let his body hair, nails, and moustache grow. He should not cleanse his body of dirt. He should keep a waterpot, deerskin and rod, wear the bark of a tree as a covering, and use garments colored like fire.		
5. Being very thoughtful, a *vānaprastha* should remain in the forest for twelve years, eight years, four years, two years, or at least one year. He should behave in such a way that he will not be disturbed or troubled by too much austerity.		
6. When, because of disease or old age, one is unable to perform his prescribed duties for advancement in spiritual consciousness or study of the *Vedas*, he should practice fasting, not taking any food.		

CHAPTER 12 ANSWERS

Fire Melts Butter

Potential Answers: The principle taught in this verse is that *unrestricted* gender mixing can make it difficult to control the senses. And therefore, the Vedic principle is to keep genders separate so that there will be minimal disturbance.

1. No; Siblings living in the same house develop a healthy affection for each other and their parents from the very beginning. Such a relationship is natural, and their association should continue to be nurtured in that way.
2. No; They should keep a healthy distance, being aware of the dangers of free mingling, and associate only when necessary.
3. No; Devotional service is the higher principle, but still she should restrict association and only interact for service purposes.
4. No; They shouldn't avoid preaching, but at the same time they should not associate intimately. They should view all women as mothers and respect them. This will avoid fanaticism or being tempted to enjoy the company of the opposite sex.
5. Ishaan makes a relevant point that sense control is the main issue.

   Ishvari also makes a valid statement that devotional service ultimately helps one restrain the senses because when one gets a higher taste in spiritual life, one gives up lower tendencies. At the same time, because we are still conditioned, we need to follow the etiquette of not freely and whimsically interacting with the opposite sex. She also makes a valid point that there should be some balance – that we shouldn't become cold and fanatical toward the opposite sex, neither should we become over familiar. Respectful dealings should be the focus, seeing each other as Kṛṣṇa's devotees and acting appropriately according to our positions in our *āśrama*.

***Understanding Celibacy** (Potential Answers)*

1. Treat them as elders/seniors and not as peers even if they may be almost your age; avoid dressing promiscuously in their presence; maintain dignity and gravity in your conversations with them, avoiding frivolous language; do not meet with a celibate alone if you belong to the opposite sex. Always be accompanied by another person of the same sex; always maintain an appropriate physical distance from celibates of the opposite sex.
2. Be aware and educated about matters of sexual abuse. Attend seminars and be curious about general norms related to the matter; always follow the etiquette mentioned in this chapter; use your common sense. If any celibate from the opposite sex is showing unneeded interest in you or is trying to attract your attention by being overtly helpful to you, trust your instincts and become cautious while dealing with them. They may turn out to be a miscreant.
3. Be wary of "celibates" who seem unnecessarily extra helpful only to you and who want to make you feel special and different from others. (If their nature is to be helpful, they would be like that to everyone, irrespective of the gender.); if any celibate of the opposite sex requests you to meet them alone, that could be a major red flag.
4. Most corporates, schools, colleges, or spiritual institutions will have a committee to whom you can lodge relevant complaints; don't let the abuser make you believe that you are to blame. Fearlessly open your heart to somebody you trust; do not be afraid to seek help.

Brahmacārī Blues

1. Because it illustrates the difficulties or struggles of being a *brahmacārī*; 2. Yes. Vidura in the *Mahābhārata* is described as a wise and honest person, and the character in this cartoon is giving Neil honest answers about *brahmacārī* life; 3. It means to merge; 4. He thinks that women are a source of misery. Although *brahmacārīs* should minimize association of women, they should view women as mothers or mother figures and show them respect; 5. Idiom; 6. He is disbelieving and has secondhand embarrassment. He facepalms; 7. He decides not to be a *brahmacārī*. He is attached to eating without restrictions, and he does not understand how to respect women.

The Four Āśramas of Life

1–25 years: Brahmacarya Āśrama

1. The *brahmacārī* should live under the care of a bona fide spiritual master.
2. He should be celibate. He should control his senses and try to avoid the association of women as far as possible.
3. He should engage himself in spiritual activities and study the Vedic literature under the direction of the spiritual master.
4. He should dress simply and wear the sacred thread.
5. He should offer whatever he has to the spiritual master.
6. He should be satisfied with eating what is necessary.
7. He should be expert in executing responsibilities and service to the spiritual master and Kṛṣṇa.

Upto 50 years: Gṛhastha Āśrama

1. After completing *brahmacarya āśrama*, a person can choose to get married and become a *gṛhastha*, a Kṛṣṇa conscious householder.
2. He should take care of his wife and children.
3. He should also provide for the other three *āśramas*.
4. He should control his senses and have intimate relations with his wife only to have children.
5. While providing for his family, he should engage them in devotional service and eventually become detached from family life and comforts.

Upto 75 years: Vānaprastha Āśrama

1. He should cut off mundane ties from his family members.
2. He should live simply, along with his wife.
3. He should become a complete celibate and live a life of austerity.
4. On becoming old and diseased, he should become detached from the body and bodily comforts in preparation to give up the body.

Upto 100 years: Sannyāsa Āśrama

1. He can straightaway enter the *sannyāsa āśrama* after the *brahmacarya āśrama* or finish his *gṛhastha āśrama* and *vānaprastha āśrama* before taking *sannyāsa*.
2. He should be a strict and complete celibate.
3. He is dependent on the *gṛhasthas* for his food and other necessities.
4. He should not own anything other than a few simple items.

Varṇāśrama Āśrama Today

1. No. A *vānaprastha* can depend on the temple *prasādam* in return for services rendered. Should avoid eating from unclean places, eating more than required, and eating at night.
2. Yes. Should be understood as not saving anything for the future. At the time of entering *vānaprastha*, should follow the example of Rūpa Gosvāmī, by dividing one's money: 50 percent distributed to qualified and pure devotees of the Lord or for the propagation of the Kṛṣṇa consciousness movement; 25 percent given to family members; 25 percent kept for personal use, in case of emergency. Shouldn't store provisions or have a large bank balance.
3. No. Should be understood as to live frugally with some austerity. Should perform austerities related to the tongue, body, and mind. Bathing two to three times a day and sleeping separately from one's spouse, and, if possible, on the floor or in a simple bed.
4. No. Should be understood as not giving too much importance to personal appearance. Should not acquire things and should live simply, without wasting time, while fixing the mind on devotional service to Kṛṣṇa.
5. No. Should be understood as living in a simple home or the temple, performing austerities for a minimum period before taking *sannyāsa*. It is the preparatory period for *sannyāsa āśrama*. Should increase austerities for self-purification, reduce bodily needs, and simplify one's life.
6. No. One should take care of the body sufficiently, because a devotee sees the body as the property of Kṛṣṇa to be used in His service. However, one should prepare for death by increasing his devotional practices and becoming more absorbed in Kṛṣṇa.

13

THE BEHAVIOR OF A PERFECT PERSON

Story Summary

Having discussed the duties of the *brahmacārīs* and *vānaprasthas*, two of the renounced stages of life, Nārada Muni began to describe the duties of the final renounced order, the *sannyāsa-āśrama*.

"After *vānaprastha* life, a person should leave home and renounce all material connections. He should travel from one place to another, passing only one night in each village. In this way, a *sannyāsī* should travel all over the world. He should dress with only a loincloth and carry only a *daṇḍa* and *kamaṇḍalu*."

"Oh, how is it possible?" asked Yudhiṣṭhira Mahārāja, aware of the many respected *sannyāsīs* he had seen all his life.

"The *sannyāsī* is completely satisfied in the self, dear King," replied Nārada Muni. "Therefore he is not dependent on any person or place. He lives on begging alms from door to door. Besides, he is a peaceful, unalloyed devotee of Lord Nārāyaṇa and a friendly well-wisher of all beings."

"Oh, please tell me more, dear Nārada. What are the other principles by which a *sannyāsī* should live?"

"A *sannyāsī* should always try to see the Supreme Lord pervading everything and see everything resting on the Supreme."

"How can he do this?" asked the curious King.

"Fully situated in the self, he should realize that unconsciousness and consciousness are merely illusions. They have no permanent existence. Only the Supreme Lord exists eternally. He pervades the entire universe in His unmanifested form. So nothing can exist without Kṛṣṇa. Realizing this, he sees Kṛṣṇa everywhere!"

"Aha!" exclaimed Yudhiṣṭhira Mahārāja.

"Since the material body is sure to be vanquished and our duration of life is not certain, we should not praise life nor death," continued Nārada Muni. "Rather, we should see that all souls are entangled in eternal time. We should observe our activities in eternal time, the cause of birth and death."

Yudhiṣṭhira Mahārāja nodded slowly, trying to absorb these eternal truths.

"In addition," said Nārada, "a *sannyāsī* should reject all mundane literature, which is a useless waste of time. He shouldn't become a professional teacher nor engage in arguments. He should not allure disciples with material benefits nor read books or give discourses as a means of livelihood. He should never accumulate material opulences.

"He doesn't even have to accept the symbols of a *tridaṇḍa* and *kamaṇḍalu* if he is peaceful, equipoised, and spiritually advanced. Actually, he shouldn't even disclose his position. He should present himself like a dumb man to society.

"I will tell you a story which illustrates this," said Nārada Muni, smiling. "Wise sages recite this ancient story, which is a discussion between Prahlāda Mahārāja and a great saintly person who was feeding himself like a python."

"Oh, please tell me!" begged the King, intrigued.

Nārada explained that a long time ago, the dearest servant of the Lord, Prahlāda Mahārāja, went on a tour with some of his confidential associates just to study the nature of saintly persons. One day, he went to the bank of the Kāverī River in the valley of Sahya Mountain. There he saw a most unusual spectacle. A saintly person was lying on the ground, covered with dirt. Prahlāda looked quizzically at him – the man's face glowed, and his eyes were as bright as stars. Prahlāda recognized him to be a deeply spiritually advanced soul, even though no one

in that place could recognize him as the person they had known. Prahlāda Mahārāja immediately offered obeisances and touched his head to the saint's feet.

Prahlāda noticed that the saintly man was quite fat. He asked, "My dear sir, you don't endeavor at all to earn a livelihood, but you have a stout body like a materialistic enjoyer. I know you don't have any money for sense enjoyment, and you're lying down because you have nothing to do. Please excuse me for asking such a question, but how then has your body become so fat?

"O *sādhu*, you appear to be learned and intelligent in every way. You speak palatable words. You see people performing all kinds of activities, yet you are lying here inactive. Why is this?"

The saintly *brāhmaṇa*'s plump face erupted in a wide grin. He said, "O best of the *asuras*, Prahlāda Mahārāja, you have transcendental eyes with which you can see a man's true character. It's obvious to me that Nārāyaṇa, the Supreme Personality of Godhead, resides within the core of your heart. My dear King, I will try to answer your questions according to what I've heard from authorities. How can I remain silent when I have this wonderful opportunity to address a rare personality like you for my own purification?

"O Mahārāja Prahlāda, I wasn't always inactive. You see, because of my insatiable material desires, I was carried away by the waves of *māyā*, engaging in various activities in various forms, life after life. In this evolutionary process, I finally received this human form of life, which can lead to heaven, to liberation, to the lower species, or to rebirth in the human form.

"In this human form, I've seen how man and woman unite for sense pleasure but they are not actually happy. Real happiness is spiritual happiness, which can only be achieved when one stops all materialistic activities. Thus, I've stopped taking part in worldly activities and am lying down here.

"The spirit souls are by nature happy because they are part and parcel of the Lord. However, they have forgotten their relationship with God, their real self-interest, and think that the body is the self. Thus the conditioned souls suffer the miseries of this material world. Just as a deer cannot see the water in a well, which is covered by grass, and runs for water elsewhere, the living being covered by the material body runs after happiness outside of himself instead of finding happiness within.

"Like this the materialist tries to find happiness and free himself from distress. However, all his plans in different bodies are ultimately baffled. This is because we live in a world in which we are faced with three kinds of miserable conditions: *adhyātmika* (miseries arising from the body and mind), *adhidaivika* (miseries arising from natural disasters), and *adhibautika* (miseries arising from society and other living beings). In all our materialistic endeavors we are faced with these miseries. So even though we may become successful in our efforts, what is the benefit of this success? We are still subjected to birth, death, old age, disease, and the reactions to our activities. Therefore, a sensible person won't put all their energies into simply making material plans only to lose it all and die in disappointment.

"I've seen how greedy rich men don't sleep at night because they fear losing their wealth. They are in constant anxiety because of governmental laws, rogues and thieves, their family members, and even themselves. Therefore, intelligent people should give up the cause of lamentation, illusion, fear, anger, attachment, and unnecessary labor. What is the cause? It's the desire for unnecessary money and prestige."

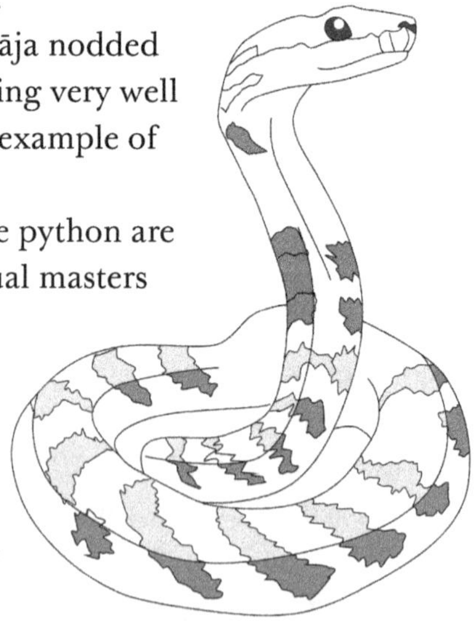

Prahlāda Mahārāja nodded in agreement, knowing very well about this from the example of his demonic father.

"The bee and the python are two excellent spiritual masters to me," continued the *brāhmaṇa*. "The python teaches me to be satisfied by staying in one place and collecting what I need. The

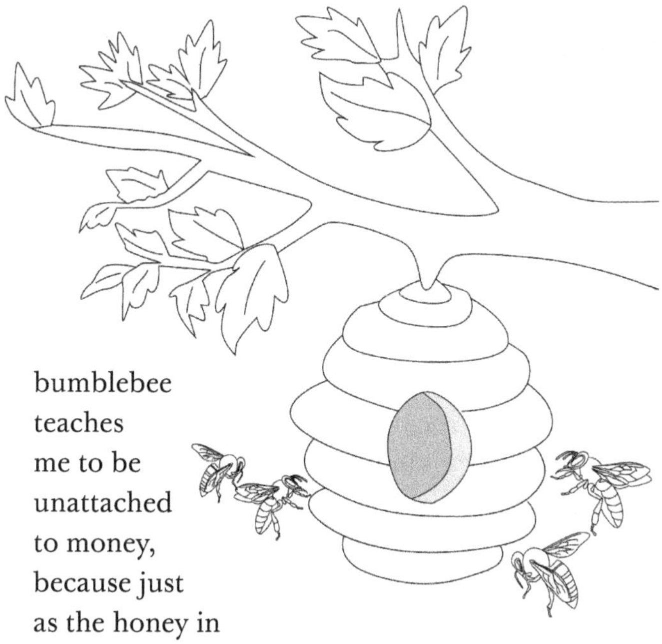

bumblebee teaches me to be unattached to money, because just as the honey in the honeycomb is taken away by force, money, which is as good as honey, can be taken away by anyone."

The *brāhmaṇa* stretched his legs and yawned widely. He continued, "I don't endeavor to get anything, but I am satisfied with whatever comes my way. If I don't get anything, I'm patient and unagitated like the python and lie down here for many days. Sometimes I eat a little and sometimes a lot. Sometimes the food is tasty and sometimes stale. Sometimes people offer me food with great respect and sometimes with neglect. Sometimes I eat during the day and sometimes at night.

"To cover myself I use whatever is available, whether it is linen, silk, cotton, bark, or deerskin. Sometimes I lie on the ground, sometimes on leaves, sometimes in a pile of ashes, and sometimes, by the will of others, in a palace on a comfortable bed with pillows."

Prahlāda Mahārāja could understand that the *brāhmaṇa* was describing different situations in different types of births. Sometimes one takes birth as an animal and sometimes as a king. In this way the *brāhmaṇa* described that sometimes he bathed himself nicely, smeared sandalwood pulp on his body, wore a flower garland and fine clothes, and traveled on a regal elephant or horse.

"I don't distinguish between good and bad," said the *brāhmaṇa*. "Some people are elevated and some are degraded, but it's not my business to praise or criticize them. I understand that being good or bad is not the goal of life – the goal is to become free from these dualities, which elevates one to higher realms or degrades one to lower species or planets. Therefore, I don't discriminate; I only desire for people's supreme welfare in Kṛṣṇa consciousness.

"A thoughtful person should realize that material existence is illusion. Only by realizing the self is this possible.

"Dear Prahlāda Mahārāja, you are such a self-realized soul and a pure devotee of the Lord. Therefore, I've described to you my journey of self-realization."

Nārada Muni ended the narration to Yudhiṣṭhira Mahārāja: "After hearing these instructions from the saintly *brāhmaṇa*, Prahlāda Mahārāja, the King of the demons, offered his obeisances and worshiped the saint. He then left for his own home, understanding what it meant to be a *paramahaṁsa*, a perfect person."

"Prahlāda Mahārāja was a *paramahaṁsa* himself even though he was a *gṛhastha*," said Yudhiṣṭhira Mahārāja, chuckling. "He showed us that in any of the *āśramas* of life, one can be a *paramahaṁsa,* an exalted soul."

Themes and Key Messages

Please go through this table of themes and key messages, with corresponding verses, and discuss each topic further.

THEMES	REFERENCES	KEY MESSAGES
The conduct, consciousness, and qualities of a *sannyāsī* determine whether he is a genuine renunciant.	7.13.1–10	A *sannyāsī* should be detached, not dependent on anything material. He should beg for alms, dress very simply, and carry a *daṇḍa* and waterpot only when necessary. Preaching is his first duty, so he travels to preach and is only interested in bringing people to Kṛṣṇa consciousness. He is completely satisfied in the self, is peaceful, and is a well-wisher to everyone. He should completely surrender to the Lord and see the Lord pervading everything. He should not read mundane literature, become a professional teacher, or indulge in arguments. He should not try to get many disciples by alluring them with material things. He should not give discourses as a livelihood nor build many temples to gain material opulence. He builds temples only to give shelter to the serious students of Kṛṣṇa consciousness and to attract souls to Kṛṣṇa.
Material desires and activities cause transmigration of the soul, and the human form is the junction, which can elevate or degrade us.	7.13.24–25	The *avadhūta brāhmaṇa* explained to Prahlāda Mahārāja that because of his material desires he was acting in different ways and struggling birth after birth in various species of life. But since he's attained the human form, he can be elevated to heaven, be degraded to lower species, or become liberated from material life. Only in the human form can one achieve *apavarga* (liberation) by becoming free from *pavarga* (material life), which is made up of the five statuses of life.
Forgetfulness of Kṛṣṇa and sense enjoyment lead to misery. Real happiness can be achieved when one gives up materialistic activities and remembers Kṛṣṇa.	7.13.26–30	Just as a deer cannot see the water in a covered well and runs after a mirage, the conditioned soul doesn't see happiness within oneself but looks for it in external things. The living beings are happy by nature because the soul is a part of Kṛṣṇa, but forgetting their relationship with Kṛṣṇa, they suffer. Therefore, the *avadhūta brāhmaṇa* adopted the lifestyle of a python, which ceases all activity. However, one can't be inactive for long. Engaging in spiritual activities that please Kṛṣṇa and help one remember Him gives the highest bliss.

THEMES	REFERENCES	KEY MESSAGES
Materialistic activities are always mixed with the three kinds of miserable conditions, so what's the use of these activities?	7.13.31–34	No one can escape the threefold miseries of life: miseries of the body and mind (*adhyātmika*), miseries caused by other living beings (*adhibhautika*), and miseries caused from natural disturbances (*adhidaivika*). If one works very hard, suffers these miseries, and then gets small material benefits, what is the value of these benefits? One still has to die and leave everything and then accept another body and continue suffering the threefold miseries. Material plans for material happiness have no real value. A rich and powerful man who is greedy to accumulate wealth suffers from insomnia, fear, and anxieties. One should therefore give up the desire for unnecessary prestige and money, the cause of lamentation and illusion.
One should be like the bee, who is unattached, and like the python, who is satisfied.	7.13.35–37	The two *gurus* of the *avadhūta brāhmaṇa* are the bee and python. The bee teaches detachment from material desires and accumulating money. Just as the bee's honey is taken away, so is a man's money. The python teaches satisfaction and not desiring to get more than needed. If one doesn't get anything, one is unagitated like a python. Only a self-realized person can realize this. A self-realized person (*paramahaṁsa*), like Prahlāda Mahārāja, is therefore equipoised to everyone, realizes that material existence is illusion, and thus retires from all material activities.

Higher-Thinking Questions

Now try to deepen your understanding of this chapter by delving into Śrīla Prabhupāda's purports and reflecting on the following questions:

1. How do you think a *sannyāsī* can renounce the world and live, as described in this chapter? What does he achieve within that gives him satisfaction? (Refer to verse 5 and purport.)

2. Why shouldn't death or life be praised as described in verse 6? What should one do instead?

3. A *sannyāsī* should generally not construct many temples. Why is this so? What is the purpose of building temples or monasteries as described by Śrīla Prabhupāda in verse 8 purport?

4. Although a *sannyāsī* should use the symbols of the *tridaṇḍa* and *kamaṇḍalu*, why is this not necessary, according to verse 9 purport?

5. According to verse 24, what is the cause of transmigration from one body to the next? Briefly explain how this happens.

6. What is spiritual evolution, as described in verse 25 and purport, compared to Darwin's theory of evolution? How can one get liberated from the evolutionary process?

7. Verse 26 purport explains that eating, sleeping, mating, and defending are different for humans? How are they different, and how can each be engaged to be different?

8. The *brāhmaṇa* ceased all materialistic activities because he knew that they don't give true happiness. Does this mean that we should give up all activity? What should we do? (Refer to verse 27 purport.)

9. Briefly explain the role of the Supersoul in fulfilling desires as described in verse 30 purport.

10. Why does good and bad have no meaning in the material world as described in verse 42 purport?

ACTIVITIES

In this section you will find many exciting things to do. These activities will get you thinking, moving, drawing, and having loads of fun.

Analogy Activity

... to bring out the scholar in you

"BEE" WEALTH WISE

In verses 35 to 37, the learned *brāhmaṇa* describes how the bee and the python taught him not to accumulate too much wealth, but to remain satisfied with what comes of its own accord. In purport 34, Śrīla Prabhupāda warns of the dangers of accumulating money: it could become the cause of lamentation, illusion, fear, anger, material attachment, material poverty, and unnecessary hard work.

Based on the teachings of his two *gurus*, the *brāhmaṇa* created a resource to encourage ordinary people to gradually become detached from accumulating unnecessary wealth. The "Bee" Wealth-Wise leaflet he created is reproduced in Resource A. This can be used as a simple preaching tool to help people develop a healthier perspective on accumulating wealth and help them understand that the Lord's service is the greatest wealth they can accumulate.

Print out Resource A and hand it to at least three adults you know. Collect their responses. Discuss what you learn from the responses in relation to the message of the learned *brāhmaṇa* and note it down in your books. Then read and fill out Resource B, the back of the leaflet. For this resource, imagine that you have a certain amount of money that you would earn from your prospective career path one day.

Resource A

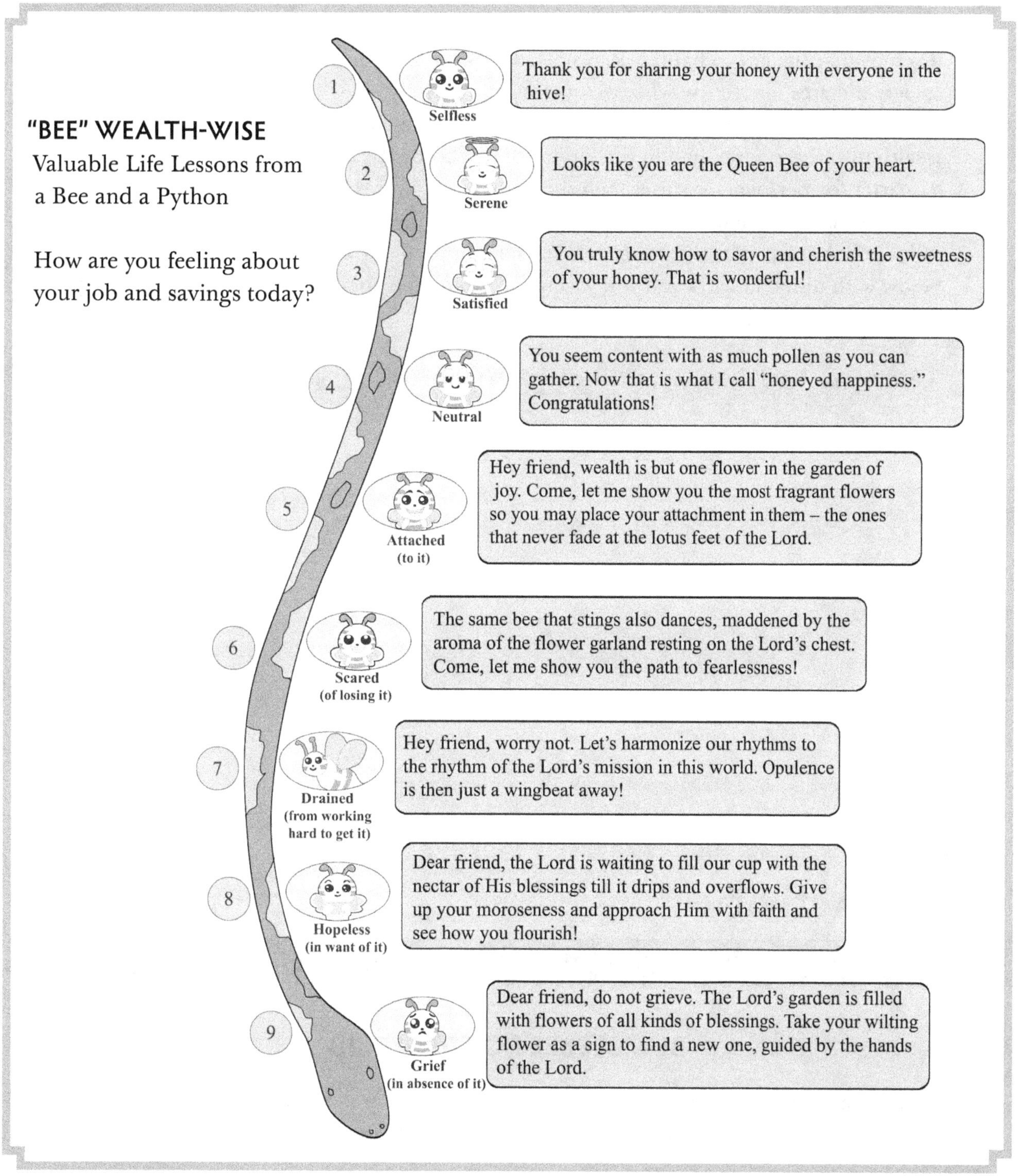

Resource B

Rūpa Gosvāmī, the leader of the six Gosvāmīs of Vṛndāvana, taught devotees a simple strategy for wealth management. If you scored more than 5 on the Wealth Wise scale, you probably are well on track to follow in his footsteps. If you scored 5 or less, you can easily make simple changes to follow his instructions.

The shelter of the Lord, of course, is the greatest wealth one can gain. Everything in this world, including material opulence, can be used in His service. The *ācāryas* teach us that the key to happiness is not possessing more and more wealth as modern society dictates, but to use what we possess more wisely.

Rūpa Gosvāmī recommends that no matter how much we have, we can divide our wealth into three parts: half in the service of the Lord, His devotees, and their mission; a quarter for personal expenses; and the remaining quarter for emergencies.

Let's make a promise (*saṅkalpa*) to follow Śrī Rūpa Gosvāmī and experience how following the *ācāryas* is the key to real satisfaction. Fill out the columns in the card below with different ways you will wisely safeguard and spend your wealth and thereby remain happy and Kṛṣṇa conscious!

Saṅkalpa 1: Lord's Mission	Saṅkalpa 2: Personal Use	Saṅkalpa 3: Wise Savings

Artistic Activity

... to reveal your creativity

BUMBLEBEE POST-IT CARD

Let's make some bumblebee art to remind us of what the bumblebee represents. The bee shows us that we shouldn't accumulate more than we need and we should be satisfied with what little we collect.

Materials: Black or any dark color sheet of paper or card; watercolor or acrylic paints, or acrylic paint markers; white outliner; black art pen; pencil; eraser; pin tacks or small magnets; chits of paper or small notebook

Directions:

1. First take your black sheet and fold it in half. If you wish to attach your chits of paper or small notebook in the center, then fold it into thirds.

2. Then with pencil draw an outline of flowers on the left panel, and the bumblebee and beehive on the right panel (Image 1).

Image 1

3. Color in the flowers. First start at the center, coloring the pollen with yellow and the flower petals in white (Image 2).

Image 2

4. With the white pen outline the stem of the flower. Color the leaves green (Image 3).

Image 3

5. Now start outlining the flower petals and leaves with the white outliner to give the finishing touches. Using the black outliner, color between the petals and the circle around the pollen to add tone and contrast (Image 4). Also add thin black lines on the flower petals.

6. Now start coloring the beehive in yellow and outline it with the white outliner. Color the bumblebee in yellow and black alternatively, and outline it with the white outliner. Add finishing touches with black pen (Image 5).

7. Now make the bee's path with white pen (Image 5).

Image 4

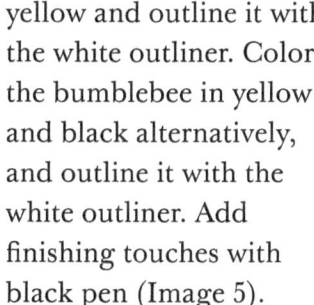

Image 5

8. Above the flowers you could paraphrase a quote from this chapter reminding you of what the bee represents (Image 6).

9. On the right panel below the beehive, pin a small sheet of paper (post chit) to make your to-do-list for the day (Image 6). Alternatively, use magnets to stick the card to the fridge or any other metallic surface.

10. You may also glue on a small recipe notebook or menu card in the center if you are making three panels (Image 8).

Image 6

Other Usage Tips:

- Pin the card on your pin board in your room and pin reminders on post chits (Image 7).
- Make a menu card for your parent or a special guest for some special day and place the menu inside as shown in Image 8.
- Pin a recipe or your favorite quotes or sayings.

Image 8

Image 7

Action Activity

... to get you moving and learning

PAVARGA MUSICAL CHAIRS

Material life is called *pavarga*, because it gives us five different states of suffering, represented by the following letters of the Devanagari script: *pa, pha, ba, bha,* and *ma.*

Pa means *pariśrama,* very hard labor.
Pha means *phena,* or foam from the mouth. (For example, sometimes horses foam at the mouth from heavy labor.)
Ba means *byarthatā,* disappointment.

Bha means *bhaya,* fear.
Ma means *mṛtyu,* death.

Think about these five states of suffering and what you feel about them. You may even think of your own or others' experiences connected to each of these suffering states.

Now, with your friends (at least six players) play a game of musical chairs to remember these five states:

- Label five chairs with each of the *pavarga* letters.
- Arrange the five chairs in a circle like you would play ordinary musical chairs.
- Start the music and let everyone run around the circle of five chairs.
- When the music stops, the players should try sitting on a chair. Those who did not get a chair are eliminated from the game.
- Each player then identifies the letter pinned on their chair, shares with the others what it stands for, and expresses any thoughts with regards to the topic.
- Once the five players share their thoughts, remove a chair, and continue the game with these remaining five players. If a player sits on the same chair with the same letter, they are challenged to say something else about the letter.
- For each round remove a chair until you have just one chair remaining with two players. The last player who sits on the chair and speaks about the letter is the winner.

Introspective Activity

... to bring out the reflective devotee in you

YOUR HAPPINESS QUOTIENT

In this activity you will reflect on your happiness in life, so you can ultimately evaluate the importance of lasting spiritual happiness.

Part 1

First calculate your happiness quotient* as follows:

Step 1: Determine how much you value your happiness factors.

Step 2: Value yourself by scoring on a scale of 1 to 10 on each of these factors.

* a concept that measures approximately the happiness each person has achieved in life.

Happiness factors:

1. Emotional: Feeling an emotional bond towards a friend or loved one.
2. Physical: Having a rigorous exercise schedule that releases "happy hormones."
3. Social: Being appreciated and praised in your family or friend circle, e.g., birthday parties.
4. Occupational: Getting pleasure from your work and career.
5. Intellectual: Getting stimulation from analyzing, critical-thinking, and solving problems.
6. Environmental: Feeling close to nature when you go for a walk or when helping with environmental issues.
7. Spiritual: Connecting with God, which makes you see yourself and life from a different angle.

Now put a value for each of these factors by circling the number in the table below, according to the importance you give them (e.g., if you give the spiritual factor great importance, then circle "5"):

	FACTORS AFFECTING YOUR HAPPINESS	NOT AT ALL				A LOT
1.	Emotional	1	2	3	4	5
2.	Physical	1	2	3	4	5
3.	Social	1	2	3	4	5
4.	Occupational	1	2	3	4	5
5.	Intellectual	1	2	3	4	5
6.	Environmental	1	2	3	4	5
7.	Spiritual	1	2	3	4	5

In the table on the next page, enter these values in the second column. Then on a scale of 1 to 10 reflect on your level of happiness in each of the factors and enter them in column 3. An example is done for you. Since our goal is to be spiritually happy and find permanent happiness, we should always give it the top priority. The rest of your values (weight) for other factors depends on your personal nature.

FACTORS OF HAPPINESS	WEIGHT GIVEN TO EACH FACTOR ON A SCALE OF 1 TO 5		YOUR HAPPINESS ESTIMATE ON A SCALE OF 1 TO 10	
	Example	Your value	Example	Your value
1. Emotional	4		8	
2. Physical	5		7.5	
3. Social	4		8.5	
4. Occupational	3		6.5	
5. Intellectual	4		8	
6. Environmental	3		7	
7. Spiritual	5		7	

Now calculate the weighted average by using this formula:
This is your happiness quotient.

$$\frac{\Sigma^{*}\ [(\text{Weight of factor}) \times (\text{estimate of factor on a scale of 1 to 10})]}{\text{Sum of weights}} = (\text{your happiness quotient})$$

Example using figures from table:

$$\frac{8{\times}4 + 7.5{\times}5 + 8.5{\times}4 + 6.5{\times}3 + 8{\times}4 + 7{\times}3 + 7{\times}5}{(4+5+4+3+4+3+5)} = \frac{211}{28} = 7.5$$

Part 2

Verse 29 gives the analogy of a deer, who, out of ignorance, cannot see the water within a well, covered by grass, but runs after water elsewhere. Similarly, the living entity covered by the material body does not see happiness within himself but runs after happiness in the material world.

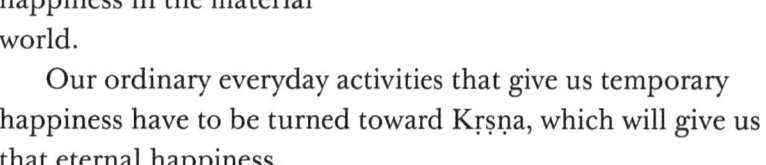

Our ordinary everyday activities that give us temporary happiness have to be turned toward Kṛṣṇa, which will give us that eternal happiness.

* Sigma symbol to indicate the sum of all terms

Below is a table with activities that can give you happiness if you keep yourself as the center. They are not necessarily negative, but reflect on how to convert them into Kṛṣṇa-centered happiness.

Self-centered happiness is temporary: A new shirt feels good till the first wash.

Kṛṣṇa-centered happiness is permanent: A new dress stitched for Kṛṣṇa gives happiness every time the Lord wears it.

SEARCHING FOR FALSE AND TEMPORARY HAPPINESS OUTSIDE YOURSELF	REAL AND PERMANENT HAPPINESS WHEN YOU CONNECT EVERYTHING WITH KṚṢṆA
1. Going to a restaurant and eating vegetarian food which is not *prasādam*.	
2. Going out with friends for a movie.	
3. Listening to music that you like.	
4. Going out for a long hard walk or trek.	
5. Shopping and buying something that pleases you.	
6. Getting some do-it-yourself kits and making a craft to decorate your house.	
7. Sending a thank-you note to someone who was kind to you.	
8. Remembering the wonderful time that you had with your friend on a holiday.	
9. Wearing a new dress or makeup and admiring yourself in the mirror, and then going out and lapping up the compliments.	

You can calculate or estimate the happiness quotient as explained in Part 1 for both the columns and see for yourself which is greater!

Happiness Quotient for temporary happiness = ____________________

Happiness Quotient for long-term permanent happiness = ____________________

Theatrical Activity

... to bring out the actor in you

SKIT: THE BHOGĪ-YOGĪ

This chapter warns us against *bhogī-yogīs*, fake renunciants posing as *yogīs*, who are mostly interested in fame, followers, and material prestige and prosperity. Enact the following humorous skit in front of your class or temple congregation.

The scene is a room with cushions on the floor. Voices of the crowd can be pre-recorded and played. Two friends, Sam and Tim, walk into the room.

Sam: Why do we have to pay for this class? Yesterday someone in the park gave me this book (holds up a copy of *Science of Self Realization*) and invited me to something called the Sunday Love Feast. And that is all free.
Tim: Don't be a scrooge, Sam. Just pay up. It'll be worth it.
Sam: It's so crowded. (They both struggle to find a place to sit.)
Tim: This *yogī* is very popular. People come from all over to see him. He's the best.
Sam: With the amount he charges, maybe he should get a better venue.
Tim: Sshh . . . he's here.
Bhogī-yogī: Today I will be auctioning off a secret *mantra* that I developed. This top-secret *mantra*, if chanted with the correct meter, will allow you to become Elon Musk's neighbor.
Background chatter: Wow! Amazing! I'd love to be Elon Musk's neighbor.
Bhogī-yogī: Let's start the bidding at ten thousand dollars.

(Sam and Tim look at each other in shock.)

Voice 1: Ten thousand dollars.
Voice 2: Fifteen thousand dollars.
Voice 3: Twenty thousand dollars.
Sam: Suckers. We would never . . .
Tim: One hundred thousand dollars. (Sam looks at him shocked.)

Bhogī-yogī: Going once, going twice, sold to the man in the blue baseball cap. Please come up and pay my assistant. All major credit cards accepted. No refunds.

Sam: (to Tim) Are you crazy? Do you even have one hundred thousand dollars?

Tim: (pulls out his credit card) Not anymore!

Bhogī-yogī: (smiles, pats Tim, and hands him a card) Here's your *mantra*. Remember to chant it every morning, precisely five minutes before the sun rises. You may not be Elon Musk's neighbor in this life but next life you definitely will be.

(Tim nods his head happily and then looks confused. He walks back to his seat and sits down dazed.)

Sam: Will Elon still be rich in his next life?

Tim: I'm not sure.

Bhogī-yogī: I will now be taking questions. Do we have any questions?

Man in the crowd: Do we have to be vegetarian to make progress in our spiritual life?

Bhogī-yogī: Well, my *guru* told me to be vegetarian every day, but in today's busy world who has time to cook? It is acceptable to eat non-veg on Tuesday, Wednesday, Friday, Saturday, and Monday and Thursday. And Sunday after the sun sets.

Sam: Didn't he just say every day of the week?

Tim: I think he did. I think he did.

Sam: Look at the time. I have that thing to do.

Tim: I also have that thing to do. To cancel that credit card transaction.

Bhogī-yogī: Leaving so soon? You didn't try my drinking water from the Himalayas. Blessed especially by me. Guaranteed to give you the strength of an elephant.

(Sam and Tim reach for the bottles.)

Sam: Don't mind if I do; it's very hot in here.

Bhogī-yogī: (with outstretched hand) That will be only ten dollars.

Sam: (splutters out the water) That's daylight robbery.

Bhogī-yogī: No, it's just good business sense.

Sam: Is this a business? I thought this was a spiritual awakening.

Bhogī-yogī: Silly boy! There's no such thing as a free lunch. If you want to become realized, you have to pay.

Sam: I think I already realized something by coming to your class.

Bhogī-yogī: I'm not surprised at all. People often have deep realizations after just one visit. What is your realization?

Sam: You're no *yogī*! Let's go, Tim. We can still make it to the Sunday Love Feast.

(They shove the water bottles into Bhogī-yogī's hand and leave.)

Bhogī-yogī: (shouting) Stop! Stop! You still owe me for the water.

Critical-Thinking Activity

... to bring out the spiritual investigator in you

THE IRONY OF EXCESS

In verse 32 the *brāhmaṇa* describes a rich man who is anxious because he possesses excess wealth. He implies that this is ironic since the rich man worked hard for wealth, thinking it would bring him happiness. Instead, he ended up unhappy.

In today's world, we find people trying to gain sensual satisfaction in several ways other than accumulating wealth. They may even end up obtaining abundance in the way of material success, but they may still end up unhappy. Here are few more examples.

Relationships

People may have many friends or followers on social media but feel very lonely personally.

Career

People may possess adequate wealth, prestige, and professional success, but their life may feel purposeless.

Fame

The famous may end up experiencing emptiness, loneliness, and stress instead of joy and fulfillment.

Perfection

Those striving for perfection, hoping to feel great satisfaction from it, often feel anxious, stressed, and insecure by a small flaw.

In each case, think about:

a) What kind of sense gratification or happiness is the person seeking?
b) Why may his pursuit bring him distress?
c) What can we, as devotees, learn from this ironic observation?

Science Activity

... to bring out the spiritual scientist in you

VEDIC AND DARWINIAN EVOLUTION

In purport 25, Śrīla Prabhupāda comments on the flaws of the modern theory of evolution of species proposed by Charles Darwin. Darwin's theory proposes that life evolves from man to human, whereas the Vedic version explains that the soul can transmigrate from human to animal and vice versa. Human life is therefore a chance for elevation or degradation. In addition, Darwin believed that life originated from matter whereas Śrīla Prabhupāda taught the Vedic version, that life originated from the Supreme Lord and not matter.

Let us try to understand what Charles Darwin proposed, and how Śrīla Prabhupāda refutes his idea.

Look at the picture below. Śrīla Prabhupāda and Darwin are writing down the key ideas of their theory. What they wrote is also shown, but some of the words are missing. Fill in the missing words.

Life most likely originated from ___________ through chemical evolution.

Different species of life come from one another. The process by which animals with helpful traits survive and create descendents, while those without these traits do not survive with time, is called ___________.

__________________ is the name of the process by which surviving plants and animals change over time to better adapt to their environment and can thus create new species.

___________ can happen only ______ way – from lower to higher species.

___________ has no role in evolution, because it is a natural process with no need of intervention by any being.

Life originated from ____________ and these individual living units are called ____________.
Different species are created by ____________ and are controlled by different ____________. Based on one's ____________, each soul is put into a different form of life.
Souls have new experiences in different bodies, and the process by which they obtain higher forms of life after passing through the lower is called ____________.
____________ can happen both ways, from ____________ to ______ species, and vice versa.
____________ acts as the ____________ and ____________ for the soul undergoing evolution in the material sphere and thus remains in charge.

Now read the above-mentioned purports, and answer the following questions:

a) Why does Śrīla Prabhupāda refute Darwin's theory strongly?
b) Why can Prabhupāda's theory be considered reasonable from a scientific viewpoint?
c) According to the *Bhāgavatam*, what can you conclude about the importance of coming to the human form of life in the evolutionary process?

Writing and Language Activities

... to help you understand better

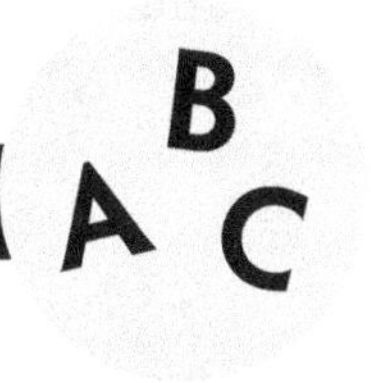

ACTION AND INACTION

The nature of the soul is to be always active; therefore, one cannot refrain from being active for even a moment (*BG* 3.5 purport). Materialistic action results in bondage and sin; therefore Arjuna wanted to avoid the war. However, Lord Kṛṣṇa states that also abstaining from one's prescribed work does not free one from reactions (*BG* 3.5); on the contrary it results in sinful reactions. So how should one act? Acting for the pleasure of the Lord does not incur any reactions; in fact, it is the soul's natural state of being. So one should do one's duties in remembrance of the Lord and dedicate one's activities to Him.

The *avadhūta* seemed inactive but was internally fully active in his service to the Supersoul. Thus his action resulted in no material reaction but only transcendental happiness.

Referring to the table below, write a paragraph on what is real action and inaction based on your study of verse 27 and purport.

	KARMĪ	KARMA-YOGĪ	JÑĀNA-YOGĪ	BHAKTI-YOGĪ
Type of action and inaction	Mostly engaged in material action (*vikarma*), prohibited by the *Vedas*.	Engages in action sanctioned by the *Vedas*, according to *varṇa* and *āśrama*, with no attachment to profit or loss.	Does not engage in materialistic sinful activities, is centered in the self, and does not actively serve the Lord. (inaction/ *akarma*)	Engages in transcendental devotional service, which is the inherent nature of the soul, and therefore frees one of all *karma*. This is real inaction (*akarma*).
Danger	Fully entangled in the cycle of *karma*, of repeated birth and death, due to disobeying the laws of the Lord.	Cannot achieve self-realization and liberation without performing devotional service.	Falls down from Brahman meditation due to lack of real activity.	No danger on this path; even little progress on this path protects one from the greatest danger.
Successful	No	No	No	Yes

NARRATIVE ESSAY: THREEFOLD MATERIAL MISERIES

This chapter emphasizes that there's no use of being successful in material activities when we still have to be reborn and suffer the threefold miseries again and again. As long as we are in the material world we cannot escape these miseries (*kleśas*): miseries of the body and mind (*adhyātmika*), miseries caused by other living beings (*adhibhautika*), and miseries caused from natural disturbances (*adhidaivika*).

Choose one of these afflictions and write a narrative about someone going through it. It could be a dramatic story of being caught in an earthquake or tornado; an emotional story of being afflicted by a terminal disease or other ailment; or a relationship story of revenge, heartbreak, or deception. Make a twist toward the end in which your central character turns to God or His devotees for higher understanding, relief, and ultimate happiness.

CHAPTER 13 ANSWERS

Your Happiness Quotient

Potential answers (Part 2):

1. Eating *prasādam* from Govindas; 2. Making reels of you and your friends in the *kīrtana melā*; 3. Enjoying *kīrtana* of famous *kīrtanīyās*; 4. Going to holy places with friends where trekking is involved; 5. Going shopping to buy jewelry and paraphernalia for the Deity; 6. Getting some craft kits to decorate Kṛṣṇa's altar; 7. Thanking Kṛṣṇa for everything by chanting extra rounds; 8. Remembering the last time you went to Vṛndāvana/Māyāpur and the pleasant experiences; 9. Decorating the Deities.

The Irony of Excess

1. a. The happiness from personal connection and relationships; b. Because of trying to obtain less meaningful but a greater number of relationships; c. We should invest time in meaningful devotee relationships, gaining inspiration and guidance from each other.

2. a. Material success and prosperity; b. Because material wealth and success cannot satisfy one completely. The spirit soul can only obtain happiness from spirit, not matter; c. We can strive for spiritual progress and success, which can satisfy us fully.

3. a. Fame; b. Because they saw only the positives and ignored the negatives of being famous, which made them disillusioned and unhappy; c. We should not aspire to be famous but rather to be humble and sincere servants of the Lord and His devotees, which brings spiritual fulfillment and bliss.

4. a. Material perfection; b. They over-endeavor; c. We should try our best but know that we are imperfect, entrapped in the material body. We are perfect when we depend on the Lord and when He uses us as His instrument.

Vedic and Darwinian Evolution

Darwin: 1. Non-living matter; 2. natural selection; 3. evolution; 4. evolution, one; 5. The Lord

Prabhupāda: 1. The Supreme Lord, soul; 2. Brahmā (the Lord's creative assistant), modes; 3. evolution/transmigration; 4. evolution, lower, higher; 5. The Lord, overseer, sanctioner

a. Darwin believed that complex life came from simple life through natural causes; i.e., through natural selection, with no divine intervention. Darwin's theory of the origin of species states that evolution occurs through gradual changes driven by environmental pressures. Darwin also believed that life could have originated from non-living matter through natural processes (primordial soup). The Vedic viewpoint rejects the notion of life arising from dead matter as well as the idea of natural evolution as an explanation for life's diversity. A divine creator is the cause of life's complexity, which cannot arise solely from natural processes, and life can only come from life.

b. Śrīla Prabhupāda received knowledge in disciplic succession, and therefore it is wisdom received through *śabda-pramāṇa*, which is the system of receiving perfect knowledge from a perfect authority, the Supreme Lord. It can therefore be trusted, just like we would trust the manual to a gadget provided by the manufacturer himself. It is not possible to prove or disprove this theory through modern observations, which are made through the imperfect senses. It has to be accepted as it is.

c. The human form is a junction between lower life forms and higher life forms in higher planets. From the human form one can inquire about the purpose of life, transcend the material realms, and reach the Lord's abode.

14

IDEAL FAMILY LIFE

Story Summary

So far Yudhiṣṭhira Mahārāja had mostly heard about the three stages of life that are favorable for spiritual advancement. "What about the householders, who occupy most of society?" the King thought.

"O great sage," Mahārāja Yudhiṣṭhira addressed Nārada Muni, "what about us who are staying at home without knowing about the goal of life? How can we easily attain liberation?"

Nārada Muni smiled and replied, "My dear King, householders must act to earn their livelihood, but instead of trying to enjoy the results of their activities, they should offer the results to Kṛṣṇa. They can understand how to satisfy Lord Vāsudeva by associating with His exalted devotees. With great respect they should hear from them about the Lord and His incarnations described in the *Śrīmad-Bhāgavatam* and other *Purāṇas*. In this way a husband can eventually become detached from his wife and children, just like a man awakening from a dream."

Yudhiṣṭhira Mahārāja nodded and said, "That's true; while asleep we may dream of friendship and love, and when we wake up, we see they don't exist. Our family and our affection for them are like a dream, and this dream will be over as soon as we die."

"Aha!" exclaimed Nārada Muni, smiling in appreciation of the King's understanding. "Therefore, a learned *gṛhastha* works only to maintain the body and soul together and is unattached to family affairs even though externally he may appear attached."

"So in other words, a *gṛhastha* should also cultivate detachment like the other *āśramas*?" asked the King.

"Exactly! An intelligent householder should live very simply. He avoids a life of excessive burden just so that he can focus on the purpose of life. He depends on the natural products of the creation for his sustenance – that which comes from rainfall, from the earth, and obtained suddenly and unexpectedly. When he focuses on serving the Lord, all of life's necessities automatically follow."

"Hmm . . ." muttered the King. "But what should we do if we get more than we require?" he asked, thinking of the royal luxuries he was born with.

"One should accept only as much wealth as required to keep the body and soul together. Anyone who accepts more is a thief and deserves to be punished by nature's laws, by facing repeated birth and death."

Yudhiṣṭhira Mahārāja's face turned grave. He asked, "Then what should we do with the excess we collect?"

"*Gṛhasthas* should contribute toward constructing temples and spreading the message of the Lord. They shouldn't over endeavor for *dharma*, *artha*, and *kāma*. They shouldn't engage in *ugra-karma*, extraneous endeavor for money and wealth but be satisfied with a simple life, dedicating their life to become Kṛṣṇa conscious.

"Seeing everyone with equal vision, they should treat innocent animals like their children and provide dogs, fallen persons, and untouchables with their needs.

"The *gṛhastha* should even engage his wife in serving guests . . . because as you know, dear King, the wife is the husband's greatest attachment, so by offering her in service to others, he can gradually give up ownership of his wife, not thinking she is his. To give up this attachment is extremely difficult, for a husband can kill others for the sake of his wife. Therefore, if one gives up attachment to his wife, he can conquer the Supreme Lord, who is not conquered by anyone. Like this, one should also give up attraction to the wife's body. Just think about it, O King, her body after death will ultimately become insects, stool, or ashes. So what is the value of this insignificant body? Rather become attracted to the Lord, who is all pervading like the sky."

Yudhiṣṭhira Mahārāja nodded and smiled. Certainly, he understood the purport of Nārada's words. The wife also needs to develop this kind of detachment.

"An intelligent person should be satisfied with taking the Lord's *prasāda* and performing the five kinds of *yajña*," Nārada continued. "After all, the Lord provides the needs of even the elephants and the ants, so what is the use of over endeavoring for material comforts? Rather, save your energy for advancing in Kṛṣṇa consciousness."

Yudhiṣṭhira Mahārāja nodded in agreement. He knew how important it was to offer sacrifice to satisfy the Supreme Lord. The greatest sacrifice or *yajña* in Kali-yuga would be the *saṅkīrtana-yajña*, by which the Lord would be just as pleased.

"The Lord is the enjoyer of all sacrificial offerings," continued Nārada, "but He is more pleased when you offer *prasāda* to qualified *brāhmaṇas* and Vaiṣṇavas, and then to other living beings, as much as you can.

"Now, dear King, there are certain auspicious times to perform religious activities, and auspicious places in which to execute them. For example, *śrāddha*, oblations to the forefathers, should be offered in the month of Bhādra during the dark-moon fortnight on certain *saṅkrānti* days. By adhering to these times, one becomes materially prosperous in one's short life. One gets permanent benefits when, during these seasonal changes, one bathes in a sacred river, chants or offers fire sacrifices, and worships the Supreme Lord, the *brāhmaṇas*, forefathers, and demigods. These rituals must be observed according to time and circumstances and the directions of the *śāstra*."

In this Kali-yuga the scriptures encourage the performance of *saṅkīrtana-yajña* – no ritualistic ceremony is successful without *saṅkīrtana*.

Nārada Muni then described the places where religious performances are successful: where Vaiṣṇavas are present; in the temple where the Lord's Deity is worshiped; where learned *brāhmaṇas* observe Vedic principles through austerity, knowledge, and mercy; where sacred rivers and lakes flow; and where the Lord performed His pastimes. Similarly, even places outside of India, where Rādhā-Kṛṣṇa Deities are worshiped, are holy places of pilgrimage and should be visited. Any spiritual activity done in these places is especially effective – the results are a thousand times better than performed in any other place.

Yudhiṣṭhira Mahārāja then inquired, "Dear Nārada Muni, you've wonderfully described the time and place to perform a religious act, but to whom should all these activities be offered? Who should be the object of all ritualistic performances?"

"O King, you more than anyone else know the answer to this question. When we were present at your Rājasūya sacrificial ceremony and when the question came up of who should be worshiped first, everyone decided that it should be Lord Kṛṣṇa, the Supreme Person. Therefore, O King of the earth, all learned scholars and saintly persons have concluded that only the Supreme Personality of Godhead, Kṛṣṇa, the root cause of existence, is the best person to whom everything must be given."

Yudhiṣṭhira Mahārāja smiled and remembered Kṛṣṇa, the friend, mentor, relative, and Lord of his life. He closed his eyes and mentally worshiped Kṛṣṇa.

"This universe is like a tree," Nārada said, "and Kṛṣṇa is the root. Simply by worshiping Him, you worship all living entities. The Lord resides in the hearts of all the species of life He has created. Thus He is known as *puruṣāvatāra*. As the Supersoul He gives intelligence to every individual according to their capacity to understand Him. So anyone wanting peace and prosperity in life should offer everything to

Kṛṣṇa, who is the real enjoyer, real friend, and real proprietor."

"Oh yes!" exclaimed the King, who had experienced great happiness and fulfillment by offering everything to the Lord. "But, dear sage, I was wondering why Deity worship was introduced in Dvāpara-yuga to replace the sacrifices performed in Tretā-yuga."

"That's a good question, O King, and is related to what I was explaining about the Supersoul in all beings. After Satya-yuga, people started disrespecting each other because they stopped seeing the Supersoul in each other's hearts. As a result, even Vaiṣṇavas and *brāhmaṇas* began quarreling among themselves. When great saintly persons saw this, they introduced Deity worship in the temples for these neophyte devotees who needed to focus their minds on Kṛṣṇa. These *kaniṣṭha-adhikārī* devotees generally value the Deity more than the devotees. Still, Deity worship purifies their hearts.

"Dear King, they don't realize that it's not just Kṛṣṇa who is the best recipient of worship. Kṛṣṇa's devotees are also fit to be worshiped. The *brāhmaṇas* and Vaiṣṇavas, especially those who preach the Lord's glories throughout the world, are as good as the Supreme Lord. In fact, just as they worship Kṛṣṇa, Kṛṣṇa worships them."

Themes and Key Messages

Please go through this table of themes and key messages, with corresponding verses, and discuss each topic further.

THEMES	REFERENCES	KEY MESSAGES
Householders should offer the results of their work to Kṛṣṇa and learn to satisfy Him through the association of great devotees.	7.14.2–4	A *gṛhastha* should work but not be attached to the fruits of his work. He must act only for the satisfaction of Kṛṣṇa (as in all the other *āśramas*). He learns how to do this by hearing from saintly devotees about the activities of the Lord and His incarnations. He also becomes purified by chanting the holy name in the association of devotees, taking *prasāda*, and hearing again and again about Kṛṣṇa from *Bhagavad-gītā*. Thus, he gradually becomes detached from affection for his wife and children, like a man waking up from a dream.

THEMES	REFERENCES	KEY MESSAGES
The *gṛhastha* lives simply and works only to keep body and soul together, giving up bodily attachments.	7.14.5–13	A householder is satisfied with what comes of its own accord to keep body and soul together. Although externally appearing attached, the *gṛhastha* should cultivate detachment. He doesn't claim to be the owner of anything. One who thinks he's the proprietor and who accumulates wealth more than necessary is considered a thief, who will be punished. He also doesn't engage in *ugra-karma*, excessive endeavor to accumulate money. A householder gives any excess money to Kṛṣṇa or the Kṛṣṇa consciousness movement for temple construction and preaching purposes. He also protects and maintains animals, considering them his own children, as well as fallen persons and untouchables. He sees his wife as the property of Kṛṣṇa and doesn't consider her his own; he gradually gives up attachment to his wife and sex enjoyment, and ultimately conquers the Supreme Lord.
The householder performs sacrifice (*yajña*) for the pleasure of the Supreme Personality of Godhead and charity to the *brāhmaṇas*; thus he can give up attachment to the body.	7.14.14–18	An intelligent *gṛhastha* is satisfied by only eating *prasāda* and by performing the five kinds of *yajña*. When he does this, he can give up attachment to the body and proprietorship in relation to the body and becomes a *mahātmā*, a great soul. He also worships the Lord as Paramātmā in everyone's hearts and performs sacrifices by offering oblations to the fire as directed by the *śāstras*. In this age the best means to satisfy the Supreme Lord is by performing *saṅkīrtana-yajña* and helping the *saṅkīrtana* movement. Kṛṣṇa is also pleased when we serve the *brāhmaṇas* by offering them *prasāda* and then distributing this *prasāda* to others.
Gṛhasthas should consider the time (*kāla*) and place (*deśa*) for performing religious activities but should know that they are only successful when *saṅkīrtana* and the worship of *brāhmaṇas* and the Supreme Lord are performed.	7.14.19–33	*Śrāddha*, or offering of sacrifice, to the forefathers are one of the religious ceremonies recommended for *gṛhasthas*, and this should be done on certain auspicious days according to the movements of the sun. However, these rituals are mostly recommended for those who are engaged in fruitive activities. Vaiṣṇava *gṛhasthas* serve the Lord and thus are promoted to His abode, whereas fruitive workers (*karmīs*) who worship the demigods and forefathers reach their abodes. (*BG* 9.25) All rituals are only successful if they begin and end with the chanting of the holy names, for *saṅkīrtana* is the recommended process for spiritual perfection in Kali-yuga. Similarly, all religious ceremonies are successful where the Vaiṣṇavas, the *brāhmaṇas*, and the Deity of the Supreme Lord are present, which make the place sacred and auspicious. The temple of Kṛṣṇa and the sacred rivers and lakes are also places where one's spiritual activities are magnified.

THEMES	REFERENCES	KEY MESSAGES
The best person (*pātra*) to whom worship must be offered is the Supreme Lord – along with His devotees – who is the resting place of existence and the Supersoul within every living being.	7.14.34–42	Kṛṣṇa is the root of everything. He is also *puruṣāvatāra*, because He resides in every living being, in every species, as the Supersoul, directing the journey of the conditioned souls and giving them intelligence to understand Him. Therefore, He is the best *pātra* (person) to whom everything must be given. (*BG* 5.29; *SB* 4.31.14) If one wants peace and prosperity, one should give everything to Kṛṣṇa, and by satisfying Him, one satisfies everyone, just as the tree is satisfied by watering the root. Therefore, among the demigods and saintly persons at Yudhiṣṭhira Mahārāja's Rājasūya sacrifice, Kṛṣṇa was chosen to be worshiped first. Worship of the *brāhmaṇas* and Vaiṣṇavas is also significant. The Lord is more pleased when we serve His devotees, whom He Himself worships.

Higher-Thinking Questions

Now try to deepen your understanding of this chapter by delving into Śrīla Prabhupāda's purports and reflecting on the following questions:

1. What is said of those who work hard day and night simply for sense gratification? Why is this so? (See verses 3–4 purport.)
2. Why is someone considered a thief if he desires more than what is required to keep body and soul together? How should we spend excess money and resources? (Refer to verse 8 and purport.)
3. Why should a *gṛhastha* not over endeavor for *dharma*, *artha*, and *kāma* as described in verse 10 and purport?
4. Referring to verse 13, explain what you think makes it easier to become detached from bodily relations.
5. Why do you think cultivation of detachment is stressed in all the *āśramas*?
6. How should people in this age perform sacrifice to please the Lord, as there are not sufficient ingredients, like ghee, for elaborate fire sacrifices? How should they use their wealth and education? (See verses 16 and 17 and purports.)
7. Are the conditions mentioned in verses 23 and 24 for performing offerings (*śrāddha*) to the forefathers applicable to Vaiṣṇavas? Why or why not? (Refer to verses 24 and 26 purport.)
8. Is temple or Deity worship enough, according to verse 29 purport? What is the correct understanding?

9. Śrīla Prabhupāda comments in verse 33 purport: "No one can become successful in fruitive activities [*karma*] or speculative knowledge [*jñāna*] without being Kṛṣṇa conscious." Why do you think that *karma* and *jñāna* are dependent on *bhakti* to be successful?

10. Why did the process of worship change from Tretā-yuga (fire sacrifices) to Dvāpara-yuga (Deity worship)? For whom is Deity worship recommended, and irrespective of our position, how should we view devotees in relation to the Deity? (See verses 39 and 40 and purports.)

ACTIVITIES

In this section you will find many exciting things to do. These activities will get you thinking, moving, drawing, and having loads of fun.

Analogy Activity

... to bring out the scholar in you

THE WAKEFUL DREAM

Verses 3 and 4 compare a *gṛhastha's* family life to a dream, and their spiritual identity to reality. Nārada Muni advises the *gṛhastha* not to get too absorbed in their "dream" life (of being a family man or woman), but to try to awaken to their "real" life with Kṛṣṇa in the spiritual world through hearing about Him. Let us understand this analogy more deeply.

Vrinda designed a dice game to help her sister Shyama understand this analogy. She also created a simple game board with odd numbers to the left, even numbers to the right, and some words in the middle.

1. The words against the odd numbers convey that material life is odd, in the same way that a dream is odd compared to reality.

2. The words against the even numbers convey that the spiritual activities (meant to "wake" the living entity) are even or fair, because they give the living entity an opportunity to understand and exist in a higher reality.

Shyama has to throw the dice. Each time, depending on the number on the dice, she needs to correlate the word to either a sleeping dream state or an awakened spiritual state and explain it. (For example, if your dice falls with two dots facing upwards, it corresponds with the word "aware" in relation to reality.) Can you play along with Shyama and help her out? Use the prompts to help you.

SLEEP/ DREAM		WAKE/ REALITY	PROMPT
⚀	False		Explain how *gṛhastha* life is false, just like a dream.
	Aware	⚁	How does spiritual activity keep a *gṛhastha* aware of reality?
⚂	Temporary		Explain how *gṛhastha* life and a dream are similar in being temporary.
	Alert	⚃	State how a *gṛhastha* can remain alert when "awake" to spiritual reality.
⚄	Forgettable		In what way are both dreams and *gṛhastha* experiences forgettable?
	Connected	⚅	How does being awake to our spiritual reality help us connect with Kṛṣṇa?

What do you think Shyama learned from the game?

Artistic Activity

... to reveal your creativity

CRAFT: A TEMPLE ALTAR

A *gṛhastha's* home should be a temple, and the altar should be the focus of the temple. In this activity you will make an altar about 12 inches tall that can house a Deity picture or Deity of four to five inches. You can increase the size as needed.

Materials: stiff cardboard; scissors; ruler; pencil; strong glue; double-sided tape; 2 gift wrapping sheets (can be of different colors); ribbons, bells, and small embellishments to decorate.

Image 1

Directions:
* measurements in inches (convert to centimeters if desired)

- Cut the following rectangles from the cardboard:
  - 7x9: two pieces
  - 6x5: two pieces; **5×5**: two pieces (for the dome)
  - 5.5x2: four pieces (for the first frame)
  - 5.5x5: one piece
  - 3.5x1.5: four pieces (for the second frame)
- Cut gift paper for all the above pieces big enough to cover it well.
- From the gift paper cut four rectangles (7x9) to make pillars.
- Cover all cardboard pieces with paper, and glue them securely (Image 1).
- Take one 7x9 rectangle. Lay it flat. This is the base.
- Use the four smaller rectangles (5.5x2) to make a frame. Glue them and also secure them with the tape. Place the frame on the base in the center (Image 2).
- Place another 7.9-inch board on the frame (Image 3).
- Roll the paper sheets (7x9 each) over a pencil and secure with the double-sided tape (Image 4). Remove the pencil.

Image 2

Image 3

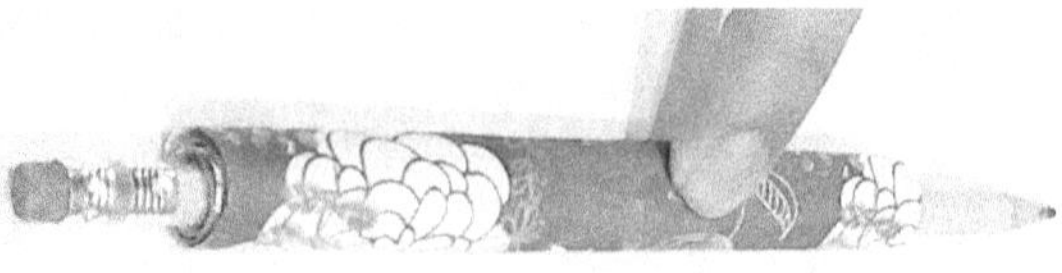

Image 4

Image 5

Image 6

- Secure the third big rectangular piece to form the back of the altar. Glue the four pillars (Image 5).
- Place the last big rectangular board to form the top of the altar (Image 6).
- Join the four rectangles (3.5x1.5) to make another frame and glue it on the top. Then add the single piece (5.5x5).
- Now only the dome is left. Cut two triangles from 6x5-inch rectangles and two from the 5x5-inch rectangles. Glue the triangles to form a dome and glue it on top (Image 7).
- Decorate the altar with embellishments of your choice.
- Now your altar is ready for your Deity or picture.

Image 7

Action Activity

... to get you moving and learning

PROMOTING THE YAJÑA FOR THE AGE

The Vedic civilization aims at satisfying the Supreme Personality of Godhead through performing *yajña*, sacrifice. This was done in Satya-yuga through meditation; in Tretā-yuga by performance of costly *yajñas*; in Dvāpara-yuga through worship of the Lord in the temple; and in Kali-yuga by performing *saṅkīrtana*, the chanting of the holy names.

Performance of *yajña* as done in previous ages is not easy in this age. The availability of qualified priests and pure ingredients for *yajña* (ghee, etc.) is rare. But the *saṅkīrtana-yajña* is easy to perform. Therefore, *gṛhasthas* and all *āśramas* are advised to help propagate the chanting of the holy name. For this, *gṛhasthas* need not leave their occupation but utilize their earnings, wealth, intelligence, mind, and words in the *saṅkīrtana* mission. Śrīla Prabhupāda engaged people from all walks of life, the educated and wealthy, since money and education are meant for the service of the Supreme Personality of Godhead.

As teenagers, you may not be earning a lot of money, but it is good to be mindful of money however little you may have so that you can efficiently use some of it in the *saṅkīrtana* movement. For this you need to learn the basic concepts of budgeting.

The first rule of budgeting is spending less than you earn!

Now try the following steps in your notebook:

Step 1: Calculate your income for a particular month by adding up all the money that comes to you in a month. For example, pocket money, some allowance, birthday gifts, money from a part time job, etc.

Step 2: Calculate the sum of all the money you spend during the month. Classify the expenses into i) Your needs (those expenses that are necessary); ii) Your wants (those expenses that are more for fun, entertainment, etc.)

Step 3: If you are spending more than what you earn, first correct it by deciding what expenses can be avoided.

Step 4: Now, resolve to keep aside a certain percentage of your income every month to contribute to the *saṅkīrtana-yajña* as your offering to the Lord and His mission. Make a list of all the contributions you could make to your local temple or preaching program. For example, *prasāda* distribution at the temple; flower offerings to the Deities; assistance to the temple devotees, etc.

Every month try to contribute the amount that you decided to set aside for one of the items in the list. It could be for the same item every month or otherwise.

If you are too young to have allowances or pocket money, you could still contribute. Carry some *prasāda*, such as fruits, sweets, or cookies, in small packets or Ziplock bags whenever you leave home. When you meet your friends or other acquaintances, give them the packed *prasāda*. Like this, you can participate in the *saṅkīrtana-yajña* and please the Lord.

Critical-Thinking Activity

... to bring out the spiritual investigator in you

CONSTRUCT CONTRASTING STORIES

This chapter extensively discusses the duties of a *gṛhastha* by discussing how a *gṛhastha* should and should not act.

You may recall that we studied the behavior of a *gṛhamedhi* in detail in Canto 3, Chapter 26.

Below is a set of cards that follows the activities of two families – the Yogi family (devotee family) and the Bhogi family (yet to become a devotee family).

1. Photocopy them and cut them out into a pack of cards.
2. Shuffle them and place them face down on a table.
3. Take turns to pick one card at a time. The card lists different everyday family situations.
4. To each situation, alternate between the most likely reaction of the Yogi and the Bhogi families.
5. Now comment on why you think the reaction was appropriate or inappropriate from the viewpoint of the *Bhāgavatam*. Also offer suggestions for Kṛṣṇa conscious reactions to these situations.

1. The family owns a small farm which they cultivate for a living. This year, the harvest has been particularly bountiful, and they have some additional income.

2. Priya, the family's teenage daughter, is about to attend her best friend's wedding. She wants to look her best and is thinking of asking her father to buy her a very expensive outfit for the occasion.

3. Shyam, the head of the family, just got a job offer that would triple his earnings. But he may need to put in eight extra hours a week at work and he knows it is likely to affect his personal and family time (including any spiritual practices).

4. Shyam's friend is going through a financial crisis, and Shyam just received a much-awaited bonus at work.

5. A big, beautiful temple of Rādhā-Kṛṣṇa is being inaugurated in the vicinity of Shyam's family. They have been invited to attend, but it is also Shyam and Kavita's wedding anniversary.

6. Aman, the family's ten-year-old son, was just exposed to an influence that does not align with their family values.

7. Priya performed poorly in her recent exams. She is also falling behind on her other routine personal and spiritual practices.

8. The local ISKCON center is conducting a free family retreat workshop over the weekend. The World Cup Final is also on the same day, at the same time.

Writing and Language Activities

... to help you understand better

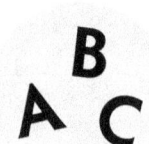

FAMOUS VEDIC HOUSEHOLDERS

Here are some famous householders from the Vedic times. Match them to the idealism they exhibited:

	HOUSEHOLDER	IDEALISM
1.	Kardama Muni and Devahuti	(a) He was committed to the truth and exemplified perfect human behavior. He maintained the *eka-patnī vrata*, the vow of having only one wife.
2.	Rāma and Sītā	(b) The wife served the husband for many years without worrying about her health and appearance. Her husband, in turn, made a heavenly flying mansion for her to live in.

	HOUSEHOLDER	IDEALISM
3.	Kṛṣṇa and Rukmiṇī	(c) Both the husband and wife showed unalloyed devotion to the Supreme Personality of Godhead when they prayed to Him for nearly a *manvantara* to have Him as their son. The Lord appeared to them three times.
4.	Sutapā and Pṛśni	(d) An ideal, chaste wife who served her five valorous husbands. They also took care of her needs.
5.	Devakī and Vasudeva	(e) This wife is known for her chastity and the advice she gave to Sītā when Rāma and Sītā visited their *āśrama* during their exile. The husband was a great mystic *yogī*, who prayed to the trinities, Brahmā, Viṣṇu, and Śiva and asked for a son. Dattātreya was born to them.
6.	Aditi and Kaśyapa Ṛṣi	(f) This couple was Sutapā and Pṛśni in their previous lives. Lord Kṛṣṇa was born to them. Throughout their life they performed austerity and lived without any complaints although Kaṁsa tortured them by imprisoning them.
7.	Draupadī and the Pāṇḍavas	(g) This couple was also Sutapā and Pṛśni in a past life. They were so austere and devoted that the Lord was born of them as Vāmana.
8.	Anasūyā and Atri Muni	(h) Although the husband had 16,108 wives, He treated all of them fairly. He served his principal wife and queen like an ordinary householder, taking care of the family and children. She also in turn always worshiped Him.

In what category of householder would you put your parents:

Ideal __________ Striving to become ideal __________

STRIVING TO BE IDEAL HOUSEHOLDERS

More characteristics of an ideal householder are given here. In the second column, with a "yes" or "no," state if the characteristic is valid today and can be followed. If not, explain in the last column in what way a compromise can be reached so that husband and wife can still be Kṛṣṇa conscious *gṛhasthas*:

	CHARACTERISTICS OF A VEDIC HOUSEHOLDER	FEASIBILITY IN MODERN TIMES	COMPROMISE THAT CAN BE REACHED
1.	Satisfied to maintain body and soul together with whatever is available and using minimum effort, according to place and time, by the grace of the Lord. Does not engage in *ugra-karma*.		
2.	Offers his wife to receive guests and serve people in general.		
3.	Listens to *Śrīmad-Bhāgavatam* in the association of devotees and slowly detaches from family and children.		
4.	Keeps cows as pets in the cow shed and does not have pet animals like dogs and cats inside the house. Protects all animals.		
5.	Does not put undue pressure of academics on children but helps them to become Kṛṣṇa conscious and to depend on Kṛṣṇa.		
6.	Gives 50 percent of earnings to Kṛṣṇa, 25 percent for family, and keeps 25 percent for emergencies.		

INTERVIEW: IDEAL GṚHASTHAS

The goal of this activity is to hear from ideal *gṛhasthas* in ISKCON and get practical understanding of this chapter. Nārada Muni gives many guiding principles for ideal *gṛhasthas*: working for the pleasure of Kṛṣṇa, associating with exalted devotees and hearing *kṛṣṇa-kathā,* cultivating detachment from wife and children, having a "simple living and high thinking" lifestyle, avoiding *ugra-karma*, developing equanimity toward all and attachment to the Lord, performing *saṅkīrtana-yajña*, and worshiping the Lord and His devotees. Reflect on these important principles and note any questions about applying them. You may also refer to the sample questions below. Using these questions, interview a few devotee householders and present your findings, either in a written report or an oral presentation to your teacher and class.

Sample questions:

1. What is your occupation and how long have you been engaged in your work?
2. How do you maintain enthusiasm to work to the best of your capacity?
3. How do you define what is needed to keep the body and soul together and what is excess accumulation of wealth?
4. How do you make the best of the association available? What qualities have helped you accept and absorb the potency of saintly association?
5. How do you manage your time so you can hear *kṛṣṇa-kathā* regularly? How do you organize your life so you can remember Kṛṣṇa throughout the day?
6. What is detachment from family members? Does it mean having no affection for them?
7. How do you serve other living entities in day-to-day life?
8. What do you do to take special advantage of holy days and holy places? Do you practice any austerities?
9. Can you share your realization from your daily *sādhana* practice, especially guidelines for chanting the holy name in your busy schedule?
10. How do you serve devotees at home, at the temple, or in holy places?

ESSAY: DEITY WORSHIP IN THE MODERN WORLD

"There is no place for temples and Deity worship in the modern world."

Write an essay refuting the statement above. Explain why the temple is considered *śreyasāṁ padam* (the best and most auspicious place). Discuss how and why *gṛhasthas* in particular can benefit from Deity service. Elaborate on how *gṛhasthas* and devotees in general can ensure they receive the auspiciousness of religious ceremonies.

Use the following verses from *Śrīmad-Bhāgavatam* for further reference: 7.14.19–33; 2.3.22; 2.9.31; 3.22.34; 6.2.41.

Then discuss how regularly you visit the temple with your friends and/or parents. Together with them brainstorm ways you can increase your visits, either weekly or monthly, by attending *maṅgala-ārati*, greetings of the Deities, or the Sunday Love Feast. After a few weeks, notice what effect increasing your visits had on you.

TIME, PLACE, RECIPIENT

In this chapter Śrīla Prabhupāda explains how nondevotees tend to see *deśa* (place), *kāla* (time) and *pātra* (recipient) when performing religious rituals, such as *śrāddha*. He also mentions that for everyone, and specifically for devotees, the chanting of the holy name should be emphasized over rituals, or in the performance of important rituals.

Imagine you are a *pūjārī* at an ISKCON center. You are being interviewed for an online podcast on the inauguration of a new temple at your location. Your interviewer asks you these three questions:

1. Have you checked the best possible time for the inauguration rituals? What effect will the time have on the Deity installation?
2. Which aspects of the rituals are most important? Why?
3. Was the site for temple construction chosen based on any special consideration?

In about 200 words, write the answers to this interview. Refer to verses 19 to 33 of this chapter for Vaiṣṇava standards on these issues.

TWO TRAIN TRACKS

The *Bhāgavatam* describes two processes that are compared to two train lines: *pāñcarātrika-vidhi* (the process of worshiping the Deity with rules and regulations), and *bhāgavata-vidhi* (the process of hearing the scripture and chanting the holy names). Let's see why Śrīla Prabhupāda describes them as two parallel train lines or tracks.

In the diagram, the train represents our journey in Kṛṣṇa consciousness, and each of the tracks on the line represents the processes mentioned above. Reflect on what it would mean if one of the tracks were removed or damaged. What would happen to the train? Relate this to Deity worship and hearing and chanting. Discuss with your class and teacher. Also discuss the importance of temples and Deity worship in ISKCON. What are the fundamental reasons for creating temples and worshiping the Deity? What is the importance of not only temple service but also devotee service. (See verse 29 purport and verse 40 purport.) Then referring to the train analogy, discuss if Deity worship alone is sufficient.

Now, use the acronym ISKCON below to write a poem related to the topic. (The poem doesn't need to rhyme.) Start each line using each letter of the acronym. Example below:

In temples grand, the Deities stand,
Service offered by loving hand.
Kirtan resounds, hearts aglow,
Consciousness lifted, souls entwined.
On tracks of worship and the holy name,
Navigating *bhakti* is like a moving train.

CHAPTER 14 ANSWERS

The Wakeful Dream

1. Dreams are false. Material experiences in *gṛhastha* life, like having opulence, a loving wife, etc., are considered false, because the eternal soul has nothing to do with these temporary relationships; 2. Just like a person who is awake is aware of what is going on around him, a person who is hearing about Kṛṣṇa is gaining knowledge and becoming aware of their spiritual reality; 3. Dreams don't last forever; they are short and come to an end; in the same way, experiences in a certain body are also temporary and end with the change of body; 4. Just as a person who is awake is alert, a person who is spiritually inclined is alert to a higher reality that can liberate him; 5. Dreams can be forgotten; in the same way, material experiences, by nature, can also be forgotten; 6. One who is awake is connected to what is happening around him. One who is practicing Kṛṣṇa consciousness is similarly connected to Kṛṣṇa.

Shyama learned the importance of cultivating spiritual life, especially for a *gṛhastha*.

***Construct Contrasting Stories** (Potential Answers)*

Yogi family: 1. They donate to the local temple; 2. Following the principle of simplicity, they convince her to find something fancy from her or her mum's wardrobe instead; 3. Shyam is likely to reconsider the attractive offer; 4. Shyam helps his friend; 5. Shyam and Kavita decide to go to the temple as part of their anniversary celebrations; 6. Shyam and Kavita explain the consequences of the influence to Aman; 7. Shyam and Kavita decide to support her with both her academic and spiritual life; 8. The family is likely to attend the retreat.

Bhogi family: Students' own answers.

Famous Vedic Householders

1-b; 2-a; 3-h; 4-c; 5-f; 6-g; 7-d; 8-e

Striving to Be Ideal Householders

1. No; Ugra-karma should be avoided, but a job which offers a secure living for one's family should be pursued so that the family is stable and peaceful to perform devotional service. Ultimately, everything can be used in the Lord's service.
2. Yes and no; The wife should be engaged in the service of guests and other family members but not with the mood of exploitation. She should be happily engaged and be protected.
3. Yes; Becoming more attached to hearing and chanting of the Lord naturally leads to detachment of material things and relationships; however, detachment does not mean complete neglect of one's family and only being concerned of one's own Kṛṣṇa consciousness.
4. Yes; Cows cannot be kept in a city residence. A group of devotees can join and start a *gośālā*, which will also be useful to the householders. Cats and dogs can be kept in the *gośālā* to protect the cows from intruders and pestilence. In modern times, pets can be kept in the home under certain guidelines.
5. Yes; Although being Kṛṣṇa conscious, some parents are ambitious for their children. Parents can guide and support children on their career path and then help them make the best decision. At the same time, they can show them how their career can be used to please Krsna.
6. Yes and no; It depends on the situation. If *gṛhasthas* can manage to do this, it is fine. With the cost of living today, this may not always be possible. However, one can get into the habit of regularly donating to the *saṅkīrtana* mission and saving for the future.

***Time, Place, Recipient** (Potential Answers)*

Students should include: 1. An auspicious time may be chosen, but it is the chanting of the holy name, the presence of the Deity and the devotees that are the most important aspects; 2. Chanting of the holy name, the presence of the Deity and pure devotees; 3. Temple may be constructed considering the location according to *vāstu-śāstra*. However, every place on the planet belongs to the Lord, so the temple can be constructed anywhere to help others connect to the Lord. The presence of the Lord makes the temple transcendental, but when it's in a holy place or around sacred rivers or lakes, its auspiciousness is magnified.

15

INSTRUCTIONS FOR CIVILIZED HUMAN BEINGS

Story Summary

Yudhiṣṭhira Mahārāja was happy to hear the glories of the *brāhmaṇas* from Nārada Muni. Nārada continued to discuss the different kinds of *brāhmaṇas* in the four *āśramas*: the *brahmacārī brāhmaṇas* are interested in studying the scripture and explaining it to others; the householder *brāhmaṇas* are attached to rituals and fruitive work; the *vānaprastha brāhmaṇas* are interested in austerities and penances and detachment from family life; and the *sannyāsī brāhmaṇas* cultivate *yoga*, especially *bhakti-yoga* and *jñāna-yoga*. If anyone desires liberation for oneself or their forefathers, one should give charity to any of these *brāhmaṇas*.

However, Nārada explained, there are different rules to observe while serving the *brāhmaṇas* and performing rituals; one has to be diligent about the time, place, and method of offering worship, charity, and service. These processes, which are *karma-kāṇḍa* and *jñāna-kāṇḍa* activities, are not easy, and devotees do not follow them. Rather, the Lord's devotees offer charity to the best of Vaiṣṇavas, devotees of the Lord. Even if they perform some rituals, they do so to uphold social standards, and they make the worship of the Lord and the chanting of His holy names the central focus. They offer *prasāda* to the Vaiṣṇavas and *brāhmaṇas* and to the forefathers during the *śrāddha* ceremony so the forefathers get spiritual benefit. Like this the devotees gain everlasting prosperity.

Nārada explained that a person aware of religious principles should never offer non-vegetarian items in the *śrāddha* ceremony. The Lord is never pleased when animals are killed in the name of sacrifice. In fact, anyone who has an awakening of spiritual knowledge will give up the process of ritualistic ceremonies.

"So, in other words, it is important that people know the purpose of religion," said Yudhiṣṭhira Mahārāja.

"Absolutely!" Nārada Muni replied, nodding with conviction. "Becoming God conscious is the topmost understanding of religious principles. And any religious principle opposed to the principle of surrendering to the lotus feet of the Supreme Personality of Godhead is considered *adharma*, or cheating religion."

"Please explain more about this," said the King.

"There are five types – the first is *vidharma*, irreligion which obstructs one from following one's true religion, surrender to the Lord; the second is *para-dharma*, religion introduced and manufactured by others; the third is *ābhāsa-dharma*, pretentious religion, which is whimsical worship of the demigods or a concocted god and neglect of one's prescribed duties in *varnāśrama*; the fourth is *upadharma*, religion promoted by someone who claims to be the follower of the *Vedas* but who is not; and the last one is *chala-dharma*, cheating religion, which is the misinterpretation of the scripture using word jugglery.

"Being a servant of Kṛṣṇa is the greatest religion!"

"Certainly!" agreed the King. "we should be satisfied with just this."

"Yes, even a poor man should not over endeavor to improve his situation but should be satisfied, like the python, with whatever he has. Anyone who is content and satisfied and who links his activities to Kṛṣṇa is always happy. But how can a materialist be happy when his heart is filled with lust and greed and wanders everywhere just wanting material wealth?

"For someone with shoes on his feet, there is no danger for him when he walks on pebbles and thorns. Everything is auspicious and safe for him. Similarly, anyone who is self-satisfied cannot be distressed; he feels happiness everywhere."

Mahārāja Yudhiṣṭhira smiled, appreciating the analogy.

"My dear King," Nārada continued, "And how is a person satisfied? He feels the presence of the Supreme Personality of Godhead within his heart and thinks of Him all the time. That is real satisfaction. A self-satisfied person can be happy even with drinking water. However, one who is driven by material desire must become a household dog to satisfy his senses.

"Um-hum," interjected Mahārāja Yudhiṣṭhira, "Greed is an overpowering impurity."

"Yes! Because of greed even a devotee or *brāhmaṇa* can lose his spiritual strength, reputation, austerity, and knowledge. Someone can satisfy his hunger and thirst by eating and drinking. And he can even extinguish his anger when he gets a reaction or is chastised. But even if a greedy person conquers all the directions of the world or enjoys everything in the world, he still won't be satisfied.

"O King Yudhiṣṭhira, many learned scholars, advisers, and presidents of learned assemblies fall down into hellish life because of not being satisfied with their positions."

Mahārāja Yudhiṣṭhira nodded, knowing well the outcome of greed as was seen among those in his treacherous family.

"So with determination one should give up lusty desires for sense enjoyment. Similarly, one should give up anger by giving up envy, one should conquer greed by discussing the disadvantages of accumulating wealth, and one should give up fear by discussing the truth.

"In the same way, one should conquer lamentation and illusion by discussing spiritual knowledge, one should overcome pride by serving a great devotee, and one should conquer envy by stopping sense gratification."

Nārada Muni continued to discuss the ways to eradicate bad habits and impurities in the heart. Then he concluded, "One must conquer the modes of passion and ignorance by developing the mode of goodness, and one should rise even above goodness to the platform of *śuddha-sattva*, pure goodness. All this can be automatically done by serving the spiritual master with faith and devotion.

"You see, dear King, the spiritual master is not an ordinary human being. He is as good as the Personality of Godhead. You receive the mercy of the Supreme Lord through the mercy of the *guru*. If the *guru* is pleased, you naturally receive the mercy of the Lord. Lord Kṛṣṇa's lotus feet are sought after by great saintly people like Vyāsa. Only a fool considers Lord Kṛṣṇa an ordinary human being.

"All rituals, regulative principles, austerities, and *yoga* are meant to control the senses and mind and come to the point of meditating on the Supreme Lord. If one cannot do this, all one's activities are useless. The Vedic ritualistic ceremonies cannot help you if you are not a devotee of the Lord. They simply entangle you more and more in material life."

Then Nārada Muni explained the process of giving up family life and living as a *sannyāsī*, a complete renunciate, practicing *yoga*, breath control, austerities, and the chanting of the *praṇava oṁkāra* to realize the Lord. However, the chanting of the Hare Kṛṣṇa *mahā-mantra* is the easiest method of self-realization in this age of Kali. There are no strict rules for chanting the holy names and anyone can benefit from it. The *mahā-mantra* can be chanted at any place or time and gives results very quickly. Like this, a devotee can immediately become a perfect *yogī* because he practices keeping Kṛṣṇa within the core of his heart. His mind naturally becomes peaceful, which helps him follow the principles of his *āśrama*.

"My dear King, this material body has a purpose – to understand the self and the Supreme Self, the Lord. A devotee uses the body for pleasing Kṛṣṇa and becoming free from material life, and the nondevotee uses the body to enjoy and become bound to the material world."

"True," agreed the King, "the body can be the cause of either liberation or bondage."

"The body is like a chariot," continued Nārada. "The senses are like the horses; the mind, the master of the senses, is like the reins; the objects

of the senses are the destinations; intelligence, which drives the mind, is the chariot driver; the ten airs in the body are the spokes on the chariot's wheels; the conditioned soul is the owner of the chariot; the Vedic *mantra praṇava* is the bow; and the pure soul is the arrow."

"Who is the pure soul targeting?" asked the King, trying to envision the chariot metaphor.

"The Supreme Being!" answered Nārada, which the King by now had guessed. "So we should use the human body to remember the Lord, regain our spiritual identity, and go back to Him. Otherwise, if we do not take shelter of the Lord, the senses, acting as the horses, and the intelligence, acting as the driver, become contaminated and bring the body, the chariot, to the path of sense enjoyment. Then the horses, chariot, and driver are thrown into a blinding dark well of material existence, in the cycle of birth and death."

Yudhiṣṭhira Mahārāja's thoughtful expression indicated that he now understood better the great importance of the human form of life.

"So dear King, we should use the body to raise ourselves to the path of *nivṛtti* – activities that purify us from material desire. On the other hand, *pravṛtti* activities, such as rituals, animal sacrifices, and welfare activities, are meant to fulfill our desires. They help the *jīva* attain the moon planet; then after enjoying, he again descends to earth through rain, becomes a herb, and then gets eaten by various living beings, leading to the next life. So the *nivṛtti* path, the path of detachment, is what we want to follow. We place ourselves at Kṛṣṇa's lotus feet, which purifies us and frees us from material desire. A *gṛhastha*, even while remaining at home, can achieve spiritual perfection of the *sannyāsī* by following his occupational duties in the *nivṛtti-mārga*."

Nārada remembered Yudhiṣṭhira's humble presentation of himself as a *gṛhastha* ignorant of spiritual life. He looked lovingly at the King and lifted his hand in a blessing pose and said, "My dear Yudhiṣṭhira Mahārāja, because of your service to the Supreme Lord, you and your brothers, the Pāṇḍavas, overcome many dangers posed by kings and demigods. By serving Kṛṣṇa's lotus feet, you conquered great enemies. By His grace may you be delivered from this material world."

Yudhiṣṭhira Mahārāja bowed his head in gratitude.

Nārada began to explain his journey on the *nivṛtti-mārga*: "Long, long ago, in another millennium of Brahmā, I was a respected Gandharva named Upabarhaṇa. In Gandharvaloka everyone is extremely beautiful, but I had such exquisite bodily features that I attracted the women of the city. Thus I was consumed by lusty desires."

Yudhiṣṭhira Mahārāja gasped, hardly believing what he was hearing.

"Once we were invited to take part in a *saṅkīrtana* festival to glorify the Supreme Lord.

Being surrounded by women, in a drunken stupor I began singing the glories of the demigods. The *prajāpatis*, the demigods in charge of the universal affairs, cursed me: 'For your offense may you immediately become a *śūdra*, devoid of all beauty!' "

The King's mouth fell open in disbelief. How was it possible that the most exalted and devoted Nārada had been in such a position?

"I then took birth as a *śūdra* from the womb of a maidservant. But I was fortunate. I served Vaiṣṇavas who were enlightened in Vedic knowledge. As a result, I became eligible to be the son of Lord Brahmā. Such is the power of serving devotees!"

Yudhiṣṭhira Mahārāja's face lit up. He remembered Lord Kṛṣṇa's instructions in the *Bhagavad-gītā* (9.32) that those who take shelter of Him, even of lower birth, can approach the supreme destination. Nārada Muni was proof of this.

"The process of chanting the Lord's holy name is also powerful. It's so powerful that even *gṛhasthas* can easily gain the ultimate destination achieved by those in the renounced order.

"My dear King, you Pāṇḍavas are so fortunate that many great saints come to your house like ordinary visitors. The Supreme Personality of Godhead, Kṛṣṇa Himself, lives with you in your house just like your brother. How wonderful it is that the Supreme Lord, sought after by exalted sages, is your well-wisher, friend, cousin, spiritual master, and your heart and soul."

Tears welled in the King's eyes as he now gazed at the Lord of his heart. Kṛṣṇa, who was the special guest and object of worship at the Rājasūya sacrifice, had been present all the time and patiently listening to their discussion. The King fell at Nārada's feet, feeling indebted to him for revealing so many wonderful truths.

With tear-filled eyes, Nārada glanced at Kṛṣṇa, closed his eyes, and prayed, "May that Supreme Lord, who is not understood even by great personalities as Lord Brahmā and Lord Śiva, who is realized by His devotees, who is the maintainer of His devotees and is worshiped by silence, devotional service, and cessation of material activities, be pleased with us."

Śukadeva Gosvāmī continued his narration to Mahārāja Parīkṣit: "Kṛṣṇa's luminous smile melted their hearts and of all those present in the assembly. In great ecstasy and love, Yudhiṣṭhira Mahārāja worshiped Kṛṣṇa and was struck with wonder that Kṛṣṇa, his cousin and friend, is the Supreme Personality of Godhead. Then Lord Kṛṣṇa and the King worshiped Nārada Muni. The sage bade everyone farewell, feeling content after imparting knowledge to Mahārāja Yudhiṣṭhira, the best of the Bharata dynasty.

"O Mahārāja Parīkṣit, I have described the varieties of living beings, including the demigods, demons, and humans, and their dynasties, who were generated from Mahārāja Dakṣa's daughters."

Mahārāja Parīkṣit bowed at Śukadeva Gosvāmī's feet, a flood of joy filling his being. Death could wait a few more days . . . all he wanted was to hear more.

Themes and Key Messages

Please go through this table of themes and key messages, with corresponding verses, and discuss each topic further.

THEMES	REFERENCES	KEY MESSAGES
Devotees are uninterested in performing rituals but are only interested in the objective of life.	7.15.1–11, 28–29	Many kinds of rituals are prescribed in the *Vedas* for *gṛhasthas* to follow, like giving in charity and performing the *śrāddha* ceremony and other sacrifices. For them to be successful one needs to follow all the rules. For example, one should give in charity to the *jñāna-niṣṭha brāhmaṇas,* the *sannyāsīs*; one should not offer meat, fish, and eggs in the *śrāddha* ceremony to the forefathers; and one should practice nonviolence and non-enviousness to animals. However, a devotee is not interested in performing rituals which are meant for elevation to higher planets. They are only interested in the objective of life, which is to stop completely the miseries of birth and death and go back to Godhead. Therefore, they perform these rituals and activities differently. For example, they offer charity to any eligible devotee, not necessarily a *brāhmaṇa*; they offer sanctified *prasāda* to the forefathers, *brāhmaṇas*, and people in general for their benefit; and they perform devotional activities for the pleasure of the Lord. These activities are transcendental because they do not incur *karma*. If performing rituals does not control the mind and senses and bring one to meditate on the Supreme Lord, it is frustrated labor.
One who has knowledge should avoid the five branches of *adharma* (irreligion) and cultivate satisfaction.	7.15.12–21	The real religious system is that of surrender to the lotus feet of the Lord. So-called *svamīs* and *yogīs* create new types of *dharma* and claim that one can follow any type of religious system because all are ultimately the same. These religious systems opposed to the progression in Kṛṣṇa consciousness are called *vidharma*, *para-dharma*, *ābhāsa-dharma*, *upadharma*, and *cala-dharma*. A devotee avoids these various cheating religious systems and endeavors to become self-satisfied. He doesn't desire material wealth and opulence and is content and happy because he connects his activities to the Supreme Lord. Like a person who doesn't get hurt by pebbles and thorns because of the shoes on his feet, the devotee doesn't feel any distress because he is self-satisfied. On the other hand, a greedy person can never be satisfied.

THEMES	REFERENCES	KEY MESSAGES
One should follow certain processes to overcome one's *anarthas* (impurities), but the best process is to surrender to and follow the instructions of a pure bona fide *guru*.	7.15.22–27	It is recommended that one consciously give up lust, greed, anger, envy, and other impurities. For example, by being determined one can give up sense enjoyment; by being determined not to envy anyone one can conquer anger; by considering the problems of wealth one can give up greed, etc. However, one can automatically conquer the senses, suffering, and *anarthas* by surrendering to the spiritual master and engaging in his service with faith and devotion. This is because the devotee attains the mercy of the Supreme Lord through the mercy of the *guru*. If the *guru* is pleased, one naturally receives the mercy of the Lord. Therefore, one should consider the *guru* as good as the Personality of Godhead.
The easiest way for a householder to become detached from family and control his mind is to chant the Hare Kṛṣṇa *mahā-mantra* and keep Kṛṣṇa within the core of his heart.	7.15.30–39	A householder becomes liberated by giving up family attachment and practicing mind control through *yoga* and other processes, like chanting the *oṁkāra*; however, the chanting of the *mahā-mantra* is the easiest process for this age, because there are no strict rules or considerations, like sitting postures, breathing, place, time, or level of the individual. The *mahā-mantra* can be chanted at any place or time and gives results very quickly. A devotee can immediately become a perfect *yogī* because he practices keeping Kṛṣṇa within the core of his heart. His mind naturally becomes peaceful by fixing it on Kṛṣṇa. This also helps to follow the principles of their *āśrama*.
For a materialist the body is the cause of bondage, and for a devotee the body is the cause of liberation.	7.15.40–46	The human body can be used in two ways: to degrade oneself into hellish conditions or to elevate oneself and go back to Godhead. The body-chariot metaphor illustrates this. Each part of the chariot is compared to the various parts of the gross and subtle body and the elements that lead one to degradation or elevation. One should pursue the spiritual path and take shelter of *guru* and Kṛṣṇa. By their mercy one can conquer the enemies of the mind, which makes one truly blissful. If one doesn't take shelter of the Lord, then the senses and intelligence bring the body to the path of sense gratification, which leads to repeated birth and death.

THEMES	REFERENCES	KEY MESSAGES
There are two paths that people either follow: the *pravṛtti-mārga* (path of enjoyment) and the *nivṛtti-mārga* (the path of liberation).	7.15.47–56, 66–67, 74	The *pravṛtti-mārga* raises one from a lower to a higher status of material life. The *nivṛtti-mārga* purifies one from material desire, making one fit for eternal life in the spiritual world. *Pravṛtti* activities include performance of rituals, animal sacrifices, and welfare activities. *Nivṛtti* activities involve cessation of material desires and enjoyment and reviving our original relationship with the Supreme Lord. One then achieves detachment from material life and attains the Lord's supreme abode. By the mercy of Śrī Caitanya Mahāprabhu, who has given the process of the chanting of the holy names, this is made very easy. A *gṛhastha*, even while remaining at home, can achieve spiritual perfection of the *sannyāsī* by following his occupational duties in the *nivṛtti-mārga*. The Pāṇḍavas and Nārada Muni's previous life are examples of this.

Higher-Thinking Questions

Now try to deepen your understanding of this chapter by delving into Śrīla Prabhupāda's purports and reflecting on the following questions:

1. Why does a devotee's performance of sacrifice give complete satisfaction as explained in verse 11 purport?
2. What is real satisfaction as described by Śrīla Prabhupāda in verse 18 purport?
3. How can one strike a balance between poverty and greed as mentioned in verse 21 purport? How can one turn material greed into a positive experience? (See verses 20 and 21 purports.)
4. Verse 24 describes various ways to overcome different kinds of suffering. What is the best way to overcome suffering as explained by Śrīla Prabhupāda in the purport? Explain how you think this happens.
5. Why shouldn't a bona fide spiritual master be considered an ordinary person? If a disciple considers the spiritual master to be ordinary, why are his efforts like the bathing of an elephant? (Refer to verse 26 purport.)
6. What is the difference between chanting the *oṁkāra* and chanting the *mahā-mantra* as described in verse 31 purport? Although they are both divine sound representations of the Supreme Lord, why do you think that the *mahā-mantra* is more beneficial in this age?

7. What is the danger of being situated on the platform of *brahma-sukha*, transcendental bliss, but not performing devotional service? (See verse 35 purport.)
8. Explain the philosophy of *acintya-bhedābheda* in relation to the Deity of the Lord. (See verse 59 purport.)
9. How are the Pāṇḍavas and the devotees in the Kṛṣṇa consciousness movement practical examples of living peacefully in the material world by the grace of Kṛṣṇa? (See verse 68 purport.)
10. Describe the three types of oneness in verses 63 to 65.
11. According to verse 71 and purport, why is the *saṅkīrtana* movement not new?
12. Why was Nārada Muni more fortunate in his position as the son of a maidservant than a Gandharva? (Refer to verse 69 and purport.)

ACTIVITIES

In this section you will find many exciting things to do. These activities will get you thinking, moving, drawing, and having loads of fun.

Analogy Activity

... to bring out the scholar in you

EXEMPLIFIED DEPENDENCE

The wise *brāhmaṇa* we met in Chapter 13 who shared the knowledge he had gained from the python and the bee again ponders deeply about the lessons they taught. He understands, as explained in this chapter (verses 15 to 18), that many devotees have set an example of being content and self-satisfied, just like the python in the analogy. By depending on Kṛṣṇa, they showed that when we live our lives completely dependent on the Lord, He certainly takes care of our needs.

Another analogy in verse 17 shows how a content devotee is free from anxiety and distress, just as a person is protected by shoes when he walks on pebbles and thorns. Such a person does not feel any discomfort and walks freely and happily. Similarly, a devotee who depends on Kṛṣṇa's protection feels happiness everywhere.

The learned *brāhmaṇa* decides to create a series of posters with some of these surrendered personalities to be displayed at the temple. The posters are reproduced in Resource A in a smaller form. Color in each poster. Also write two lines under the sketch, preferably using poetic rhythm, to describe how each devotee exemplified dependence on Kṛṣṇa to fulfill both bodily and spiritual needs.

Resource A

Mādhavendra Purī

Rūpa and Sanātana Gosvāmīs

Śukadeva Gosvāmī

Raghunātha dāsa Gosvāmī

Śrīla Prabhupāda

Refer to the following prompts to help you construct your verse for each personality:

1. Mādhavendra Purī never asked anyone for food and was happy with what came of its own accord.
2. Rūpa and Sanātana Gosvāmīs lived under a different tree every night and were satisfied with offering whatever they could acquire without much endeavor.
3. Śukadeva Gosvāmī did not stay in a *gṛhastha's* place for even the time it took to milk a cow.
4. Raghunātha dāsa was satisfied with a cup of buttermilk every alternate day and didn't aspire for any material comfort.
5. Śrīla Prabhupāda left for America with just forty rupees in hand.

Can you now tell why these devotees were satisfied? [Hint: See verse 18 purport]

Artistic Activity

... to reveal your creativity

EXPRESSIVE CHARCOAL ART

Van Gogh and other artists used various bold and expressive strokes to convey a deeper emotion and energy in their artwork. The body-chariot metaphor in this chapter is meaningful and active, and therefore we will paint it expressively. The goal is to create an energetic drawing.

Materials: charcoal stick or pencil; fixative to avoid smudging; pencil; eraser; if coloring use colors of any water-based media and a few brushes; printout/tracing/drawing of the chariot in Resource at the end of this chapter.

Steps:

1. Before you begin, think intently about using the body-chariot metaphor as an arrow to reach the Lord's lotus feet. Meditate on the need for determination, mercy, and perseverance to achieve this exalted goal.

2. Using the image below as a guide, begin with your printout or copy of the Resource at the end of the chapter, first adding strokes on the horses with the charcoal.
3. Remain focused on your intent stated in step 1. Make free but expressive marks controlling the shape and direction of each stroke.
4. After practicing on the horse, you can complete the chariot the same way in charcoal or watercolor paint.
5. Try to invoke drama, mystery, and energy in your artwork using shadows, light, and movement. For example, darken the area under the chariot to add an eeriness, which represents irreligion.

6. You can add action in the sky by using long curvy strokes or an eagle to depict farsightedness. Be creative and bold.
7. Spray the fixative on the charcoal artwork. For the watercolor painting, let the colors dry before framing it.

Introspective Activity

... to bring out the reflective devotee in you

DRIVING THE CHARIOT

Print the drawing of the chariot as in the art activity. Label the parts of the chariot which represent the body as given in verses 40 to 46. Reflect on how this chariot can go in the right direction by following the path given by Śrīla Prabhupāda and in the wrong direction of painful degradation when following the path of irreligion.

Now label other important parts, like the mind, intelligence, and senses and think more deeply about how each controls the other. For example, reflect how the intelligence (the chariot driver) uses the mind (the reins) to control the senses (the horses).

Then see in your own life how you (the chariot driver) can help steer each of these parts toward the destination.

First reflect on your body. For example, the ten life

airs are the spokes of the wheel; when the life airs are balanced, you are physically and mentally healthy. Reflect on whether you get enough sleep and rise early, eat nourishing *prasāda*, and exercise to take care of your health. The body is an instrument of service to Kṛṣṇa, and keeping it fit and sharp helps us progress. Make notes on how you can improve and maintain it.

Similarly, for the mind reflect if you absorb your mind in reading the scriptures and chanting the holy names. Evaluate what can agitate the mind and give rise to unnecessary desires and attachments. Note any teachings from this chapter that can help you fix your mind.

Then reflect on how intelligence is sharpened by the study of scriptures and hearing from advanced devotees. Recall a situation in which your intelligence guided your mind from being lazy or wanting to engage in temporary enjoyment.

How you are able to control the intelligence, mind, and senses will determine your consciousness, which is described as the cause of bondage or liberation in verse 41. Reflect on how your consciousness changes on a particular day. How is it related to your body, intelligence, mind, and senses? Become aware that when we are connected with the Lord and His mercy incarnation, the spiritual master, and advanced devotees, how our consciousness rises and we have clarity and focus.

Also reflect on how we drive the chariot will determine how the chariot moves. Similarly, how we steer our intelligence and mind in the right direction, our senses and body follow in the same manner.

Action Activity

... to get you moving and learning

A GAME OF GREED

Play this game to see how greed entices you to do things which you will not do normally.

Collect or make the following items before playing:

1. Different money notes in your currency. You can use false currency done on paper.
2. Various coupons:
   - Movie tickets for two
   - Dinner at a high-class restaurant for two
   - Air ticket and stay for two days in a popular tourist spot
   - Coupons of purchase for some branded items
   - Coupons for exchange of the latest mobile phone in the market
   (Add more items of your choice)

How to play:

1. Each player will start with a fixed amount of money and a fixed number of coupons. Each person will have a different coupon. The number of coupons can vary. Each player can have less or more according to their wish.
2. Each player is allowed a few minutes to come to the podium of their class and market their wares (his coupons). This person plays the role of Māyā.
3. Using marketing skills, the player should be able to entice the audience and sell their coupons.
4. Who are the winners?
   a) The person with the largest amount of cash at hand (greed for money).
   b) The person with the largest number of coupons (greed for sense gratification).

Discussion:
After the game is over, each player can talk about their experience – how the marketing agent, Māyā, attracted them, how they resisted the temptation, and how they thought they could use their money and coupons in a more effective way.

Of course, the "winners" should first talk about how their thought process worked!

Note: This is a fun game with lot of shouts from the audience, especially meant for teenagers.

Critical-Thinking Activity

... to bring out the spiritual investigator in you

NIVṚTTI IN HOUSEHOLD LIFE

In Chapter 7 we discussed both the *pravṛtti* and *nivṛtti mārgas*. Recall what you learned.

This chapter describes how the Pāṇḍavas and Nārada (in a previous life) were elevated to the highest stage of devotional service by adopting *nivṛtti-mārga*, or the path of renunciation adopted by *sannyāsīs*. They showed by example that *gṛhasthas* can follow *nivṛtti-mārga* and attain perfection. With your teacher and class, discuss both their stories in as much detail as possible.

Divide your study group into two teams, A and B. (If you are self-studying, you could do this activity with a parent or a mentor.) You will play a game that brings out the exalted qualities of the Pāṇḍavas and boy Nārada, which will help you understand how they followed the *nivṛtti* path even in *gṛhastha-āśrama* and attained loving devotional service to Kṛṣṇa.

1. Team A first calls out a quality of a person on the path of *nivṛtti.*
2. Team B should explain one way/pastime in which either the Pāṇḍavas or boy Nārada showed that quality. If they succeed, they get a point.
3. The teams then swap. Team B should now mention one quality of a person on the path of *nivṛtti.*
4. Team A explains one way/pastime in which either the Pāṇḍavas or boy Nārada showed the quality. If they succeed, they get a point.
5. The game can go on as long as both teams can call out qualities. The team that gets the most points wins.

After the game, evaluate how you and your family can follow the path of *nivṛtti* as exemplified by these devotees.

Writing Activities

... to bring out the writer in you

LIMERICK: THE GREATEST ENEMY

A limerick is a humorous five-line poem. Read the following limerick:

There was a young man from Nux
Who loved to collect old books
He collected so many
But didn't look in any
And now his education he overlooks

"Even if a greedy person has conquered all the directions of the world or has enjoyed everything in the world, still he will not be satisfied." (*SB* 7.15.20)

Greed, caused by the mode of passion, is referred to as the greatest enemy. Choose your greatest enemy – what are you most greedy to have (except *prasādam*)? Now write a limerick about how this greed is dangerous.

To understand the dangers of greed, read verses 18 and 19.

Hints on writing a limerick:

- Limerick poems tell a candid, funny story with quirky words that don't necessarily make sense. You can invent your own words as long as their meaning is implied.
- The first line of the limerick sets up the character(s) and setting of the poem.
- Limerick poems have an AABBA rhyme scheme. This means the first, second, and last lines rhyme while the third and fourth lines rhyme separately.
- The last line is the punchline.

After you write your limerick, reflect on how greed can affect your spiritual life. How can you overcome greed? Discuss with your class, teacher, or parents.

ESSAY: A GREEDY PERSON IS NEVER SATISFIED

Verse 20 describes that when a person is hungry and thirsty, food and water will satisfy him, and when a person is angry, chastisement or a reaction will remove that anger, but if a person is greedy nothing will satisfy him. Refer to the analogy activity in this chapter, which shows how a devotee is always satisfied. Greed and satisfaction are opposed to each other; therefore a greedy person is never satisfied.

Write a narrative essay (fiction or non-fiction) to illustrate this theme, possibly using the analogies related to self-satisfaction in this chapter, and show how a greedy person is never satisfied. Also include the dangers of greed, referring to verses 18 to 21.

LETTER: TOPMOST YOGĪ

A householder becomes liberated by giving up family attachment and practicing mind control through *yoga* and other processes, like chanting the *oṁkāra*; however, the chanting of the *mahā-mantra* is the easiest process for this age, because there are no strict rules or considerations, like sitting postures, breathing, place, time, or level of the individual. The *mahā-mantra* can be chanted at any place or time and gives results very quickly.

Imagine in an earlier birth, you were a *yogī* chanting the *oṁkāra,* having the goal of attaining liberation. Let us imagine that you are able to write and send letters to your other self in this earlier age and receive letters as well.

You just received a letter from the *yogī*, who excitedly explains the process you followed as a *yogī* then. Now, as a practicing *bhakti-yogī*, you want to send a reply to him explaining how your chanting of the *mahā-mantra* is the easiest process for this age. You will have to explain how this age is different from the age he practiced as a *yogī*, how having strict rules like sitting postures, breathing, place, etc., will not work in this age, and how the *mahā-mantra* is the most merciful, easiest, sublime, and the only relevant process in Kali-yuga.

Be creative about the situations in previous ages. It can be a funny letter or it can take the tone of a serious debate, or it can be a simple narration of situations in both ages.

You may want to remember that a devotee always practices keeping Kṛṣṇa within the core of his heart. Thus he becomes a topmost *yogī* as his mind is always fixed on Kṛṣṇa.

Language Activities

... to help you understand better

FIVE KINDS OF ADHARMA

Verses 12 to 14 describe the five branches of irreligion, or *adharma*. Can you think what entices a person to follow one of the five kinds of *adharma*? In other words, what is the greed in each of these *dharmas* which are opposed to Kṛṣṇa consciousness? Also give an example of each in the table below.

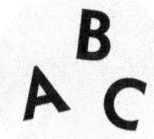

	TYPES OF ADHARMA	EXPLANATION	EXAMPLES	ENTICEMENTS
1	Vidharma	Fashionable ideas that look attractive and stop one from following one's own religious system.		
2	Para-dharma	Religious systems manufactured and introduced by others or performing someone else's occupation or duties that does not fit one's *dharma* or nature.		
3	Ābhāsa-dharma	Religious systems that appear like a shadow, or an imitation, of the real *dharma* of Kṛṣṇa consciousness. Pretentious religion.		

	TYPES OF ADHARMA	EXPLANATION	EXAMPLES	ENTICEMENTS
4	Upadharma	Religions that oppose the principles of the *Vedas* while followers claim to be followers of the *Vedas*.		
5	Cala-dharma	Misinterpretation of the *Vedas* by using word jugglery.		

What is the real religious system explained by Śrīla Prabhupāda in his purports to these verses?

GREED: NEGATIVE OR POSITIVE?

Although we think of greed, *laulyaṁ*, as negative, it can also be positive. Greed for material things and sense gratification will lead you away from Kṛṣṇa consciousness. Greed for Kṛṣṇa and His devotees' association will help you progress in Kṛṣṇa consciousness.

In the table, positive and negative greeds are jumbled up. Put a tick in the right column:

	TOPIC	+VE GREED	-VE GREED
1	Mother made lovely cookies. Gopala stuffs his shirt pocket with cookies and goes to play. Soon he comes back complaining of stomach-ache. Mother chastises him for eating so many cookies without permission.		
2	Raghunātha Dāsa Gosvāmī walked for 12 days to reach Puri and have *darśana* of Mahāprabhu. He couldn't wait to see the Lord.		
3	Little Radha was very fond of kachoris. Mother made a jar full of kachoris and offered it to the Lord. She went out for some work. Little Radha put her hand in the jar and took a handful of kachoris. As she tried to bring her hand out of the jar, her hand got stuck. The mouth of the jar was too small. She would have to let go of all the kachoris but one, to take out her hand. But Radha wanted all the kachoris! She was wondering what to do when mother came back and caught her red handed!		

	TOPIC	+VE GREED	-VE GREED
4	Joe goes to a mall. In a big shop he sees the SALE sign. He knows that he will get things cheap, so he goes in. He buys stuff for $700, but the salesperson says that if he buys for $1000 he can get a gift coupon. So he buys stuff for $300 more. The gift coupon that he gets is a purchase coupon for $100. He is tempted to buy some more. He buys stuff for $150. He comes back to the counter and pays the coupon and the extra $50. Joe started buying for $700 but ended up buying for $1150.		
5	Many of Śrīla Prabhupāda's disciples endured many difficulties in opening temples, preaching, distributing books, and traveling. They wanted to do more and more service to please their spiritual master.		
6	Gajru, the milkman, decided to sell his bucket of milk. With the money he wanted to buy another cow. Then he would have more milk, more money . . . He would then marry, and his wife would bring him a glass of hot milk. Gajru imagined the milk to be too hot, so he got angry and pushed her. His leg hit the bucket of milk, which fell and spilt all the milk on the floor.		

RITUAL TO SPIRITUAL

The *Vedas* prescribe various rituals for householders. Lord Kṛṣṇa in *Bhagavad-gītā* states that acts of sacrifice, charity, and austerity should not be given up. According to one's *varṇa*, a devotee householder may have to engage in certain rituals daily or during special circumstances in life, such as birth, marriage, and death in the family. However, devotees are not interested in pursuing rituals for any gross or subtle material gain. Their objective is to serve the lotus feet of Kṛṣṇa and seek Kṛṣṇa's blessings for spiritual advancement.

The acronym SPI when added to "RITUAL" transforms rituals into SPIRITUAL activities, which increase devotion to the Lord.

"S" stands for Supreme Personality of Godhead, Śrī Kṛṣṇa, who possesses all energies and resources.

"P" stands for our position as parts and parcels of Lord Kṛṣṇa and our priority to serve the Lord and each other, as someone dear to Kṛṣṇa.

"I" stands for the intention to please and serve Kṛṣṇa.

Using this acronym, write a few lines explaining how to properly perform three of the rituals listed at the end of this activity. You may use other examples. One example is included below.

Example: Giving charity on birthdays or anniversaries
Ritual: Give charity to gain material benefits, like name, recognition, and material prosperity.
Spiritual: Give charity to *brāhmaṇas* and Vaiṣṇavas who propagate and protect spiritual culture, and donate towards cow protection and book distribution for the benefit of all. The mood is to please Lord Kṛṣṇa by becoming His instrument and using His resources in His service.

Examples of rituals:

1. Marriage
2. *Śrāddha* ceremony for ancestors
3. *garbhādhāna-saṁskāra* (for conception of a child) and other *saṁskāras* of a child's development
4. Initiation ceremony with fire sacrifice
5. Fasting on certain holy days
6. Daily worship of Deities
7. Daily chanting of *mantras* and holy names

THE POWER OF THE GURU

(This activity has three parts, so you can complete them at three different stages or times.)

Two sisters, Guru-śakti dāsī and Guru-bhakti dāsī, are discussing with their spiritual master about how to eliminate undesirable qualities (*anarthas*) in their hearts. Their *guru* refers them to verses 22 to 25 in this chapter. They then made up a table to identify some of the vices mentioned in these verses and how they can be overcome. Now they are reflecting on how each action can remove each *anartha*. Can you help them fill the table? You may first discuss with your class and teacher. (An example is done for you.)

A.

ANARTHAS	ACTION TO OVERCOME	EXPLANATION
Lusty desires	Make determined plans	
Anger	Give up envy	
Greed	Discuss disadvantages of accumulating wealth	
Fear	Discuss the truth	
Lamentation and illusion	Discuss spiritual knowledge	
Pride	Serve a great devotee	
Envy	Stop sense gratification	When one does not strive for enjoying the senses and competing with others for material gains, name, and status, one is not envious of those who have these things.
Oversleeping	Develop mode of goodness	

B. Then the sisters studied verse 25, which states that if one serves the spiritual master with faith and devotion, one automatically can conquer the lower modes and overcome these *anarthas*. Let's see how this is possible.

Śrīla Prabhupāda discusses the difference between the *guru* and the Lord in verse 27 purport. He explains that the spiritual master is called *sevaka-bhagavān*, the servitor Personality of Godhead, and Kṛṣṇa is called *sevya-bhagavān*, the Supreme Personality of Godhead who is to be worshiped.

The *Gurvaṣṭakam*, by Śrīla Viśvanātha Cakravartī Ṭhākura, glorifies the unique aspects and qualities of the spiritual master. If you don't know the words of the *Gurvaṣṭakam*, find the words and translation and learn to sing them. Then referring to the following last two verses, explain how and why you can easily remove the *anarthas* from the heart (as discussed in part A) by serving the *guru* with faith and devotion.

sākṣād-dharitvena samasta-śāstrair
uktas tathā bhāvyata eva sadbhiḥ
kintu prabhor yaḥ priya eva tasya
vande guroḥ śrī-caraṇāravindam

The spiritual master is to be honored as much as the Supreme Lord, because he is the most confidential servitor of the Lord. This is acknowledged in all revealed scriptures and followed by all authorities. Therefore I offer my respectful obeisances unto the lotus feet of such a spiritual master, who is a bona fide representative of Śrī Hari [Kṛṣṇa].

yasya prasādād bhagavat-prasādo
yasyāprasādān na gatiḥ kuto 'pi
dhyāyan stuvaṁs tasya yaśas tri-sandhyaṁ
vande guroḥ śrī-caraṇāravindam

By the mercy of the spiritual master, one receives the benediction of Kṛṣṇa. Without the grace of the spiritual master, one cannot make any advancement. Therefore, I should always remember and praise the spiritual master. At least three times a day I should offer my respectful obeisances unto the lotus feet of my spiritual master.

C. Then, after understanding the power of the *guru*, the sisters write a *Vyāsa-pūjā* offering to their *guru*, glorifying his qualities and compassion and describing what they've learned about the *guru's* mercy in relation to conquering lower tendencies and *anarthas*. Referring to verse 28 purport, they also explain how they get even greater results by serving the spiritual master.

You may begin as follows and complete your offering in your notebook:

Dear Guru Mahārāja,

Please accept my humble obeisances. All glories to Your Divine Grace. All glories to Śrīla Prabhupāda.

On this glorious occasion of your appearance, we thank you for the spiritual gifts you've given us. From the *Śrīmad-Bhagavatam* and the *Gurvaṣṭakam* we've learned that the *guru* is a confidential servant of the Lord. So by serving you the Lord will be . . .

CHAPTER 15 ANSWERS

***Nivṛtti* in Household Life** (*Potential Answers*)

They did not have material desires; they did not perform rituals to gain material gifts or to go to higher planets; they did not cultivate knowledge to simply do word jugglery; they loved the Lord and followed His instructions; they had faith in the plan of the Lord; they trusted that the Lord would protect them under all circumstances.

Five Kinds of Adharma

1. Marxists and communists; so-called *yogīs* and *svamīs*; a person is enticed by using free will for anything, ultimately leading nowhere.
2. New-age cults; philosophers or "*gurus*" teaching concocted philosophies; people following occupations against their nature; people getting enticed by flowery language or false promises and ideologies; getting enticed by the duties of other *varṇas*, like *brāhmaṇa* acting like a *kṣatriya*, *śūdra* acting like a *brāhmaṇa*, etc.
3. Fake *gurus* who attract followers with their talk, magic tricks, etc.; enticed by whimsical worship of the demigods or a concocted god for material gain; neglect of one's prescribed duties.
4. Māyāvādīs (impersonalists); get enticed by the commentaries of the *Vedānta-sūtras*, believing they are followers of the *Vedas*, but their conclusions of God are impersonal. They choose to emphasize certain statements that support their beliefs.
5. Fake *gurus*, *yogīs*, and scholars; followers get enticed by flowery language and by the misinterpretation of the *Gītā's* message. When Kṛṣṇa says something, they interpret it to mean something different, often denying Kṛṣṇa's supremacy and personality.

Real religion is surrendering to the Supreme Personality of Godhead and understanding one's position as a servant of Him.

Greed: Negative or Positive?

1. -ve; 2. +ve; 3. -ve; 4. -ve, 5. +ve; 6. -ve

Ritual to Spiritual

To make the rituals spiritual, students should recommend adding the spiritual elements of chanting the holy name, offering *prasāda* to ancestors, or doing any other aspect of devotional service.

The Power of the Guru

A. (*Potential Answers*)

Lusty desires: with determination, we can plan our day in such a way that we are engaged in Kṛṣṇa's service and thus be less likely to lust after material things; Anger: we are less prone to get angry if we are not envious of others. Because of lusting to be like other materialistic people, we get angry if we don't get what we want, and then we get envious of those who have what we want. So if we control lust, then we can control anger and envy; Greed: if we discuss the miseries arising from accumulating excessive wealth and the dangers of becoming attached to wealth and sense enjoyment, then we can control greed; Fear: discussing the spiritual truths of one's eternal existence in relation to the Supreme Lord and how the Lord is one's eternal friend and well-wisher, we can overcome fear, being confident about the Lord's protection and presence in our life; Lamentation and illusion: acquiring spiritual knowledge of this material world and life in relation to our *karma*, real identity, and purpose in life, we can remove the illusion that we are the enjoyers, the proprietors, and controllers of everything; we will thus not lament when we lose something; Pride: a great devotee can remove our pride by chastising us or reminding us of our eternal position as humble servants of Kṛṣṇa. By serving such devotees, we can also learn from their example of being a humble servant; Oversleeping: by doing activities in the mode of goodness, we will be less likely to oversleep because we will be motivated and enthusiastic to get up in the morning to do those things we like.

Parts B and C: Students should explain that when we serve the pure devotee or spiritual master, we please him, and by pleasing him, Kṛṣṇa is pleased. When we please Kṛṣṇa, He gives us the strength to overcome all internal obstacles and impurities. Thus even if we are not successful by our own endeavors, our service and surrender to the *guru* automatically helps us overcome *anarthas*. By following the *guru's* instructions, the *guru* blesses us with knowledge and intelligence to be successful in our spiritual practices and overcome our shortcomings. But more than this, we develop our love for the Lord and cross over this ocean of material existence and return home, back to Godhead.

RESOURCE FOR ART ACTIVITY: THE CHARIOT

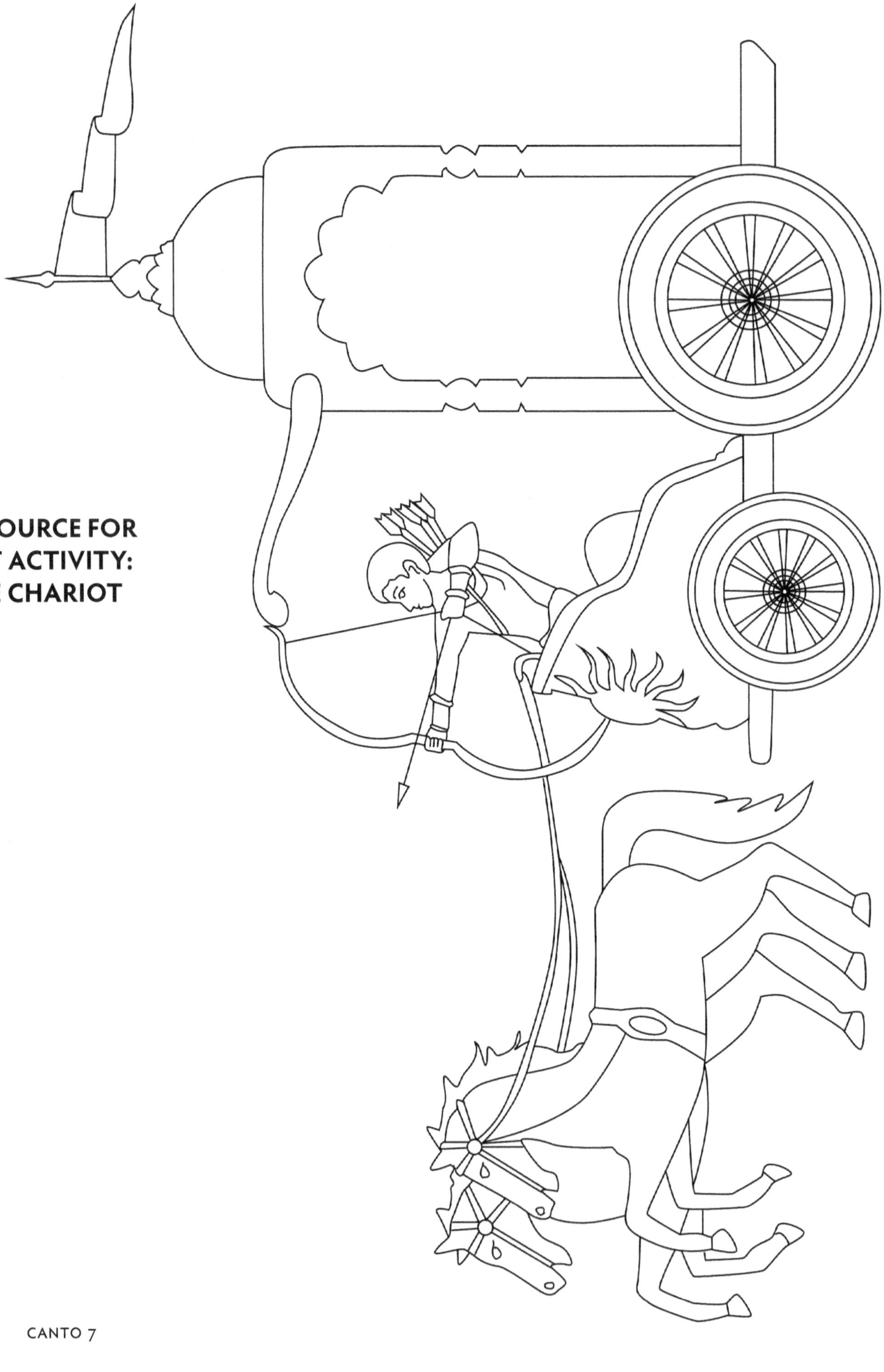

www.ingramcontent.com/pod-product-compliance
Lightning Source LLC
Chambersburg PA
CBHW080322080526
44585CB00021B/2437
* 9 7 8 1 7 3 6 9 6 1 0 7 0 *